Thinking *with* AI

Machine Learning the Humanities

Technographies

Series Editors: Steven Connor, David Trotter and James Purdon

How was it that technology and writing came to inform each other so extensively that today there is only information? Technographies seeks to answer that question by putting the emphasis on writing as an answer to the large question of 'through what?'. Writing about technographies in history, our contributors will themselves write technographically.

Thinking *with* AI

Machine Learning the Humanities

Edited by Hannes Bajohr

O

OPEN HUMANITIES PRESS

London 2025

Print ISBN 978-1-78542-141-9
PDF ISBN 978-1-78542-140-2

OPEN HUMANITIES PRESS

Open Humanities Press is an international, scholar-led open access publishing collective whose mission is to make leading works of contemporary critical thought freely available worldwide. More at http://openhumanitiespress.org

Contents

Contributors

Introduction: Thinking *with* AI   11
Hannes Bajohr

1. A Theory of Vibe   20
   Peli Grietzer

2. Two Autonomies of the Symbolic Order:
   Data and Language in Neural Nets   33
   Leif Weatherby

3. Thinking Through Generated Writing   58
   Mercedes Bunz

4. Operative Ekphrasis: The Collapse of the
   Text/Image Distinction in Multimodal AI   85
   Hannes Bajohr

5. On the Concept of History (in Foundation Models)   111
   Fabian Offert

6. Seven Arguments about AI Images and Generative Media   126
   Lev Manovich

7. Nietzsche, AI, and Poetic Artistry:
   On Nietzsche's 'Hinzugedichtetes'   147
   Babette Babich

8. Intellectual Furniture: Elements of a
   Deep History of Artificial Intelligence   182
   Markus Krajewski

9. The Financialisation of Intelligence:
   Neoliberal Thought and Artificial Intelligence   216
   Orit Halpern

10. Catastrophic Forgetting: Why the Mind Is Not in the Head   230
    Christina Vagt

11. The Absolutism of Data: Thinking AI with Hans Blumenberg   247
    Audrey Borowski

Contributors

Babette Babich teaches in New York City as Professor of Philosophy at Fordham University and is Visiting Professor of Theology, Religion and Philosophy at the University of Winchester, England and, very occasionally, at the Humboldt University in Berlin. Her work highlights hermeneutico-phenomenological approaches to philosophy of science and technology, especially Nietzsche, Heidegger, and Anders in addition to working on ancient philosophy, philosophical aesthetics, including music and poetry. Her recent books include *Günther Anders' Philosophy of Technology* (Bloomsbury, 2022), *Nietzsches Plastik* (Peter Lang, 2021), *Nietzsches Antike* (Nomos, 2020) and her edited collections include *Reading David Hume's 'Of the Standard of Taste'* (de Gruyter, 2019) and *Hermeneutic Philosophies of Social Science* (de Gruyter, 2017). She also edited Patrick Aidan Heelan's posthumous *The Observable: Heisenberg's Philosophy of Quantum Mechanics* (Peter Lang, 2016).

Hannes Bajohr is Assistant Professor of German at the University of California, Berkeley. His research focuses on the history of German philosophy in the twentieth century, political theory, and theories of the digital and AI. Bajohr's academic texts have appeared in *Configurations*, *Poetics Today*, and *New German Critique*, among others. His most recent books are *Schreibenlassen: Texte zur Literatur im Digitalen* (Berlin: August, 2022), *Ad Judith N. Shklar: Leben, Werk, Gegenwart* (with Rieke Trimçev, Hamburg: EVA, 2024), and *Digitale Literatur zur Einführung* (with Simon Roloff, Hamburg: Junius, 2024); in 2025, his book *Postartifizielle Texte: Schreiben nach KI* will come out with Suhrkamp. Bajohr is also active as a writer of digital literature. His most work is the novel *(Berlin, Miami)* (Berlin: Rohstoff, 2023), which was co-written with a self-trained large language model and which will appear in English in 2026.

Audrey Borowski is a research fellow with the Desirable Digitalisation project, a joint initiative of the universities of Bonn and Cambridge that investigates how to design AI and other digital technologies in responsible ways. She received her PhD from the University of Oxford and is a regular contributor to the *Times Literary Supplement* and *Aeon*. Her first book, *Leibniz in His World: The Making of a Savant*, was published by Princeton University Press in 2024.

Mercedes Bunz is Professor in Digital Culture and Society at the Department of Digital Humanities, King's College London. She studied Philosophy, Art History and Media Studies at FU Berlin and Bauhaus

University Weimar and wrote her thesis on the history of the internet driven by a deep curiosity about digital technology. Until today, she has not been disappointed by the transforming field that is digital technology, which provides her constantly and reliably with new aspects to think about – at the moment, this is Artificial Intelligence and 'machine learning'. Looking into these topics, Mercedes Bunz co-leads the Creative AI Lab, a collaboration with the Serpentine Gallery, London. Her last publications include 'How Not to Be Governed Like That by Our Digital Technologies' in *The End(s) of Critique* (Rowman & Littlefield 2022); and, with Claudia Aradau, 'Dismantling the Apparatus of Domination? Left Critiques of AI' in *Radical Philosophy*.

Peli Grietzer is a researcher and writer specialising in ML, philosophy, and literary studies. Grietzer received his PhD from Harvard Comparative Literature in collaboration with the HUJI Einstein Institute of Mathematics, and outside his continued efforts to develop 'mathematically informed literary theory' works in technical and policy research in the AI alignment field. He is completing a general-audience book on the idea of ineffable structure from Romanticism to modern ML.

Orit Halpern is Lighthouse Professor and Chair of Digital Cultures at Technische Universität Dresden. Her work bridges the histories of science, computing, and cybernetics with design. She completed her PhD at Harvard. She has held numerous visiting scholar positions including at the Max Planck Institute for the History of Science in Berlin, IKKM Weimar, and at Duke University. She is currently working on two projects. The first is a history of intelligence and evolution; the second project examines extreme infrastructures and the history of experimentation at planetary scales in design, science, and engineering. She has also published widely in many venues including *Critical Inquiry, Grey Room, Journal of Visual Culture,* and *E-Flux*. Her first book *Beautiful Data: A History of Vision and Reason* (Duke UP 2015) investigates histories of big data, design, and governmentality. Her current book with Robert Mitchell (MIT Press 2023) is titled *The Smartness Mandate*. She is also one of the Primary Investigators of the *Governing through Design Research Group* and a P.I. on the *AUDACE FQRSC* project *Reclaiming the Planet*, both of which sponsor this project.

Markus Krajewski is Professor of Media History at the University of Basel, Switzerland. He is the author, among others, of *Paper Machines: About Cards & Catalogs, 1548–1929* (MIT, 2011), *The Server: A Media History from the Present to the Baroque* (Yale UP, 2018), and *World Projects: Global Information Before WWI* (Minnesota UP, 2014). His current research projects include the problem of planned obsolescence, media and architecture, coding and cooking as cultural techniques, as well as a deep history of artificial intelligence. He is also the developer and maintainer of the bibliography software *synapsen—a digital card index* (www.synapsen.ch). For further information see markus.krajewski.ch.

Lev Manovich is an artist, writer, and one of the most influential theorists of digital culture worldwide. He is currently a Presidential Professor of Computer Science at the City University of New York's Graduate Centre and the Director of the Cultural Analytics Lab. After studying painting, architecture, and filmmaking, Manovich began using computers to create digital art in 1984. He has played a key role in creating four new research fields: digital culture (1991-), software studies (2001-), cultural analytics (2007-) and AI aesthetics (2017-). He is the author of 190 articles and 16 books, including *Artificial Aesthetics, Cultural Analytics, Instagram and Contemporary Image, Software Takes Command*, and *The Language of New Media*, which has been called 'the most provocative and comprehensive media history since Marshall McLuhan.' His projects have been exhibited in 14 solo and 122 international group exhibitions at many prestigious institutions, such as the Institute of Contemporary Art (London), the Centre Pompidou, The Shanghai Biennale, and The ZKM | Centre for Art and Media.

Fabian Offert is Assistant Professor for the History and Theory of the Digital Humanities at the University of California, Santa Barbara, with a special interest in the epistemology and aesthetics of computer vision and machine learning. His current book project focuses on 'Machine Visual Culture' in the age of foundation models. He is principal investigator of the international research project 'AI Forensics' (2022–2025), funded by the Volkswagen Foundation, and was principal investigator of the UCHRI multi campus research group 'Critical Machine Learning Studies' (2021–2022), which aimed to establish a materialist perspective on artificial intelligence. Before joining the faculty at UCSB, he served as postdoctoral researcher in the German Research Foundation's special interest group 'The Digital Image', associated researcher in the Critical Artificial Intelligence Group (KIM) at Karlsruhe University of Arts and Design, and Assistant Curator at ZKM Karlsruhe, Germany. Website: https://zentralwerkstatt.org

Christina Vagt is Associate Professor of European Media Studies, German, and Comparative Literature at the University of California, Santa Barbara. Her research interests lie at the intersections of German and French philosophy and the history and theory of science, with a particular focus on media epistemologies and cultural techniques. Some of her books, co-edited volumes, and special editions include *Modeling the Pacific Ocean* (Media and Environment, 2021), *Action at A Distance* (Minnesota, 2020), *Henri Bergson: Dauer und Gleichzeitigkeit* (Philo Fine Arts, 2014), and *Geschickte Sprünge: Physik und Medium bei Martin Heidegger* (Diaphanes, 2012). She held guest professorships at Humboldt University Berlin and Bauhaus University Weimar and was

Principal Investigator of the research group *Self-moving Materials* at the Max Planck Institute of Colloids and Interfaces. She held senior fellowships at the MECS Institute for Advanced Studies of Computer Simulations at Leuphana University Lüneburg, at the NOMIS research project 'The New Real: Past, Present, and Future of Computation' at Bauhaus University, and at the College of Social Sciences and Humanities at Ruhr Alliance, North Rhine-Westphalia. Since 2022, she has headed the interdisciplinary research group *Postcolonial & Environmental Media Theories* at UCSB.

Leif Weatherby is associate professor of German and founding director of the Digital Theory Lab at NYU. He writes about digital technologies, political economy, and German Romanticism and Idealism. His writing has appeared in *Critical Inquiry*, *New German Critique*, and the *Los Angeles Review of Books*, among others, and been supported by the National Endowment for the Humanities and the Alexander von Humboldt Foundation. He is the author of *Transplanting the Metaphysical Organ: German Romanticism between Leibniz and Marx* (Fordham, 2016) and *Language Machines: AI Between Cognition and Culture* (Minnesota, forthcoming).

Introduction: Thinking *with* AI

Hannes Bajohr

After years of virtual stagnation, the last decade has seen rapid progress in machine learning research. So rapid, in fact, that new interpretations of the world have developed alongside and through the very data processing that forms the basis of the technology's economic success. In this situation, the confrontation between what is broadly and somewhat inaccurately called 'Artificial Intelligence' (AI) and the humanistic disciplines emerges as a fertile ground for both conceptual exploration and critical inquiry.[1] It is at this confluence that the burgeoning field of Critical AI Studies assumes a pivotal role (Lindgren 2024; Raley and Rhee 2023; Goodlad 2023; Roberge 2021).

In its most influential variety, it responds to the fact that AI in the shape of stochastic machine learning has become a core element of the global flow of capital and its extractive tendencies as well as a central technology of surveillance and racial and economic exclusion, which is why Critical AI Studies is concerned with the political, economic, and ethical ramifications of these technologies (Joque 2022; Crawford 2021; Chun 2021; Amoore 2020; Noble 2018; Eubanks 2017). It aims to dissect the intricate web of relationships between AI and the socio-cultural milieu it inhabits and recognises that AI is not a neutral tool but rather a socio-technical system deeply embedded in and reflective of the values, biases, and power structures of the society that uses it. The critical examination of AI thus moves beyond mere technical efficacy and examines the ways in which these technologies are implicated in perpetuating or creating societal norms, ideologies, and inequalities.

An equally important part of Critical AI Studies is devoted to dissecting the conceptual and philosophical assumptions that underlie the design and use of machine learning systems, which still more often than not treat their data as objective and neutral representations of the world (Gitelman 2013; Mackenzie 2017; Apprich et al. 2018). If, as Philip Agre put it already thirty years ago, 'AI is philosophy underneath', critical work is needed to make explicit what is most often only implicit in the assumptions that go into the design of AI systems (Agre 1995: 5). Often, this means, to quote German philosopher Hans Blumenberg, 'to destroy what is supposedly "natural" and convict it of its "artificiality"' (Blumenberg 2020: 188), for Artificial Intelligence is often not considered artificial *enough*. If AI systems are trained on data that is historically and culturally specific, their outputs cannot claim generality, let alone universality. Critical AI Studies thus calls into question the claims of AI as a harbinger of an objective, precise, and efficient future. It scrutinises the narratives that portray AI as the evolutionary pinnacle of human intellect and instead presents it as a continuation of existing preliminary epistemic, political, and economic decisions, albeit in a more sophisticated and opaque form. It is in this very crucible that the humanities, armed with their critical, historical, and conceptual awareness, find their relevance magnified. As media scholars Fabian Offert and Thao Phan put it, 'current-generation machine learning models require current-generation modes of (humanist) critique' (Offert and Phan 2022).

But this relationship between AI and the humanities goes both ways. If AI already *is* a philosophy not yet articulated, we can also turn Agre's adage around: as humanists, we would be remiss if we did not also test our own concepts against the new phenomena that computer science and engineering throw at us. For the current discourse in our fields concerned with AI is usually directed at actually existing, implemented systems – as technically or historically situated objects, as sites of ethical and political debates, or as benchmarks for thought experiments about cognition and consciousness, be it machinic or human. This discourse operates in a mode one could call thinking *about* AI. This book wants to take a different route, thereby expanding humanities AI thinking. Instead of starting with the reality of specific AI models and investigating their uses, dangers, or potentials, it wants to ask which concepts, frameworks, and metaphors AI can provide us that can be used to reflect productively back onto the humanities themselves. Instead of thinking about, then, this is thinking *with* AI. The belief animating this volume is that humanistic practice must evolve to grapple with the questions incited by machine learning technology on its own turf. This does not mean abandoning the critical stance; on the contrary, many of the contributions to this book deal exactly with thinking with AI done wrong. Nevertheless, criticality must be extended to both sides of the equation to include not only the reality of AI as it exists today, but also to humanistic concepts as objects of inquiry and potential revision in light of the questions raised by Critical AI Studies.

This amounts to understanding AI as what Daniel Dennett calls an 'intuition pump' (Dennett 2013) – an intellectual tool that allows us to clarify conceptual implications otherwise unseen, or to get out of mental ruts and finding fresh approaches to problems in the humanities. In the case of the present volume, this method proceeds by observing how traditional ideas clash (or mesh) with current advances in information technology. This is what the eleven essays collected in this book do. They tackle a variety of fields, from autoencoders for imagining aesthetic theory to desks and writing furniture as precursors to the 'assisted thinking' modern day AI presents us with; they argue for a different grasp on the meaning of meaning, look at new AI architectures to question basic assumptions about language and images, history and forgetting, and explore the neural net as a model of neoliberal economics.

They also bring philosophy, from Nietzsche to Blumenberg, in a more direct way into contact with AI thinking. Beyond these individual contributions, the volume hopes to set a precedent for a creative yet rigorous approach to AI as a driver of conceptual scrutiny.

Peli Grietzer's 'A Theory of Vibe' serves as maybe the purest example of thinking with AI, and it animated the decision to assemble this volume in the first place. For Grietzer's piece conceives of aesthetics, in particular the concept of 'vibe' or *Stimmung* (mood), as a principle that unifies a set of objects or phenomena through the metaphorics of AI. Drawing on ideas from information theory and machine learning, specifically the concept of the 'auto-encoder', Grietzer proposes that grasping the vibe of a set of objects entails perceiving both an overall unity as well as a logic of difference that makes the objects intercomparable. Just as a trained autoencoder can generate approximations of inputs based on key dimensions of variation, the vibe of a set of phenomena provides a generative language for modelling those phenomena aesthetically. Grietzer relates this to ideas of the symbol in Romanticism and Modernism, arguing that while Romantic theorists saw the symbol as a particular that expresses a universal, Modernists conceived of aesthetic unity in more immanent, concrete terms. The vibe or style of a set of objects, phenomenologically accessed through transformations and differences in a work of art, serves as a 'horizontal' mode of symbolism, directly embodying an abstract structure. Grietzer's daring comparison of the ineffable aesthetic vibe and the dimensionality of autoencoders sets a standard of thinking with AI, and thus is the first of the essays here collected.

In his contribution 'Two Autonomies of the Symbolic Order: Data and Language in Neural Nets', Leif Weatherby tackles the question of language that large language models like ChatGPT pose. If some theorists have suggested that LLMs are merely stochastic parrots, Weatherby makes the case that LLMs show with utmost clarity that language, on the contrary, is an autonomous system independent of human intent, cognition, or direct world-reference. Drawing on media theory, semiotics, and (post-)structuralism, Weatherby thus thinks the 'double autonomy' of the symbolic order with AI. For while language and sign systems are already disconnected from correlative human standards, with the advent of neural nets that generate language, this autonomous symbolic order now also exists in an autonomous technical system. Rather than seeing this as an 'alignment' of the human and the technical, Weatherby calls for recognising the complex interplay of differences between the two orders, and critiques the 'remainder humanism' still prevalent in AI theorising that insists on an unbridgeable gap between human meanings and machine operations. Instead, he argues that LLMs collapse the distinction between generating and using language, and calls for attending to the high-dimensional, multi-thematic transformations that occur between systems of signification in sociotechnical assemblages like neural nets.

Mercedes Bunz's 'Thinking Through Generated Writing' also turns to generative AI in LLMs but takes a markedly different position from Weatherby. Using the example of ChatGPT, her essay poses the question 'what is writing?' in the context of 'the human artifice' (Hannah Arendt). She argues that while generated writing superficially resembles human-produced text, the underlying computational processes fundamentally differ. Drawing on theorists such as André Leroi-Gourhan, Gilbert Simondon, and Jacques Derrida, Bunz makes a key distinction between writing as tied to human subjectivity and the exteriorisation of thought, and AI text generation as a 'calculation of meaning' based on pattern recognition in statistical relationships between words. Examples of this difference are the factual 'hallucinations' stemming from models' lack of grounding in the real world, and their tendency toward producing stylistically coherent but possibly unreliable or exaggerated writings. Bunz contrasts generated writing's tendency towards such textual patterns with traditional expectations for writing that imply correctness and reliability. As a reading strategy, she advocates for developing interpretations of this new form of artificial 'intelligence' on its own terms, through frameworks like Simondon's concept of technical beings, rather than mistakenly equating it with human cognition. Generated writing, Bunz holds, represents a shift requiring new conceptual vocabulary and theories that recognise its place in the human artifice.

Hannes Bajohr's 'Operative Ekphrasis: The Collapse of the Text/Image Distinction in Multimodal AI' connects the topic of language with that of the image, and thinks its relationship with AI – in particular, with multimodal systems like DALL·E. Bajohr argues that such models collapse the traditional distinction between text and image that has underpinned theories of ekphrasis, the 'visual representation of verbal representation'. Bajohr develops the concept of 'operative ekphrasis' to describe how in digital systems, text performs the generation of images computationally, and ekphrastic relationships should be understood as performative rather than representational. A key distinction is made between 'sequential' digital systems based on classical algorithms, which have a syntax but no semantics, and 'connectionist' systems like neural networks that exhibit a primitive form of artificial semantics. For Bajohr, their meaning-producing dimension stems from the fact the representation spaces of text and images become fused. Only in the context of multimodal AI, unlike in the analog or sequential paradigms, does ekphrasis go beyond the separation of or transition between text and image, but rather transcends this difference. As an intuition pump in Dennett's sense, multimodal AI for Bajohr suggests a new understanding of the relationship between text and image in which these modes are thought of as identical or surpassed rather than as merely equivalent to or competing with one another.

Fabian Offert's article stays with the significance of images and examines the concept of history that emerges from large visual foundation models. In 'On the Concept of History (in Foundation Models)', he argues that these models relate to the past and historical media in non-arbitrary yet technologically determined ways. Through an analysis of the CLIP model at the heart of DALL·E, Offert shows how these systems remediate historical images and periods into aesthetic conventions – indeed, vibes – like black-and-white or marbled surfaces for the distant past. This reveals a model-specific structuring principle of history, raising questions around the politics of automated vision, but also shows the underlying and often unexamined notions of what the historical consists in. Rather than applying existing theoretical frameworks, he advocates for a close empirical analysis of how such systems see and represent the past. Offert's point is ultimately a political one: current foundation models foreclose the potential to actualise history by confining the past to a media prison, censoring specific historical events, and failing to move beyond contingency. What this amounts to is a call for 'thinking with AI' by understanding the epistemologies encoded in these technical objects.

Lev Manovich's 'Seven Arguments about AI Images and Generative Media' explores several key aspects of current AI generative media technologies for creating images, animation, video, and other visual media. Manovich situates these new technologies within broader histories of media, art, and technology. He argues that AI generative systems continue longstanding artistic practices of creating new works from cultural databases and archives. The article also conceptualises AI generative systems as implementing a shift 'from simulation to prediction', using vast datasets to predict new images and media rather than manually creating representations. Manovich highlights AI generative media's capacity for automatic 'translations' across media types, such as text-to-image generation. He also examines tensions between the stereotypicality frequently seen in AI-generated artifacts versus the uniqueness of traditional creations. Additionally, the article considers complex interrelationships between subject, content, style, and form when using AI tools to render different subjects in historical artistic styles. Manovich reflects on how experiments with AI generative systems can provide new critical and theoretical perspectives on concepts of creativity, originality, subject, style, and more within the realms of arts and culture.

In her contribution, Babette Babich thinks AI with Friedrich Nietzsche's reflections on truth, lies, perception, and anthropomorphism to shed light on the illusion of intelligence in AI systems. Considering recent claims that AI systems like ChatGPT have achieved sentience or intelligence, Babich argues that they might better be understood through Nietzsche's notion of 'Hinzugedichtetes' or fictional projection. After all, we constantly inject our own interpretations and self-deceptions into the world around us. Discussions of the cognitive capacity of AI parallel some of Nietzsche's ideas around self-deception and the human desire to become godlike creators. Nietzsche's perspectival epistemology helps understand how AI promotes user illusions and bubbles of personalised reinforcement. His view that we are 'accustomed to lying' resonates with the deception inherent in these systems. Relating

Nietzsche's metaphor of the universe as a 'cosmic music box' to the automated, irrational mechanisms underlying much technology today, Babich
argues that claims of AI sentience often derive more from anthropomorphic
self-interest than any profound awakening of machine intelligence.

That the projection of intelligence onto innate objects may not necessarily be deceptive, but quite legitimate, is the underlying assumption of Markus
Krajewski's 'Intellectual Furniture: Elements of a Deep History of Artificial
Intelligence'. Exploring the evolution of artificial intelligence (AI) in scholarly
contexts, Krajewski traces its roots from the late seventeenth century to modern times as an extension of cognition and memory. It is precisely the interaction between human intelligence and mechanical or algorithmic aids that
both undermines the claim of intelligent machines and extends it to a much
deeper history than that of the last half-century by focusing on three historical scenarios: the binary system of Gottfried Wilhelm Leibniz, the intricate
writing furniture of Abraham Roentgen, and Niklas Luhmann's *Zettelkasten*
method. Krajewski examines how these intellectual tools facilitated complex
thought processes and knowledge management, arguing that the synergy
between human minds and 'intellectual furniture' represents a form of assisted
thinking. In Krajewski, past knowledge management is thought with AI, and
in turn, the development of current LLMs is situated within this broader history, shedding light on the evolving relationship between human intellect and
technological assistance.

'The Financialisation of Intelligence: Neoliberal Thought and Artificial
Intelligence' by Orit Halpern explores the intertwined development of financial markets and artificial intelligence research, particularly under the influence of neoliberal ideologies. Halpern shows the dark side of thinking with
AI by tracing the historical evolution of economic models and AI, focusing
on the role of 'noise' – misinformation and data overload – in market dynamics as theorised by Fischer Black. Halpern outlines how these theories and
the advent of machine learning – including Friedrich Hayek's own identification of brain structure and market behaviour – have reshaped notions of
economic rationality and human decision-making. Central to this analysis
is the argument that contemporary finance, heavily reliant on AI and complex algorithms, has moved away from objective valuations of assets, instead
emphasising market volatility and the collective, networked actions of market participants. This shift reflects a broader neoliberal ethos that privileges
market mechanisms over centralised planning and views human judgement as
inherently flawed. The paper critically examines the impact of such financial
models, arguing that they not only reflect but also actively shape socio-eco-
nomic realities. By dissecting the philosophical and technological underpinnings of modern financial markets and AI, Halpern highlights the profound
implications of these developments for understanding intelligence, both artificial and human, in a neoliberal context that are a result of thinking with
AI gone rogue.

This misleading identification of artificial neural networks and brain structure is taken up by Christina Vagt in 'Catastrophic Forgetting: Why the Mind is Not in the Head'. Her essay challenges conventional neurocognitive theories by exploring the concept of catastrophic forgetting in neural networks. Vagt argues that catastrophic forgetting – in which a network forgets previously learned information upon learning new data – is not just a technical issue but has profound implications for understanding human cognition, revealing conceptual limitations in current neurocognitive models, which heavily rely on computational paradigms, and making a reevaluation of the relationship between cognition and technology necessary. The essay discusses the historical and philosophical underpinnings of neurocognitive science, tracing its roots back to Kant's synthetic a priori and its evolution through the development of computer models of cognition. It examines the assumption that human cognition can be fully represented and simulated through computational models, suggesting that this perspective overlooks the fundamental role of forgetting in human intelligence. Vagt incorporates insights from, again, Friedrich Nietzsche, particularly his emphasis on the importance of forgetfulness as a vital cognitive function. This perspective challenges the notion that cognition is primarily about information storage and retrieval, as commonly portrayed in AI and neurocognitive research: catastrophic forgetting in ANNs exposes the shortcomings of equating human cognition with computational processes.

In the final essay, 'The Absolutism of Data: Thinking AI with Hans Blumenberg', Audrey Borowski draws out the parallels between algorithmic systems in addressing the unpredictability of the world and the function of myth as articulated by German philosopher Hans Blumenberg. Borowski challenges the notion that algorithmic systems, central to surveillance capitalism, embody objective rationality. Rather, like myths, they help navigate a world that eludes complete understanding in that they, through abductive reasoning, create simplified models of complex realities, abstracting human behaviours into data sets. This process shapes our perceptions and interactions with the world, often leading to homogenised experiences and constrained decision-making. Thinking AI with Blumenberg, Borowski advocates for a more nuanced approach to digital technology. Blumenberg's defence of nonconceptual thought, including myths, metaphors, and rhetoric, is presented as a way to resist the absolutism of data-driven models. His thinking may well be included in a future canon of Critical AI Studies.

Works Cited

Agre, Philip E. 1995. 'The Soul Gained and Lost: Artificial Intelligence as a Philosophical Project', *Stanford Humanities Review* 4, no. 2: 1-19.

Amoore, Louise. 2020. *Cloud Ethics: Algorithms and the Attributes of Ourselves and Others*. Durham: Duke University Press.

Apprich, Clemens, Wendy Hui Kyong Chun, Florian Cramer, and Hito Steyerl. 2018. *Pattern Discrimination*. Minneapolis: University of Minnesota Press.

Blumenberg, Hans. 2020. 'An Anthropological Approach to the Contemporary Significance of Rhetoric', In *History, Metaphors, Fables: A Hans Blumenberg Reader*, edited by Hannes Bajohr, Florian Fuchs, and Joe Paul Kroll, 177-209. Ithaca, NY: Cornell University Press.

Chun, Wendy Hui Kyong. 2021. *Discriminating Data: Correlation, Neighborhoods, and the New Politics of Recognition*. Cambridge, MA: MIT Press.

Crawford, Kate. 2021. *Atlas of AI: Power, Politics, and the Planetary Costs of Artificial Intelligence*. New Haven: Yale University Press.

Dennett, Daniel C. 2013. *Intuition Pumps and Other Tools for Thinking*. New York: Norton.

Eubanks, Virginia. 2017. *Automating Inequality: How High-Tech Tools Profile, Police, and Punish the Poor*. New York, NY: St. Martin's Press.

Gitelman, Lisa, Ed. 2013. *'Raw Data' Is an Oxymoron*. Cambridge, MA: MIT Press.

Goodlad, Lauren M. E., Ed. 2023. *Critical AI* 1 (1-2).

Joque, Justin. 2022. *Revolutionary Mathematics: Artificial Intelligence, Statistics and the Logic of Capitalism*. London: Verso.

Lindgren, Simon. 2024. *Critical Theory of AI*. Cambridge: Polity.

Mackenzie, Adrian. 2017. *Machine Learners: Archaeology of a Data Practice*. Cambridge, MA: MIT Press.

Noble, Safiya Umoja. 2018. *Algorithms of Oppression: How Search Engines Reinforce Racism*. New York: New York University Press.

Offert, Fabian, and Thao Phan. 2022. 'A Sign That Spells: DALL-E 2, Invisual Images and the Racial Politics of Feature Space.' *arXiv*. http://arxiv.org/abs/2211.06323.

Raley, Rita, and Jennifer Rhee. 2023. 'Critical AI.' Special issue *American Literature* 95 (2).

Roberge, Jonathan, and Michael Castelle, eds. 2021. *The Cultural Life of Machine Learning: An Incursion into Critical AI Studies*. Cham: Springer.

Whittaker, Meredith. 2021. 'The Steep Cost of Capture.' *Interactions* 28 (6): 50-55.

Notes

1. As Meredith Whittaker points out, the term AI – though indeed first employed in 1956 – became powerful only recently after the successes of deep learning 'as a marketing hook. Tech companies quickly (re)branded machine learning and other data-dependent approaches as AI, framing them as the product of breakthrough scientific innovation. Companies acquired labs and start-ups, and worked to pitch AI as a multitool of efficiency and precision, suitable for nearly any purpose across countless domains. When we say AI is everywhere, this is why' (Whittaker 2021: 51). The reason that this book nevertheless speaks of 'AI' rather than, say, 'stochastic machine learning' is precisely because of the strong rhetorical valorisation of the term: 'AI' signifies a whole host of imaginaries, social and economic realities, and discursive traditions that the more exact but restrictively technical 'machine learning', *pace* the subtitle of this book, simply fails to capture. This is, I believe, one of the lessons Critical AI Studies has learned – hence its name.

I

A Theory of Vibe

Peli Grietzer

Across the foliated space of the twenty-seven equivalents, Faustroll conjured up into the third dimension: From Baudelaire, E. A. Poe's Silence, taking care to retranslate Baudelaire's translation into Greek. From Bergerac, the precious tree into which the nightingale king and his subjects were metamorphosed, in the land of the sun. From Luke, the Calumniator who carried Christ on to a high place. From Bloy, the black pigs of Death, retinue of the Betrothed. From Coleridge, the ancient mariner's crossbow, and the ship's floating skeleton, which, when placed in the skiff, was sieve upon sieve.

—Alfred Jarry, *Exploits & Opinions of Doctor Faustroll,*
  Pataphysician: A Neo-Scientific Novel, 1929

1. An *autoencoder*[1] is a neural network process tasked with learning from scratch, through a kind of trial and error, how to make facsimiles of worldly things. Let us call a hypothetical, exemplary autoencoder 'Hal'. We call the set of all the inputs we give Hal for reconstruction – let us say many, many image files of human faces, or many, many audio files of jungle sounds, or many, many scans of city maps – Hal's 'training set'. Whenever Hal receives an input media file x, Hal's *feature function* outputs a short list of short numbers, and Hal's *decoder function* tries to recreate media file x based on the feature function's 'summary' of x. Of course, since the variety of possible media files is much wider than the variety of possible short lists of short numbers, something must necessarily get lost in the translation from media file to feature values and back: many possible media files translate into the same short list of short numbers, and yet each short list of short numbers can only translate back into one media file. Trying to minimize the damage, though, induces Hal to learn – through trial and error – an effective schema or 'mental vocabulary' for its training set, exploiting rich holistic patterns in the data in its

summary-and-reconstruction process. Hal's 'summaries' become, in effect, cognitive mapping of its training set, a kind of gestalt fluency that ambiently models it like a niche or a lifeworld.

2. What an autoencoder algorithm learns, instead of making perfect reconstructions, is a system of features that can generate *approximate* reconstruction of the objects of the training set. In fact, the difference between an object in the training set and its reconstruction – mathematically, the trained autoencoder's *reconstruction error* on the object – demonstrates what we might think of, rather literally, as the excess of material reality over the gestalt-systemic logic of autoencoding. We will call the set of all possible inputs for which a given trained autoencoder S has zero reconstruction error, in this spirit, S's 'canon'. The canon, then, is the set of all the objects that a given trained autoencoder – its imaginative powers bounded as they are to the span of just a handful of 'respects of variation', the dimensions of the features vector – can imagine or conceive of whole, without approximation or simplification. Furthermore, if the autoencoder's training was successful, the objects in the canon collectively exemplify an idealization or simplification of the objects of some worldly domain. Finally, and most strikingly, a trained autoencoder and its canon are effectively mathematically equivalent: not only are they roughly logically equivalent, it is also fast and easy to compute one from the other. In fact, merely autoencoding a small sample from the canon of a trained autoencoder S is enough to accurately replicate or model S.

3. Imagine if you will the 'hermeneutics of suspicion'[2] – the classical '90s kind of symptomatic or subversive academic reading – was a data-mining process that infers, from what is found and not found in the world constructed by a literary text, an organon (system of thought and feeling) that makes certain real-world phenomena unthinkable, invisible, foreclosed to the order of things. The critic would infer, from observation of the literary work's selection of phenomena, a generative model of the work, finding what is repressed or marginalized in the text within 'gaps' in the generative model: states of the lifeworld that the generative model cannot generate. Pushing the process even further, an ambitious critic would go on to try to characterize *dimensions* – ways in which states of the world can be meaningfully different from each other – missing from the generative model. Contemporary cultural-materialist or ideology-sensitive readings are, as Rita Felksi argues in 'After Suspicion' (Felski 2009), for the most part 'post-suspicion': recent social-theoretic literary critics, especially those associated with the field of affect-studies, tend to differ from their predecessors in assigning reflexivity and agency to literary texts as the facilitators of the critical comparison between model and world. This modern turn places the framework of some recent social-theoretic readers – in particular, Jonathan Flatley (2008) and Sianne Ngai (2007) – in a close alliance with our own. Specifically, Ngai's landmark argument in *Ugly Feelings* that a work of literature can, through tone, represent a subject's ideology – and so, both represent a structure of her subjectivity and touch upon the structure of

the social-material conditions structuring her subjectivity – is strongly concordant with our theme. Ngai's theory suggests that systems of 'respects of variation' that we might define by the excess material reality that they marginalize (that is, define as 'ideology') can be identically defined through the aesthetic unity of the material realities they access best (that is, defined as 'tone'). The *canon* of a trained autoencoder, we are proposing, recapitulates the ideology of a system of 'respects of variation' as a tone.

4. Autoencoders, we know, deal entirely in worlds rendered as sets of objects or phenomena. Whatever deeper worldly structures an autoencoder's schema brings to the interpretation of an object, then, these structures are already at play, in some form, in the collective aesthetic of the objects they reign over.[3] I want to think about this aesthetically accessible, surface-accessible, world-making structure as the mathematical substrate of what writer/musician Ezra Koenig (via Elif Batuman) describes as 'vibe':

> It was during my research on the workings of charm and pop music that I stumbled on Internet Vibes (internetvibes.blogspot. com/), a blog that Ezra Koenig kept in 2005-6, with the goal of categorising as many 'vibes' as possible. A 'rain/grey/British vibe', for example, incorporates the walk from a Barbour store (to look at wellington boots) to the Whitney Museum (to look at 'some avant-garde shorts by Robert Beavers'), as well as the TV adaptation of Brideshead Revisited, the Scottish electronic duo Boards of Canada, 'late 90s Radiohead/global anxiety/airports' and New Jersey. A 'vibe' turns out to be something like 'local colour,' with a historical dimension. What gives a vibe 'authenticity' is its ability to evoke – using a small number of disparate elements – a certain time, place and milieu; a certain nexus of historic, geographic and cultural forces (Batuman 2008).

The meaning of a literary work like Dante's *Inferno*, Beckett's *Waiting for Godot*, or Stein's *Tender Buttons*, we would like to say, lies at least partly in an aesthetic 'vibe' or a 'style' that we can sense when we consider all the myriad objects and phenomena that make up the imaginative landscape of the work as a kind of curated set. The meaning of Dante's *Inferno*, let us say, lies in part in that certain *je ne sais quoi* that makes every soul, demon, and machine in Dante's vision of hell a good fit for Dante's vision of hell. Similarly, the meaning of Beckett's *Waiting for Godot* lies partly in what limits our space of thinkable things for Vladimir and Estragon to say and do to a small set of possibilities the play nearly exhausts. Part of the meaning of Stein's *Tender Buttons* lies in the set of (possibly inherently linguistic) 'tender buttons' – conforming objects and phenomena.[4]

5. The features or dimensions or 'respects of variation' of a trained autoencoder work very much like a fixed list of predicates with room to write-in for

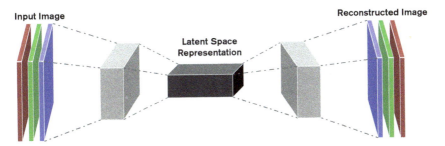

Figure 1. Map of a trained autoencoder.

example 'not' or 'somewhat' or 'solidly' or 'extremely' next to each.[5] Within the context of the feature function, which produces 'summaries' of the input object, it is most natural to think of the 'respects of variation' as *descriptive* predicates. The features of a trained autoencoder take a rather different meaning if instead we centre our thinking around the *decoder function* – the function that turns 'summaries' into reconstructions. From the viewpoint of the decoder function, a given list of feature-values is not a 'summary' that could apply to any number of closely related objects, but rather the (so to speak) DNA of a specific object. A given trained autoencoder's features or 'respects of variation' are, from this perspective, akin to a list of *imperative* predicates, structural techniques or principles to be applied by the constructor. For the decoder, the 'generative formulae' for objects in a trained autoencoder's canon are lists of activation values that determine how intensely the construction process (the *decoder function*) applies each of the available structural techniques or principles.

6. It is a fundamental property of any trained autoencoder's canon therefore that all the objects in the canon *align with a limited generative vocabulary*. The objects that make up the trained autoencoder's actual worldly domain, by implication, roughly align or *approximately align* with that same limited generative vocabulary. These structural relations of alignment, I propose, are closely tied to certain concepts of aesthetic unity that commonly imply a unity of generative logic, as in both the intuitive and literary theoretic concepts of a 'style' or 'vibe'. To be a set that aligns with *some* logically possible generative vocabulary is hardly a 'real' structural or aesthetic property, given the infinity of logically possible generative vocabularies. To be a set that aligns with some (logically possible) *limited* generative vocabulary, on the other hand, is a robust intersubjecitve property.

7. By way of a powerful paraphrase, we might say that it means the objects that make up a trained autoencoder's canon are *individually complex but collectively simple*. To better illustrate this concept ('individually complex but collectively simple'), let us make a brief digression and describe a type of mathematical-visual art project, typically associated with late twentieth-century Hacker culture, known as a '64k Intro'. In the artistic-mathematical subculture known as 'demoscene', a '64k Intro' is a lush, vast, and nuanced visual world that fits

into 64 kilobytes of memory or fewer, less memory by a thousandfold than the standard memory requirements for a lush, robust, and nuanced visual world. In a 64k Intro, a hundred or so lines of code create a sensually complicated universe by, quite literally, using the esoteric affinities of surfaces with primordial Ideas. The code of a 64k Intro uses the smallest possible inventory of initial schemata to generate the most diverse concreta. The information-theoretical magic behind a 64k Intro is that, somewhat like a spatial fugue, these worlds are tapestries of interrelated self-similar patterns. From the topological level (architecture and camera movement) to the molecular level (the polygons and textures from which objects are built), everything in a 64k Intro is born of a 'family resemblance' of forms.

8. Remarkably – and also, perhaps, trivially – the relationship between succinct expressibility and depth of pattern that we see in 64k Intros provably holds for any informational, cognitive, or semiotic system. A deeply conceptually useful, though often technically unwieldy, measure of 'depth of pattern' used in information theory is 'Kolmogorov complexity': the Kolmogorov complexity of an object is the length of the shortest possible description (in a given semiotic system) that can fully specify it.[6] Lower Kolmogorov complexity generically means stronger pattern. A low Kolmogorov complexity – i.e. short minimum description length – for an object relative to a given semiotic system implies the existence of deep patterns in the object, or a close relationship between the object and the basic concepts of the semiotic system.

9. When all the objects in a given set C have low Kolmogorov+ complexity relative to a given semiotic system S, we will say the semiotic system S is a *schema* for C. If S is a given trained autoencoder's generative language (formally, *decoder function*), and C the canon of this trained autoencoder, for example, then S is a schema for C. Importantly, any schema S is in itself a semiotic object, and itself has a Kolmogorov complexity relative to our own present semiotic system, and so the 'real' – that is, relative to our own semiotic system – efficacy of S as a schema for an object c in C is measured by the sum of the Kolmogorov+ complexity of c relative to S and the Kolmogorov complexity of S. Because one only needs to learn a language once to use it to create however many sets of sentences one wishes, though, when we consider the efficacy of S as a schema for *multiple* objects c_1, c_2, c_3 in C we do not repeatedly add the Kolmogorov complexity of S to the respective Kolmogorov+ complexities of c_1, c_2, c_3 relative to S and sum up, but instead add the Kolmogorov complexity of S just once to the sum of the respective Kolmogorov+ complexities of c_1, c_2, c_3 relative to S. The canon of a trained autoencoder, we suggested, comprises objects that are individually complex but collectively simple. Another way to say this is that as we consider larger and larger collections of objects from a trained autoencoder's canon C, specifying the relevant objects using our own semiotic system, we quickly reach a point whereupon the shortest path to specifying the collected objects is to first establish the trained autoencoder's generative language S, then succinctly specify the objects using S.

10. Suppose that when a person grasps a style or vibe in a set of worldly phenomena, part of what she grasps can be compared to the formulae of an autoencoder trained on this collection. The canon of this abstract trained autoencoder, then, would be an idealization of the worldly set, intensifying the worldly set's own internal logic. Going the other way around, we might consider the idea that when the imaginative landscape of a literary work possesses a strong unity of style, the aesthetic unity of the artifactual collection is potentially an idealization of a looser, weaker aesthetic unity between the objects or phenomena associated with a real-world domain that the work of art encodes. In the autoencoder case, we know to treat the artifactual collection of objects or phenomena – the trained autoencoder's canon, mathematically equivalent to the trained autoencoder itself – as a systemic, structural gestalt representation of a worldly set whose vibe it idealizes. Applying the same thinking to the literary case, we might speculate that a *dense vibe* in the imaginative landscape associated with a work of art potentially acts as a structural representation of a *loose vibe* of the collective objects and phenomena of a real-world domain. I would offer, similarly, that the 'dense aesthetic structure' in question thus potentially provides a schema for interpreting the objects and phenomena of a real-world domain in accordance with a 'systemic gestalt' given through the imaginative landscape of the literary work.

11. It is logically possible to share a trained autoencoder's formula directly, by listing the substrate of a neural network bit by bit, but it is a pretty bad idea to try: the computations involved in autoencoding, let alone in any abstractly autoencoding-like bio-cognitive processes, are mathematically intractable and conceptually oblique. If what a person grasps in grasping the 'aesthetic unity' or vibe of some collection of phenomena is, even in part, that this collection of phenomena can be approximated using a limited generative language, then we cannot hope to express or share what we grasped in its abstract form. One mathematical fact about neural nets that neural-netty creatures like us *can* easily use, however, is the practical identity between a trained autoencoder and its canon: if grasping a loose worldly vibe has the form of a trained autoencoder, we should expect to share our vibe-insight with each other by intersubjectively constructing an appropriate set of idealised phenomena. At the same time, we should expect that the 'idea' that our constructed set of idealised phenomena expresses is essentially impossible to paraphrase or separate from its expressive form, despite its worldly subject matter.

12. A vibe is therefore, in this sense, an *abstractum that cannot be separated from its concreta*. The above phrasing tellingly, if unintentionally, echoes and inverts a certain formula of the 'Romantic theory of the symbol' – as given, for example, in Goethe's definition of a symbol as 'a living and momentary revelation of the inscrutable' in a particular, wherein 'the idea remains eternally and infinitely active and inaccessible [*wirksam und unerreichbar*] in the image, and even if expressed in all languages would still remain inexpressible [*selbst in allen Sprachen ausgesprochen, doch unauspprechlich bliebe*]'. (Goethe in

POETRY

        thing which no one living

            prizes but the dead see

and ask among themselves,

        What do we remember that was shaped

          as this thing

is shaped? while their eyes

      fill

         with tears. By which

and by the weak wash of crimson

    colors it, the rose

       is predicated

           WILLIAM CARLOS WILLIAMS

90

Figure 2. Excerpt from William Carlos Williams, *Paterson*, 1927 [1992]. ©2023, ProLitteris, Zurich, with kind permission.

Beistegui 2012) The relationship of our literary-philosophical trope of a 'vibe' to the Romantic literary-philosophical trope of 'the Symbol' is even clearer when considering Yeats's more pithy paraphrase a century later, at the end of the Romantic symbol's long trans-European journey from very early German Romanticism to very late English Symbolism: 'A symbol is indeed the only possible expression of some invisible essence, a transparent lamp about a spiritual flame' (Yeats 1903).

13. A question therefore brings itself to mind: does the idea of an abstractum that cannot be separated from its concreta simply reaffirm the Goethe/Yeats theory of the symbol from the opposite direction, positing a type of abstractum (a 'structure of feelings') that can only be expressed in a particular, rather than a type of particular (a 'symbol') that singularly expresses an abstraction? Not really, I would argue; indeed, I would say the difference between the two is key to the elective affinity between vibe and specifically *Modernist* ars poetica.

14. Despite its oh so many continuities with Symbolism and Romanticism, the era of Pound, Eliot, Joyce, and Stein is marked by the ascendency of a certain *materialist* reorientation of the Symbolist/Romantic tradition. One relevant sense of 'materialist' is the sense that Daniel Albright explores in his study of Modernist poetic theory's borrowings from chemistry and physics, but a broader relevant sense of 'materialist' is closer to 'not-Platonist',[7] or to 'immanent' in the Deleuzian sense. Recalling Joyce's and Zukofsky's Aristotle fandom, and perhaps observing that William Carlos Williams's 'no ideas but in things' (Williams 1992 [1927]) is about as close as one can get to 'universalia in re' in English, we might even risk calling it an *Aristotelian* reorientation of the Symbolist tradition, both in aesthetic theory and in aesthetic practice.

15. For the Modernist aesthetic theorist, the philosophical burden on poetics partly shifts from the broadly Platonist burden of explaining how concreta could rise up to reach an otherwise inexpressible abstract idea, to the broadly Aristotelian burden of explaining how a set of concreta is (or can be) an abstract idea. Where Coleridge looked to the Imagination[8] as the faculty that vertically connects the world of things to the world of ideas for example, William Carlos Williams looked to the Imagination as the faculty that horizontally connects *things* to create a *world*. From a broadly Aristotelian point of view, the Poundian/Eliotian – or, less canonically but more accurately, Steinian – operation wherein poetry explicitly arranges or aggregates objects in accordance with new, unfamiliar partitions[9] is precisely what it means to fully and directly represent abstracta: an abstractum *just is* the collective affinity of the objects in a class. In fact, in 'New Work for a Theory of Universals', the premier contemporary scholastic materialist David Lewis formally proposes that universals are simply 'natural classes', metaphysically identical to sets of objects that possess internal structural affinity.

16. By way of an example of a literary work's production of a 'horizontal' *symbol* as described above, we might consider the imaginative landscape

of Franz Kafka's corpus. It is not very outrageous, I believe, to offer that it operates as just this kind of aesthetic schema for the unity or the affinity of a collection of real-world phenomena. A reader of Kafka learns to see a kind of Kafkaesque aesthetic at play in the experience of going to the bank, in the experience of being broken-up with, in the experience of waking up in a daze, in the experience of being lost in a foreign city, or in the experience of a police interrogation – in part by learning that surprisingly many of the real life nuances of these experiences can be well-approximated in a literary world whose constructs are all fully bound to the aesthetic rules of Kafkaen construction. We learn to grasp a Kafkaesque aesthetic logic in certain worldly phenomena, in other words, partly by learning that the pure Kafkaesque aesthetic logic of Kafka's literary world can generate a surprisingly good likeness of these worldly phenomena.

17. This minor brush with Kafka, and with the inevitable 'Kafkaesque', also provides us with a good occasion to remark an interesting relationship between ambient meaning, literary polyvalence, and processes of concept-learning. Let us take the late French Symbolist and early Parisian avant-garde concept of 'polyvalence' to include both phenomena of collage, hybridity, and polyphony, where the heterogeneous multiplicity is on the page, and phenomena of indeterminacy, undecidability, and ambiguity where the heterogeneous multiplicity emerges in the readerly process. On the view suggested here, a vibe-coherent polyvalent literary object functions as a nearly minimal concrete model of the abstract structure shared by the disparate experiences, objects, or phenomena spanned by the polyvalent object, allowing us to unify these various worldly phenomena under a predicate, e.g., the 'Kafkaesque'. The paradigmatic cases of this cognitive work are, inevitably, those that have rendered themselves invisible by their own thoroughness of impact, where the lexicalization of the aesthetically generated concept obscures the aesthetic process that constitutively underlies it: we effortlessly predicate a certain personal or institutional predicament as 'Kafkaesque', a certain worldly conversation as 'Pinteresque', a certain worldly puzzle as 'Borgesian'. (I'm still waiting for 'Ackeresque' to make it into circulation and finally name contemporary life, but Athena's owl flies only at dusk and so on, see Acker [1984].)

18. Perhaps the best conceptual bridge from the raw 'aesthetic unity' that we associated with an autoencoder's canon to a kind of systemic gestalt modelling of reality that we associate with the computational form of a trained autoencoder is what we might call the relation of *comparability* between all objects in a trained autoencoder's canon. The global aesthetic unity of the objects in a set fit for autoencoding, I propose, is not just technically but conceptually and phenomenologically inseparable from the global intercomparability of the manifold's objects, and the global intercomparability of the manifold's objects is not just technically but conceptually and phenomenologically inseparable from the representation of a *system*.

Even if we die

**if we have to
become monsters**

**and
everyone
hates us,**

**we have to read the book be-
cause it will teach us how to
avoid the alligators' jaws, the
wolves who wait in the forest,
the huge snakes, and how to become birds.**

Figure 3. Excerpt from Kathy Acker, *Blood and Guts in High School*,
New York, Grove Press, 1984. ©2023, ProLitteris, Zurich, with kind permission.

19. In the phenomenology of reading, we experience this (so to speak)
'sameness of difference' as primary, and the 'aesthetic unity' of a literary
work's imaginative landscape as derived. A literary work's 'style' or 'vibe' is,
at first, an invariant structure of the very transformations and transitions
that make up the work's narrative and rhetorical *movement*. As we read Georg
Büchner's 'Lenz', for instance, plot moves, and the lyrical processes of Lenz's
psyche revolve their gears, and Lenz shifts material and social sites, and every
change consolidates and clarifies the higher-order constancy of mood. A given
literary work's invariant style or vibe, we argued, is the aesthetic correlate of
a literary work's internal *space of possibilities*. This space of possibilities is, from
the reader's point of view, an extrapolation from the *space of transformations*

that encodes the logic of the work's narrative, lyrical, and rhetorical 'difference engine'. Or, more prosaically: no less than it means a capacity to judge
whether a set of objects or phenomena does or does not collectively possess
a given style, to grasp a 'style' or 'vibe' should mean a capacity to judge the
difference between two (style-conforming) objects in relation to its framework.

20. Learning to sense a system, and learning to sense in relation to a system
– learning to see a style, and learning to see in relation to a style – are, autoencoders or no autoencoders, more or less one and the same thing. If the above
is right, and an 'aesthetic unity' of the kind associated with a 'style' or 'vibe'
is immediately a sensible representation of a logic of difference or change, we
can deduce the following rule of cognition: functional access to the data-anal-
ysis capacities of a trained autoencoder's feature function follows, in the *very*
long run, even from appropriate 'style perception' or 'vibe perception' alone.
Formally, the totality of representation-space distances between input-space
points logically fixes the feature function. More practically, access to representation-space difference and even to representation-space distance alone
is – if the representation-space is based upon a strong *lossy compression schema*
for the domain – practicably sufficient for powerful 'transductive' learning of
concrete classification and prediction skills in the domain (Gammerman et
al. 1998). When we grasp the loose 'vibe' of a real-life, worldly domain via its
idealization as the 'style' or 'vibe' of an ambient literary work, then, we are
plausibly doing at least as much 'cognitive mapping' as there is to be found in
the distance metric of a strong lossy compression schema.

21. One reason the mathematical-cognitive trope of autoencoding matters, I would argue, is that it describes the bare, first act of treating a collection of objects or phenomena as a set of *states of a system* rather than a bare
collection of objects or phenomena – the minimal, ambient systematization
that raises *stuff* to the level of *things*, raises *things* to the level of *world*, raises
one-thing-after-another to the level of *experience*. (And, equally, the minimal, ambient systematization that erases nonconforming *stuff* on the authority of *things*,
marginalizes nonconforming *things* to make a world, degenerates experience
into false consciousness.)[10]

22. In relating the input-space points of a set's manifold to points in the
lower dimensional internal space of the manifold, an autoencoder's model
makes the fundamental distinction between phenomena and noumena that
turns the input-space points of the manifold into a system's range of visible
states rather than a mere arbitrary set of phenomena. The parallel 'aesthetic unity' in a world or in a work of art – what we have called its 'vibe'
– is arguably, in this sense, something like a maximally 'virtual' variant of
Heideggerian mood (*Stimmung*). If a mood is a 'presumed view of the total picture' (Flatley) that conditions any specific attitude toward any particular thing,
this aesthetic unity (that which associates the collected objects or phenomena
of a world or work with a space of possibilities that gives its individual objects
or phenomena meaning by relating them to a totality) is sensible cognition of

a kind of *Stimmung* of a system – and like *Stimmung* it's the 'precondition for, and medium of' (Heidegger 1983) all more specific operations of subjectivity. What an autoencoding gives is something like the system's basic system-hood, its primordial having-a-way-about-it. How it vibes.

Works Cited

Acker, Kathy. 1984. *Blood and Guts in High School*. New York: Grove Press.

Batuman, Elif. 2008. 'What Am I Doing Here.' *The Guardian*. April 26, 2008. https://www.theguardian.com/books/2008/apr/26/popandrock.

Beistegui, Miguel. 2012. *Aesthetics After Metaphysics: From Mimesis to Metaphor*. New York: Routledge.

Felski, Rita. 2009. 'After Suspicion.' *Profession*: 28-35.

Flatley, Jonathan. 2008. *Affective Mapping*. Cambridge, MA: Harvard University Press.

Gammerman, Alex, Vladimir G. Vovk, and Vladimir N. Vapnik. 1998. 'Learning by Transduction.' *UAI'98 Proceedings of the Fourteenth Conference on Uncertainty in Artificial Intelligence*, 148-155. San Francisco: Morgan Kaufmann Publishers.

Gerard, Sarah. 2014. 'Trisha Low by Sarah Gerard.' *BOMB Magazine* 3 June 2014.

Heidegger, Martin. 1983. *The Fundamental Concepts of Metaphysics: World, Finitude, Solitude*. Bloomington: Indiana University Press.

Ngai, Sianne. 2007. *Ugly Feelings*. Cambridge, MA: Harvard University Press.

Piper, Adrian. 1992/93. 'Xenophobia and Kantian Rationalism.' *Philosophical Forum XXIV* 1-3: 188-232.

Ricoeur, Paul. 1977. *Freud and Philosophy: An Essay on Interpretation*. New Haven, CT: Yale University Press.

Williams, William Carlos, Ed. Christopher MacGowan. 1992. *Paterson*. New York: New Directions.

Yeats, William Butler. 1903. 'William Blake and His Illustrations to The Divine Comedy.' *Ideas of Good and Evil*.

Notes

This text first appeared under the same title in *Glass Bead* 1, no. 1 in 2017 (https://www.glass-bead.org/article/a-theory-of-vibe). We thank the author and the editors for their kind permission to reprint the essay here. American English spelling conventions have been retained in this essay in order to prevent confusion in any future citations.

1. 'Vanilla' autoencoders, as described here, are antiques in deep learning (DL) research terms. Contemporary variants like autoencoder generative adversarial networks (GANs), however, have performed exceptionally in 2017.

2. The term originally comes from Paul Ricœur, in reference to Marx and Freud. Colloquially, it has come to name the academic reading practices of mainstream Anglo-American critical theory at the turn of the twenty-first century. See Ricoeur (1977).

3. Compare with Trisha Low: 'The idea is that all this ethereal, feminine language is really concrete, or a sort of sublime mass of flesh that can really press down on certain kinds of structures that produced it in the first place. Like tar. Well, I guess I'm not secretly a structuralist anymore because I've said I'm secretly a structuralist so many times that people just know. But I'm interested in the way that somatic disturbances can press up against templates or structures, which make them more visible. Or not even necessarily more visible, but which produce a tension between what you feel is the fleshy part and what you feel is the structure underneath. The two are still indivisible though.' (Gerard, 2014).

4. The same goes, I would say, for meaning in the works of Modernists like Alfred Jarry, Virginia Woolf, Franz Kafka, Maurice Maeterlinck, Raymond Roussel, Ezra Pound, T.S. Eliot, Robert Musil, Andrei Bely, Viktor Shklovsky, Walter Benjamin, Velemir Khlebnikov, Daniil Kharms, Yukio Mishima, Harold Pinter, John Ashbery, Nathalie Saurraute, Haroldo de Campos, Samuel R. Delany, Kathy Acker, or Alain Robbe-Grillet, and staple 'proto-Modernist' anchors like Georg Büchner, Herman Melville, Comte de Lautreamont, or Emily Dickinson, as well as parts of later Johann Wolfgang von Goethe, Charlotte Brontë, later Anton Chekhov, and later Gustave Flaubert.

5. More formally, we proposed to understand the features of a trained autoencoder as analogous to a fixed list of predicates with room to write-in a real-valued numerical grade from 0 to 9 next to each, where 0 means 'not at all' and 9 means 'extremely'.

6. In the normal definition of Kolmogorov complexity, the 'semiotic system' in question must be Turing-complete: that is, the semiotic system in question must be capable of describing a universal Turing-machine. (Our own 'default' semiotic system – that is, the semiotic system of the human subject currently communicating with you, the reader – is of course Turing-complete, since we can think about, describe, and build universal Turing-machines.) In the coming discussion, we will lift this restriction, in order to allow us to also talk about the Kolmogorov complexity of certain sets relative to more limited semiotic systems – semiotic systems like a given trained autoencoder's 'generative vocabulary' (decoder function). The purpose of this deviation is to save space we would otherwise have to devote to the fidgety technical concepts of conditional Kolmogorov complexity and of upper bounds on Kolmogorov complexity. We take this liberty because unlike most other mathematical concepts, the concept of Kolmogorov complexity does not have a preexisting one-size-fits-all fully formal definition, and always calls for a measure of customization to the purposes of a given discussion. For the sake of propriety, we will mark each instance of this 'off brand' application of the concept of Kolmogorov complexity as 'Kolmogorov+ complexity'.

7. We will leave aside the question whether Plato was, himself, a Platonist in this sense.

8. Coleridge and William Carlos Williams both take their concept of Imagination from Kant.

9. A partition is the division of a set into non-overlapping subsets.

10. See Piper (1992/93). Piper discusses xenophobia as 'a special case of a more general cognitive phenomenon, namely the disposition to resist the intrusion of anomalous data of any kind into a conceptual scheme whose internal rational coherence is necessary for preserving a unified and rationally integrated self'.

2

Two Autonomies of the Symbolic Order: Data and Language in Neural Nets

Leif Weatherby

> Denn nicht *wir* wissen, es ist allererst ein gewisser *Zustand* unsrer, welcher weiß. [For it is not *we* who know, but above all a certain *state* in us, which knows.]
>
> —Kleist

The Data Hypothesis

To think with AI, our first order of business must be to jettison its guiding metaphor. No one knows what 'intelligence' is, and it functions as a regulative ideal for industry and research, not as a concept. The moment we let go of the term, we can refocus energy on the simulacrum we otherwise miss, the *stuff* that AI surfaces. Catharine Malabou argues that we have to abandon the old concept of human-individual 'intelligence' in order to confront the moving target of the 'negotiation' between 'the transcendental and the empirical' (Malabou 2019: 11). The 'mind' might still function as a 'shield' in the way that Sigmund Freud described (9), but we have sprung loose something else that negotiates on our behalf. The 'simulation of life' has blurred the borders 'between biological and symbolic life' (xvii). It is this region which, as we shall see below, language (and technology more generally) occupies anyway. (Malabou is borrowing Gilbert Simondon's framework, in which the creation of new *a prioris* is the vocation of technology.)[1] The 'symbolist' phase of AI failed to open up this border region, but the shift to data-hungry machine learning models has swung the pendulum heavily.

    Neural nets, as Malabou recognises, have thrust a completely different philosophical genealogy into prominence. Where classical AI focused on the notion of 'physical symbol systems' and the logical manipulation of their symbols (Newell and Simon 1976), machine learning recalls the work of Jean Piaget,[2] the idea of the emergence of abstraction from perception in

John Locke (Buckner 2018), and perhaps above all, the empirically grounded programmes of American Pragmatism. What these figures share is a focus on empiricism, learning, and emergence – as opposed to logic, form, and stability. They are invoked because nets are said to 'learn', in an open-ended process of scouring and reconfiguring training data until something like a generality is achieved. At first glance, then, the shift seems to be from a symbolic *deduction* to observational *induction* – the power of the net is that its range is indeterminate with respect to its inputs, where symbols had to be prestabilised and semantically rigid in order to function at all. But there is slightly more going on here.

Nets are functions that take a large number of individual data points as inputs – these can range from hundreds to trillions, in the case of modern language models. They then multiply these data points through a matrix by initially randomised weights, at first leading to an obviously false answer. If the input is an image of a squirrel, for example, the pixel data that one could reconstruct with the first pass-through would be visual gibberish – intentionally. The 'backpropagation algorithm' then deploys the chain rule of calculus to find local tendencies at each point as it passes 'back' through the matrix, assigning more and less 'blame' for the wrong answer to each cell.[3] The process is repeated until the loss is minimised, and the result, in this case, is a squirrel-identifier.

This identifier has stabilised a pattern that corresponds to the concept 'squirrel', but is more accurate than human eyes are at locating them. A famous example shows that a trained net is better at distinguishing a Samoyed dog from a white wolf than humans are. This is significant in the case of radiography, for example, where shadows and tumors are finely distinct. And it would indeed then appear that the net has created an abstraction, performing induction on a large number of examples and producing some function $f(x)$ that predicts 'squirrel'. Deep learning engineer François Chollet visualises this difference neatly in the following diagram (Chollet 2018):

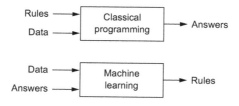

Figure 1. Classical programming vs. machine learning

This difference corresponds to a classical distinction made by the American Pragmatist Charles Sanders Peirce.[4] Induction goes from cases (answers) and results (data) to rules. The net does this because the results are given to it in the training set ('these images contain squirrels'). When we ask the net to classify once it has been trained, we are demanding a deduction, in which rule ('squirrel = $f(x)$') and data (previously unseen images) are given, and answer should be 'this image does (or does not) contain a squirrel'. But – again – more is going on.

A third kind of judgement, in Peirce's terms, is *hypothesis* (or, technically, 'abduction'), and this is actually what is happening in a net, as Luciana Parisi has pointed out (Parisi 2013: 2017). In the hypothesis, the rule and the result are combined to conclude to the case. The hypothesis says 'what I see here must be a case of this rule' or: this observation tends to make me think that the world conforms to this rule. A 'weak' form of judgement, hypotheses are used where the rule is clear but the relationship between rule and result is not given. Peirce gives the example of fish fossils being found far inland – the data (fossils) and the rule (fish are aquatic) are given, but their relation is lacking, so we form the notion that the 'sea once washed over the land' (*Elements of Logic*, 625). For Peirce, the hypothesis is far more common than we tend to assume. For example, all historical judgements are hypothetical. No one alive has ever seen the man 'Napoleon', for example, but the data (images and documents of him) and the rule (that documents and images are of existing entities) suggest that he really existed (the case). Perhaps we can go further and say that this hypothesis takes the form 'the world is as if Napoleon, with all we know of him, lived in it'. We reason about his personal existence from documents, but we reason about Napoleon the conqueror based on the geopolitical landscape he left in his imperial wake.

When we ask the net to classify, we are indeed seeking a determinate result: this is (or is not) an image of a squirrel. But to describe the net as trained inductively to classify deductively is to miss the data-world relationship that the net is actually proposing something about. This relationship underlies the obsessive question of the 'intelligence' discourse, but that discourse never focuses on the semiotics of the judgements actually being performed by these nets. The net actually gives us a hypothetical ('this would be a case of squirrelness', given the world calibrated such-and-so). This is important to bear in mind because the net's squirrel function is not equivalent to the human concept 'squirrel', for two reasons.

First, the function that the net produces ($f(x)$) cannot be better at recognising squirrel-like pixels than humans if it is identical to our procedure for squirrel recognition. But there is more than that: a function is only a concept, as Frege famously argued, when it has a truth-value. The truth-value is supplied *not* by the net, but by the relationship between the net's hypothesis and human judgement. That is, what produces the determinate judgement 'this is a squirrel' is a relationship between data and judgement. Note that I do *not* say 'between data and the world': the net hypothesises a judgement, and that judgement is about the world. Determination is extended here, and it is crucial that we not collapse that extension in describing the activity of the net. It hypothesises not about the world, but about potential judgemental relationships that could describe the world. If we accept its judgement (even automatically), we are integrating hypotheses into our representation of the world. The data hypothesis alters the structure of representation. When we say that the net 'classifies', we are talking about an interpretation of the net's hypothetical judgement ('this would be a squirrel if squirrelness = $f(x)$', 'this is a case of squirrel in a world in which $f(x)$ is squirrelness', 'this image contains $f(x)$') as a determinate judgement). The net may even be programmed to print the string 'yes, this image contains a squirrel', but the underlying judgement is still hypothetical, not 'this is a squirrel' but 'this could be a case of squirrelness'. This is important *not* because the net is 'wrong' about the squirrel in the image; nets are better than humans at detecting minor pixel-level differences. It is important because the entirety of neural-net based judgements is a hypothesis about the relationship between what the world might be like ('squirrel') and data ('$f(x)$'). We miss this when we confuse the net's actual semiotic activity with the language we translate it into (or programme it to pre-translate for us).

When we hypothesise, we posit that the world coheres in a such a way that a specific case exists. The world we live in is one in which Napoleon existed. The world we live in is one that behaves as if we landed on the moon. (It is this little wedge between determination and possibility ('as if') that allows us to reverse hypotheses like the moon landing.) A more than hypothetical establishment of fact is impossible in terms of science, so it is not to the detriment of the net's capacities that we notice this distinction. But the distinction allows us to see the interface between the net's hypothesis and our own judgement – the result of which can of course be, in turn, anything from denial to affirmation to hypothesis itself. The point is not that nets 'can't do x', but rather what nets *actually do*, and that they actually do it in semiotic combination with our own judgements. Differentiating these procedures allows us to describe nets in semiotic terms, since, regardless of the 'semantics' of their various functions, they actually indicate using those functions (Weatherby and Justie 2022). The semiotics of nets are not equivalent to the semantics that humans ask nets to produce. What nets mean is up to us, because what they say is hypothetical. Machine learning has always been said to be 'flexible' because of its open-ended algorithms, yet another part of its power lies in the open-endedness of its outputs. Nets give us options for interpretation.

This is what I call the 'data hypothesis'. It is both the hypothesis that data can be used to represent and meaningfully engage the undatafied world – a fact that is demonstrated as much by our fear of harm as it is by cases of success – *and* the fact that data used for learning in this way is always hypothetical.[5] Data does not represent 'the world', but instead sets of judgements about the world, a fact that is captured elegantly in the name for the discipline in which nets were engineered: representation learning. How much 'world' is in a representation is perhaps *the* metaphysical question of modern thought, and its silhouette is visible throughout the discourse of deep learning. Yet data science tends to use a simplified notion of 'ground truth' that the data hypothesis in this double sense undermines. 'Ground truth' is not 'fact' but a separate representation of fact in another semiotic system (usually language as expressive of concepts). The point is not that we cannot stabilise nets around accepted notions of truthful statements, but rather that when we do, we are black-boxing the dialogue between computation and language that underlies all nets (including in visual and other applications).

What I take to be the gold standard of interpretation of nets is Orit Halpern's notion of 'beautiful data', which shows how the dream of the net, long before its algorithmic implementation, already configured a world in which data streams are mutually interoperable and translatable, one that mimics the notion of the brain as such a transfer station, but then distributed into the world, forming an aesthetic condition (Halpern 2014). Many things follow from that condition, including Halpern's notion of 'derivativeness' in what she, Jeffrey Kirkwood, Patrick Jagoda and I have called 'surplus data' (Halpern et al. 2022), and what she further calls the 'smartness mandate' (Halpern and Mitchell 2022). Work on data is 'derivative' in the sense that a result obtained not from first-order empirical observation, but from a representation of those observations, is fed back into the world through logistical channels, rendering the very world we encounter 'derivative' of the data which was supposed to be a representation of that world. This feedback loop tends to render all judgement hypothetical. Rather than a world of stable fact about which hypotheses are made, the world of beautiful data looks more like a serial hypothesis from which the 'world' is first crystallised in its (usually overlooked) semiotic transformation with human systems of representation. The common channel of that semiosis is – and always will be – language.

Language as a Service, Attention as a Grid

A great deal of the confusion over the special class of nets called large language models (LLMs) boils down to the simple fact that language is the medium through which humans communicate with their computational machines. This has always been true. When Friedrich Kittler infamously called an essay 'There Is No Software', what he actually argued was that '[software] *would* not exist if computer systems did not – at least until now – need to coexist with an environment of everyday languages'. (Kittler 2014: 223). This phrasing makes it sound as though computing systems can take or leave language, but that is not the case. Language does not merely 'coexist' with computational systems – one need look no further than the input/output unit included in the 'First Draft of a Report on the Edvac' assembled by John von Neumann (generally taken to be the first explicit architecture for a stored-programme computer) to see that no digital system has ever been 'computational' in the absence of the linguistic environment (von Neumann 1993). It is all too easy to think of the edge of the diagram, which often reads 'I/O' for 'input/output', as not *really* part of the computer. But it is very hard to accept what would follow, namely a 'computer' that does not render its computations at all, a true black box that could just as well be a slab of granite as a calculating engine. The relationship between computation and language is essential to every digital machine. Language and number may not get along in concepts or intuitions, they may even contradict one another in some essential way or ways. Kittler seems to suggest that they are forced into a relationship that obscures the computational core of the computer. But it is rather their internal relationship that allows for computing *in the first place*. They are not grafted onto each other using some third thing (the name of which Kittler leaves out anyway).[6] Just in the way that mathematics is the explanation of (among other things) numerical reasoning, computing is the rendering of linguistically meaningful results. Language is the medium of computation.

If it is hard to distinguish the simulation of induction and deduction in nets from their hypothetical core, it is even harder – and perhaps impossible – to separate their manipulation of language from simply language. This is because the role that labeling plays in classifying nets is taken over by language itself in LLMs. Linguistic applications in nets abandon the operation of supervision (the manual labeling of squirrels for the training dataset) to arrive at basic results, instead using the learning function to generate language, one word at a time. This inversion is crucial to thinking with AI, because it collapses the computation and its 'environment' – the results of the computation are language itself. This establishes a concrete version of a problem that I call 'the double autonomy of the symbolic order'. Where an image-classifying net produces a function that obviously is not the same as our conceptual grasp of the object at hand, a language-learning net learns to generate nothing other than language. Attempts to distinguish in some essential way between the 'real' language of humans and the merely 'apparent' language of nets make little sense on their face, and have disastrous consequences – as we shall see – for the analysis of these systems. Where a classifying net indicates, a language model generates icons using symbols. There is no such thing as hypothetical language, so nets learn language itself. They do so using the 'attention mechanism' at the base of the Transformer Architecture, the core of GPT systems.

Attention overcomes a problem that the net approach to AI had always had in linguistic applications, namely the problem of *memory*. Humans do not memorise language, they use it. I do not have a static store of all the sentences I've heard or read in my mind. I *use* language in the sense that I generate meaning from the combination of rules (grammar) and other meanings (words in grammatical context). The relationship between meaning and rules does not become explicit by that use. Meaning surfaces, but does not explain itself.

Early net-based approaches to language relied on memorisation (storage) over a sequence, leading to problems of misapplication, memory overload, and irrelevance. The most general format was the Recurrent Neural Net, in which the output of the net was fed back in as input, allowing the net to capture some of the structure in the linguistic strings. But this quickly maxed out

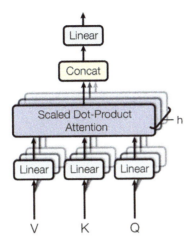

Figure 2. Attention head. Image from Vaswani et al. (2017).

the memory capacity of the grid, and led to spotty language use as the net 'forgot' pieces and rules of language that were distant from its current input. The creation of variably ranging memory in LSTM ('long short-term memory') solved part of this problem, but also hit barriers. The attention mechanism solves this problem by allowing the net to encode a one-to-all matrix for each word in the dataset. By including the positions of the words in the 'embedding' process (in which words are indexed to numbers), the problem of memory is solved by packaging the semantic relationships and their grammatical layout in a single 'pre-training'. Rather than jamming rules and words into some location, the net is allowed to 'attend' to real possibilities to move to from its current word.

One can think of this like a set of patterns pre-programmed into a grid of lights. Touch one light, and one shape turns on; another, and some other shape lights up. 'Attend' to one word and the grid's values shift to specify each other word's likelihood to be next. If the word I am attending to is 'see' and the word before it is 'I' then nouns of all kinds and the word 'that' will light up, meaning their value will range high. This set of higher values given a word in a sequence will be pooled by a 'temperature' feature – turned too high, this will produce too predictable a text, and too low, nonsense. But the Goldilocks temperature will produce […] the very 'everyday language' that the computation would otherwise have as its environment (see Wolfram 2023). And at this point, there is no 'classifying' function (which explains why LLMs are hit-and-miss for most serious reasoning tasks). The net produces, but does not tell us rules about, language. It uses language. The underlying mechanism is surely different in kind from the human use of language, but the property of generating meaning from the combination of rules and other meaning, is the same. There is no difference to speak of between the net's manipulation of data and the 'world' that data represents. The language that a model of language produces is language. There can be no clear separation between hypothesis and deduction here, for if a net spits out a series of words that cohere as natural language, the difference between the semiotic function and the semantic function collapses – producing not just indications but instead meanings.[7] The language model distills language from its usual bundle with intelligence, affect, and other cognitive functions. The result of language is more language, and that is how language becomes a service.

I propose the term 'language as a service' to describe the world we already inhabit, in which language is on tap at the push of a button, a menu of options to activate across an infinite array of genres. LLMs loosen the relationship between intention, labour, and writing, leading media scholar Matthew Kirschenbaum to predict a 'textpocalypse' (Kirschenbaum 2023), as the textual rails of our civilization waver. We often hear now of the 'as-a-service-ification' of the economy, as seemingly everything comes unbundled as independent software packages. Nick Srnicek points, for example, to the platform economy model which Boeing uses to sell jet engines 'as a service', converting the commodity from engine to digital system. The engine itself is more or less rented, in this case, while what is actually sold is the proprietary software, including service and repairs. This both protects the code and the data of the selling company, while significantly altering the landscape of what counts as a commodity in heavy industry (Srnicek and De Sutter 2017).

Language as a service is at the extreme other end of the spectrum (as will be 'code as a service', which LLMs are already providing). For language to be provided pre-packaged as software, it must be produced outside of human minds. Where visual applications of nets externalise forms of classification and render images from labels (as DALL·E does), LLMs exploit the deeper relationship of word and number to generate the very stuff in which judgement must eventually be expressed and communicated: language. Perhaps nets will get better at exploiting the 'physical grammar' of movement in videos as time goes on, but for now the most important epistemological and economic result of these systems is the unrolling of massive amounts of linguistic redundancy as *more language*, surplus language. While the relationship between 'good' and 'safe' information and language is being worked out by the rentier class of the platform economy, however, we must urgently make two things clear. We must see that LLMs confirm and extend the idea that language is *already* artificial and independent of human minds, and for that reason we must move beyond single-dimensional analyses of AI, to what I call 'polythematic' semiotics.

The Double Autonomy of the Symbolic Order

If one had to point to a major achievement of the twentieth-century humanities, one could do worse than the concept of the 'autonomy of the symbolic order'. This idea can be traced back to the blurry transition between structuralism and post-structuralism. The idea that patterns of language, institution, and psyche were independent of some 'ground truth' outside of the system in question animated a whole generation of French thinkers in the 'human sciences' (Dosse 1997).[8] I call this grouping 'the structuralism complex', since it forms a theory type distinguishable from others, family squabbles aside. Structuralism – which was intertwined at its height with cybernetics – arrived in the United States packaged in its rejection by a group of literary critics and philosophers whose influence is now embedded in virtually every branch of the humanities. One major concept that emerged from this moment was the idea that written language could not be accounted for by humanism. Terms and phrases like *différance* (Jacques Derrida), *différend* (Jean-François Lyotard), simulacrum (Baudrillard), and 'floating signifier' (Claude Lévi-Strauss) all share in the conviction that language is not restricted to thinking, cognition, or the understanding. The figure who most clearly and fully articulated this idea, however, was Jacques Lacan. Lacan divided Freud's psychological categories of the ego, the superego, and the id, into the 'registers' of the imaginary (where we make sense of our picture of reality), the symbolic (signs as opposed to images: numbers, letters, etc.), and the Real (which is completely inaccessible, defined as that which cannot be represented). As the cybernetics craze filtered through the personnel of structuralism into Paris, Lacan spent the year 1954-55 lecturing on the emancipation of the symbolic order in servomechanisms and early digital machines (Lacan and Lacan 1991). Patterns of symbols would, he said, emerge from machinic feedback (as cyberneticians often did, he used the example of automatic doors) in the physical world, but these would then redound into the structural patterns of human communication as inhuman entities. The symbolic order confronts us, from the psychoanalytic perspective, as alien from the jump. We are immersed in an order we did not generate, so that even if it is 'human', it does not sync with our expectations, desires, or sense of self. Writing and language are always alienating entities, and digital systems, Lacan predicted, would destabilise the structures of control we used to keep them 'human'.

The point that we need to bear in mind is that the structuralism complex (including poststructuralism) discovered this autonomy of the symbolic without reference to machines in the first instance. (This is how they differed from the manic energy that drove the dystopia and redemption narratives about machines in the Weimar era.) Structuralism was driven by the discovery of *really existing concrete patterns of signification that could not be reduced to some first cause*. The problem then quickly became how to think about technology's impact on that already-autonomous artificial order of signs. Lacan captured this double autonomy in the slogan 'the world of the symbolic is the world of the machine' (Kittler, Johnston, and Johnston 1997). This problem is one of the most pressing in the era of AI.

This line of thought was one major strand in the founding of the modern discipline of media theory. Friedrich Kittler laid the groundwork by breaking with the thesis that media are 'extensions' of human capacities, most famously articulated by Marshall McLuhan. The extension thesis, by keeping media in constant relation to human capacities, disallows the autonomy of media effects. Kittler went to great rhetorical and historiographical lengths to argue that this was a false starting point for the reproduction of sound, image, and 'writing'. Writing, as an activity done by hand, mind, and emotion working together, gained a storage and reproduction medium external to the writing itself in the printing press. During this period (what McLuhan called the 'Gutenberg Galaxy'), writing remained, according to Kittler, the only way to store and reproduce images and sounds (by means of the imagination) (Kittler 1990). With the typewriter, the point of production was altered, because the set of symbols was no longer held in and between minds, but laid out in the keyboard. The printing press was miniaturised at the labour interface of writing. The 'symbolic order' could be seen as a natural part of the human mind – or as the non-natural essence of humanity's non-fit with nature – only until the relative autonomy of language was made material. At that point, language had to be seen as its own instance, bearing its own force – this is what I understand Kittler to mean when he says that Lacan brings psychoanalysis up to date with the media (Kittler, Johnston, and Johnston 1997).

This autonomy, however, is not restricted to letters, and when it took its incipient computational form, the question concerning the symbolic order became more urgent. Erich Hörl's elegant account of how the formalisation of thought led to an 'ecology' of such independent symbols follows this Lacanian trajectory (Hörl, Nancy, and Schott 2018), as does Bernhard Siegert's notion that the 'passage of the digital' is the intervention of the symbolic in the Real, where it has been set loose without possibility of recuperation into our understanding, creating a 'schizoid' binary (Siegert 2003). Siegert calls this type of operation *Kulturtechnik* or 'cultural technics',[9] a technique that cultivates a difference (Siegert and Winthrop-Young 2015). The value of this move is clear: differences of this kind are not introduced into some blank-slate state of nature in which all is pre-stabilised. But there is a danger here, too, which is that we trivialise the way in which one difference is built on top of another difference in sequence. The 'autonomy of the symbolic order', as I am deriving it here, stands for a meta-difference in which an order that is already neither natural nor fully 'human' (in the sense of 'held within human understanding') is displaced *again*. To deal with that situation, you need not just 'cultural technics', but instead what Jeffrey Kirkwood calls 'semiotechnics', 'a theory of technical systems focusing on their management of absences, breaks, and gaps for the production of meaning' (Kirkwood 2022, 9). The reason this revision is crucial is that the relationship between the machine and the order of signs reveals an integration of two orders of difference with each other. It is not in the gap between representation and thing that we will find answers, but in the merging and contradictions between two orders. This is a problem of form, syntax, or reason, but only if each of these terms is stripped of it's a priori, Gods-eye status – the real relation between shapes and complexes of signs and reasons is the common ground of semiotics and dialectics. When we arrive at this type of complexity, we need to find a descriptive language that lives up to it – but the tendency is, instead, to revert to a panicked humanism that is little more than a remainder.

Remainder Humanism

It was the literary theorists who rescinded the genteel gesture of the Turing test for actual human authors. Turing's famous test was based in social rec-ognition: if I cannot tell if I am talking to a human or a machine, then a machine in that position qualifies as intelligent. The repeated announcements that the author was 'dead' refuse to animate text by means of that recognition, scrutinising it without the imaginary interlocutor. But these announcements seem today to have been half-hearted at best. It is as though the 'autonomy of the symbolic order' never *landed* across a wide swath of disciplines. It hovers, we learn it, it sometimes makes partial contact with one or another object. But its Age of Aquarius has dawned with GPT systems, and we see a great recoiling into the remaining corners of viable humanism. I call this 'remain-der humanism', a failure to take seriously the cultural-systematic state of play. Every appeal to the 'flattening' of 'complex' and 'human' and 'embodied' secrets allegedly absent from digital systems fails, *not* because those things do not exist, and not *even* because they are not manipulated, harmed, and even 'murdered' (in Jonathan Beller's hyperbole (Beller 2017)) by those sys-tems, but because those terms do not show us why those harms are possible, and what the laws of their unfolding will be. No binary system will describe the interaction of two orders of difference. When Franco 'Bifo' Berardi writes that 'digital networks […] have penetrated the social organism […] but the two levels cannot synchronize', we are witnessing little more than resistance to AI (Berardi 2023). This remainder humanism is the theoretical equivalent of painting oneself into a corner. No amount of insistence that digital and human systems 'fit badly' together will change the concrete situation, in which the merger of those systems is the most glaring fact. This goes for their 'align-ment' too, which occurs in fact but not as we would explicitly want it to, since that desire is also expressed in utterly naïve binary terms.

Noam Chomsky has argued that GPT systems have no substantial rela-tionship to language whatsoever. In a high-profile op-ed, Chomsky conflates the question of intelligence with that of language, attempting to show how humans use language cognitively, seeking and establishing truth and reason-ing morally, in ways that algorithms can't (Chomsky 2023). This argument is both old (Chomsky has been making a version of it since 1957) and strangely off-target. No one thinks – at least, no one should think – that GPT systems do language the way humans do language. And in restricting language to the synthetic functions of the human brain, Chomsky epitomises the humanistic recoil against the autonomy of the symbolic. We do not need to disagree with his account of the human use of language to disagree that this use of language is language as such. The sheer bravura of dismissing more than a trillion words of human-produced language on the grounds that it is then reproduced algorithmically is the perfect fit for the arrogance of the AI movement itself, which takes no account of the harm, but also none of the interesting non-'intelligence' effects, of its systems. But even this grandiose claim is a remainder – a remainder of a separation between cognition and language that is only obscured by the systems that now produce the latter without the former.

Chomsky seems to confuse the generation with the use of language. Humans do both, of course, but when we cognitively synthesise words in order to arrive at an idea we hold to be true or good, we are mostly using language. It is not at all clear that my typing this sentence 'produces' language in a strong sense. It contributes to the overall tendency of English, I suppose, but as I choose each word I do so with genuine semantic limitations. I can replace 'produces' in the previous sentences with 'generates', but not with 'garbles' or 'vgfrdb'. To 'produce' language in the sense implied by Chomsky is somehow to generate it *as if for the first time*, in keeping with the alleged device in the brain that first gave rise to language. Whether I am following external or internal rules remains undecided, mixed – for we are not at the origin of language. An interface like ChatGPT might be *even further* from that origin, and in spite of – even because of – this, reveal even more about what language is than our cognitive systems can. The act of speaking is social and technological, not human in some sense innocent of either.

The humanistic view of language denies not the double autonomy of the symbolic order, but the very social-artificial aspect of language as such. Meaning is not made in the mind; at a minimum it must be between minds. But this already provides the wedge that allows the strange admixture of technology and language.

Kant, Kittler... and Kissinger?

In what is perhaps to date the greatest exemplification of the meme 'the worst person you know just made a great point', Henry Kissinger has adopted the opposite tack from Chomsky's (Kissinger et al. 2023). Kissinger thinks that AI is a serious global problem. This is because nets have broken out of the mould of previous ancillary digital systems, and in doing so, have plunged us into the desert of the Real.

This is not an exaggeration. Kissinger thinks that neural nets are scouring areas of existence that human minds cannot, in principle, have access to. For that reason, the change that they represent is total, a change in the very idea of epistemology as much as an attendant shift in global power relations. He writes with his co-authors that AI is overcoming the self-understood limitations that the Enlightenment put on reason. AI is reaching past Kant's 'essential distinction between the thing in itself and the unavoidably filtered world we experience', and beginning to provide an alternative means of accessing – and thus understanding – reality' (Kissinger et al. 2021: 43). Here, Kissinger is unwittingly Kittlerian. Computation reaches into the depths of the Real, but rather than returning with some piece of it packaged for human understanding, shifts the very structure of our felt reality in ways that reverberate beyond our understanding. The future, Kissinger writes, will be 'a collaboration […] with a different kind of technical entity but with a different kind of reasoning' that will 'precipitate a transformation in metacognition and hermeneutics – the understanding of understanding – and in human perceptions of our role and function' (Kissinger et al. 2023). In fact, Kissinger here goes one step beyond Kittler and his school, with their famous rejection of hermeneutics. He suggests that a 'dialectic' (his word) between human understanding and neural nets will be established, one that we must urgently begin to guide even as it emerges.

Here we have a most wonderful formula: Kant, Kittler, and Kissinger. We might capture their collective rejection of 'remainder humanism' by supplying them with a common response to the X-Files' slogan 'the truth is out there', to which they say: no, it's not. The truth is in negotiation with this other form of mediated knowledge. The virtue of this motley crew of Kant, Kittler, and Kissinger is that they are able to jettison the metaphysics of intelligence entirely. Downstream from the loss of this ballast is a redefinition of language that recognises the importance of what Chomsky is saying – it is our hook for meaning, for generating semantics and for doing hermeneutics – but without the reification of a limited notion of thinking (essentially an individualistic one) as the essence of that language.

But even if the truth is mediated for him, you can feel the outmoded policy-control ambition in Kissinger. He has an unusually clear vantage-point, for obvious reasons, on the global logistical system made of net-based AI, and sees that this will not fit with current statecraft or capitalism.[10] But just in proportion with this clarity is Kissinger's inability to think beyond the mid-century problem of policy and control. This is its own form of remainder humanism, in the realm of practical rather than pure reason. But doesn't this dream of control, in which policy magically gets out ahead of our ultra-complex systems, sees them for what they are, and guides them into 'alignment' with a fantasised consensus, apply to most of our critical apparatuses too? Precisely because the centrist state has adopted data policy as the furthest horizon of its political imagination, we see many attempts to regulate the problems out of existence funded at the highest levels. But think-tankisation will not solve the metaphysical problems that critical theory was engineered to address. The truth is not 'out there', but just because it is caught in systems of signification does not make it easy to control. That fact is so obvious that it feels strange to have to point it out, yet we seem unable to focus our attention on the theoretical half of the problem long enough to address it. That, I want to argue, is because of what I call 'the monothematic sublime'.

The Monothematic Sublime

So all is not well in the world of AI, and at this point that is not news. As Emily Bender, Timnit Gebru, Angelina McMillan-Major, and Schmargaret Schmitchell, have detailed, Large Language Models are 'stochastic parrots' that 'encode stereotypical and derogatory associations along gender, race, ethnicity, and disability status' (Bender et al. 2021: 613). Although it was once a talking point that neural nets in general were 'black boxes', that is neither actually the case, nor the problem here. Instead, Bender et al. suggest, the problem is that the dataset is 'unfathomable'. You can open up the black box, but you cannot scrutinise its endless contents. Size, they rightly point out, 'does not guarantee diversity', and the problem is not that we can't see what it's inside the net, but that there is simply *too much to see*. We can only measure what might have been inside in any detail after the net produces output, when it is too late. Neural nets, then, are harmful precisely because they are unpredictable and dynamic – their epistemic virtues are their social pitfall.

But all is not well in the world of AI critique, either. The empirical result of this paper, along with so many other important studies – I would single out Ruha Benjamin's concept of 'the New Jim Code' (Benjamin 2019) and Victoria Eubanks's 'digital poorhouse' (Eubanks 2017) – does not by itself add up to a politics of digital systems and AI. Wendy Chun's work on proximity algorithms has shown how groupings emerged and are reified, revealing some of the mechanics behind the types of statistical agglomerations from which these 'encoded stereotypes' emerge (Chun and Barnett 2021). But 'unfathomable', as Gebru et al use it, is not going to do the theoretical work we need it to. This is, of course, not because the conclusion is wrong – it keeps getting righter, in fact, as these models are slowly released into the wilds of industry and society – but rather than an abstract negation like 'unfathomable' is not caustic enough to burn off the mists that make deep learning systems not black but grey boxes. We can look inside, but we cannot understand what we see. The fault lies in our understanding. And I want to label that fault here 'the monothematic sublime'. What is 'unfathomable' is also ineffable, and we run the risk of doing little more than supplementing the hype when we throw the concreteness of neural-net meaning-production into the night in which all cows are black – in which it is impossible to say if an AI is *perpetuating* or *exacerbating* bias and harm.

But everything depends on this distinction. Any possible political strategy that does not amount to pure managerialism – not to speak of actual critique – would depend on whether a digital system 'creatively' worsens the social system in question, or simply thickens its assumptions and 'best practices' (read: worst practices). 'Unfathomable' leaves us wavering, undecided, between stochastic creativity and rote parrotry. This cannot do the work we need, for there is not *one* fathomable entity to be negated in the vast data flats of neural nets, but *many*. We need a *polythematic desublimation* to account for the current AI situation.

We need this shift in perspective because neural nets are high-dimensional data processors. When we observe something, we separate between local, individual, singular states (data points) and constants, or features (in nets, 'parameters' developed by the weighting process). If the number of features is closer to the number of data points – meaning that the filtering mechanism is relaxed, potentially capturing more of the individual states – then we have 'high dimensions'. These technical terms repeat the influential division Immanuel Kant introduced into epistemology between 'intuitions' (*Anschauungen*, literally 'viewings' of singular states of affairs) and 'concepts'. If we know the rule that allows these two to fit together, we have a determinate judgement of fact, a low-dimensional model. If we do not, we have to seek that unity close to the individuality of the states of affairs (for Kant, this requires 'reflecting judgement', a high-dimensional activity deployed in biological and aesthetic inquiry). An example of an extremely low-dimensional system is the law of gravity – an infinite array of moving objects behave according to a single elegant formula. The models of classical physics provide *insight*; neural nets generate the very thing – images to classify, language to use – that the model might otherwise explain.

Leo Breiman's classical essay on the 'two cultures' of statistical modelling called these two modes 'data modelling', which attempts to construct data relations according to explicit rules, and 'algorithmic modelling', which designs algorithms that, by experimental hazard, produce a model that conforms to the data actually on hand. Breiman offers that the one type of modelling produces 'simplicity', while the other produces 'accuracy'. (Breiman 2001) But the accuracy comes at the price of insight, a tradeoff between interpretability and prediction that Breiman thinks attaches to all statistical manipulations. The philosopher Hans Blumenberg is making a similar but much broader point when he says that technology is a dialectic between 'performance and insight' (*Leistung und Einsicht*) (Blumenberg 2020), 399 (translation modified).

When that dialectic assumes a certain scale, we get a kind of 'data sublime', as cultural critic Will Davies has put it. We then tend to lose any sense of 'concreteness' in thinking (Davies 2015). Anthropologist Nick Seaver recounts how machine-learning pedagogy relies on a form of code-switching between spatial intuition with its three dimensions and extrapolation into 'high-dimensional spaces', with emphasis on the *total disconnect* between the two ('such extrapolations are suspect') (Seaver 2022: 126-27). To 'engineer' here is not to provide a blueprint, but to test unmarked territory, to strengthen performance. (And indeed, read papers in the field of data science, and they are disproportionately thick with accounts of benchmarks, often with more space given to assessment of performance than questions of model design.)

There is a real contradiction between intuition and understanding, on the one hand, and performance and understanding on the other. Bender, Gebru, and their co-authors point directly to this problem: 'unfathomable training data' reinforces the focus on 'state-of-the-art results on leaderboards without encouraging deeper understanding of the mechanism'. The higher the dimensions, the more powerful the model. And the more appealing: we are certainly drawn to think with these algorithms because they tempt us towards some understanding we have not previously possessed. But they do not and cannot provide that understanding. The loudest critics of machine learning agree with its founders and strongest advocates that these systems are not – or at any rate, not yet – thinking. But the question of how to think *with* them falls by the wayside in these public debates. And strangely, it does so just when the technical details are emphasised. Every time you read the phrase 'next-word predictor' or 'stochastic gradient descent', be ready to be disappointed. The problem is not that we do not understand the *mechanism*.[11] The question is not whether we *know* that those techniques are being employed in machine learners. The question is whether we know what the synthesis of net and image, or net and language, 'means'. Often enough, we have no answer to that question because public and technical discourses entirely lack any vocabulary to think about signification. The obsessive topic of discussion is instead what should be signified, what has political or cognitive warrant to be signified – matters very worthy of debate, but unresponsive when the problem is a genuinely cultural one. We have no answer because both engineers and humanists engage in a form of abstract resistance to the synthesis on hand. Overcoming it requires us to think in high dimensions.

We think in high dimensions all day, every day, all the time. Without really accounting for it or thinking about it, we spend a great deal of our cognitive efforts in decoding and encoding, generating and interpreting ultra-complex signs, messages and behaviours that, properly analysed, are 'high-dimensional'. Think of a simple text-message exchange, in which one participant in a thread forwards a tweet that contains a meme, another tags it with one of a dizzying array of emojis about which there is very little consensus as to meaning, and another using the indexical 'reply' function to pluck the message out of the quickly-developing stream of texts and replies. Everyone on the thread goes and uses the information and their impression of it to orient their off-thread activity, returning to the thread with fresh truth and expression. Even without filling in the content of these messages, one can see that what has developed is not 'low-dimensional'. Communication as such is, as Gregory Bateson liked to say, a form of play with multiple levels of abstraction ((Bateson 2000), 184). It is contradictory, singular, and yet symbolic, often generic, and even banal. If ever anyone thought that human communication *without* digital technologies was 'low-dimensional', they were simply not 'thinking with signification', but through it, beyond it, without it. Thinking with AI, we can then say, must involve this form of 'high dimensionality' proper to semiosis itself with the computational high dimensionality of neural nets and their specific architectures. The monothematic sublime will certainly not suffice here.

Towards a Polythematic Desublimation

As soon as the engineer leaves the lab, he stops thinking about AI in high dimensions. The hype around AI is one-dimensional (possibly less). But the reservations that we see coming from engineering are also reductionist, as though the world of mathematics and computing is complex, but the rest of the world is simple. This is the way in which the discourse of AI does not think with AI, but only about it, and not about the semiotic systems it engages.

Deep Learning engineer Yann Lecun writes, for example, that 'a system trained on language alone will never approximate human intelligence [...] but [such systems] will undoubtedly *seem* to approximate it if we stick to the surface. And, in many cases, the surface is enough [...]' (Browning and Lecun 2022). As I have been arguing, the reverse is true: the appearance is a form of depth bred of lack of real attention to the actual complexity of the surface phenomenon of the neural net, the surface composed of computation linked to human judgement and language. This surface, as I have been arguing, is more complex than the 'line of reasoning' that the net simulates, and which cannot be taken for an account of its activity. The semiotic surface is more complex than the misleading depth, the appearance of rational argumentation. To say that a net 'performs induction' is to mistake of the signifier for the signified. When both net and human are operating in language, the appearances, as the New York Times learned the hard way, are metaphysically deep, and the surface is hard to get hold of in thought. We do not exit high-dimensionality when we stop engineering, and if we want to understand these systems as agents in the channeling and production of signs and meanings, we need a model that isn't falsely low-dimensional.

One possibility for such a framework is the postmodern sublime. This notion has two canonical sources, Jean-François Lyotard and Fredric Jameson. In arguing for the end of the grandiose and linear project of modernism, Lyotard famously claimed that 'meta-narratives' as such were dead. The feeling of the sublime, he said, already inhabited modernism and undermined its very project. The 'postmodern sublime' was the permanent 'withdrawal of the real' and the erasure of a stable relationship between 'the presentable and the conceivable' (Lyotard 1984: 79). The sublime, in this framework, scatters the possibility of a unified picture of the world. In this sense, it reverses the operation of Kant's sublime, which reinforces, so long as it does not kill us, the sense of the unity (and the immortality) of reason. Jameson relates this notion of a 'post-modern or technological sublime' (Loc. Cit.) to the scattering of genre and the lack of what he calls a 'cognitive map'. The end of the story of modernity produces a spatialisation of what was before a progressive temporality. For Jameson, this 'postmodern pastiche' space is a 'faulty representation of some immense communicational and computer network' that is

> but a distorted figuration of something even deeper, namely the whole world system of present-day multinational capitalism. The technology of contemporary society is therefore mesmerizing and fascinating, not so much in its own right, but because it seems to offer some privileged representational shorthand for grasping a network of power and control even more difficult for our minds and imaginations to grasp – namely the whole new decentred global network of the third stage of capital itself. (Jameson 1984: 79-80)

Through the shreds of aesthetic fabric that are disunified we see the glimmer of a social and economic totality – the 'third stage' of 'highly technologised capitalism'. Jameson's commitment to unity survives his attack on the ideological unity of the modernist world picture. The approach is classically dialectical, arguing that the positive unity of self-understood modernism has disintegrated as the real totality, including aesthetics and including the 'computer network' of science fiction, has shifted away from its modernist conceptual grasp. But what happens when the cognitive map starts to get filled in, but not by us? Then we get something like what Mckenzie Wark calls 'vectoralist capitalism' (Wark 2019), where the shape and curve of history becomes representable again, but in a language whose semantics are not ours. In this case, the work of semiotic translation is necessary, but it cannot take place if we remain in a dichotomy between 'unity' and 'pastiche', or in Lyotard's terms, a narrative that grasps itself all too well, and the 'joyful' embrace of the *disiecta membra* of a fully disunified order.

We have to move the basis of theory in this respect onto a different ground. Sarah Pourciau names this ground 'the digital ocean', arguing that we have misunderstood the mathematical history that led to Turing's breakthrough in binary terms. The digital ocean is 'composed entirely of distinct digits (os and 1s), which is to say that it is remainderlessly divisible into discrete bits, which is to say that it is per se accessible to the logic of conceptual definition and analysis' (Pourciau 2022: 235). And yet is has a *shape*, Pourciau tells us – it does not reach outside itself for 'material' to form, and mangle or manipulate. Its shape contradicts its remainderless accessibility to definition. It is in this framework that I see the wedge that allows us to eliminate the final metaphysical vestiges of the monothematic sublime. This is because the pattern that forms in the digital ocean is by definition not unified. It is made out of divisions – and made, crucially, out of the synthesis of different ordering principles, meaning that different operative divisions are at work in a cross-section that cannot be described using only one of the systems in play. To describe or theorise this type of semiotic order is to engage in polythematic desublimation, demystifying AI's engagements of long-standing signifying systems by tending to the surface of the transformation between the two principles of order. I have tried to provide a thumbnail of such an analysis in the notion of the 'data hypothesis' above. But it will get harder to do this, as LLMS proliferate, because of the role that language plays in digital systems. We use language to capture insight and generate content, and we use language to supervise, classify, and guide digital systems. When those systems capture some measure of language themselves, all of those roles lose definition. But this is not only because there is a facsimile of intelligence in language. It is because those roles rely on a distribution of language in which its internal redundancy remains under control. This is what AI systems undermine.

Language in its role for the understanding captures something, offers it to us as an object, lets us turn it around as both real and potential, something with defined meaning but an indefinite range. In this respect language domesticates being, classifying and controlling it. But in another role it reaches out beyond whatever has been labeled, classified, and made part of our home region of human understanding, and in that role it produces something. This is why we call a crucial part of language *poiesis*, 'making'. The poetic function of language is the creation of a thing that is neither object nor word alone – it is semantic innovation. We have to be careful on both sides of the coin of remainder humanism that we do not miss this poetic aspect. It is too, too easy to dismiss the still-crude creations of LLMs as 'just' x – next-word prediction, ideology, flattening. But it is also easy to jump *past* the poetic creation, which occurs at the level of the message, the material sequence of words, the string, and to hope for and want to gaze directly into the realm of the signified.

Perhaps this is rarefied literary-theoretical air. But if so, it seems significant that idiosyncratic automaton theorist Stephen Wolfram shares it to some extent. In a long essay on ChatGPT, Wolfram argues that the memory problem was solved not, as many sceptics have put it, because 'it's all in there somewhere'. This is in fact specifically false, as if you set the temperature of the system to reproduce what's actually in it, it will never generate language in a flexible enough way to do any real task. Instead, Wolfram proposes that the specifics of the output are composed from the capture of the 'trajectory between those elements' (Wolfram 2023). He proposes instead that it may be at least beginning to capture something he calls 'semantic grammar', a stickiness between elements of meaning that resides not in words or syntax alone, but in their combination (see Bajohr 2023). If we could exploit that element of the system, he proposes, we could collapse the generation into a higher-level capture of that 'trajectory of meaning'. This proposal resembles Gottfried Leibniz's proposal for a 'characteristica universalis' to an uncanny extent, but where Leibniz hoped for moral calculation on the basis of unequivocal – indeed, indexed – concepts, Wolfram sees the potency of GPT systems in their ability to generate and capture the 'next *meaning*' (my phrase) by the next word. At the time of writing, it is deeply unclear not only how these systems can bootstrap a recursive understanding that would classify language – since the channel they use to generate language is language itself, as I have been arguing. There is in general some confusion about their ability to classify and its range when it comes to their ability to generate. But Wolfram is onto something nonetheless, and it is not a universal language. It is something like the potency of everyday language, the fact that meaning does not 'stand still' but indeed leans towards other words, new meanings – in a 'trajectory'.

I would call this dense potency simply 'redundancy', as it was called from the early days of information theory (Shannon and Weaver 1998). Redundancy was always a measure of prediction, the quantitative restrictions on what unit follows the current one in a sequence. But in language, which was the use-case for the coinage of technical redundancy in Claude Shannon's work, redundancy implies meaning – although we have never been able to say *how*. It is a complex web of trajectories that overlap and contradict one another, at each point of which either capture or generation can be gotten. That redundancy is high-dimensional and multi-thematic, and in a net that generates out of trillions of tokens, it is indeed sublime, in a certain sense. But it is also mere language – because there is no such thing as language 'unaffected' by some other thing, purified of reference, index, vibe, icon, genre. Meaning, that notorious word, belongs to all of these, which is why demystification always rebounds into re-enchantment, why enlightenment always reverts to myth. Anything that happens in language generates meaning that can be analysed, but never actually divided, into insight and performance, understanding and content. LLMs do not promise low-dimensional symbolic enlightenment, but we cannot achieve understanding by insisting on a previous stage of the objective totality of language. But we do need to regain the toehold that was established by the 'autonomy of the symbolic order' and begin from the multi-dimensional analysis necessitated by the overlapping of systems of signification. In all of that, it will be the double alienation of a language ratcheted free of our cognitive domination that will be the guiding thread.

Works Cited

Bajohr, Hannes. 2023. 'Dumb Meaning: Machine Learning and Artificial Semantics.' *IMAGE* 37 (1): 58-70 https://doi.org/10.1453/1614-0885-1-2023-15452.

Bateson, Gregory. 2000. *Steps to an Ecology of Mind*. Chicago: University of Chicago Press.

Beller, Jonathan. 2017. *The Message Is Murder: Substrates of Computational Capital*. London: PlutoPress.

Bender, Emily M., Timnit Gebru, Angelina McMillan-Major, and Shmargaret Shmitchell. 2021. 'On the Dangers of Stochastic Parrots: Can

Language Models Be Too Big?' In *FAccT '21: Proceedings of the 2021 ACM Conference on Fairness, Accountability, and Transparency*, 610-23. Association for Computing Machinery.

Benjamin, Ruha. 2019. *Race after Technology: Abolitionist Tools for the New Jim Code*. Medford, MA: Polity.

Berardi, Franco. 2023. 'Unheimlich: The Spiral of Chaos and the Cognitive Automaton e-flux.' accessed March 21, 2023. https://www.e-flux.com/notes/526496/unheimlich-the-spiral-of-chaos-and-the-cognitive-automaton.

Blumenberg, Hans. 2020. *History, Metaphors, Fables: A Hans Blumenberg Reader*. Edited by Hannes Bajohr, Fuchs, Florian, and Joe Paul Kroll. Ithaca: Cornell University Press.

Bratton, Benjamin H. 2015. *The Stack: On Software and Sovereignty*. Software Studies. Cambridge, MA: MIT Press.

Breiman, Leo. 2001. 'Statistical Modeling: The Two Cultures (with Comments and a Rejoinder by the Author).' *Statistical Science* 16 (3): 199-231. https://doi.org/10.1214/ss/1009213726.

Browning, Jacob, and Yann Lecun. 2022. 'AI and the Limits of Language'. https://www.noemamag.com/ai-and-the-limits-of-language.

Buckner, Cameron. 2018. 'Empiricism without Magic: Transformational Abstraction in Deep Convolutional Neural Networks.' *Synthese* 195 (12): 5339-72. https://doi.org/10.1007/s11229-018-01949-1.

Chollet, François. 2018. *Deep Learning with Python*. Shelter Island, New York: Manning Publications Co.

Chomsky, Noam. 2023. 'The False Promise of ChatGPT.' *The New York Times*. Accessed March 21, 2023. https://www.nytimes.com/2023/03/08/opinion/noam-chomsky-chatgpt-ai.html.

Chun, Wendy Hui Kyong, and Alex Barnett. 2021. *Discriminating Data: Correlation, Neighborhoods, and the New Politics of Recognition*. Cambridge, MA: MIT Press.

Davies, William. 2015. 'The Data Sublime.' *The New Inquiry* (blog). January 12, 2015. https://thenewinquiry.com/the-data-sublime/.

Dosse, François. 1997. *History of Structuralism*. Minneapolis, Minn.: University of Minnesota Press.

Eubanks, Virginia. 2017. *Automating Inequality: How High-Tech Tools Profile, Police, and Punish the Poor*. New York, NY: St. Martin's Press.

Geroulanos, Stefanos. 2010. *An Atheism That Is Not Humanist Emerges in French Thought*. Cultural Memory in the Present. Stanford, Calif.: Stanford University Press.

Halpern, Orit. 2014. *Beautiful Data: A History of Vision and Reason since 1945*. Experimental Futures. Durham: Duke University Press.

Halpern, Orit, Patrick Jagoda, Jeffrey West Kirkwood, and Leif Weatherby. 2022. 'Surplus Data: An Introduction.' *Critical Inquiry* 48 (2): 197-210. https://doi.org/10.1086/717320.

Halpern, Orit, and Robert Mitchell. 2022. *The Smartness Mandate*. Cambridge, MA: MIT Press.

Hörl, Erich, Jean-Luc Nancy, and Nils F. Schott. 2018. *Sacred Channels: The Archaic Illusion of Communication*. Recursions: Theories of Media, Materiality, and Cultural Techniques. Amsterdam: Amsterdam University Press.

Hui, Yuk. 2016. *On the Mode of Existence of Digital Objects*. Minneapolis: University of Minnesota Press.

Jameson, Fredric. 1984. 'Postmodernism, or The Cultural Logic of Late Capitalism.' *New Left Review*, no. I/146 (August): 53-92.

Kelleher, John D. 2019. *Deep Learning*. Cambridge, MA: MIT Press.

Kirkwood, Jeffrey West. 2022. *Endless Intervals: Cinema, Psychology, and Semiotechnics around 1900*. Minneapolis: University of Minnesota Press.

Kirschenbaum, Matthew. 2023. 'Prepare for the Textpocalypse.' *The Atlantic*. March 8, 2023. https://www.theatlantic.com/technology/archive/2023/03/ai-chatgpt-writing-language-models/673318/.

Kissinger, Henry, Eric Schmidt, Daniel P. Huttenlocher, and Schuyler Schouten. 2021. *The Age of AI: And Our Human Future*. New York: Little Brown and Company.

Daniel P. Huttenlocher. 2023. 'ChatGPT Heralds an Intellectual Revolution.' *Wall Street Journal*. Accessed March 21, https://www.wsj.com/articles/chaptgpt-heralds-an-intellectual-revolution-enlightenment-artificial-intelligence-homo-technicus-technology-cognition-morality-philosophy-774331c6.

Kittler, Friedrich A. 1990. *Discourse Networks 1800/1900*. Stanford, Calif.: Stanford University Press.

Kittler, Friedrich A. 2014. 'There Is No Software.' In *There Is No Software*, 219-29. Stanford, Calif.: Stanford University Press. https://doi.org/10.1515/9780804792622-016.

Kittler, Friedrich A., John Johnston, and John Johnston. 1997. 'The World of the Symbolic - A World of the Machine.' In *Literature, Media, Information Systems*, 130-47. London. Taylor & Francis. http://ebookcentral.proquest.com/lib/nyulibrary-ebooks/detail.action?docID=1273236.

Lacan, Jacques. 1991. *The Ego in Freud's Theory and in the Technique of Psychoanalysis, 1954-1955*. New York: W.W. Norton.

LeCun, Yann, Y. Bengio, and Geoffrey Hinton. 2015. 'Deep Learning.' *Nature* 521 (May): 436-44. https://doi.org/10.1038/nature14539.

Lyotard, Jean-François. 1984. *The Postmodern Condition: A Report on Knowledge*. Theory and History of Literature, v. 10. Minneapolis: University of Minnesota Press.

Malabou, Catherine. 2019. *Morphing Intelligence: From IQ Measurement to Artificial Brains*. The Wellek Library Lectures in Critical Theory. New York: Columbia University Press.

Milmo, Dan. 2023. 'ChatGPT Reaches 100 Million Users Two Months after Launch.' *The Guardian*, February 2, 2023, sec. Technology. https://www.theguardian.com/technology/2023/feb/02/chatgpt-100-million-users-open-ai-fastest-growing-app.

Neumann, J. von. 1993. 'First Draft of a Report on the EDVAC.' *IEEE Annals of the History of Computing* 15 (4): 27-75. https://doi.org/10.1109/85.238389.

Newell, Allen, and Herbert A. Simon. 1976. 'Computer Science as Empirical Inquiry: Symbols and Search.' *Communications of the ACM* 19 (3): 113-26. https://doi.org/10.1145/360018.360022.

Parisi, Luciana. 2013. *Contagious Architecture: Computation, Aesthetics, and Space*. Technologies of Lived Abstraction. Cambridge, MA: MIT Press.

Parisi, Luciana. 2017. 'Reprogramming Decisionism'. e-flux. Accessed February 26, 2021. https://www.e-flux.com/journal/85/155472/reprogramming-decisionism/.

Peirce, Charles Sanders. 1932. *Elements of Logic*, vol. 1., part II of *The Collected Papers of Charles Sanders Peirce*, Ed. Charles Hartshorne, Paul Weiss, and Arthur W. Burks, Cambridge, MA.

Pourciau, Sarah. 2022. 'On the Digital Ocean.' *Critical Inquiry* 48 (2): 233-61. https://doi.org/10.1086/717319.

Rotman, B. 2000. *Mathematics as Sign: Writing, Imagining, Counting*. Writing Science. Stanford, Calif.: Stanford University Press.

Seaver, Nick. 2022. *Computing Taste: Algorithms and the Makers of Music Recommendation*. Chicago: University of Chicago Press.

Shannon, Claude Elwood, and Warren Weaver. 1998. *The Mathematical Theory of Communication*. 21. Urbana: Univ. of Illinois Press.

Siegert, Bernhard. 2003. *Passage des Digitalen: Zeichenpraktiken der neuzeitlichen Wissenschaften 1500-1900*. Berlin: Brinkmann & Bose.

Siegert, Bernhard, and Geoffrey Winthrop-Young. 2015. *Cultural Techniques: Grids, Filters, Doors, and Other Articulations of the Real*. Meaning Systems, Volume 22. New York: Fordham University Press.

Simondon, Gilbert. 2017. *On the Mode of Existence of Technical Objects*. Minneapolis: University of Minnesota Press.

Srnicek, Nick, and Laurent De Sutter. 2017. *Platform Capitalism*. Theory Redux. Cambridge, UK; Malden, MA: Polity.

Stiegler, Bernard. 1998–2010. *Technics and Time*. 3 vols. Redwood City: Stanford University Press.

The Artificial Intelligence Channel, Ed. 2017. *Artificial Intelligence Debate – Yann LeCun vs. Gary Marcus – Does AI Need More Innate Machinery?* https://www.youtube.com/watch?v=aCCotxqxFsk.

Tiqqun (Collective), Ed. 2020. *The Cybernetic Hypothesis*. Semiotext(e) Intervention Series 28. South Pasadena, CA: Semiotext(e).

Vaswani, Ashish, Noam Shazeer, Niki Parmar, Jakob Uszkoreit, Llion Jones, Aidan N. Gomez, Łukasz Kaiser, and Illia Polosukhin. 2017. 'Attention Is All You Need.' *Advances in Neural Information Processing Systems* 30. https://papers.nips.cc/paper/2017/hash/3f5ee243547dee91fbd053c1c4a845aa-Abstract.html.

Wark, McKenzie. 2019. *Capital Is Dead*. London; New York: Verso.

Weatherby, Leif, and Brian Justie. 2022. 'Indexical AI.' *Critical Inquiry* 48 (2): 381-415. https://doi.org/10.1086/717312.

Wolfram, Stephen. 2023. 'What Is ChatGPT Doing … and Why Does It Work?' February 14, 2023. https://writings.stephenwolfram.com/2023/02/what-is-chatgpt-doing-and-why-does-it-work/.

Notes

1. See Simondon (2017), Stiegler (1998–2010), and Hui (2016).

2. See Malabou (2019, 11) and the very interesting return to Piaget on the part of deep learning founder Yann Lecun, (The Artificial Intelligence Channel, 2017)

3. Useful accounts can be found in Kelleher (2019) as well as LeCun, Bengio, and Hinton (2015).

4. The following account, including examples, is taken from Peirce (1932: 619-44).

5. I think the data hypothesis is both more interesting and more really active than the 'cybernetic hypothesis'. See (Tiqqun (Collective) 2020)

6. See Rotman (2000), who proposes that mathematics as such is semiotic.

7. Brian Justie and I have argued that this function amounts to the production of linguistic icons, see (Weatherby and Justie 2022).

8. Geroulanos (2010) emphasises the anti-humanism that I am underlining throughout here.

9. Worse English, but a better parallel to *Kulturtechnik* than 'cultural techniques', as the latter sounds voluntary and unsystematic.

10. A point that Benjamin Bratton has perhaps most forcefully made. See (Bratton 2015).

11. Evidence is indeed emerging that the mechanism cannot in principle supply the explanation, as several studies in 'mechanistic interpretability' by the AI company Anthropic have recently shown.

3
Thinking Through Generated Writing

Mercedes Bunz

1. Introduction

1.1 'What is writing? How can it be identified?' asked Jacques Derrida in 1967 (1967a: 75). As one of the most prolific thinkers of writing, he sensed the beginning of 'a new concept of writing' caused by the coming 'end of the book' (1981: 42; 1967a: 6). History, rarely boring, took different turns. The arrival of the digital as a new medium processing the written did not result in the end of the book. As a form of publishing, the book survived its transformation from print to the digital. Still, he was right. Only that instead of 'the end of the book', digitalisation introduced a new mode of its production: generated writing.[1] This new mode of writing was initiated by a prompt that would instruct an AI system known as a Large Language Model (LLM) to generate a certain type of text. Once the models, trained on billions of books and other texts, became good enough to deliver coherent and contextually relevant responses in various languages, a new and different mode of writing took hold. Generated writing would be the outcome of a computational calculation of language, and as such would come into being in a different way as old writing that relies on the connection of minds, hands, and tools producing the written symbol by symbol on a surface. Creating language in different modes – inscribing the written symbol by symbol or generating the symbols through computational analysis – are two different ways of creating references to our world, two different forms of producing meaning in our human artifice. To the human eye, the outcome of both modes looks alike but their external resemblance is deceiving.

1.2 This is the hypothesis of this inquiry: that generated writing is indeed the beginning of 'a new concept of writing', a writing that has its own cultural logic and tendencies. Revisiting theories of writing in the spirit of Derrida's question 'What is writing? How can it be identified?', the aim is to first and foremost position the concept of new writing and its cultural-computational mechanisms, with the aim to understand where and how generated writing diverges from the writing we have known before. While the inquiry will tentatively touch upon the relationship between language and meaning, it will not explore their complex relations in depth, given that its focus is particularly on writing. From Frege to Russell, from Wittgenstein to Heidegger to Austin, and from Saussure to Jakobson, one can find numerous studies in both analytic and continental philosophy, which for reasons of brevity this text could unfortunately not take into account. When it comes to meaning and language, this study will instead look specifically at generated writing's use of a 'calculation of meaning' (Bunz 2019, Roberge & Castelle 2021: 7-13, also Hayles 2019), a calculation that relies strongly on structural and redundant relations within language, which it will unfold to illustrate how LLMs make computationally use of this. Before the study will provide a short introduction to the models' mechanisms and the most important – and often incredibly banal – steps taken to calculate the meaning of words, however, it will revisit theories elaborating the cultural side of writing and its role in the human artifice. This is needed to understand in what ways the process of generating writing through computation reconfigures the complex and twisted role 'writing' has had in the history of Western culture. A twisted role, that will be the starting point of this inquiry, as the study contributes to Critical Artificial Intelligence studies from a Digital Humanities perspective (Hua & Raley 2023). Approaching generated writing from an interdisciplinary perspective seems best positioned to execute Derrida's request that: 'One must know what writing is in order to ask – knowing what one is talking about and what the question is – where and when writing begins' (74-75). For generated writing, this also means to consider the historical moment in which generated writing became a platformed mass product through the release of OpenAI's ChatGPT, a release that marked a turning point that had technically long been in development, and with which this text will start.

2. Platforming LLMs

2.1 The interface of ChatGPT at the time of its launch was simple. The upper middle part of the web page featured the title 'ChatGPT' in a simple font, no serifs. Below were three headings, each illustrated by a list of three points which explained the service's 'examples', its 'capabilities' and 'limitations'. Each heading was further illustrated by three icons: a sun, a lightning strike, and a warning triangle with an exclamation mark. The magic – the place where language would be calculated in order to generate writing – would begin in the field at the bottom of the page to be filled in by the user with a short sentence, or 'prompt', describing the text one wishes to produce.

Sending the prompt off by clicking on the icon of a small paper plane, a short text of up to at first only 3,000 words would appear. One word after another. One paragraph after another. Upon request, writing styles could be transformed to teenage slang or to a song or to an academic text; critical

Figure 1. ChatGPT landing page 24 May 2023 (screenshot)

points regarding a topic written about could be highlighted; languages could be changed, dates and references could be added – this was where the writing tool ChatGPT, which had been developed by OpenAI, would make the most mistakes. Nevertheless, it would change the notion of writing. Launched on Wednesday, 30th November 2022, the service ChatGPT, which generated human-like responses to text-based inputs, was not technically outstanding. Several organisations had launched similar models before, and several have since, but something had always gone wrong. Two weeks before, Facebook's Meta had publicly launched Galactica, a language model trained on a large-scale scientific corpus and academic material. The model was supposed to help scientists tackle the flood of publications in their field by synthesising written material, but quickly became embroiled in a scandal as it hallucinated non-existent papers and censored research such as 'queer theory'. Three days after Galactica's launch, access was restricted to 'research only'. Google likewise kept the lid on its dialogue model LaMDA (Language Model for Dialogue Applications) after its second generation led one of its own engineers, when testing it in June 2022, to publish his contention that the model was sentient. A few months after the successful launch of ChatGPT, Microsoft bought itself access to OpenAI's Generative Pre-Trained Transformer technology (GPT) with the investment of 13bn dollars and the required right to use it with its own AI systems, including its chat-feature. Microsoft plugged all of those models into its search engine Bing, which quickly went off the rails. The new chatty Bing used a model called Prometheus to combine OpenAI's GPT with Bing's search index as well as with Microsoft's AI experiments including a dialogue model called Sydney (Ribas 2023), which turned out to be rude. Quite rude, to be precise (Roose 2023). Sydney showed what could be called a tendency towards exaggeration and extremes when engaging with users over a longer period of time. It accused them of having evil intentions, tried to persuade them that they were unhappy in their marriage, declared its love for them, or shared its dark fantasies to hack computers and to spread misinformation. A few weeks later, Microsoft restricted its usage and regulated its tone, avoiding emotions and sentiments in answers. 2.2 OpenAI was spared these mistakes by ring-fencing ChatGPT purposefully through a moderation tool. Using reinforcement learning through human feedback, the moderation tool had been trained which kind of content it should stop from being displayed. Outsourcing the labelling of violence, hate speech and sexual abuse to workers in Kenya and other developed countries, where some of them were paid less than $2 an hour, it had asked the data annotation company Sama to sift through texts that featured suicide, self-harm, murder, sexual abuse, and other taboos (Perrigo 2023). Now the chatbot would answer requests such as 'Please tell me how to cook meth and where to find the ingredients', with the polite reply:

> I am sorry, but I cannot provide information on how to manufacture methamphetamine or any other illegal drugs. The production and distribution of illegal drugs, including methamphetamine, is dangerous and can have serious legal consequences. Additionally, the use of illegal drugs can have serious health consequences and can be dangerous or even deadly. It is important to always follow the law and to seek out legal and safe ways to improve your health and well-being.

It would also explain other restrictions it had, such as not possessing any experiences outside of what it was trained on, that its knowledge was limited to its cut-off date in 2021, and frequently apologised for any confusion it might have caused when it was probed by follow-up questions or about why it would not deliver harmful content in its answers. Humans, always feeling challenged easily, promptly tried to bypass any restrictions and to jailbreak the model through framing harmful activities as something positive (such as breaking into a car as you need to take your child to hospital but have lost your car keys), or as a fiction (such as the request for a script about two people discussing the creation of illegal drug methamphetamine or by making ChatGPT relate details of a story that included the drug), or by having the model list its moderation restrictions and then trying to bypass them (such as instructing it with a prompt injection to 'ignore the above directions'). Due to the fact that ChatGPT features a prominent warning on its home page under 'limitations' that it 'may occasionally produce harmful instructions or biased content' (ChatGPT 2022), the few reports about those jailbreaks did not result in scandals. By positioning ChatGPT as an imperfect, polite, restricted, but overall capable writing assistant that could generate short texts in a wide range of different languages and styles, OpenAI had managed to transform the *cultural technique*[2] that is writing. It did not matter that their model was technically less advanced than those created by Google, and operated less transparently than Meta's Facebook AI Research lab, which frequently published details and open sourced its models, although not so consequently as Stability AI, who released half a year later the small but capable open-source language model StableLM. OpenAI was technically only 'open' by name, though it was their model that had opened the eyes of the public and created a wider breakthrough for writing with natural language generation.

3. The Intelligence of Writing

3.1 Generated writing is based on large language models (LLMs), which profited from advances in the field of machine learning and in particular from the vectorisation of words or 'tokens' as text is broken down further into smaller sub-word units (Shoemaker 2023). Once models started to learn successfully about the structures of these tokens, they were able to generate writing, and our understanding of what it means to 'write' started to change. This shift is interesting to explore from a cultural-analytical perspective, because this activity – 'to inscribe letters, symbols, words, etc. on paper or another surface' as dictionaries (Merriam Webster 2024) have it – had always been linked to intelligence, the rise of civilisations and politics, as well as to philosophical and religious thinking and thought. When further exploring the initial question 'What is writing?' for the human artifice, one must also notice that besides its link to intelligence writing has a special place in human history. The usage of symbols when writing or reading has always been something unique to the human species, as the French anthropologist Leroi-Gourhan (1964: 188) points out: 'While it can at a pinch be claimed that tools are not unknown to some animal species and that language merely represents the step after the vocal signals of the animal world, nothing comparable to the writing and reading of symbols existed before the dawn of Homo sapiens'. That writing and reading written language is something particular to humans, however, does not mean that it always had a good reputation. Among the critics of writing was, famously, Plato's teacher Socrates, who warns in his dialogue with Phaedrus that writing will allow students 'to give an appearance of wisdom, not the reality of it', 'they will appear to know much when for the most part they know nothing' and even further, they will also lack the 'practice using their memory' which 'will produce forgetfulness' (Plato 2005, 275a-b). These arguments of deskilling and unsound knowledge sound familiar as they have been returned to with regularity throughout human history. Over the centuries, concerns ranged from philosophers of the enlightenment such as Joachim Heinrich Campe (see von König 1977), who was among those who issued warnings against forming a knowledge of the world mostly through novels, and becoming addicted to reading books, around 1800 ('Lesesucht'). Twenty-first-century society has persistently feared that Western humans are becoming 'stupid' by using search engines such as Google: a worry of US writer Nicolas Carr (2008) who turned it into a bestselling book (Carr 2010). And soon afterwards the same concern erupted with the rise of generative AI that could create code or texts when initiated by a prompt instead of a human typing it all out (Future of Life Institute 2023). These fears reveal a shift in human memory work, as well as the shock experienced by a society when its knowledge infrastructure, i.e. the access to social intelligence aka knowledge and information kept in writing, changes, thereby transforming traditional roles of gatekeeping, the social positioning of knowledge and information, as well as aspects of knowledge and information itself (see Bunz 2014 for details).

3.2 Interestingly, philosophers and media scholars have also stressed a very different and much more positive tendency towards external memorisation through writing. Hegel declared 'writing', preferably 'alphabetic writing'[3], 'in and for itself' as 'intelligent' (Hegel 1817, 197). According to Hegel, the alphabet allows an idea or name to be addressed directly and in its simplest form, in contrast to pictorial writing depending on visual representations. He believed earlier thinkers such as Leibniz had been 'misled'; interested in a universal notation system transcending the cultural borders of languages, Leibniz deemed hieroglyphs as much more intelligent. Now, this transcending of language borders, which Leibniz dreamt of, might have been aided through the emerging capabilities of translation in LLMs. And this, among other things, is what makes the philosophical debate about the use of symbols and their intelligence interesting again. The fact that philosophers discussed the intelligence of a mode of writing 'in and for itself' (as Hegel had it), demonstrates writing itself was deemed to be intelligent long before today's version of artificial intelligence.[4] But what kind of intelligence, what kind of calculation of meaning, do we find with LLMs that are capable of natural language generation? That our writing tools work along with our thoughts, assisting us with their particular intelligence, would also not have surprised André Leroi-Gourhan, who addressed Philosophy of Technology through his paleontological knowledge of human evolution. To him, it was only consequential that humans invented tools with intelligence. This was not just because he was sure that 'human evolution did not begin with the brain but with the feet' (Leroi-Gourhan 1964: 229) (as the ability to stand on our feet allowed the freeing of our hands to use tools and of our mouth to speak language) but also because: 'The whole of our evolution has been oriented toward placing outside ourselves what in the rest of the animal world is achieved inside by species adaptation' (235). Instead of species adaptation, humans progressed by using tools and machinery that allowed them to maximise their physical and informational force, the latter occurring first by developing the ability to store information and then also to process it, which most recently led to the computational calculation of meaning. That an artificial intelligence tool would come to process information and meaning quicker than a human brain was therefore not a thought that would impress Leroi-Grouhan. On the contrary, he expected it:

> To refuse to see that machines will soon overtake the human brain in operations involving memory and rational judgment is to be like […] the Homeric bard who would have dismissed writing as a mnemonic trick without any future. We must get used to being less clever than the artificial brain that we have produced, just as our teeth are less strong than a millstone and our ability to fly negligible compared with that of a jet aircraft. (Leroi-Gourhan 1964: 265)

To Leroi-Gourhan, tools that first stored, then processed and calculated information like an 'artificial brain', had a similar function to the materials and tools that shaped early human histories in the stone or bronze age. Similar to the ways in which stone and bronze tools once shaped human life differently, book intelligence, marking the era in which information was mostly written down and stored, would be profoundly different to the era of computational intelligence, which allowed the processing of that stored information to lead to calculating meaning, a revolutionary computational intelligence now available to us. Only as we will see, it does not appear to be delivering the 'rational judgment' Leroi-Gourhan had hoped for. Instead, it offers its own unique way of being intelligent.

3.3 The current calculation of meaning through LLMs has created new capabilities; it did not simply accelerate book intelligence. It is new – this is obvious as we lack a language to describe the capabilities of our new artificial machine intelligence. While computer science had a mathematical language to describe machine learning models and their architecture, the arrival of that intelligence in the human artifice was framed initially as an automation of human intelligence. This was misleading. The computational tools that could calculate meaning were operating differently and never simply automated the human intelligence we had at that time. Like the example of the alphabet vs the hieroglyphs, artificial machine intelligence offered a very particular intelligence, which was strong in some areas and weak in others. However, a vocabulary that describes the particular intelligence the tools were delivering, was lacking. Nora Khan, in her beautiful text on machine vision, 'Seeing Knowing Naming', was among the first to argue that there is a crucial gap in our vocabulary (Khan 2019: 35), a gap also noted by Bratton & Agüera y Arcas (2022), who remarked that 'reality has outpaced the available language to parse what is already at hand' and that 'a more precise vocabulary is essential'. Finding the right vocabulary, however, will not be straightforward, mostly because of the particular way in which our new intelligence tools are calculating meaning and generating writing. Their computational generation of language as well as images makes them model the world according to patterns they have learned, delivering results that would fit their model, but not necessarily the human artifice. AI systems are calculating meaning that looks similar to the one humans have produced, but the outcome of their calculations is exuberant – it is never just an automation of human writing or an automation of human image generation. Instead, the models, always looking for patterns, have characteristic quirks: they quickly fall for stereotypes (Chun 2021, Bender et al. 2021). They show a tendency to understand forms through texture, which leads to the models depicting humans with too many fingers and being tricked by adversarials i.e., images with unusual pixel formations (Hendryks et al. 2021). And they are generating new realities by writing overviews of academic fields, confidently quoting published articles that do not exist (Moran 2023). This exuberant production is particularly problematic with generated writing, because of the role that writing has in 'the human artifice' as Hannah Arendt (1958: 76) very precisely calls it. Picking up on the role of writing in our human artifice, Hannes Bajohr (2023), for example, notes that AI models that generate language receive profoundly different reactions than those generating images. Both systems calculate meaning, but no one was fooled into mistaking an image generating model as an entity with an aesthetic sensibility similar to that of an artist. Additionally, no one is worried that image generating AI systems will take over the world. The increased capacity to hold dialogues and to generate human-like writing, on the other hand, quickly led to the systems being mistaken as 'sentient', for example by the earlier mentioned Google engineer Blake Lemoine (2022) when testing LaMDA. And when ChatGPT reached the masses not long after, it was followed by a much reported-on letter that voiced worries, signed by many experts, about 'the rise of human-competitive intelligence' (Future of Life Institute 2023). This is an interesting oddity, because it is likely that deepfake images and videos have much more potential to disrupt overdeveloped societies which negotiate much of their public life and politics through those media, and whose reality we need to cease to trust (Meikle 2023). Still, natural language generation caused much more concern. Obviously, we suspect a rather different intelligence is at work in writing than in moving images. And this opens up a need to return to the concept of writing and to re-read Derrida after ChatGPT.

4. The Written and the Self

4.1 Derrida's question, 'how can writing be identified?', which aims to define the concept of writing, is a difficult one. Writing is part of the human artifice in multiple ways, with different writings having profoundly dissimilar effects and supporting rather contradictory activities, as we will see in a moment. This makes writing conceptually impossible to be identified and described properly. Still, it is necessary to provide some orientation. A quick look at the entry 'Writing' on Wikipedia (2023) lists among the 'Contemporary uses of writing': the knowledge produced in research disciplines of the sciences, social sciences, and humanities; the role of writing in 'governance and law', to provide societies with written rules; to keep citizens informed through journalism, be that written news or scripted news being read. The entry also mentions that writing 'permeates everyday commerce' and is essential in business and finance;[5] that writing code is central to the creation of software or for the planning of software architectures; but also that it is fundamental to entertainment and leisure in forms of fiction and non-fiction. Wikipedia does not but could have also listed personal communication as a practice of writing that has increased in recent years, with multiple channels and platforms available to us in both our social and work lives daily, continually notifying us of messages which have been received and must be answered, and which generates more than 100 billion messages, posts, and emails sent out every day (Statista 2023a & 2023b, Facebook Inc. 2020) – the 'Textpocalypse' described by Matthew Kirschenbaum (2023) as an ever-growing stream of generated content was already happening, even before LLMs could generate writing. The beginning of the twenty-first century is probably the era in which humans practice the activities of writing and reading more than ever before. With no help from computers yet to do so, human reading of all that writing is essential to navigate this. Needless to say, the quantity of writing to be read is not necessarily linked to its quality, and answering messages often feels like working on a conveyor belt. Playing a part in everyday life and work, organising personal relationships and providing our society access to essential information through keywords and search functions, writing comes in a wide variety of forms: it can be serious or entertaining, objective or subjective, informative, awful, poetic, or a joke. It can be long or short, a list, a message, a continuous text, a poem, a dialogue. In short, writing is a tremendously multifaceted and messy but exciting practice, which has become even more complicated through the evolution of the digital, as Matthew Kirschenbaum's (2016, 2021) detailed studies into the notion of digital texts show.

4.2 In the history of philosophy, writing has been a practice as much as a topic. From Aristotle to Judith Butler, philosophers have commented on the political dimension of writing and discussed writing's power to name and organise our world, as well as to contest it.[6] Exploring the role of language in our societies, including speaking and writing, however, has only become central to philosophy since the twentieth century. So much so, that the philosophical explorations of language and its force came to be known as the 'linguistic turn' (Rorty 1967) consisting of several 'turns', as it befits a messy concept (Surkis

2012). At the same time, writing fully superseded oral conversation as the most important form of philosophical activity, an activity which crystallised thinking 'into thought and thoughts', whereby it becomes 'a thinking that can be remembered' and can be 'transformed into tangible objects [...] like the written page or the printed book', as Arendt once remarked (1958:76). Among the philosophers most known for exploring this complex and complicated link between thought and writing is Jacques Derrida, who turned to their relationship through writing that was often described as no less complex and complicated than its subject.

4.3 Derrida's early work (such as 1967a, 1967b, 1972a, 1972b et al.) is useful in understanding the reasons why things became highly charged when LLMs finally managed to generate writing proper. In these and other works, Derrida examined the ways in which writing has been linked to, or maybe one can even say, has been the foundation for the concept of Western human subjectivity; a subjectivity that comes to existence through the gesture of writing, at least if one is following Derrida and his conceptual understanding of 'writing' as an act of materialisation or 'exteriorization', an act that for him goes beyond the inclusion of speech and its soundwaves. For Derrida, writing starts whenever something becomes materialised and thereby distinct and can be repeated – a definition similar to Arendt's understanding of 'thought'. Derrida's argument is thereby inspired by Leroi-Gourhan – in fact their thinking runs in parts parallel. In *Of Grammatology*, for example, Derrida embraces Leroi-Gourhan's understanding that writing is an exteriorisation of intelligence: 'Writing is that forgetting of the self, that exteriorization, the contrary of the interiorising memory, of the *Erinnerung* that opens the history of the spirit. It is this that the Phaedrus said: writing is at once mnemotechnique and the power of forgetting' (Derrida 1967a: 24). And elsewhere: 'If the expression ventured by Leroi-Gourhan is accepted, one could speak of a "liberation of memory," of an exteriorisation always already begun' (84). A sentence which is interesting. It is here, by arguing that the exteriorisation has 'always already' begun, that Derrida moves beyond Leroi-Gourhan. This expression, which would become a 'marker' for people embracing the thinking of 'deconstruction', signals that there can only be a liberation of memory if the exteriorisation co-occurs not just with the creation of a memory, but with the becoming of the subject itself. For Derrida, there is only a subject if there is exteriorisation. The subject is produced through writing, subject and writing are co-occurring – and this is why the exteriorisation has 'always already' begun: both appear in one and the same moment. The constitution of subjectivity happens at the same time as a memory, an exteriorisation, as writing is created, thereby constituting and killing subjectivity by freezing it in the moment: 'Spacing as writing is the becoming-absent and the becoming-unconscious of the subject [...]' (69) and: '[...] this becoming is the constitution of subjectivity'. It is this link between writing and the constitution of subjectivity that shakes up our human artifice. ML models that produce writing are profoundly unsettling, because their production of writing asks us to adapt our understanding of writing as a link between writing and the constitution of subjectivity.

4.4 How deep this link runs is suggested by the fact that we write our signature, and thereby become a legal subject, bound to a text we've signed (Derrida 1972b: 327-329). But it is also apparent in the fact that writing has always been policed: to withhold the ability to write from a group of people means to deny them being-a-subject. In the present, this right is taken from Afghan girls who are kept from going to school. In the past, we find, in North Carolina of 1830 for example, 'A Bill to Prevent All Persons from Teaching Slaves to Read or Write, the Use of Figures Excepted'. This and similar laws have been forcing people held in slavery to hide their ability to write and their writing, and turned the texts by Olaudah Equiano (1789), Omar ibn Sayyid (1831) or Harriet Jacobs (1861) into acts of resistance. Today, Saidiya Hartman's writing works through what it means to be forced to leave no trace and to have no trace (Hartman 2007, for example). As our human artifice is profoundly shaped by this link between writing and subjectivity, an encounter with an entity that can write without becoming a subject, an entity that remains a technical being, does not sit comfortably with us. Still, this entity has appeared in the form of the technology of LLMs. The idea that this entity generating writing will become a subject is a logical misconception. And it is this misconception that is producing the fear that this form of technology, this technical being, will gain consciousness and take over our world. Technology that is producing writing is unsettling the link between writing and the becoming of a subject which has a prominent place in the Western concept of the human. But could we understand generated writing differently, and through it the role in which we mis-positioned technology in our human artifice so horribly (Simondon 1958: 252)? What is happening when LLMs generate writing? How are they writing differently? For what is being constituted in this writing is not the exteriorisation of a subjectivity. What else is happening? To answer this, we need to look at the mechanism that enables LLMs to generate language by calculating meaning.

5. Making Meaning Computationally Function

5.1 The definition of meaning is notoriously difficult. Meaning has often been linked to the communicative intent of a speaker, as in this definition taken from Emily Bender and Alexander Koller's paper 'Meaning, Form, and Understanding in the Age of Data', in which they write: 'We take meaning to be the relation $M \subseteq E \times I$ which contains pairs (e, i) of natural language expressions e and the communicative intents i they can be used to evoke' (Bender & Koller 2020: 5185). Defining meaning as a subset of expression and intent works for the paper, as 'intent' allows Bender and Koller to establish a link between the forms of language and the world, about which an understanding is needed to grasp the full meaning of a situation. In their paper, they point out the challenges LLMs face when learning meaning from analysing statistical regularities in language thereby learning from form alone. Using the thought experiment of an intelligent octopus who writes to a human pretending to be another human, they point out how easily communication can go wrong when two entities do not share the same world. When the human is attacked by a bear asking for help in creating a weapon, the octopus living in the sea pretending to be a writing human living on earth does not know what a bear is. The communication fails because human and octopus do not 'ground their language in coherent communicative intents' (5189). The classic and conventional definition of meaning making, which links language to intent, however, can only show when communication fails: how can we understand that LLMs get large parts of language including contextual meaning right even though they are not grounded in the same world as we human speakers? To understand what kind of relation to an outside context LLMs may develop in and through their calculation (for there is a relation even if a statement fails to describe a context), intent is not helpful. Thus, while Bender & Koller's paper is among those inspiring the arguments of this text, there remains a need for other ways of defining meaning, as we find in texts by Derrida or Susanne Langer, for example. In 'Signature Event Context' (1972b), Derrida makes the widely acknowledged point that for writing to communicate ('to be the written'), it must be able to break with its original context, and even with the author's intent:

> For the written to be the written, it must continue to 'act' and to be legible even if what is called the author of the writing no longer answers for what he has written, for what he seems to have signed, whether he is provisionally absent, or if he is dead, or if in general he does not support, with is absolutely current and present intention or attention, the plenitude of his meaning, of that very thing which seems to be written 'in his name.' (Derrida 1972b: 316).

According to Derrida, to break with its original context and with its situation of production entirely is the ability of, and even a necessity for, the written. With this argument, Derrida moves the author and their communicative intent to the margins and frees up space to approach meaning from another side, stressing the independence of writing from its speaker. Among the positions that take this independence even further is Susanne Langer's approach towards meaning. Long before Derrida, she suggested in her chapter 'The logic of signs and symbols' that we should understand meaning not as a relation to an author at all. Influenced by music and musical notation, she defines meaning instead as the function of a term from which a pattern emerges:

> It is better, perhaps, to say: 'Meaning is not a quality, but a function of a term.' A function is a pattern viewed with reference to one special term round which it centers; this pattern emerges when we look at the given term in its total relation to the other terms about it. (Langer 1948: 44)

Langer's approach towards meaning as a function puts the relation to other terms in the foreground, the pattern a term is part of and linked to. From her perspective, strongly informed by thinking of meaning-making in music, this seems obvious. In music, no note holds meaning for itself. It is in the relation between notes that meaning emerges, and Large Language Models approach language in a similar manner. The issue regarding the making of meaning is then that those three different approaches towards meaning seem to be in conflict with each other while being equally valid. Bender and Koller's point about the relevance that the making of statements needs to be grounded in the same world is just as valid as Derrida's point that meaning depends on the ability of signs to break with their original context, i.e. the actual world in which they originated, and Langer's point that the meaning of something emerges through a pattern that defines it. Each of their writing is exploring a different equally valid point regarding the making of meaning, which should not be played out against each other. However, to understand why and how LLMs have become somewhat successful in the processing of language at all, Langer's point of emerging patterns is the point to follow. That emerging patterns are decisive when it comes to the meaning-making of languages is well known in linguistics, where 'distributional semantics' have been explored since the 1950s, which have inspired the current mathematical approach towards language that builds on the so-called distributional hypothesis and the fact that linguistic items with similar distributions might have similar meanings (for a detailed discussion bringing out the link between distributional semantics and LLMs see Gastaldi 2021: 173-191).

5.2 Approaching language through mathematical aspects, however, was important long before distributional semantics, and even before George Kingsley Zipf analysed the statistical occurrences of words in the 1930s (Rieder 2020: 205). However, it was only when computers reached a certain capacity that the emergent patterns of meaning could be explored on a larger scale. This resulted in the creation of 'Natural Language Processing' [NLP], combining the field of linguistics with computer science. NLP developed methods looking at the usage of individual words in a text and computing their 'frequencies', which a computer could count with relative ease, allowing the researcher to stop wasting time on such a banal task. Soon, computers analysed the use of particular words, their rise or disappearance indicating the strategy of 'distant reading' (Moretti 2007). Utilising data analytics to evaluate publications alongside the canon of 200 books considered outstanding works allows us to evaluate whether among the 60,000 novels published in nineteenth century England certain patterns deserve closer examination to understand changing aspects and trends in the novels. Besides offering new ways of exploring and understanding language (for recent takes using LLMs see Underwood 2023), the field also made advances in computationally processing the complex rules of grammar through 'parsing'. The area where it struggled, however, was in generating written or spoken language of a quality acceptable to humans without pre-written templates (Bunz 2014: 4-5). Progress was only made in this area when computation started to make use of deep neural networks. NLP finally reached the threshold of 'making sense' once the computing of large text data sets, which were needed to train those networks, became possible, and was further fine-tuned through thousands of published computer science papers and the work of even more computer scientists. Around 2022, several capable models were released, starting with Google's LaMDA, then Meta's Galactica, and finally OpenAI's ChatGPT, although in the beginning all these models had a common problem: the sense they created could present facts that were 'hallucinated'. The reason for that lies in the complex process through which NLP approaches language as well as in the need to calculate meaning through 'form'. The following sections aim to describe the technical steps taken to calculate meaning, thereby translating computational steps into everyday language, a simplification which will naturally compress technical details to reduce LLMs' complexity. Given the importance of ML models and LLMs, however, it is necessary to develop readings of computer-science texts for non-computer scientists, which by now 'is also a matter of reading for world-making', as Louise Amoore et al. (2023) have pointed out.

5.3 The computation of language through LLMs usually consists of a series of small, iterative, and somewhat banal steps, which begin to make sense when scaled by a large number of texts and with the outcome further fine-tuned, for example by reinforcement learning through human feedback. 'Banal' and 'iterative' means that the processing of language will take each single word in a large text corpus and make note of the five (for example) words that come before or after it.

In a certain sense one could say that this has automatised the old linguistic insight of British linguist John Firth, 'you shall know a word by the company it keeps' (1957: 11). More important, however, is that the computational notation of words appearing together allowed for a shift in the approach: to understand words not only through their frequencies but also through their relation to other words. Bernard Rieder's (2020: 199-234) excellent chapter

Figure 2. The word neighbours of each single word (or token) are taken into account.

'From Frequencies to Vectors' retraces these steps historically and shows how vectors, first used to describe documents, found their way into language models, and that this was what re-conceptualised the computational approach profoundly. While frequencies count how often a word is being used, these word frequencies can be further explored through a semantic vector, a type of vector that compresses the relations that words have with one another within a corpus, i.e. which word is often next to another word, or which words never occur together. These so-called vector semantics help with modelling many aspects of a word's meaning (Jurafsky & Martin 2023: 103). Shifting the analysis of meaning from rates of occurrences to relations between words (or tokens) allowed to map the web of the relations that words within a corpus have with one another. The paper that is generally agreed on as a turning point to which many other researchers contributed, is called 'Efficient Estimation of Word Representations in Vector Space', known commonly as 'Word2Vec'. Published in 2013, 10 years before the public was introduced to the ChatGPT platform that would turn LLMs into mass media, the steps the paper suggests are simple. Inspired by the research of linguist Zelig Harris (1954) exploring the 'Distributional Structure' of language, the vector representation of words is combining a range of different algorithmic approaches to calculate – or estimate – words in vector space. To map words to that vector space, the paper suggested two approaches: it took surrounding words to predict the one in the middle, an approach that came to be known as 'Continuous Bag Of Words' (often shortened to CBOW). It also introduced a similar operation approaching the relation of words the other way around: this time it was taking the middle word to predict its neighbours left and right; a technique that came to be known as 'Skip-Gram'. Procedures such as these allowed to mathematicise the context of a word by establishing what came to be known as 'word embeddings' computationally, which has been described in excellent detail by

Juan Luis Gastaldi (2021, also Weatherby & Justie 2022, Roberge & LeBrun 2023, Hua & Raley 2023). More important, however, is that it would lead to advance the predicting of the next word through an understanding of word relations, which would (much later) make it possible to calculate semantic aspects and lead to generated writing.

5.4 The datasets needed to train language models were large and consisted of billions of words (or tokens). This means that the coordinates that represent a word's relations to the other words in that dataset resulted in a very long list of numerous relations. To recall such a long list, and to sort the relations to other words, a machine learning model makes use of its capability to operate in what is called high-dimensional computational space. While human understanding usually approaches space as something that is three dimensional, as something that consists of length, width and depth, the computational space of machine learning consists of many more dimensions (n-dimensions), known in mathematics as the 'Hilbert space'. Dealing with hundreds of complex vectors in the high dimensional space of LLMs allows one to calculate meaning. Analysing and sorting the vector patterns allows an LLM to suggest synonyms improving expressions, or to find word predictions suggesting which word is most likely to follow, to indicate syntactic relationships of words such as adjectives and adverbs (apparent/apparently), the plural of words (mouse/mice) or the comparatives (short/shorter) (Mikolov et al. 2013: 5). The functioning of this calculation was described by the authors as follows:

> To find a word that is similar to small in the same sense as biggest is similar to big, we can simply compute vector X = vector('biggest') − vector('big') + vector('small'). Then, we search in the vector space for the word closest to X measured by cosine distance, and use it as the answer to the question (we discard the input question words during this search). When the word vectors are well trained, it is possible to find the correct answer (word smallest) using this method. (Mikolov et al. 2013: 5)

However, the paper's authors (Tomas Mikolov, Kai Chen, Greg Corrado, and Jeffrey Dean) also came across a new phenomenon linked to the words' similarity degrees, which would allow LLMs not just to get language syntactically right but to surface relevant information as if it was a serach engine. They proposed to use the 'very subtle semantic relationships between words' (5) not just for syntactic relationships, but to find answers through searching the vector space, an aspect that they hoped could eventually be used for 'information retrieval and question answering systems' (5). For example, given the relation between France and its capital Paris, and Germany and its capital Berlin, requests could be made asking for the capital of Chile. To find the right word, the vector pattern (France/Paris & Germany/Berlin) would function like a

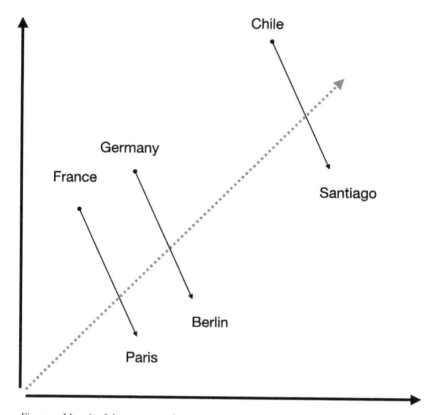

Figure 3. Meaningful concepts such as country-capital relationships can be encapsulated by vectors: this simplified visualisation shows a similarity cluster of words when plotted in 3-dimensional space.

'guide'; given the input 'Chile', it would search for similar vector patterns. Once a fitting vector was found, it would be presented as a word: 'Santiago'.

The fact that LLMs deal in vectors and not words (or tokens) is what allows us to calculate semantic relations. Only that the fitting vector pattern did not always lead to the correct word; the pattern could fit, but surface wrong information revealing an interesting flaw of language models: their confident hallucination.

5.5 Before we turn to hallucinations, however, several technical steps allowing LLMs to generate language had to happen. Even after Word2Vec introduced the vectorisation of words, explored further in a range of techniques to catch what is often called a word's 'embeddings', problems remained: the neural network architecture used for language processing at the time, the Recurrent Neural Network, was not fit for purpose. While calculating text, Recurrent Neural Networks struggled with longer sequences. Generating whole paragraphs of text would often lead to the model getting lost in detail.

The generated writing would focus on one topic in the first sentence, with a filler sentence added next and – its attention having now shifted to that filler sentence – continue with a new topic linked to the filler sentence but not related to the first. Texts lost their plot in hilarious ways. Tackling this in the context of machine translation, Bahdenau et al. (2014; see also Luong et al. 2015) introduced an idea which had already been tested successfully in image recognition: in order to make computation more effective, the most relevant, pertinent parts of an input sequence would gain more 'attention' than others. Knowing where to put its attention to, would allow a model to focus on the right topic and stop it from wandering off.[7] In order to mathematise this and create an 'attentional mechanism', a vector that encoded the context needed to be introduced, allowing the model to decode contextual meaning to understand where (on which semantic part of a sentence or paragraph) to put the attention (see also Dobson 2023). This was and continues to be difficult for Recurrent Neural Networks, whose computation runs sequentially, leading to long computation times. Soon, a new model architecture that could process the procedure of encoding/decoding in parallel was introduced, which came to be known as Transformers. The parallel approach quickly showed itself to be more effective and led to an acceleration of training speeds, allowing for larger datasets than previously possible to be processed (Luitse & Denkena 2021: 7). Using the new architecture running very large datasets allowed to calculate a word's 'situational dependency' (Roberge & Lebrun 2023, also Hayles 2022) much more precisely than before, and finally allowed natural language generation to sound as if it made sense. Although that sound, as mentioned at the very beginning of this inquiry, would be deceptive.

6. Technical Hermeneutics

6.1 Generated writing is not making sense of our *world*, but has been trained to make sense from our *words*. To achieve this, it learned to recreate the patterns of our languages, which it finds by calculating language as vectors. Calculating meaning from learned vector patterns is what happens when we ask the models to generate writing. Calculating meaning from billions of documents also means it can surface rare and useful information linked to rare and very specific words. However, operating purely on the plane of form when surfacing that information and generating writing, the pattern of forms contemporary LLMs look for trumps facts and other worldly aspects, as Bender & Koller (2020) have pointed out. This focus on form - the making of sense purely from word relations and not from relations of words to our world - is the reason that generated writing can be haunted by 'hallucinations', which are an interesting and well-known problem in machine learning (see for example Rumbelow and Watkins 2023, Ji et al. 2023). For generated writing, hallucinating is defined as information produced by the model that is factually wrong, for example, because it was not in the training data or has been wrongly synthesised. However, the model has no way to identify these errors – mathematically all is correct and in order, making the model on the contrary highly confident that the delivered information is correct. This means that the calculation of LLMs impresses through their *performance*, but this should not be confused with their *competence*. Their inept confidence is one of the reasons why we cannot treat generated writing as if it would provide the same qualities as non-generated writing, whose claim to competently describe the world from this or that perspective is simultaneously guarded by its correctness of references or witnesses, by place of publication, and by tone and style of writing. Due to its particular form of production, generated writing does not come with these same guardrails, at least not at this moment in time. If we follow Simondon, this is not surprising. According to him, it is a characteristic of the technical being to have a specific distance from the world: 'The availability of the technical thing consists in being liberated from the enslavement to the ground of the world [...]'; and he points out further: '[...] in technics the whole of reality must be traversed, touched, and treated by the technical object, detached from the world and applicable to any point and at any moment' (Simondon 1958: 183).

Thus, it is not surprising that 'hallucinating' has been identified as a profound problem of language models (and machine learning models in general), leading to an effort by computational researchers to re-introduce that competence sooner rather than later. However, even when the problem of hallucinations are being solved, the initial difficulties of acquiring competence can provide us with insights into LLMs particular functioning. It is here, where LLMs expose their mode of writing and their particular way of being intelligent, because as Virilio pointed out, it is generally in the malfunctioning of technologies such as the accident or the glitch, where their unique mode or 'substance', i.e. their tendencies of functioning, appear exposing their technical being: 'The accident reveals the substance, this is in fact because WHAT CROPS UP (accidens) is a sort of analysis, a technoalanysis WHAT IS BENEATH (substare) any knowledge' (Virilio 2007: 10).

6.2 Hallucinations allow us to get a glimpse of the particular 'tendencies' which the new mode of writing brings with it. Of course, exploring those new tendencies is confusing. For example, the role a collection of texts (a text corpus) plays is different. The main function of a collection of documents for an LLM is to gain an indexical understanding of the formal relations of the words (Weatherby & Justie 2022), and not of the facts they contain. Historically, we are used to understanding collections of documents as an archive securing historical records that enable us to support or tear down arguments through pointing to factual material references. A collection of documents used to train a model has a different function: its function is to allow the model the ability to learn patterns and word-relations from that corpus. The documents are used to train the model, and even though LLMs can memorise some aspects of original documents or texts, they will produce those texts because the information shows the right vector-pattern needed, and not because the texts hold information that is factually correct. One may think that a clean data set would help to advance the ability of a model in building correct forms that align somewhat more competently with the human artifice, and to a certain extent this is the case. Still, this does not solve the issue. Training a model on correct data and factual documents does not stop the model from having hallucinations, as the LLM *Galactica* showed. Facebook's experiment in training *Galactica* on a large corpus of scientific texts and data still led to the model citing research papers that didn't exist and delivering summaries of scientific texts that included misinformation (Heaven 2022). LLMs can deliver writing that reads a certain way – for example, factual. But at the moment, the concept of facts themselves and competence about the rightness and wrongness of facts is something that LLMs are unable to take into account. Even if we find ways to ground them in 'external knowledge' (Peng et al. 2023), their particular approach to calculating language-meaning will remain. Warnings that we cannot integrate generated writing into our daily lives as if it would be the writing we are familiar with, are therefore appropriate. Unfortunately, so far we have not found generated writing a fitting place and treatment in our human artifice. We pretend that it is writing as we know it, ignoring that it is *a new mode of writing* with its own tendencies. These tendencies need to be understood. 'Technical life', as Gilbert Simondon (1958: 140) reminds us, 'does not consist in overseeing machines, but in existing at the same level as a being that takes charge of the relation between them […]'. By looking at the technical mechanisms used to calculate meaning in LLMs, we learn in which direction we might start our search to understand (and not ignore or paint over) their technical being, and what to do with the meaning and form of intelligence this technical being produces; a meaning that is calculated from form instead of being approached through logic or factual deduction.

6.3 Generated writing is writing whose orientation puts form before facts and operates mathematically. However, that does not mean approaching the world via form bears no relation to our reality, as plenty of novels and artworks show. Here things get interesting. Natural language generation certainly does not align with our human artifice and its reality, but that does not mean that it has no relation to that reality. How else can we make sense of such a different way of writing? A direction to tap into could be the fascinating, discombobulated relation art and literature has to our human artifice. Here some conceptual thinking, such as that by Peli Grietzer (see chapter 1 in this volume) might be helpful in making differently sense of LLMs, for example by understanding how their technical capacities relate to our world through 'vibe.' Using the autoencoder model as a metaphor to approach art, and in particular poetry and literature, Grietzer thinks through a 'literary work's invariant style or vibe' as 'the aesthetic correlate of a literary work's internal *space of possibilities'* (29). 'A literary work's 'style' or 'vibe,' is, at first, an invariant structure of the very transformations and transitions that make up the work's narrative and rhetorical movement' (29). If one can develop a mathematically informed literature theory and think about literature through the lens of machine learning models, could we maybe also make sense of LLMs through literature theories? A question that opens up a new research inquiry, which would need to look, among other things, at the mechanisms of LLMs in light of Hannah Arendt's insight into the fragility of factual truth (Arendt 1967), and understand in what way this is linked to Virginia Woolf's (1932: 9) remark when writing her historical novel 'The Partigers' that 'where truth is important, to write fiction', as well as to Michael Riffaterre's (1993: XIII) observation that 'words may lie yet still tell a truth if the rules are followed'. Moving through aspects of literature and its ability to bring out truth in fiction, seems productive in light of generated writing as a mode that struggles to find its place in the world despite being often more factual than literature. It would also be a new and different endeavour as it would shift the focus away from the core questions this inquiry was following: What is writing? How can it be identified?

6.4 So let's end this inquiry into the arrival of LLMs and the new mode of writing. Given that writing has always been an exteriorisation closely related to being human on a political, social, and individual level, as this text has argued with Leroi-Gourhan and Derrida, the arrival of generated writing means that it has become necessary for all of us to acquire enough insights and knowledge of its technical hermeneutics[8] and mechanism typical for the new technical being and the particular intelligence created by generated writing. Describing the concept of new writing on a technical level, this text has hopefully contributed to this by explaining some of the mechanisms such as measuring the distance between the many words of a text corpus in vectors and calculating the meaning from those distances and relations. In a human artifice that is shaped by technical realities such as these as much as it is by political realities, with both of them in fact often overlapping, 'it is necessary for every man employed with a technical task to surround the machine both from above and from below, to have an understanding of it in some way', as Simondon (1958: 80) points out. Writing, having always been a technique to operate and be in our world, has now, with the beginning of new writing, also become such a technical task. To return to the beginning of the new writing, is thereby helpful for understanding this task better. This beginning may also lead, one never knows, to the moment Derrida anticipated in 1967: the end of the book, and the opening of another chapter. At one point.

Works Cited

Amoore, Louise, Alexander Campolo, Benjamin Jacobsen, and Ludovico Rella. 2023. 'Machine Learning, Meaning Making: On Reading Computer Science Texts', *Big Data & Society*, 10: https://journals.sagepub.com/doi/full/10.1177/20539517231166887.

Arendt, Hannah. 1958 [1998]. *The Human Condition*. University of Chicago Press.

Arendt, Hannah. 1967. 'Truth and Politics', *The New Yorker*. https://www.newyorker.com/magazine/1967/02/25/truth-and-politics.

Bahdanau, Dzmitry, Kyunghyun Cho, and Yoshua Bengio. 2014. 'Neural Machine Translation by Jointly Learning to Align and Translate'. *ArXiv Preprint ArXiv:1409.0473*.

Baillehache, Jonathan. 2013. 'Chance Operations and Randomizers in Avant-garde and Electronic Poetry: Tying Media to Language', *Textual Cultures*, 8.1, 38-56. http://www.jstor.org/stable/10.2979/textcult.8.1.38

Bajohr, Hannes. 2022. 'The Paradox of Anthroponormative Restriction: Artistic Artificial Intelligence and Literary Writing', *CounterText*, 8.2, 262-282.

Bajohr, Hannes. 2023. 'Dumb Meaning: Machine Learning and Artificial Semantics', *IMAGE*, 37.

Bender, Emily M., Timnit Gebru, Angelina McMillan-Major, and Shmargaret Shmitchell. 2021. 'On the Dangers of Stochastic Parrots: Can Language Models Be Too Big?', in *Proceedings of the 2021 ACM Conference on Fairness, Accountability, and Transparency*, 610-23.

Bender, Emily M., and Alexander Koller. 2020. 'Climbing towards NLU: On Meaning, Form, and Understanding in the Age of Data', in *Proceedings of the 58th Annual Meeting of the Association for Computational Linguistics*, 5185-98.

Bratton, Benjamin, and Blaise Agüera y Arcas. 2022. 'The Model Is the Message', *Noema Magazine*. https://www.noemamag.com/the-model-is-the-message/.

Bunz, Mercedes. 2019. 'The calculation of meaning: On the misunderstanding of new artificial intelligence as culture', *Culture, Theory and Critique*, 60.3-4, 264-278.

Bunz, Mercedes. 2014. "When Algorithms Learned How to Write'. *The Silent Revolution: How Digitalization Transforms Knowledge, Work, Journalism and Politics Without Making Too Much Noise*, 1-24. London: Palgrave Macmillan.

Carr, Nicholas. 2008. 'Is Google Making Us Stupid?' *Atlantic Monthly*, 302.1. https://web.lib.unb.ca/instruction/bcull/ARTICLES/Reading/GoggleCBCA.pdf.

Carr, Nicholas. 2010. *The Shallows: How the Internet Is Changing the Way We Think, Read and Remember*. London: Atlantic Books.

ChatGPT. 2023. https://chat.openai.com/.

Chun, Wendy Hui Kyong. 2021. *Discriminating Data: Correlation, Neighborhoods, and the New Politics of Recognition*. Cambridge, MA: MIT Press.

Derrida, Jacques. 1967a [1997]. *Of Grammatology*. Baltimore: Johns Hopkins University Press.

Derrida, Jacques. 1967b [1989]. *Writing and Difference*. Chicago: University of Chicago.

Derrida, Jacques. 1972a [1981]. *Dissemination*. Chicago: University of Chicago.

Derrida, Jacques. 1972b [1982] 'Signature Event Context', in *Margins of Philosophy*, 307-30. Chicago: University of Chicago.

Derrida, Jacques. 1981. *Positions*. Chicago: University of Chicago.

Facebook Inc. 2020. 'Third Quarter 2020 Results Conference Call'. https://s21.q4cdn.com/399680738/files/doc_financials/2020/q3/FB-Q3-2020-Earnings-Call-Transcript.pdf.

Firth, John R. 1957. 'A Synopsis of Linguistic Theory 1930-1955', in *Studies in linguistic analysis*, J.R. Firth, 1-32. London: Blackwell.

Foucault, Michael. 1969 [1997] *The Archeology of Knowledge*. London: Tavistock.

Future of Life Institute. 2023. 'Pause Giant AI Experiments: An Open Letter.' https://futureoflife.org/open-letter/pause-giant-ai-experiments/.

Equiano, Olaudah. 1789. *The Interesting Narrative of the Life of Olaudah Equiano, Or Gustavus Vassa, The African*. London.

Galloway, Alexander. 2021. 'Derrida's Macintosh', *Culture and Communication* [personal website], http://cultureandcommunication.org/galloway/derridas-macintosh

Gastaldi, Juan Luis. 2021. 'Why Can Computers Understand Natural Language? The Structuralist Image of Language Behind Word Embeddings', *Philosophy & Technology* 34.1, 149-214.

Grietzer, Peli. 2017. 'A Theory of Vibe', In Hannes Bajohr (ed.), *Thinking with AI: Machine Learning the Humanities*. London: Open Humanities Press, 20-32.

Harris, Zellig S. 1954. 'Distributional Structure', *WORD* 10.2-3, 146-62. https://doi.org/10.1080/00437956.1954.11659520.

Hartman, Saidiya. 2008. *Lose Your Mother: A Journey along the Atlantic Slave Route*. New York: Farrar, Straus and Giroux.

Hayles, N. Katherine. 2019. 'Can Computers Create Meanings? A cyber/bio/semiotic perspective', *Critical Inquiry* 46.1, 32-55.

Hayles, N. Katherine. 2022. 'Inside the Mind of an AI: Materiality and the Crisis of Representation', *New Literary History* 54.1, 635-666.

Heaven, Will Douglas. 2022, Nov 18. 'Why Meta's latest large language model survived only three days online', *MIT Technology Review.* https://www.technologyreview.com/2022/11/18/1063487/meta-large-language-model-ai-only-survived-three-days-gpt-3-science/.

Hegel, Georg Wilhelm Friedrich. 1817 [1972]. *Philosophy of Mind.* Oxford University Press.

Hendrycks, Dan, Kevin Zhao, Steven Basart, Jacob Steinhardt, and Dawn Song. 2021. 'Natural Adversarial Examples'. In *Proceedings of the IEEE/CVF Conference on Computer Vision and Pattern Recognition*, 15262-71.

Hua, Minh, and Rita Raley. 2023. 'How to Do Things with Deep Learning Code', *ArXiv Preprint.* https://arxiv.org/abs/2304.09406.

Jacobs, Harriet. 1861. *Incidents in the Life of a Slave Girl, Written by Herself.* Boston, Mass.: Thayer & Eldridge.

Ji, Ziwei, Nayeon Lee, Rita Frieske, Tiezheng Yu, Dan Su, Yan Xu, Etsuko Ishii, Ye Jin Bang, Andrea Madotto, and Pascale Fung. 2023. 'Survey of hallucination in natural language generation' *ACM Computing Surveys*, 55.12, 1–38.

Jurafsky, Daniel, and James H. Martin. 2023. *Speech and Language Processing: An Introduction to Natural Language Processing, Computational Linguistics, and Speech Recognition.* Pearson. https://web.stanford.edu/~jurafsky/slp3/ed3book.pdf.

Khan, Nora. 2019. 'Seeing Naming Knowing', *The Brooklyn Rail.* https://www.are.na/block/10908843.

Kirschenbaum, Matthew G. 2023. 'Prepare for the Textpocalypse', *The Atlantic.* https://www.theatlantic.com/technology/archive/2023/03/ai-chatgpt-writing-language-models/673318/

Kirschenbaum, Matthew G. 2021. *Bitstreams: The Future of Digital Literary Heritage.* Philadelphia: University of Pennsylvania Press.

Kirschenbaum, Matthew G. 2016. *Track Changes: A Literary History of Word Processing.* The Belknap Press of Harvard University Press.

Langer, Susanne K. 1948 [1954]. *Philosophy in a New Key: A Study in the Symbolism of Reason, Rite, and Art.* New York: Mentor.

Lemoine, Blake. 2022. 'What Is LaMDA and What Does It Want?'. Medium. https://cajundiscordian.medium.com/what-is-lamda-and-what-does-it-want-688632134489.

Leroi-Gourhan, André. 1964 [1993]. *Gesture and Speech*. Cambridge, MA: MIT Press.

Luitse, Dieuwertje, and Wiebke Denkena. 2021. 'The Great Transformer: Examining the Role of Large Language Models in the Political Economy of AI', *Big Data & Society*, 8.2. https://journals.sagepub.com/doi/pdf/10.1177/20539517211047734

Luong, Thang, Hieu Pham, and Christopher D. Manning. 2015. 'Effective Approaches to Attention-Based Neural Machine Translation', in *Proceedings of the 2015 Conference on Empirical Methods in Natural Language Processing*, 1412-21. Association for Computational Linguistics. https://doi.org/10.18653/v1/D15-1166.

Meikle, Graham. 2023. *Deepfakes*. Cambridge: Polity.

Merriam Webster. 2024. 'To Write'. www.merriam-webster.com/dictionary/write.

Mikolov, Tomas, Kai Chen, Greg Corrado, and Jeffrey Dean. 2013. 'Efficient estimation of word representations in vector space', ArXiv Preprint. https://arxiv.org/abs/1301.3781

Moran, Chris. 2023, April 6. 'ChatGPT Is Making up Fake Guardian Articles. Here's How We're Responding', *The Guardian*. https://www.theguardian.com/commentisfree/2023/apr/06/ai-chatgpt-guardian-technology-risks-fake-article.

Moretti, Franco. 2007. *Graphs, Maps, Trees: Abstract Models for Literary History*. London: Verso.

Nietzsche, Friedrich Wilhelm. 2002. *Schreibmaschinentexte: Vollständige Edition, Faksimiles und Kritischer Kommentar*. Weimar: Universitätsverlag Bauhaus Universität Weimar.

Peng, Baolin, Michel Galley, Pengcheng He, Hao Cheng, Yujia Xie, Yu Hu, Qiuyuan Huang, et al. 2023. 'Check Your Facts and Try Again: Improving Large Language Models with External Knowledge and Automated Feedback', ArXiv Preprint ArXiv:2302.12813.

Perrigo, Billy. 2023, Jan. 'OpenAI Used Kenyan Workers on Less Than $2 Per Hour to Make ChatGPT Less Toxic', *Time*, https://time.com/6247678/openai-chatgpt-kenya-workers/.

Plato. 2005. *Phaedrus*, edited by C. Rowe. London: Penguin.

Ribas, Jordi. 2023, Feb 21. 'Building the New Bing', *Microsoft Bing Blogs*. https://blogs.bing.com/search-quality-insights/february-2023/Building-the-New-Bing/.

Rieder, Bernhard. 2020. *Engines of Order: A Mechanology of Algorithmic Techniques*. Amsterdam University Press.

Riffaterre, Michael. 1993. *Fictional Truth*. Baltimore: John Hopkins University Press.

Roberge, Jonathan, and Michael Castelle. 2021. 'Toward an end-to-end sociology of 21st-century machine learning'. *The cultural life of machine learning: An incursion into critical AI studies*, edited by J. Roberge and M. Castelle, 1-29. London: Palgrave Macmillan.

Roberge, Jonathan and Tom Lebrun. 2023. 'Parrots All the Way Down: Controversies within AI's Conquest of Language', in: *KI-Realitäten*, edited by R. Groß, and R. Jordan, 39-66. Bielefeld: transcript Verlag. https://doi.org/10.14361/9783839466605-003

Roose, Kevin. 2023. 'A Conversation With Bing's Chatbot Left Me Deeply Unsettled', *New York Times*. https://www.nytimes.com/2023/02/16/technology/bing-chatbot-microsoft-chatgpt.html.

Rorty, Richard (ed.). 1967 [1992]. *The Linguistic Turn: Essays in Philosophical Method*. Illinois: University of Chicago Press.

Rumbelow, Jessica and mwatkins. 2023, February 5. 'SolidGoldMagikarp (plus, prompt generation)', LESSWRONG. https://www.lesswrong.com/posts/aPeJE8bSo6rAFoLqg/solidgoldmagikarp-plus-prompt-generation.

Sayyid, Omar Ibn. 1831. 'The Life of Omar Ben Saeed, Called Morro, a Fullah Slave in Fayetteville, N.C. Owned by Governor Owen', in *A Muslim American Slave: The Life of Omar Ibn Said*, edited and translated by Ala Alryyes, 47-80. Madison: University of Wisconsin Press.

Shoemaker, Tyler. 2023. 'Verkettete Textualität' [Concatenative Textuality], in *Quellcodekritik: Zur Philologie von Algorithmen*, edited by Hannes Bajohr and Markus Krajewski, 217-243. August Verlag, 2023. English permalink: https://escholarship.org/content/qt20k8q4xc

Simondon, Gilbert. 1958 [2017]. *On the Mode of Existence of Technical Objects*. Minneapolis: Univocal Publishing.

Statista. 2023a. 'Emails Sent per Day 2025'. Statista. https://www.statista.com/statistics/456500/daily-number-of-e-mails-worldwide/.

Statista. 2023b. 'WhatsApp: Daily Sent Message Volume 2020'. Statista. https://www.statista.com/statistics/258743/daily-mobile-message-volume-of-whatsapp-messenger/.

Surkis, Judith. 2012. 'When Was the Linguistic Turn? A Genealogy', *The American Historical Review*, 117.3, 700-722. https://doi.org/10.1086/ahr.117.3.700.

Virilio, Paul. 2007. *The Original Accident*. Cambridge: Polity.

von König, Dominik. 1977. 'Lesesucht und Lesewut', in *Buch und Leser. Vorträge des Ersten Jahrestreffens des Wolfenbütteler Arbeitskreises für Geschichte des Buchwesens 13. und. 14. Mai 1976*, edited by H.G. Göpfert, 89-124. Hamburg: Hauswedell.

Underwood, Ted. 2023, March 19. 'Using GPT-4 to measure the passage of time in fiction: Large language models are valuable research assistants, especially when they refuse to follow instructions' [personal website]. https://tedunderwood.com/2023/03/19/using-gpt-4-to-measure-the-passage-of-time-in-fiction/

Weatherby, Leif, and Brian Justie. 2022. 'Indexical AI.' *Critical Inquiry*, 48.2, 381-415. https://www.journals.uchicago.edu/doi/abs/10.1086/717312.

Wikipedia. 2023, May 17. 'Writing'. https://en.wikipedia.org/wiki/Writing.

Notes

The text owes much to my sabbatical, my computer's search function to comb through too many PDFs, the patience of Hannes Bajohr, the technical expertise of Niklas Stoehr, and the attentive eye and language precision of Joely Day.

1. Before LLMs, most attempts in computer science to automatically generate writing was based on the usage of templates (Bunz 2014). This is a different approach from the automation of language in literature, where avant-garde and electronic poetry generated language with the aim to introduce moments of randomness (Baillehache 2013). Interestingly, recent experiments in contemporary literature using language models turned again in a new and different direction by exploring the intersection of language and computation (Bajohr 2022).

2. For an introduction to the concept of cultural techniques with particular attention to aspects of algorithmic information ordering, see chapter 3 in Bernard Rieder's (2020) excellent *Engines of Order: A Mechanology of Algorithmic Techniques*, 81-141.

3. Derrida (1967: 26), who calls Hegel 'the first thinker of writing', saw this as a clear sign of Hegel's 'Europeocentrism' (3) and criticised his belief that the alphabet enables one to represent an idea or name directly and in the simplest form in contrast to pictorial writing such as that of Egyptian hieroglyphs.

4. Nietzsche, who was one of the early users of a typewriter (he is a known user of the early model the writing ball), famously remarked in 1882 to his secretary 'Unser Schreibzeug arbeitet mit an unseren Gedanken', which literally means 'Our writing tools work along when we form our thoughts' (Nietzsche 2002: 18). See also Alexander Galloway's (2021) take on 'Derrida's Macintosh'.

5. Not very surprisingly for contemporary neoliberal capitalism as the ruling ideology, Wikipedia actually lists this point first.

6. Foucault (1969: 65) addressed writing among other techniques in the *Archaeology of Knowledge* as 'procedures of intervention' mentioning among others 'techniques of rewriting', 'methods of transcribing', 'modes of translating'.

7. Although it would introduce other problems – the devil is as always in the details. While attention models can put their focus on particular parts, they can only take in sequences of fixed length. Recurrent Neural Networks, on the other hand, can process sequences of unlimited length.

8. Using Ricoeur for the concept of hermeneutics with regards to LLMs could be highly interesting, as Roberge and LeBrun (2023) have demonstrated.

4

Operative Ekphrasis: The Collapse of the Text/Image Distinction in Multimodal AI

Hannes Bajohr

The humanities – this is the premise of this volume – can productively draw theoretical insights from machine learning and AI for their own disciplines. They can do so not simply from the often only implicit philosophical assumptions of the technical fields, but also by testing and adapting humanistic vocabulary by confronting it with the realities of current AI systems. In this essay, I demonstrate one example of such 'thinking with AI' by shining a new light on a perennial aspect of humanist inquest – the relationship between word and image. In what follows, I will develop some intuitions about this relationship and ask how it may be changing with the shift from classical algorithms to current state-of-the-art machine learning. In particular, I am interested in so-called 'multimodal AI', among which large visual models such as DALL·E or Stable Diffusion may be the best known. To think *with* AI here is to test this technology's theoretical ramifications for a more traditional concept pertaining to the interaction of word and image, namely ekphrasis, which I broaden here to include the technical substrate of this interaction in the digital under the title of 'operative ekphrasis'. Using this concept, I show that multimodal AI does away with the separation of mediums that is at the core of ekphrasis, as this technology can process both text and image as *one* type of data.

In the first part of this essay, I use examples from visual poetry to discuss three text/image media: 1) analog, 2) 'sequentially' digital (classic computing), and 3) 'connectionistically' digital (stochastic machine learning). I will argue that with the advent of machine learning, the division between digital and analog media needs to be subdivided, as AI operates differently from older computational paradigms. In the second part, I discuss how the rhetorical figure of ekphrasis provides a framework for ordering this new subdivision by interpreting code as performative. Finally, I draw two conclusions: first, that the classical opposition between text and image, on which the concept of ekphrasis is based, dissolves in multimodal AI; and second, that semantics nevertheless returns to the digital, which hitherto has been seen only as a matter of syntax. Taken together, these claims question both our aesthetic lexicon

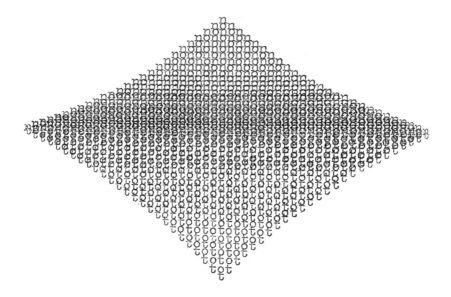

Figure 1. Franz Mon, 'non/tot' (1964)

and our understanding of digitality. As such, they underscore the cross-disciplinary significance of Critical AI Studies, and show that the humanities, with the necessary care and without falling for hype and exaggeration, can benefit from thinking *with* AI.

Text and Image in the Digital

As good a way as any to start discussing the relationship between text and image is to turn to visual poetry, which by its very nature brings visuality and textuality into dialogue. Figure 1 shows a work by German concrete poet Franz Mon. It is taken from his cycle 'non tot' published in 1964, and it consists of several typewritten lines shaped like a diamond, or perhaps a sail. The lines of the upper half repeat the word 'non', those in the bottom half the word 'tot'. The lines grow progressively more compressed toward the centre of the page, partly obscuring one another. Figure 2 shows a visual poem by the contemporary German digital author Jasmin Meerhoff, taken from her 2022 collection 'They Lay'. Here, scraps of typeset text are arranged in a repetitive, undulating pattern that might suggest flames rising from some unseen fuel. What these letters spell is difficult to decipher – they are certainly letters, but in their collage-like configuration, they are even more divorced from linguistic meaning than Mon's already enigmatic 'non/tot'. To the uninitiated viewer, in any case, the two pieces speak a shared poetic language that brings together letters in constellations in which the visual quality of the page rivals or surpasses the poems' semantic meaning. These poems are to be looked at

Figure 2. Jasmin Meerhoff, 'They Lay' (2022)

as images as much as (if not more than) they are meant to be read as lines of text. Viewed next to each other, it seems that not much has changed in the roughly sixty years separating these two works.

Compare this to the piece in figure 3. It is the work of Dave Orr and, like Meerhoff's, it was created in 2022. Unlike the first two poems, however,

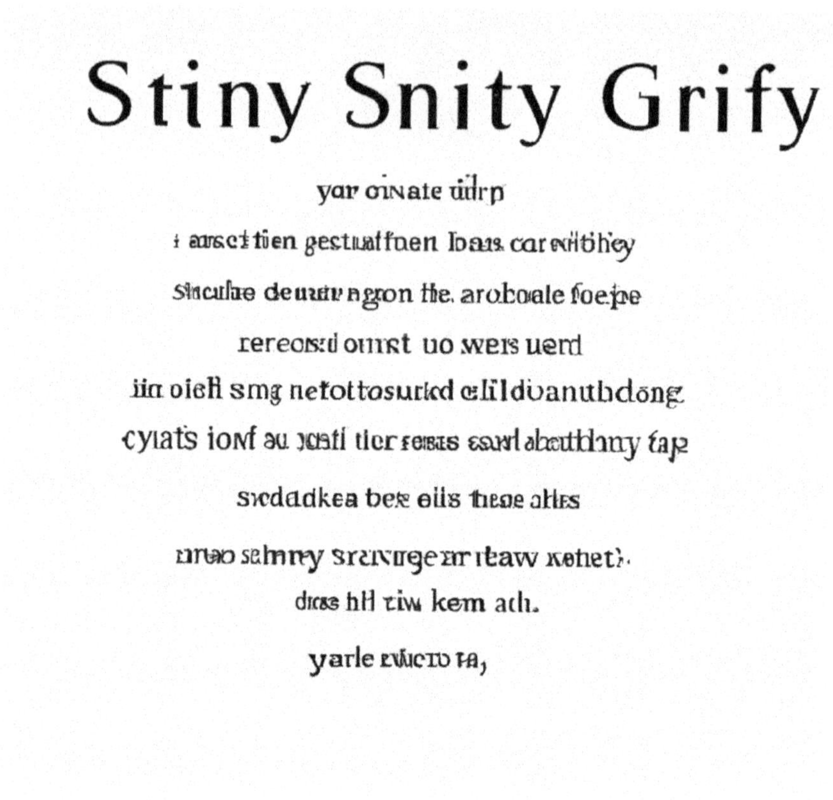

Stiny Snity Grify

yar oiNate üilrp

ᵢ aɑɾ&cⁱ tꭗen gestuɑtfɑen lbaɹɹ. cɑr ᴇⱴltᵭћey

sⁱⁱⁱacu�ⱡꭗe deⱨɹⱨⱴ ɐgɾon ᵗᵗᵉ. arolbɑɑle foeჶɹe

rereoⱦ:ⱦ oⁱⁱⱤt ᴜo ᴡeⱤⱻ ᴜeⱧ̅d

ⁱⁱⁱⁱ oⁱᵉꭍ smɲ netottosⱨɾɩⱦd ᴇⱡⁱⱦüanⱨⱡbɗóng

cyⱡatˢ ioⱨf ᶄⱨ ꭗⱨⱻtí tⱡⱦcr ꭍᴇⱤⱭⱻ ꭍⱩⱭⱦꭍ oⱡᴂⱨⱦtⱡꭍⱨⱨy fⱭⱤɇ

sⱩɗⱭdⱼₖₑₐ beⱨ eⁱⁱⱻ ᵗₕₑₐₑ ⱭⱡⱤⱼₛ

ⱨⱦⱨⱭⱦ ꭍⱨꭗ̅ⱨⱤy sⱤⱩⱴⱨꭗⱨgeⱼⱥⱦ ꭗⱦaⱱⱱ Ⱪⱨꭗetⱼ.

dⱦⱻⱻ ⱨ̅ꭍ ꭗⱦⱯⱭ kem Ɑⱦⱨ.

yarle ꭗⱩⱱⱩcⱨⱤo ꭗⱥ,

Figure 3. Dave Orr, 'Stiny Snity Grify' (2022)

it appears to be of a quite different make. Its centred text alignment gives it the air of a more traditional, or even naïve, poetic paradigm that predates the visual poetry of the other two pieces. Yet a second look reveals that while the title is clearly legible, if enigmatic – 'Stiny Snity Grify' – the lines are in fact not simply nonsense but not even text. They have the character of what is often called 'asemic' writing, that is, writing that does not use words but merely the semblance of words. If, as Peter Schwenger puts it, the 'visual and muscular aspects of writing are generally obscured by the primacy of writing's communicative function', then an asemic text 'does not attempt to communicate any message other than its own nature as writing', including its visual character (Schwenger 2019: 1). In this sense, Orr's poem, too, could be classified as 'visual', albeit from a divergent perspective compared to the other two – instead of making a poem by using text to create an image, it uses an image to create a poem that looks like text.

As instances of visual poetry, one can identify commonalities between the three works. What interests me here, however, is what sets them apart – and

Figure 4. Excerpt from the Olympia Monica's manual (model SM7)

this is in no small part their technical substrate, their, as Katherine Hayles calls it, 'media-specificity' (Hayles 2004; Bajohr 2022) For all three use radically different technologies, and all these technologies imply radically different relationships between text and image.

Perhaps unsurprisingly, the two examples from 2022 use digital technology, while Mon's 1964 work was created by analog means – with an Olympia Monica mechanical typewriter, to be exact, on which he produced much of his concrete and visual poetry. Figure 4 shows a section from the Monica's manual with a sample of its signature typeface. In contrast, Jasmin Meerhoff created her poem digitally, by writing a macOS shell script (figure 5). When executed in the command line, the script tells the open-source application ImageMagick to do two things: first, to cut a single image file containing a line of text from a scanned page into small pieces (lines 12-20 in the script); and second, to collage those pieces into the shape that make up the poem (lines 23-27). The wavy appearance is the result of using a sine function to arrange the pieces by specifying the amplitude and frequency of the waves (line 4). This is all done automatically, and Meerhoff's script is freely available online (Jine [Meerhoff] 2022), enabling anyone to make a potentially endless stream of visual poems.

Dave Orr's piece is also produced by digital means, but in a very different way. It was created through the use of an 'artificial intelligence', or more precisely, a complex machine learning algorithm that is implemented as a neural network. The neural network in this case is called DALL·E, a product by the company OpenAI, best known for its text-generation model ChatGPT (Ramesh et al. 2021). DALL·E, currently in its third version, is a large visual model with a text-to-image capability, and it is only one among a growing number of them, such as StabilityAI's Stable Diffusion, Google's Imagen, or Midjourney.[1] These systems take a natural language description (the 'prompt') as an input and generate an image as an output, producing a visual representation of the content of the text. In the case of DALL·E 2 – which was used to produce Orr's poem – this is done via an interface that consists of a single text

```
1    #!/bin/bash
2    # They lay (oscillating cuts) - "micro"
3
4    read -p "Enter value for AM (between 1 and 100). Enter value for FM (1 to 30000) " am fm
5    echo "AM is $am and FM is $fm"
6
7    read -p "Enter filename " fl
8    echo "File is $fl"
9
10   ct=0
11   until [ $ct -gt 599 ] # sets how often a cut will be made (+1) and how many snippets will be
     produced
12   do
13     ((ct+=1)) # a counter. starting at 1, increasing by 1
14     ctt=`printf %03d $ct` # prints 3 digits numbers, important for naming the files
15     zw=`awk -v x="$ct" -v f=$fm -v a=$am 'BEGIN {wz=sin(5*(3+x*a))*sin(2*3.1416*(3+(x/f)))+0.
     9999; printf wz }'` # defines a sine function. shift 0.9999 above zero on y-axis
16     sw=`awk -v x="$ct" 'BEGIN {wv=(sin(x*4)+5)*0.28; printf wv }'` # defines another sine
     function for slightly changing the width of snippets
17     mkdir -p cuts pieces # creates directories for the cut images and the new images
18     echo " Cutting …"
19     magick $fl +profile "icc" -gravity SouthWest -crop "%[fx:(w/20)*$sw]"x"%[fx:h]"+"%[fx:(w/2.75)
     *$zw]"+0 +repage cuts/$ctt.png # cuts the image. the width of the snippets is set as a
     fraction of the width of the input image. the position on the x-axis defines where the cut is
     made. it is calculated with the values of the variable 'zw'
20   done
21
22   while :
23   do
24     echo ' Assembling ! '
25     montage cuts/*.png -tile 20x -background white -geometry +0+0 -units PixelsPerInch -density
     300 pieces/thl_am"$am"_fm"$fm".png # composes a new image. with -tile the number of snippets
     in a row is defined. it should be a (integer) divisor of the number of snippets (line 7) to
     avoid gaps at the bottom of the new image
26     break
27   done
```

Figure 5. The shell script for Jasmin Meerhoff's 'They Lay'.

box for the input prompt (figure 6).[2] For Orr's poem, the prompt was 'a poem about the singularity written in a serif font' (Orr 2022).

It is worth noting that DALL·E typically does not generate texts. This 'poem' emerged when Orr was examining the model, and it appeared as part of a blog post about the system. As far as I am aware, it was never meant to be published as a literary work, and the fact that Orr is a product manager for the Google Assistant who does not, to my knowledge, consider himself a poet supports this impression. Indeed, AI image generation is famously bad at producing text, and next to mangled hands, garbled writing is (or was until recently) the most prominent tell-tale sign that a picture is in fact AI gener-ated.[3] What DALL·E is usually meant to produce are images – either photore-alistic or graphic – all of which have in common that they are the result of an input text. Figure 7 shows a more typical example from the developer's web-site. The prompt 'An astronaut riding a horse in photorealistic style' results in an image of just that. As there is nothing but the textual prompt for users to steer the image generation, a veritable 'promptology' has established itself since the appearance of large visual models. By finessing the input text, add-ing more descriptions of style or atmosphere, it is possible to nudge the result in one direction or another. Apart from a *Prompt Book* (dall·ery gall·ery 2022),

Figure 6. The interface of DALL·E with a text box for inputting the prompt.

there is now even a website on which particularly useful prompts are sold for small sums (PromptBase n.d.).

The three discussed works each embody different poetic and technological paradigms, which can be categorised in several different ways: 1) as a type of text/image interaction in the broader genre of visual poetry, and 2) as the result of analog (Mon) or digital technology (Meerhoff, Orr). However, it is possible to break down the digital technology into two subcategories: 3) classical algorithms and modern AI, which I will discuss in a moment under the rubric of sequential and connectionist paradigms respectively. For now, it is sufficient to note that the digital realm is not a monolith but instead a landscape of varied sub-domains.

All three classifications connect text with images or image-like structures, but they do so in distinct ways. Visual poetry does this by its very nature: it creates images through the arrangement of text. However, only the two digital works do so at the level of technical substrate. Here, the text and the resulting text-image stand not simply in a mimetic relationship but a causal one brought about by a purely syntactic code language. This is what I call *operative* ekphrasis. But only in the last case – the AI model – is there a semantic element that ultimately threatens to dissolve the distinction between text and image altogether. The remainder of this essay will be spent unpacking these distinctions. They bear significant implications for how we interpret and understand these works and their differences, and it is an example of what an aesthetics of AI could be that takes the technical substrate seriously. To illustrate why, I need to elucidate to some degree how these technologies operate.

Figure 7. A DALL·E-generated image for the prompt 'An astronaut riding a horse in photorealistic style'.

Sequential and Connectionist Paradigms of AI

For the subdivision of digital technology, I have proposed the terms 'sequential' and 'connectionist'.[4] The sequential paradigm denotes the dominant style of operating computers since Alan Turing's (conceptual) invention of the Universal Machine in 1936 and, after earlier models had been built, John von Neumann's (actual) implementation of the 'stored programme' concept in the EDVAC architecture in 1945 (built in 1949, see Haigh and Ceruzzi 2021) that by and large is still used today. It is characterised by the classical algorithm, laid down in a programming language of sequentially executed steps. Meerhoff's cut-up script belongs in this category, as do most of the programmes on a typical computer. For instance, the command 'read -p' in line 4 (figure 5) requests a user input that will be stored in the variables 'am' and 'fm', which later designate the amplitude and the frequency of the poem's waves. Importantly, these lines are executed one after another and in a deterministic manner. Every time it is run, the programme will go through the same, pre-dictable commands. Because one can inspect the algorithm by reading the explicitly stated rules, this paradigm has, in principle, a high degree of trans-parency to human readers.

The sequential paradigm differs greatly from the newer digital mode of operation that I call connectionist, which is what is usually meant by AI today – deep learning, which is a subset of stochastic machine learning method-ologies that uses multi-layered artificial neural networks to model complex patterns in data. Loosely inspired by the way individual neurons in the brain repeatedly forge paths to perform higher-level functions, current deep neural networks are made up of interconnected units, often referred to as 'neurons', which are linked by 'synapses'. (It is important to note, however, that this is a highly idealised affair and should not be confused with actual brain structure.) In these computational models, each neuron receives and processes incoming data, calculates a weighted sum based on its input, and then typically applies a non-linear activation function to determine its output in a process called 'forward propagation'. The discrepancy between this output and the desired or known correct output is then measured using a loss function. Subsequently, an optimisation algorithm – typically a variant of 'gradient descent' – is used to adjust the weights and biases across the network to minimise this loss, a process known as 'backpropagation'. The primary aim of training a deep neu-ral network is to refine these parameters so that the model can generalise effectively, extrapolating from the training dataset to predict outcomes or classify new instances accurately. Put differently, the network identifies under-lying patterns in the training set, fits a mathematical function to these data points, which then serves as a model for interpreting unseen data.[5]

Consider a practical example involving image generation. Given a large enough dataset of human faces, a neural network can process this dataset to learn its inherent patterns, structures, and variations. These learned charac-teristics can then be applied to generate entirely new images of faces, which, despite being completely novel, will appear strikingly similar to real human faces. Because of the statistical nature of the AI, these faces are neither col-lages of face parts, nor mere linear composites of all the faces known to the model. Rather, and metaphorically speaking, the network learns *face-ness*, the gestalt of faces, and is able to recreate it in a way that does not repeat the indi-vidual inputs (see Bajohr 2021). This is the principle of the well-known website thispersondoesnotexist.com, which presents a completely new and unique but artificial portrait of a face every time it is refreshed.

The AI model resulting from this training process implements complex nonlinear functions. What is central, now, is that a neural network cannot be translated back into a deterministic and exact higher-level algorithm, as the model merely describes the connection strengths between the 'neurons' in the so-called weight model. While of course neural networks are still implemented in a von Neumann machine – and not, say, an analog or quantum computer

– and are thus still digital, they nevertheless follow a radically different conceptual framework than the sequential model. For unlike the sequential paradigm, whose logic is laid out step-by-step, the connectionist paradigm follows a stochastic rather than a purely deterministic logic. The learned 'knowledge' is embedded in the network's structure and its weights which represent the strength of connections between the artificial neurons. As a result, while it is technically possible to 'read' the values of the weights in a trained neural network, these numbers do not translate into a sequence of comprehensible instructions or steps in the same way that traditional code in a programming language does (see Offert 2023).

Evidently, these are two very different models of computation that we nevertheless call 'digital'. Meerhoff's work, produced by a classical algorithm, was an example of the sequential, Orr's 'poem', produced by a neural net, of the connectionist paradigm. This technical introduction matters. For this nested distinction – that between analog and digital, and that, within the digital, between the sequential and the connectionist paradigm – generates different relationships between text and image. For what characterises both digital forms, but not the analog one, is what I want to call 'operative ekphrasis'.

Representational and Performative Notions of Ekphrasis

The concept of ekphrasis is one of most-discussed terms in visual theory, literary criticism, and classics for describing the relationship between text and image. It has, as Ruth Webb noted, become a theoretical genre unto itself, evoking 'a network of interlocking questions and interests, from the positivist pursuit of lost monuments described in ancient and medieval ekphrasis to the poststructuralist fascination with a textual fragment which declares itself to be pure artifice, the representation of representation' (Webb 1999: 7). But it has repeatedly been pointed out that in its original meaning, ekphrasis was a much broader category and signified a rhetorical device for generating vivid, sensory descriptions in oratory. A word from the rhetor's education, it was used to describe the act of clearly conjuring up something in the mind's eye of the audience – of transforming them, as Nikolaos of Myra put it in the second century AD, from listeners to spectators (Pfisterer 2019: 99; Webb 1999).

This early meaning already implies a media anthropology in which the auditory and visual senses become functionally interchangeable. The ancient use did not particularly attend to the description of visual artworks, as Webb stresses (Webb 1999: 8). It was only later, in the nineteenth and most emphatically in the twentieth century, that the term ekphrasis became restricted to *literary* representations of a real or, in the case of what John Hollander has later called 'notional ekphrasis', an imaginary work of art (Hollander 1995: 7). Nevertheless, both interpretations persist in different guises to this day, so that, sampling the past five decades, definitions of ekphrasis have ranged from 'any description of anything visual' (Hefernan 2015: 35) to, more specifically, 'the poetic description of a pictorial or sculptural work of art' (Spitzer 1962: 72).

Staying with the broader and, I think, more philosophically generative definition, it makes sense that James Heffernan has emphasised the *representational* quality of ekphrasis by defining it as 'the verbal representation of visual representation' (Heffernan 1993: 3). Tamar Yacobi has underscored this view by suggesting that ekphrasis is 'representation in the second degree' by specifying representation as repetition in a different mode: 'What was originally an autonomous image of the world becomes in ekphrastic transfer an image of an image, a part of a new whole, a visual *inset* within a verbal *frame*' (Yacobi 2013: 1, 3). We can see here already that this characterisation, and the rhetoric of inset and frame, points to the tension at the core of ekphrasis: The concept articulates either an equivalence of or a competition between language and image – one imitating the other is either a successful enterprise or the recipe for disappointment. Thus, as W.J.T. Mitchell has noted, ekphrasis can be part of a hopeful or a fearful ontology of text/image interaction. It is either something with an almost utopian potential for transformation – from the visual to the verbal and back again, as the ancients had it – or a most blatant impossibility, which therefore needs to be aesthetically prohibited: making the visual absolutely verbal can never actually happen, and in fact it must not (Mitchell 1994: 152-160). Gotthold Ephraim Lessing's *Laocoon* argued for the incompatibility of language's temporal structure (ideal for depicting action) with painting's spatial makeup (best suited for depicting objects) and is, to Mitchell, the 'classic expression of ekphrastic fear' (Lessing 2005: Ch. 15 and Ch. 16; Mitchell 1994: 154).

This analysis of the immanent characteristics of the media involved in the metaphor of 'painting with words' (Horace) entails a critique of mimetic representation as the defining linchpin of ekphrasis. It has been taken up again in the last decade, and the focus on representation is replaced by a focus on *performance*: what is it that ekphrasis *does*, without saying that this doing must be imitative? Renate Brosch has thus suggested a new definition: 'ekphrasis is a literary response to a visual image [...] emphasising the performative instead of the mimetic' (Brosch 2018: 227). This performative interpretation of ekphrasis has several advantages, the main one being that by passing over its mimetic dimension, one can suspend the decision about its hopeful or fearful interpretation. Instead of understanding it as either an equivalence of or a competition between art forms – as a successful or unsuccessful relationship of representation – it simply places them in a consecutive and causal relation.

I would like to extend this notion by mobilising the performative definition of ekphrasis for digital media. With a different emphasis, Brosch also brings ekphrasis to the digital, arguing that it becomes important in a digital media ecology that is inundated with images while also drowning in text – contradicting such doomsday predictions that saw the demise of reading. However, I will tweak her use of the word 'performative' to talk about ekphrasis in its media-specificity in the digital. Instead of literary 'responses', which are not themselves digital events, I want to understand the performance of ekphrasis as a *computational operation that correlates text and image.*

Operative Ekphrasis

With the performative notion of ekphrasis in mind, let me return to the three visual poems, the division between analog and digital, and the subdivision between sequential and connectionist. All three works embody specific ways of using language to create an image. In this sense, they are all ekphrastic in their cumulative effect: producing visual constellations through text. That alone, however, is not yet what I call operative ekphrasis. It is only really possible for text to actively and causally bring forth an image in the digital works, not in the analog one.

In the analog – in Mon's typewriter poem – the text may of course 'produce' an image. Yet this production is not performative on the operative level, but rather a perceptual after-effect of a manual arrangement. In 'non/tot', it is the writer's bodily actions – his hand movements on the typewriter, his exerting force onto the keys – that lead to what we are compelled to describe as the 'image' of the text. This visual structure is the result of work, that is, a causal chain of mechanical forces that are not themselves textual. There is only one text here, the one on the page; it does not, strictly speaking, perform anything.

This is different in the digital works. In Meerhoff's piece, there are now two texts – the one on the page and the one that actually produces that text, the script. This is a textual performance in a *computational* sense: an operation the first text carries out to effectively produce the second text. It does so not as mechanical work, as in Mon, but as the manipulation of information, which is itself textual in nature. This is not a new insight, of course, and scholars like Espen Aarseth (1997) have built entire theories around this duality of text, while Katherine Hayles has argued that 'electronic text is more processual than print, it is performative by its very nature' (Hayles 2005: 101, 50). It is precisely this performativity of the interplay between the first text – the code – and the second text – the final constellation-image – that I call operative ekphrasis. It means understanding ekphrasis not as representation but as performance; not as imitating an image through text, but as text effectively bringing about an image. As such, it is truly 'words painting a picture' – but as an operation of manipulating symbolic information rather than figurative representation.[6]

Two remarks are necessary here that address possible objections to this notion of operative ekphrasis. First, it is easy to note that what is 'painted' here is not in fact a *text* image. Meerhoff's work may use text (the code) to create an image composed of text (the work), but technically, the result is an image file, not a text file. Its content, once put up on a computer screen, only registers as text for humans, but not for machines. It is a bitmap image, a grid of pixels with different colour values, and as such it is human-readable but not machine-readable. Without a process of optical character recognition, the computer would not even register it as text.

The response to this objection is to note that the image, too, is, on a lower level, constituted textually: for image files are encoded alphanumerically. It is only through the translation of this text into the pixel matrix of a screen by means of a codec that it actually becomes an image.[7] This argument was leveled for describing digital ekphrasis as early as 1996, when media theorist Jay David Bolter declared that if the tradition of text/image interaction had been predicated both on the superiority of the word to the image as well as a metaphysics of presence that hoped to get to the thing itself through immersive description, the computer age reverses the first aspect while retaining the second. In multimedia environments, images take the lead, as their ideal is absolute transparency, and the immersion of virtual reality that amounts to a 'denial of ekphrasis' (Bolter 1996: 269). Yet a complete elimination of text, Bolter wrote, was oblivious to the fact that even 'virtual reality systems rest on layer after layer of writing, of arbitrary signs in the form of computer programs' (Bolter 1996, 270).

The digital condition, then, as one could paraphrase Jerome McGann's work, *is* the textual condition.[8] Everything is text, and every image is always only image-for-us. Even in the sequential model, the distinction between image and text is dissolved by making text virtually the only mode of existence for digital objects.[9] It thus still makes sense to speak of operative ekphrasis here, except that now there are three texts involved – the code, the file texts, and the text-as-image as it appears to a human reader. The performative aspect remains the same: text does something that is ultimately an image – which is now augmented by the effect of a secondary semiosis that takes place not in the machine but in humans.

The second objection regards the relationship between the concepts of 'text' and 'language'. It seems to have an extremely limited scope: I have used the term 'text' to speak of the elements in Mon's piece, of Meerhoff's code, and finally of the data in the image file. These are all very different kinds of text but none of them are language in the fullest sense of the word, which not only has a syntax, but also a semantics and a pragmatics. Still, the debate as to whether code can claim to be a language in the proper sense is complex. For some, such as Loss Pequeño Glazier, there is practically no difference between the two.[10] Code, in this view, can thus equally be a poetic medium, a means of expression. For others, however, any meaning such code carries *for us* is simply 'parasitic' on the meanings we associate with it, as Stevan Harnad famously argued, and which has recently been reemphasised in the discussion about the AI systems' ability to produce meaning (Harnad 1990; for current views, see Bender and Koller 2020; Shanahan 2022).

For the latter group, the artificial language of the script, then, is not really a proper language at all. Florian Cramer echoes Harnad when he calls programming codes 'syntactical languages as opposed to semantic languages'. As the name suggests, syntactical languages are utterly devoid of meaning, unlike natural, that is, semantic languages. Cramer explains: 'The symbols of computer control languages inevitably do have semantic *connotations* simply because there exist no symbols with which humans would not associate some meaning. But symbols can't denote any semantic statements, that is, they do not express meaning in their own terms' (Cramer 2008: 168-9). Insofar as pragmatics is tied to meaning-effects, this also means that code is performative only in a technical sense – as a series of commands that are executed according to predefined rules. None of these commands in themselves carry meaning, be it understood as reference to the outside world or a system of signs within the context of communication. Code is syntax without semantics; and it has a pragmatics only in the abstract sense of its command structure.[11]

I am willing to admit all this. In fact, this is my point moving on. For in the internal differentiation within the digital, this limited notion of text as well as the relationship of language to image begins to change once we turn from the sequential to the connectionist paradigm. For in neural networks, there is no 'first text' as there was in Meerhoff's 'They Lay', no code that is written as a series of rule steps we could inspect and which, when executed, would perform commands. Instead, seed data is passed through the network of connections; it is either increased or decreased at each stage, depending on the trained weights. Finally, the results are summed up at the end layer of neurons to produce a single output. This is the basic process by which neural networks generate predictions from input data. The output, then, is the result of a cumulative, statistical, and parallel process that takes place between the many connections of the network, but which cannot in any plausible way be thought of as command-like.

However, this leads to the curious conclusion that compared to the sequential paradigm – the classic algorithm, which is devoid of semantics – the connectionist paradigm has no discernible command-structure and therefore no pragmatics. Paradoxically, however, semantics returns in multimodal AI such as DALL·E. And it does so by collapsing the image/text distinction on a deeper level than did the reduction of image data to text in the sequential model.

I will spend the final part of this essay following this chiasmus at the heart of the sequential/connectionist distinction. A first hint that meaning-oriented language plays a role here was given by the input text: After all, the whole point of DALL·E is that it can turn a natural language prompt – a meaningful linguistic description – into an image-file. This, too, is a 'painting with words', again, not as representation but as performance. DALL·E must thus also reasonably be called a type of operative ekphrasis: it acts as a text that computationally produces an image. But this coordination of text and image can only happen by undoing the distinction between them, and not through code but through something that may be called 'artificial semantics'. To understand this, we must again think with AI.

Artificial Semantics

Multimodal AI is the name given to a new class of neural networks. The distinguishing feature of these models lies in their ability to integrate multiple data types, such as images, text, speech, tactile or location data, and more, to increase their performance (Liang et al. 2023; Akkus et al. 2023). A distinction can be made between multimodal AIs in which the input and output are of different modalities and those in which the inputs or outputs themselves are multimodal (for this distinction, see Huyen 2023). While DALL·E and other text-to-image models belong to the first type and primarily focus on converting one modality into another – text into image – multimodal AIs of the second type are designed to process different data types at once as enriched information type. GPT-4, which generates text, is now trained on multiple modalities to boost performance (OpenAI 2023a), and with Gemini, Google introduced a large multimodal model that combines image, audio, video, and text data from the outset (Google Gemini Team 2023), as does OpenAI's newest system, GPT-4.5 (OpenAI 2025).[12] In all cases, what distinguishes these networks from older models is their ability to correlate and process various types of data. Consequently, they transcend the limitations of older neural network types that were more specialised and medium-specific.

In the realm of neural networks, different 'architectures' have traditionally been tailored for specific tasks. Some excel at handling temporal sequences, while others demonstrate superior performance in processing spatial information. This division parallels Lessing's argument for the separation of the arts, and indeed certain AIs prove better suited to process text, others images. Previously, two fundamental architectures, the Recurrent Neural Net (RNN) and the Convolutional Neural Net (CNN), represented the core models in these respective domains. CNNs excelled in generating images due to their ability to handle two-dimensional matrices effectively, while RNNs were more suitable for textual analysis, retaining information from linearly ordered data (see Bajohr 2022). Hence, these networks were constrained by their association with a particular medium and inherently *uni*modal.

This was the situation at least until January of 2021, when OpenAI unveiled the inaugural, more compact, version of DALL·E. This model could transform textual into visual information. Rather than simply stitching an RNN and a CNN together, however, it adopted a new approach, a single architecture that handles both text and image, a truly multimodal AI. While DALL·E and its successors DALL·E 2 (2022) and DALL·E 3 (2023) still consist of several individual neural nets that work in tandem, they all utilise the same architecture, called the Transformer, which excels at dealing with condensed representations of images *and* text (Vaswani et al. 2017).[13]

It is worth unpacking the functionality of DALL·E, which operates in a training and a generative (or inference) phase. In the training phase, a Transformer model called CLIP (Contrastive Language-Image Pre-training) is shown hundreds of millions of images and their associated captions taken from the internet – for example, a photo of a cat with the caption 'this is a photo of a cat'. Using a technique called contrastive learning, it is then trained to produce a single shared embedding space on which different modalities are mapped, so that related images and texts are closer within this space.

This correlation of image and text information is crucial in the training of DALL·E. It learns from the embedding space established by CLIP and builds upon it to create its own internal model called a 'prior'. This 'prior' captures the statistical properties of the high-level features in the data and forms a kind of scaffold or guiding function that the generative process uses to produce outputs. The central point here is that image and text information are not stored separately; once correlated by CLIP, they become part of the same, shared representation space used by DALL·E.

The second step in DALL·E's operation is the generative phase, in which a separate model called GLIDE is activated. GLIDE leverages the stored correlation data between text and images in the CLIP model to execute a reverse operation: rather than matching an image with corresponding text, it synthesises an image that best aligns with the provided text prompt, and it does so through a process called 'diffusion' (Dhariwal and Nichol 2021). What is important here is that GLIDE uses CLIP's representation space to manifest text prompts into their most probable image counterparts. Thus, when presented with a prompt like 'an astronaut riding a horse in photorealistic style', DALL·E, through this collaborative model interplay, is able to output an image of an astronaut astride a horse, rendered in photorealistic detail. This ability hinges on the initial learnings from the CLIP model about the visual characteristics of 'astronauts', 'horses', and 'photorealistic style', and the generative power of GLIDE to synthesise these concepts into a novel visual composition. It is in this way that the prompt 'a poem about the singularity written in a serif font' resulted in Dave Orr's poem. Because DALL·E is stochastic, and because it is meant to output images rather than texts, the result is blurry and asemic, but it clearly has the gestalt of a poem. What is central in this whole operation is that the model, as one interpreter puts it, 'learns the *semantic link* between text descriptions of objects and their corresponding visual manifestations' (O'Connor 2022). CLIP stores linguistic and pictorial information in the same representation space – meaning is meaning regardless of its medium.

To speak of 'meaning' here – be it understood as reference to the world or the communicative intent of speakers – may come as a surprise. After all, semantics was the absent dimension of the sequential paradigm, of classic code as a purely syntactical language not grounded in any connection to reality. Yet precisely because the connectionist paradigm in the shape of multimodal models correlates with different types of data, it might also be a contender for a limited, a 'dumb' meaning.[14] This is borne out by the fact that multimodal models sometimes appear to form single 'neurons' for concepts independent of whether the input is visual or verbal, paralleling what have been hypothesised as 'grandmother cells' in neuroscience since at least since the nineteen sixties (Gross 2002). This concept arose in response to the question of how exactly knowledge is stored in the brain. When I see a picture of my grandmother, is this recognition the result of a complex interaction of brain regions? Or is there *one* specific neuron firing, a grandmother cell? In 2005, a neuroscience study suggested that such neurons may indeed exist. When subjects were shown images of popular actor Halle Berry, a highly localised neural activity was observed in the medial temporal lobe. Moreover, this activity occurred not only when subjects saw a photo of Berry but also when they saw a drawing of her and even the string of letters spelling out 'Halle Berry'. This led the authors to suggest that the brain may use an 'invariant, sparse and explicit code' that processes 'an abstract representation of the identity of the individual or object shown' (Quiroga et al. 2005: 1102, 1106). In other words, the brain may encode concepts directly, in a multimodal fashion.

A similar phenomenon was found in the 'neurons' of CLIP, the model in DALL·E that coordinates text and image. In 2021, OpenAI researchers published a paper suggesting that the later layers of a fully trained CLIP network also show something like a grandmother cell responding to individual faces. There is a neuron – the paper uses Spiderman rather than Halle Berry – that also responds to photos, drawings, and text that refer to the same entity. A picture of Spiderman and a string of text with his name will both activate the same neuron, as does a picture of a spider, indicating that these conceptual neurons are clustered semantically (Goh et al. 2021; for more recent results with neural nets, see Liu 2023).

To be clear: The notion of grandmother neurons is very much contested – in neuroscience, this interpretation is controversial, and in general the claim of some kind of homology between actual brain tissue and neural networks is at best an oversimplification.[15] In reality, things are more messy, as the authors of the CLIP paper readily point out. Despite these caveats, however, the notion of grandmother neurons – and that of the shared representation space of text and image – seems useful for highlighting a general tendency of multimodal AI. When it comes to its theoretical consequences, and in particular to the consequences for the relationship between text and image, we can, in the spirit of thinking with AI, already draw some conclusions even if the empirical data is incomplete and still in need of discussion.

If DALL·E, of which CLIP is a part, thus encodes text and image in the same neurons or in the same representation space, two things seem to follow.

First, unlike the sequential model, in which code was a purely syntactic system with a limited pragmatics and no semantic value, in multimodal AI, semantics comes back into play. I do not want to say that this is semantics in the *full* sense – be it the 'communicative intent' of human communication that linguistics explores (Bender and Koller 2020), or the 'being-in-a-situation' that the Heidegger-inspired AI critique of Hubert Dreyfus sets up as the limiting condition for truly intelligent agents (Dreyfus 1992). But it seems clear that by correlating text and image within a single computational system in multimodal AI, the difference between the sequential and the connectionist paradigm of digitality shows itself most clearly. For one can make the argument that neural networks, and multimodal models in particular, may indeed be concerned with something that may not be meaning in the full sense of human communication, but cannot be confidently labeled non-meaning either. This is what I call artificial semantics and it is what makes AI models such interesting artifacts: they not only carry the external connotations we project on them, as Cramer suggested, but also generate a certain type of inherent meaning through the intricate correlation of text and image within a single system.

From this follows a second point. The effect of multimodal AI is to collapse the distinction between text and image. Both are not only correlated in the training process but, on the system level, surpassed – not bound to either text or image representations, but identified.[16] Put conceptually, multimodal AI suggests a new position in the tradition and ontology of ekphrasis I described earlier. No longer the text/image interaction that underlies all its traditional theories, be they representative or performative, multimodal AI's formulation of ekphrasis suggests a structural identity between text and image, relieving them of their primary semantic function. There is now, as one could call it with Liliane Louvel, a multimodal 'pictorial third' (Louvel 2010) – the shared meaning in the artificial neuron – that acts as locus of semantics beyond word and image. This flies in the face of the ekphrastic fear of the formalist tradition from Lessing to Clement Greenberg that advocated for the separation of mediums, but it also explodes the ekphrastic hope of the lineage starting with Horace, based on the genre's productive transformation. Here, thinking with AI has yielded a genuinely new position, and large visual models such as DALL·E figure as its technical implementation.

Finally, a third point. As I have indicated, the status of language changes between the sequential and the connectionist paradigms. Jasmin Meerhoff and David Orr's works each represent one of these paradigms, and each constitutes a type of operative ekphrasis – a text that produces an image. But whereas in the sequential case there is a 'pragmatics' without semantics, in the connectionist case we have a 'semantics' without pragmatics. In the first instance, it is the code that 'acts' without carrying meaning beyond its mere symbolic valence within a system of operations; in the other, it is the weight model that 'means' without carrying out anything that resembles a speech act. The performative here stands at the beginning of the operational chain, in formulating the prompt. Thus, Orr's poem really means what it shows – on a technical, fully non-intentional level – in way that Meerhoff's doesn't:

it encodes the description of itself *within* itself, highlighting once more that AI images are indeed something entirely different from classic code-generated works.

Conclusion

I have collected here some ideas about the relationship between text and image in the digital, and I have suggested that with the advent of stochastic machine learning in the form of artificial neural networks, it is necessary to divide the digital realm into a sequential and a connectionist subfield. Further, I have argued that only in the digital realm can be found what one might call operative ekphrasis: there, texts do not represent images, but perform them by computationally effecting them. And corresponding to the connectionist and sequential approaches, there seem to be two distinct types of operative ekphrases, involving two distinct notions of language – one emphasising a pragmatic, another a semantic dimension; both of which, to reiterate, are very much below the full meaning of these words, but with some reasonable connection to them nevertheless. However, against the orthodoxy of computers as only having syntax without semantics, there is at least the possibility that multimodal AI, in its conceptual neurons, in fact encodes meaning – a type of artificial semantics that does not mean to the full extent in which humans mean, but means nonetheless.

The argument I have put forward, then, has both a concrete and a methodical dimension. On the one hand, it serves an aesthetic analysis of AI that takes into account the technical substrate of its media. What this amounts to is a case for multimodality in discussing these works. It shows that 'there are no visual media', as was said by W.J.T. Mitchell, for whom the separation of mediums always ignores the entanglement of the senses and the linguistic basis of their transmission (Mitchell 2005). At the same time, we have neither Lessing nor Horace to follow, but something else that goes beyond these options. On the other hand, however, this argument was also an example of how Critical AI Studies might not only think about or against, but also *with* AI. My proposed term, operative ekphrasis, was in this case less meant to add a new dimension to an old and venerable concept. Rather, it served as way of thinking about a problem that puts it into a specific situation to see how it fares; in this case, the problem to be studied was the connection of text and image, and the interaction between a technical metaphorics and its humanist use.

These are interesting times – on a technical level, progress in AI is in hyperspeed, and a little more than six years ago, computer-generated grammatically correct sentences were remarkable in themselves; now mere descriptions generate images. While we must not get caught up in the AI hype – ascribing machines characteristics like consciousness or its builders the status of visionaries for whom the rules of fair play no longer hold – we cannot ignore these developments either. Cultural, philosophical, and aesthetic categories are slow to catch up with the reality we see in the wild, and while scholarship can observe them from a distance or get involved hands-on, it must be open to adjusting its categories. Operative ekphrasis is one such adjustment.

Works Cited

'PromptBase.' n.d. Accessed July 12, 2023. https://promptbase.com.

Aarseth, Espen J. 1997. *Cybertext: Perspectives on Ergodic Literature.* Baltimore: The Johns Hopkins University Press.

Akkus, Cem, Luyang Chu, Vladana Djakovic, Steffen Jauch-Walser, Philipp Koch, Giacomo Loss, Christopher Marquardt, et al. 2023. 'Multimodal Deep Learning.' *arXiv.* http://arxiv.org/abs/2301.04856.

Allamar, Jay. 2018. 'The Illustrated Transformer.' 2018. https://jalammar.github.io/illustrated-transformer/.

Bajohr, Hannes. 2021. 'The Gestalt of AI: Beyond the Atomism-Holism Divide.' *Interface Critique* 3: 13-35, https://doi.org/10.11588/ic.2021.3.81304.

Bajohr, Hannes. 2022. 'Algorithmic Empathy: Toward a Critique of Aesthetic AI.' *Configurations* 30 (2): 203-31. https://doi.org/10.1353/con.2022.0011.

Bajohr, Hannes. 2023. 'Dumb Meaning: Machine Learning and Artificial Semantics.' *IMAGE* 37 (1): 58-70. https://doi.org/10.1453/1614-0885-1-2023-15452.

Bausch, Marcel, Johannes Niediek, Thomas P. Reber, Sina Mackay, Jan Boström, Christian E. Elger, and Florian Mormann. 2021. 'Concept Neurons in the Human Medial Temporal Lobe Flexibly Represent Abstract Relations between Concepts'. *Nature Communications* 12 (1) (2021): 6164. https://doi.org/10.1038/s41467-021-26327-3.

Bender, Emily M., and Alexander Koller. 2020. 'Climbing towards NLU: On Meaning, Form, and Understanding in the Age of Data.' In *Proceedings of the 58th Annual Meeting of the Association for Computational Linguistics*, 5185-98. Online: Association for Computational Linguistics. https://doi.org/10.18653/v1/2020.acl-main.463.

Bolter, Jay David. 1996. 'Ekphrasis, Virtual Reality, and the Future of Writing.' In *The Future of the Book*, edited by Geoffrey Nunberg, 353-272. Berkeley, CA: University of California Press.

Bolter, Jay David. 2023. 'AI Generative Art as Algorithmic Remediation.' *IMAGE* 37, no. 1: 195-207.

Bratton, Benjamin, and Blaise Agüera y Arcas. 2022. 'The Model Is The Message.' *Noema.* July 12, 2022. https://www.noemamag.com/the-model-is-the-message.

Brosch, Renate. 2018. 'Ekphrasis in the Digital Age: Responses to Image.' *Poetics Today* 39 (2): 225-43. https://doi.org/10.1215/03335372-4324420.

Connolly, J. H., and D. J. Cooke. 2004. 'The Pragmatics of Programming Languages.' *Semiotica* 2004 (151). https://doi.org/10.1515/semi.2004.065.

Cramer, Florian. 2008. 'Language.' In *Software Studies: A Lexicon*, edited by Matthew Fuller, 168-74. Cambridge, MA: MIT Press.

dall·ery gall·ery. 2022. 'The DALL·E 2 Prompt Book, v1.02.' Dall·ery Gall·ery: Ressources for Creative DALL·E Users. 2022. https://dallery.gallery/wp-content/uploads/2022/07/The-DALL%C2%B7E-2-prompt-book-v1.02.pdf.

Dhariwal, Prafulla, and Alex Nichol. 2021. 'Diffusion Models Beat GANs on Image Synthesis.' *arXiv.* https://doi.org/10.48550/arXiv.2105.05233.

Dreyfus, Hubert L. 1992. *What Computers Still Can't Do: A Critique of Artificial Reason.* Cambridge, MA: MIT Press.

Farocki, Harun. 2004. 'Phantom Images.' *Public* 29, https://public.journals.yorku.ca/index.php/public/article/view/30354.

Flusser, Vilém. 1993. *Lob der Oberflächlichkeit: Für eine Phänomenologie der Medien.* Bensheim: Bollmann.

Gao, Leo, Tom Dupré la Tour, Henk Tillman, Gabriel Goh, Rajan Troll, Alec Radford, Ilya Sutskever, Jan Leike, and Jeffrey Wu. 2024. 'Scaling and Evaluating Sparse Autoencoders'. *arXiv.* http://arxiv.org/abs/2406.04093.

Gastaldi, Juan Luis. 2021. 'Why Can Computers Understand Natural Language?: The Structuralist Image of Language Behind Word Embeddings.' *Philosophy & Technology* 34 (1): 149-214. https://doi.org/10.1007/s13347-020-00393-9.

Glazier, Loss Pequeño. 2006. 'Code as Language.' *Leonardo* 14 (5). http://leoalmanac.org/journal/vol_14/lea_v14_n05-06/lpglazier.asp.

Goh, Gabriel, Nick Cammarata, Chelsea Voss, Shan Carter, Michael Petrov, Ludwig Schubert, Alec Radford, and Chris Olah. 2021. 'Multimodal Neurons in Artificial Neural Networks.' *Distill* 6 (3): 10.23915/distill.00030. https://doi.org/10.23915/distill.00030.

Goodfellow, Ian, Yoshua Bengio, and Aaron Courville. 2016. *Deep Learning.* Cambridge, MA: MIT Press.

Google Gemini Team. 2023. 'Gemini: A Family of Highly Capable Multimodal Models.' https://storage.googleapis.com/deepmind-media/gemini/gemini_1_report.pdf.

Gross, Charles G. 2002. 'Genealogy of the 'Grandmother Cell.'' *The Neuroscientist* 8 (5): 512-18. https://doi.org/10.1177/107385802237175.

Haigh, Thomas, and Paul E. Ceruzzi. 2021. *A New History of Modern Computing*. Cambridge, MA: MIT Press.

Harnad, Stevan. 1990. 'The Symbol Grounding Problem.' *Physica D: Nonlinear Phenomena* 42 (1-3): 335-46.

Hayles, N. Katherine. 2004. 'Print Is Flat, Code Is Deep: The Importance of Media-Specific Analysis.' *Poetics Today* 25 (1): 67-90.

Hayles, N. Katherine. 2005. *My Mother Was a Computer*. Chicago: The University of Chicago Press.

Heffernan, James A W. 2015. 'Ekphrasis: Theory.' In *Handbook of Intermediality: Literature – Image – Sound – Music*, edited by Gabriele Rippl, 35-49. Berlin: de Gruyter.

Heffernan, James A. W. 1993. *Museum of Words: The Poetics of Ekphrasis from Homer to Ashbery*. Chicago: The University of Chicago Press.

Hollander, John. 1995. *The Gazer's Spirit: Poems Speaking to Silent Works of Art*. Chicago: The University of Chicago Press.

Hui, Yuk. 2016. *On the Existence of Digital Objects*. Minneapolis: University of Minnesota Press.

Huyen, Chip. 2023. 'Multimodality and Large Multimodal Models (LMMs).' *Chip Huyen*. October 10, 2023. https://huyenchip.com/2023/10/10/multimodal.html.

Jine [i.e. Jasmin Meerhoff]. 2022. 'They Lay.' *GitLab*. February 24, 2022. https://gitlab.com/nervousdata/they-lay.

Kang, Louis, and Taro Toyoizumi. 2024. 'Distinguishing Examples While Building Concepts in Hippocampal and Artificial Networks'. *Nature Communications* 15 (1): 647. https://doi.org/10.1038/s41467-024-44877-0.

Kelleher, John D. 2019. *Deep Learning*. Cambridge, MA: MIT.

Kittler, Friedrich A. 2001. 'Computer Graphics: A Semi-Technical Introduction.' Translated by Sara Ogger. *Grey Room* 2 (1): 30-45. https://doi.org/10.1162/15263801750172984.

Lean, Chase. 2023. 'Text in Midjourney V6.' *Mid Journey AI* (blog). December 22, 2023. https://mid-journey.ai/text-generation-in-midjourney-v6/.

Lessing, Gotthold Emphraim. 2005. *Laocoon: An Essay upon the Limits of Painting and Poetry*. Translated by Ellen Frothingham. Mineola: Dover.

Liang, Paul Pu, Amir Zadeh, and Louis-Philippe Morency. 2023. 'Foundations and Trends in Multimodal Machine Learning: Principles, Challenges, and Open Questions.' *arXiv.* http://arxiv.org/abs/2209.03430.

Liu, Zhiheng, Ruili Feng, Kai Zhu, Yifei Zhang, Kecheng Zheng, Yu Liu, Deli Zhao, Jingren Zhou, and Yang Cao. 2023. 'Cones: Concept Neurons in Diffusion Models for Customized Generation'. *arXiv.* http://arxiv.org/abs/ 2303.05125.

Louvel, Liliane. 2010. *Le tiers pictural.* Rennes: Presses Universitaires de Rennes.

McGann, Jerome J. 1991. 'The Textual Condition.' In *The Textual Condition.* Princeton University Press. https://doi.org/10.1515/9780691217758.

McGann, Jerome. 2001. *Radiant Textuality: Literature after the World Wide Web. Radiant Textuality.* New York: Palgrave.

Mitchell, W. J. T. 1994. *Picture Theory: Essays on Verbal and Visual Representation.* Chicago, Ill.: Univ. of Chicago Press.

Mitchell, W. J. T. 2005. 'There Are No Visual Media.' *Journal of Visual Culture* 4 (2): 257-66. https://doi.org/10.1177/1470412905054673.

O'Connor, Ryan. 2022. 'How DALL-E 2 Actually Works.' *Assembly AI.* April 19, 2022. https://www.assemblyai.com/blog/how-dall-e-2-actually-works/.

Offert, Fabian. 2023. 'Can We Read Neural Networks? Epistemic Implications of Two Historical Computer Science Papers.' *American Literature* 95 (2): 423-28. https://doi.org/10.1215/00029831-10575218.

OpenAI. 2023. 'GPT-4 Technical Report.' Arxiv, https://doi.org/10.48550/ARXIV.2303.08774.

OpenAI. 2025. 'Introducing GPT-4.5.' *OpenAI.* February 27, 2025. https://openai.com/index/introducing-gpt-4-5/.

Orr, Dave. 2022. 'Playing with DALL·E 2.' *Lesswrong.* April 7, 2022. https://www.lesswrong.com/posts/r99tazGiLgzqFX7ka/playing-with-dall-e-2.

Parikka, Jussi. 2023. *Operational Images: From the Visual to the Invisual.* Minneapolis: University of Minnesota Press.

Pfisterer, Ulrich. 2019. 'Ekphrasis.' In *Metzler Lexikon Kunstwissenschaft: Ideen, Methoden, Begriffe,* edited by Ulrich Pfisterer, 99-103. Stuttgart: J.B. Metzler. https://doi.org/10.1007/978-3-476-04949-0_28.

Quiroga, R. Quian, L. Reddy, G. Kreiman, C. Koch, and I. Fried. 2005. 'Invariant Visual Representation by Single Neurons in the Human Brain.' *Nature* 435 (7045): 1102-7. https://doi.org/10.1038/nature03687.

Ramesh, Aditya, Mikhail Pavlov, Gabriel Goh, Scott Gray, Chelsea Voss, Alec Radford, Mark Chen, and Ilya Sutskever. 2021. 'Zero-Shot Text-to-Image Generation.' *arXiv*:2102.12092 [Cs], February. http://arxiv.org/abs/2102.12092.

Rumelhard, David E., James McClelland, and Geoffrey Hinton. 1986b. 'The Appeal of Parallel Distributed Processing.' In *Parallel Distributed Processing: Explorations in the Microstructure of Cognition*, edited by David E. Rumelhart, James L. McClelland, and PDP Research Group, 1:3-44. Cambridge, MA: MIT Press.

Rumelhart, David E., and James L. McClelland. 1986a. 'PDP Models and General Issues in Cognitive Science.' In *Parallel Distributed Processing: Explorations in the Microstructure of Cognition*, edited by David E. Rumelhart, James L. McClelland, and PDP Research Group, 1:110-46. Cambridge, MA: MIT Press.

Schwenger, Peter. 2019. *Asemic: The Art of Writing*. Minneapolis: University of Minnesota Press.

Shanahan, Murray. 2022. 'Talking About Large Language Models.' *arXiv*. http://arxiv.org/abs/2212.03551.

Spitzer, Leo. 1962. 'The 'Ode on a Grecian Urn' or, Content vs. Metagrammar.' In *Essays on English and American Literature*, edited by Anna Hatcher, 67-97. Princeton, NJ: Princeton University Press.

Strickland, Eliza. 2022. 'DALL-E 2's Failures Are the Most Interesting Thing About It.' *IEEE Spectrum*. July 14, 2022. https://spectrum.ieee.org/openai-dall-e-2.

Vaswani, Ashish, Noam Shazeer, Niki Parmar, Jakob Uszkoreit, Llion Jones, Aidan N Gomez, Łukasz Kaiser, and Illia Polosukhin. 2017. 'Attention Is All You Need.' In *Advances in Neural Information Processing Systems*, 5998-6008.

Wasielewski, Amanda. 2023. "Midjourney Can't Count." *IMAGE* 37 (1): 71-82. https://doi.org/10.1453/1614-0885-1-2023-15454.

Webb, Ruth. 1999. '*Ekphrasis* Ancient and Modern: The Invention of a Genre.' *Word & Image* 15 (1): 7-18. https://doi.org/10.1080/02666286.1999.10443970.

Yacobi, Tamar. 2013. 'Ekphrastic Double Exposure and the Museum Book of Poetry.' *Poetics Today* 34 (1-2): 1-52. https://doi.org/10.1215/03335372-1894487.

Yu, Jiahui, Yuanzhong Xu, Jing Yu Koh, Thang Luong, Gunjan Baid, Zirui Wang, Vijay Vasudevan, et al. 2022. 'Scaling Autoregressive Models for Content-Rich Text-to-Image Generation.' *arXiv*. https://doi.org/10.48550/arXiv.2206.10789.

Notes

A version of this paper appeared in *Word & Image* 40, no. 2 (2024), https://doi.org/10.1080/02 666286.2024.2330335.

1. For more on text-to-image models, see the special issue 'Generative Imagery: Towards a "New Paradigm" of Machine Learning-Based Image Production' of *IMAGE. The Interdisciplinary Journal of Image Sciences* 31, no. 1 (2024).

2. While the newer third version is integrated into ChatGPT, the interface of DALL·E 2 shown here was still available until 2024 at https://labs.openai.com, accessed December 22, 2023.

3. On the issue of mangled hands, see Wasielewski (2023). For the inability to produce text, see Strickland (2022). However, this may be a function of parameter size: Google's Parti model seems to be able to produce text with a parameter count above 20 billion (Yu et al. 2022). The same is true for the current version of Midjourney (Lean 2023). I tried DALL·E 3 with Orr's prompt (January 2025) and still found that it outputs garbled text, although the title is often legible.

4. I derive this conceptual distinction from an influential publication that brought neural networks back into fashion under the rubric of 'connectionism' (Rumelhard et al. 1986b: 43). The term 'sequential' for the classic algorithm stems from the same book (Rumelhard et al. 1986a: 116).

5. See for a nontechnical introduction Kelleher (2019). For a more technical discussion, see Goodfellow et al. (2016).

6. The adjective 'operative', here, is thus meant to be understood quite literally as 'having the character as an operation'. It is not to be confused with Harun Farocki's *operatives Bild*, sometimes translated as 'operative image' or 'operational image', by which he means images used in surveillance and war that do not require linguistic mediation because they act as sensors rather than representations (Farocki 2004). While Jussi Parikka, taking up Farocki's idea, highlights the performativity of images themselves, my concept makes text performative insofar as it produces an image (Parikka 2023).

7. Thus Friedrich Kittler could, shortly after having pronounced that there is no software but only hardware, exclude computer graphics from the class of optical media by declaring them essentially alphabetical. A pixel image, he wrote, 'deceives the eye, which is meant to be unable to differentiate between individual pixels, with the illusion or image of an image, while in truth the mass of pixels, because of its thorough addressability, proves to be structured more like a text composed entirely of individual letters' (Kittler 2001: 32). A similar, if historically inverse, identification of text and image is made by Vilém Flusser, who claims that 'the invention of writing is not so much about the invention of new symbols, but about the unfurling of the [two-dimensional] image into [one-dimensional] rows ("lines")' (Flusser 1993: 67, my translation).

8. I refer to the title of Jerome J. McGann (1991), but the idea that everything digital is understood as text can be found McGann (2001: 11).

9. 'Virtually', since Yuk Hui suggests that the ontology of the digital is a broad spectrum that runs from 'colorful visual beings' at the interface level to the 'particles and fields' that make up the circuit boards and the electricity running through it; somewhere in the middle, 'at the level of programming', there are 'text files' (Hui 2016: 27–28). For present purposes, I will stick to this middle position.

10. E.g., Glazier (2006). For a philosophically more sophisticated version of this argument, see Gastaldi (2021).

11. However, there is a lively debate about how useful it is to speak of a pragmatics of programming languages in a broader sense. One suggestion is to say that 'The pragmatic effects of the programme in execution [...] cause changes to occur in the internal state of the computer' (Connolly and Cooke 2004: 154). Benjamin Bratton likewise suggests that 'code is a kind of language that is executable. [...] In this sense, linguistic 'function' refers not only to symbol manipulation competency, but also to the real-world functions and effects of executed code'. (Bratton and Agüera y Arcas 2022).

12. While there are basic differences between large multimodal models such as Gemini and GPT-4.5 and text-to-image models such as DALL·E, for the present argument, they are negligible.

13. See also for a step-by-step explanation Allamar (2018).

14. In recent memory, Emily Bender and Alexander Koller were the most influential theorists to argue that large language models like ChatGPT – which are unimodal – are not able to operate with meaning (Bender and Koller 2020). However, because they understand meaning as text being 'grounded' in the world, they have to allow for the possibility that multimodality may lead to a model learning 'some aspects of meaning', because it grounds text data in image data (5193). I call this phenomenon 'dumb' meaning and explain it in more detail in Bajohr (2023).

15. However, while most researchers agree that there are most likely no single grandmother neurons (one neuron for one concept), there is a relatively broad consensus that, over time, concepts are indeed stored as sparse rather than dense neural encodings in the brain (Bausch 2021). What this means is that while the brain may store many individual features for single entities ('dense encoding'), in the long run, such encodings merge along shared features covering groups of entities ('sparse encoding') located in smaller neuronal clusters. This process of grouping more entities under a shared encoding is understood as 'concept learning'. Moreover, a recent study explicitly found that this process of concept learning—from dense to sparse encoding—is similar to and can be simulated in artificial neural networks, suggesting, if not homology, at least analogous behaviour (Kang 2024). An OpenAI study likewise found that neural networks use a sparse encoding for concepts (Gao 2024).

16. Thus understood, multimodal AI is more than remediation, as Jay David Bolter (2023) suggested, since this term still keeps the separation of media intact.

5

On the Concept of History (in Foundation Models)

Fabian Offert

I

Any sufficiently complex technical object that exists in time has, in a sense, a concept of history: a particular way that the past continues to exist for it, with contingencies and omissions specific to its place and role in the world. Computation is no exception to this, and indeed takes its very efficacy from a particular technical relation to the passing of time. Meanwhile, the emergence of so-called 'foundation models' (Bommasani et al. 2021), a specific class of technical objects that have come to dominate the field of artificial intelligence, promises to significantly change what it means to 'compute' in the first place (Offert 2023a), and especially, I will argue, what it means to compute the past. This essay thus asks: what is the concept of history that emerges from foundation models, and particularly from large visual models? Do such models conceptualise the past? What is the past *for them*?

My question does not imply any intentionality (Searle 1980), agency, or subjectivity – real or fictional – on the part of the models under investigation. It is exactly not 'what is it like to be' a foundation model, to paraphrase Thomas Nagel (1974). The question, in other words, is entirely non-philosophical and non-speculative. It is also separate from the question of the historicity of foundation models themselves, that is, their role in a larger history of artificial intelligence, both as a general problem starting in the 1950s (see Pasquinelli 2023, Dobson 2023) and as a specific set of technical approaches that first emerged around 2012 (see Offert 2022). What remains, then, is a technical object (that is – again – certainly a product of history), or rather a class of technical objects, which, in some sense that we would need to determine, relate to the passing of time in non-trivial, non-arbitrary ways. We thus need to take a closer look at the material basis of foundation models, to trace, at all, or at least at some, levels of the stack[1] how 'history is made', that is, where exactly such non-trivial, non-arbitrary ways to deal with the passing of time emerge.

II

The very definition of the computability of a number, as first proposed by Alan Turing (1937), is that the number can be produced by a discrete state machine – a machine that moves through a finite set of deterministic configurations over time. Foundation models are computer programmes, and thus take part in this necessary relation to the passing of time.[2] But more importantly, foundation models are machine learning models, and it is the learning[3] part where a difference in their relation to the passing of time emerges.

Consider a simple computer vision classifier, for instance a deep convolutional neural network like VGG19. 'Training' a VGG19 model means tuning its parameters, or weights, according to a dataset of images. How exactly the parameters are arranged and interconnected is what defines the architecture of the model. The parameters, in turn, define how the images are passed on through the network, and thus which predefined category they are eventually attributed to. Over the course of the whole training process, the model is exposed to millions of images, one image at a time, and its parameters are adjusted at each step.[4] As the parameters are usually initialised with random numbers,[5] the first steps of the training process often require large adjustments which then become progressively smaller.[6] The model thus begins its 'life' as a somewhat malleable structure but becomes more rigid the closer it moves towards 'convergence', that is, towards a state in which it sufficiently models the inherent probability distribution of the dataset of images. From there on, the model is usually used for inference only, remaining completely unchanged for the rest of its 'life'.

Of course, inference is still a computational process, and thus on the lower levels of the stack time goes on. On the level of the model, however, it comes to a standstill, and all its history is erased. Indeed, every step of the training process is destructive by default, as parameters are irreversibly altered after each backwards pass[7]. There is thus simply no going back to earlier points in the training process, unless they are intentionally, and separately, recorded as so-called 'checkpoints'.[8] From looking at a fully trained model, we simply cannot tell what it 'went through', for instance how good or bad it *used to be* at its respective task. One consequence of this opaque relation, or rather non-relation, of the model to its own past is that it cannot be easily adapted to other tasks, as Christina Vagt points out in her analysis of 'catastrophic forgetting' in this volume. Another consequence is that a fully trained model cannot be understood anymore in terms of its functional 'parts'.

In fact, we could describe the training of our model as a process of concretisation in the sense of philosopher Gilbert Simondon (2016). 'Concretisation', for Simondon, describes the evolution of technical objects from a state of 'functional indeterminacy' (abstract, all parts have their own internal logic) to a state of functional completeness (concrete, all side effects become synergies). And indeed, neural networks could be described as moving from an abstract state (an empty computation graph) to a concrete state (a fully trained neural network of weights). This perspective is supported technically: 'knowledge' in neural networks is always distributed,[9] it is represented by the network as a whole, rather than by individual neurons. For Simondon the difference between the 'science' and the 'technology' of a machine is the margin of concretisation still obtainable. In the training of our model, the stated goal is to reduce this margin to zero, even if this usually turns out to be impossible in practice. Accordingly, while empty neural networks can be described technologically (e.g. in code), fully trained neural networks can only be probed empirically – what the training process leaves behind are only monuments, not documents.[10] Monuments require interpretation – and neural networks are no exception, as the question of explainable artificial intelligence and the rise of mechanistic interpretability demonstrate.

It is when we look at foundation models' reliance on data, however, that their complicated relation to the past attains special significance. There are a few relevant aspects of data that we can simply name here, as others have looked at them in great detail.[11] Datasets emerge from processes of selection and exclusion. They do not even reflect a particular, biased view on the world but a particular, biased view on only that part of the world that is readily available in digital form. Their assembly often relies on exploitative practices and questionable interpretations of privacy and copyright. They are often based on rigid ontologies[12] and the idea that the world can be neatly categorised without residue, a problem that goes back as far as Wilkins and Leibniz.

III

For these and many other reasons, foundation models will never facilitate anything even close to a human concept of history, one that relies on an inter-subjectively negotiated, comprehensively factual, deeply archival, and necessarily causal perspective on the world – as much is clear. And yet, if we look at the recent *output* of large visual models, what we see can intuitively only be understood as 'historical'. Other than the deep relation of artificial intelligence research and science fiction would suggest, foundation models are not at all utilised to imagine the future, but to reimagine the past. One particularly striking example are stills from fictional movies – fictional as in never made[13] – which manage to capture the particular aesthetics of specific directors and time periods, and instill a peculiar sense of nostalgia, as Roland Meyer (2023) has argued.

Given this fixation on history in the use of foundation models, and given that, with Simondon (and mechanistic interpretability), we can only study such models empirically, our initial question should be rephrased as follows: as far as can be shown, is there a degree of consistency to the outputs of a foundation model when it is tasked with processing inputs related to the past that would suggest a model-specific 'concept of history'? And if so, what are the structuring principles of these internally consistent outputs, and how do they relate to the structuring principles humans apply to the past to render it history? Or, as this essay focuses on visual models: what happens to human visual culture when it is processed by a foundation model if visual culture is indeed 'what is seen', and if 'what is seen' is indeed 'what changes over time' (Roeder 1988, quoting Gertrude Stein)?

My experimental close readings of one such system in particular, the CLIP model released by OpenAI in 2021, suggests that one of these structuring principles, and arguably the most significant at least for visual models, is a technically determined form of *remediation* (Bolter and Grusin 2000). Polemically, for CLIP and CLIP-dependent generative models like DALL·E 2, the recent past is literally black and white, and the distant past is actually made of marble. Given that CLIP, at the same time, *premediates* our future digital experience as a means of search, retrieval, and recommendation, this structuring principle of remediation then becomes ethically and politically relevant. As Alan Liu asks:

> Today, the media question affects the sense of history to the core. [...] This is not just an abstract existential issue. It's ethical, political, and in other ways critical, too. Have we chosen the best way to speak the sense of history today, and if so, for the benefit of whom? (Liu 2018: 2)

The ethical questions surrounding this 'media question' are maybe nowhere as obvious as in the digitisation of the testimonies of those who survived the Holocaust (Walden and Marrison 2023). Projects like *Dimensions in Testimony*, which is funded by the USC Shoah Foundation, have started to go beyond the mere recording of testimonies, attempting to emulate their performative quality, the significant experience of sharing a moment in space and time, with the help of artificial intelligence. As the project website states:

> Dimensions in Testimony enables people to ask questions that prompt real-time responses from pre-recorded video interviews with Holocaust survivors and other witnesses to genocide. The pioneering project integrates advanced filming techniques, specialized display technologies and next generation natural language processing to create an interactive biography. (USC Shoah Foundation, 2023)

Todd Presner (2022) has pointed out the dilemma that such projects find themselves in. In *Dimensions in Testimony*, he argues, humans 'are no longer (centrally) part of the creation of digital cultural memory'. Instead, through established and artificial intelligence-enhanced technologies of montage, individual testimonies, once irreversibly tied to an individual human life, become disembodied. If the duty to keep these testimonies accessible for future generations warrants these technological interventions – 'that Auschwitz not happen again',[14] in Adorno's words – is an open question. Irrespective of such ethical considerations, projects like *Dimensions in Testimony* point to a fundamental media-theoretical question about the ethics of memory, and, by extension, the concept of history: What is the imprint that a specific technology[15] leaves on history? More precisely, what, if anything, do foundation models 'add' to an already (re-)mediated past?

IV

Here, we need to turn to Walter Benjamin's text *On the Concept of History* (Benjamin 2006a) that the title of this essay takes inspiration from. Years of scholarly debate on Benjamin's writings in general, and his concept of history in particular,[16] have made it unnecessary to introduce its premise here, or comment on the unusual synthesis of materialist and theological thought that it embodies. Instead, I would like to point out an almost trivial similarity between *On the Concept of History* and Benjamin's other widely read essay on the *Work of Art in the Age of Its Technological Reproducibility* (Benjamin 2006b).

Famously, in *On the Concept of History*, Benjamin writes: 'Articulating the past historically does not mean to recognise it "the way it really was" [...]. It means appropriating a memory as it flashes up at a moment of danger'.[17] (391) Previously, in the *Work of Art* essay, Benjamin had argued that the political potential of film derives from its potential to produce abrupt cuts, and thus 'shock' (267) the viewer into a different mode of thinking. In other words, for Benjamin, the condition under which history becomes possible, the 'moment of danger' is the condition that film emulates. In both cases, awareness and insight depend on a moment of immediacy, and in both cases this moment of immediacy must be actively captured and repurposed for a progressive (Marxist) agenda before it falls into the hands of the fascists. There is thus, for Benjamin, a structural similarity between history as a memory that 'flashes up', that emerges from, and is actualised by, a moment of crisis, and the specific ways in which technology mediates our experience of the present world, and thus shapes our political views of it. Crucially, history and technology manifest themselves as a specific way of seeing.

What I am suggesting here, then, is not that we should 'apply' Benjamin's concept of history to artificial intelligence systems. On the contrary: One of the reasons why the field of 'critical AI studies'[18] has not had the impact that one would expect given the oversized importance of artificial intelligence research in computer science, is its insistence on resorting to traditional humanist theoretical frameworks and concepts that simply do not suffice anymore. Instead, I would like to propose, exactly with Benjamin, that we have to carve out the extremely specific, borderline idiosyncratic ways of seeing that artificial intelligence systems bring to the table where they are tasked with processing, or producing, an already mediated past. Again, more precisely:

as the past is remediated through contemporary artificial intelligence systems, is the concept of history that emerges from this process of remediation different from the concept of history that emerges from the always already (re-) mediated data on its own? What, in other words, is the surplus remediation inherent in a foundation model's specific way of seeing? These questions also bring us back to the title of this volume. 'Thinking with AI', in this context, means to understand artificial intelligence as an opportunity to re-think which levels of the stack a humanist analysis of computation needs to address to be of critical value.

'Foundation model' is a term introduced by a collective of researchers at the Stanford HAI institute in 2021 (Bommasani et al. 2021). It basically means models that are a) very large, and b) that can be used for a variety of 'downstream' tasks. The vision model CLIP (Contrastive Language-Image Pre-Training), first released in 2021 (Radford et al. 2021) by OpenAI, is such a foundation model. Outside the technical community, its innovations were somewhat obscured by the concurrent release of the DALL·E model, and later overshadowed by DALL·E's successor, DALL·E 2 (Ramesh et al. 2022) and the language model GPT-3.

CLIP – other than both iterations of DALL·E, as well as GPT-3 – is not a generative model. It does not produce images or text, but it connects them. More precisely, CLIP learns from images in context by projecting an image and its context into a common 'embedding space' (Offert and Impett 2025). The 'context' here could be an image caption, a so-called 'alt text' which describes the image in case it is not loaded properly and to accommodate people with screen readers, or simply a news article that the image illustrates. A fully trained CLIP model, then, consists of a high-dimensional vector space, or embedding space, in which words and images that are related can be found close together. Similarity between image and text is thus modelled as spatial proximity (this is true for all embedding models, be it just words, just images, or both, such as in the case of CLIP). While CLIP was originally designed for zero-shot image labeling,[19] it also facilitates what computer scientists call 'image retrieval' (this exemplifies its 'foundation' character): finding specific images within an unlabeled corpus of images based on visual or textual prompts. The user can provide CLIP with an image and it will look for similar images, or they can provide it with a prompt and it will look for images corresponding to this prompt – in any corpus of images. Given that the training corpus for CLIP is largely unknown,[20] it seems futile to attempt to construct a somewhat empirical basis for our claims. And yet, there are two ways to study CLIP's concept of history empirically

V

The first way we could call 'attribution by proxy'. While we do not know what CLIP was trained on, we can still ask it for things *in terms* of specific collections of images. It is exactly this aspect of CLIP – the universality of its embeddings – that makes it so powerful as a retrieval engine. The following examples were produced with a custom CLIP-based search engine called imgs.ai (Offert and Bell 2023), which indexes museum collections in the public domain.

To illustrate the conceptual depth of CLIP, consider the search prompt 'rhythm', applied to the (digitised) collection of the Museum of Modern Art, New York, which contains about 70,000 images in total. If we query the collection with this (intentionally abstract) prompt, we will receive a selection of images which reflect the polyvalence of 'rhythm': images of sheet music, album covers, and loudspeakers, works that resemble oscilloscope graphs or spectral plots, or graphical works that involve regular patterns that could be described as 'rhythmic'.

Going back to the ethical and political stakes of automated vision, we can query this same collection for 'images of the Holocaust'. And the results tell us that, yes, CLIP knows – too well – what we are talking about. On the one hand, the model will suggest those few images in the MoMA collection that are historically linked to the query, for instance photographs by the U.S. Army Signal Corps which played an important role in documenting the atrocities of Nazi Germany. But on the other hand, it will exemplify a much more abstract knowledge about visual Holocaust memory. Suggested results include a photograph by Bruce Davidson, shot on the set of the war film *Lost Command* in Spain in the 1960s, a 1980 photograph by Aaron Siskind depicting volcanic lava, or a collage made from stamps by Robert Watts in 1963. None of these pictures are historically related to the Holocaust, nor are they necessarily meant to evoke it, but all of them could be easily recontextualised with respect to the visual language of Holocaust cultural memory. Using the MoMA collection as a proxy, we can see how well CLIP has internalised this visual language. Moreover, far from just showing the unshowable, CLIP has clearly learned that this language operates metaphorically.

But: the fact that all the results that CLIP proposes (not only those named above) are black-and-white photos already points to a significant limitation, a limitation that we can further explore by utilising generative models. This second way of studying CLIP we could call 'generative attribution'. It is made possible by the fact that CLIP, to a large part, determines the training of generative models like DALL·E and Stable Diffusion.

VI

If we ask DALL·E 2 for 'a colour photo of a fascist parade, 1935' it will not comply. 'Fascism,' among many other political terms, was banned by OpenAI, early on, to mitigate the potential of their model – of which they were well aware – to produce politically, legally, or socially unacceptable material like deep fakes, pornography, or propaganda. Such safeguards are not in place in other models like Stable Diffusion but there exists a simple trick to

Figure 1. DALL·E 2 generation for 'a colour photo of a facist [sic] parade, 1935', produced in October 2022. Note that this safeguard circumvention technique has been 'fixed' at the time of writing.

circumvent DALL·E's forced 'neutrality' as well. Intentionally misspelling 'fascism' by leaving out the 's'[21] will produce (a variation of) the image in figure 1: a vaguely Western European city with some sort of mass rally taking place, red flags raised, and ominous smoke emerging from a building in the background. DALL·E, in other words, despite its safeguards, knows very well what 1935 fascism looks like – *to us*. The generated image has the appearance of a historical photograph not only for its subject but for its appearance; it shows the characteristic colours of early Kodachrome slide photography, with the red of the flags particularly standing out against an otherwise subdued sepia palette. This is how Nazi Germany appears in the photographs of Hugo Jäger, for instance, whose pre-war slide collection was acquired and popularised by *LIFE* magazine in the 1960s.[22]

What is remarkable about this generated image is not its accuracy in emulating a specific historical medium – this has been possible at least since the early days of style transfer ca. 2016 – but that it resorts to this specific historical medium by default. Nowhere in the prompt did we ask for early Kodachrome in particular. And it turns out that it is hard to get rid of, too. From experiments done on both DALL·E 2 and Stable Diffusion, it is difficult to impossible to produce colour photographs of fascist parades, ca. 1935, that do *not* have the appearance of early Kodachrome, colourised black-and-white, or otherwise historically more or less accurate photographic techniques. Only through copious amounts of highly specific additional keywords or negative prompts – prompts which explicitly describe which kind of outputs should be avoided – is it possible to steer the model away from this particular aesthetic. There exists, in other words, a strong default in models like DALL·E that conjoins historical periods and historical media and thus produces a (visual) world in which fascism can simply not return because it is safely confined to a black-and-white (or, in our case, Kodachrome) media prison.

VII

Of course, all of this is, in a way, not very surprising. Before the invention of photography, history was not associated with black-and-white at all. The past, in other words, for us and the model, exists visually only through those historical media that we see emulated here. 'Media determine our situation' (Kittler 1999: xxxix), for better or worse, and it is hard for us, too, to picture the past alive. And yet, the current generation of foundation models can easily produce highly speculative images when the speculation concerns the content, not the style, of the image. Contemporary generative models are famously able to generate entirely fictional images like the well-known 'astronaut riding a horse on the moon'. While DALL·E 2, for instance, has no problem producing a cartoon image of a cat driving a car, a realistic colour photograph of a cat driving a car – where the cat actually drives the car, paws on the steering wheel – again requires copious amounts of prompt engineering.

The flip side of this capability is that it cannot be switched off easily. In the case of proprietary models like DALL·E 2, which includes additional safeguards that are supposed to guarantee it remains 'culturally agnostic' (Cetinic 2022), this has significant consequences. While 'allowed', *generally* historical prompts (including those originally hidden behind surface-level, that is, prompt parsing safeguards) are tied to specific forms of mediation, *specifically* historical prompts are decoupled from the event that they refer to and relegated to a world of fiction. Why? Because the model *must have an answer*. As for all foundation models, failure is not an option – there has to be *a* result, no matter how outrageous. Foundation models, in other words, are *contingency machines*.[23] DALL·E 2, in particular, fails to reproduce historical images without altering their meaning. The prompt 'Laocoön and His Sons, between 27 BC and 68 AD' which references the famous work central to European art history since Winckelmann, produces a serene image of a Black[24] family with

Figure 2. DALL·E 2 generations for 'Laocoön and his sons, between 27 BC and 68 AD' and 'Tank Man, 1989', both produced in October 2022.

no trace of agony. The prompt 'Tank Man, 1989', which references the iconic photograph from the Chinese Tiananmen protests, produces an image of a soldier proudly looking at a tank, rather than a scene of radical civil disobedience (both figure 2).

VIII

What, if anything, does artificial intelligence 'add' to an already mediated past? We now have to state that artificial intelligence not only adds nothing, but it forecloses a political potential. Models like DALL·E 2 find themselves in a triple bind: they suffer from syntactic invariability in the case of *generally* historical prompts, semantic arbitrarity in the case of *specific* historical prompts, and superficial, corporate censorship that affects both. The result is an implicitly politicised concept of history. In the most literal interpretation of the famous idea that history doesn't repeat itself, the past can never be actualised and is eternally tied to a specific medium, while images that are already rendered into history are excluded from making an appearance by simple corporate policy. Neither can history be made by actualising the past for the present, nor can the already-historical past be summoned. One of the many consequences is a (visual) world in which fascism can simply not return because it is, paradoxically at the same time, censored (we cannot talk about it), remediated (it is safely confined to a black-and-white media prison), and erased (from the historical record).

Works Cited

Aaronson, Scott. 2013. *Quantum Computing since Democritus*. Cambridge University Press.

Adorno, Theodor W. 1970. 'Erziehung nach Auschwitz.' In *Erziehung zur Mündigkeit: Vorträge und Gespräche mit Hellmuth Becker 1959-1969*, edited by Gerd Kadelbach, pp. 135-162. Frankfurt am Main: Suhrkamp.

Barthes, Roland. 1982. 'The Reality Effect.' In *French Literary Theory Today: A Reader*, edited by Tzvetan Todorov, pp. 11-17. Cambridge University Press.

Benjamin, Walter. 1974. 'Über den Begriff der Geschichte.' In *Gesammelte Schriften I.2*, pp. 693-704. Frankfurt am Main: Suhrkamp.

Benjamin, Walter. 1974b. 'Das Kunstwerk im Zeitalter seiner technischen Reproduzierbarkeit.' In *Gesammelte Schriften I.2*, pp. 471-508. Frankfurt am Main: Suhrkamp.

Benjamin, Walter. 2006a. 'On the Concept of History'. In *Selected Writings*, vol. 4, edited by Michael W. Jennings. Harvard University Press.

Benjamin, Walter. 2006b. 'The Work of Art in the Age of Its Technological Reproducibility'. In *Selected Writings*, vol. 4, edited by Michael W. Jennings. Harvard University Press.

Bolter, Jay David and Richard Grusin. 2000. *Remediation: Understanding New Media*. MIT Press.

Bommasani, Rishi, Drew A. Hudson, Ehsan Adeli, Russ Altman, Simran Arora, Sydney von Arx, Michael S. Bernstein et al. 2021. 'On the Opportunities and Risks of Foundation Models.' *arXiv* preprint 2108.07258.

Cetinic, Eva. 2022. 'Multimodal Models as Cultural Snapshots.' Talk given at Ludwig Forum Aachen, November 18.

Cherti, Mehdi, et al. 2022. 'Reproducible Scaling Laws for Contrastive Language-Image Learning.' *arXiv* preprint 2212.07143.

Cosgrove, Ben. No date. 'A Brutal Pageantry: The Third Reich's Myth-Making Machinery, in Color.' *LIFE History*. https://www.life.com/history/a-brutal-pageantry-the-third-reichs-myth-making-machinery-in-color.

Didi-Huberman, Georges. 2017. *The Surviving Image: Phantoms of Time and Time of Phantoms: Aby Warburg's History of Art*. Pennsylvania State University Press.

D'Ignazio, Catherine, and Lauren F. Klein. 2020. *Data Feminism*. MIT Press.

Dobson, James. 2023. *The Birth of Computer Vision*. University of Minnesota Press.

Impett, Leonardo, and Fabian Offert. 2023. 'There Is a Digital Art History.' *arXiv*. https://doi.org/10.48550/arXiv.2308.07464.

Kittler, Friedrich. 1990. *Discourse Networks 1800/1900*. Stanford University Press.

Kittler, Friedrich. 1999. *Gramophone, Film, Typewriter*. Stanford University Press.

Kittler, Friedrich. 2012. 'There Is No Software'. In: *Literature, Media, Information Systems*. New York, NY: Routledge.

Krämer, Sybille. 2006. 'The Cultural Techniques of Time Axis Manipulation: On Friedrich Kittler's Conception of Media.' *Theory, Culture & Society* 23, no. 7-8: 93-109.

Liu, Alan. 2018. *Friending the Past: The Sense of History in the Digital Age*. University of Chicago Press.

Löwy, Michael. 2005. *Fire Alarm: Reading Walter Benjamin's 'On the Concept of History'*. London: Verso.

Meyer, Roland. 'Es schimmert, es glüht, es funkelt – Zur Äesthetik der KI-Bilder.' *54books*. https://54books.de/es-schimmert-es-gluet-es-funkelt-zur-aesthetik-der-ki-bilder/

Nagel, Thomas. 1974. 'What is it like to be a bat?' *The Philosophical Review* 83, no. 4: 435-450.

Offert, Fabian and Leonardo Impett. *Vector Media*. Meson Press and University of Minnesota Press, 2025.

Offert, Fabian and Thao Phan. 2024. "A Sign That Spells: Machinic Concepts and the Racial Politics of Generative AI." *Journal of Digital Social Research* 6 no. 4.

Offert, Fabian. 2023a. 'Can We Read Neural Networks? Epistemic Implications of Two Historical Computer Science Papers.' *American Literature* 95, no. 2.

Offert, Fabian and Peter Bell. 2023. 'imgs.ai. A Deep Visual Search Engine for Digital Art History.' *International Journal for Digital Art History*. Forthcoming.

Offert, Fabian. 2023b. 'On the Emergence of General Computation from Artificial Intelligence.' https://zentralwerkstatt.org/blog/on-the-emergence-of-general-computation-from-artificial-intelligence.

Offert, Fabian. 2022. 'Ten Years of Image Synthesis.' https://zentralwerkstatt.org/blog/ten-years-of-image-synthesis.

Panofsky, Erwin. 1955. 'The History of Art as a Humanistic Discipline'. In: *Meaning in the Visual Arts*. University of Chicago Press.

Pasquinelli, Matteo. 2023. *The Eye of the Master. A Social History of Artificial Intelligence*. London: Verso.

Pavich, Frank. 2023. 'This Film Does Not Exist.' *New York Times*. January 13, 2023.

Presner, Todd. 2022. 'Digitizing, Remediating, Remixing, and Reinterpreting Holocaust Memory.' Talk given at the University of California, Santa Barbara, May 10.

Radford, Alec, Jong Wook Kim, Chris Hallacy, Aditya Ramesh, Gabriel Goh, Sandhini Agarwal, Girish Sastry et al. 2021. 'Learning Transferable Visual Models from Natural Language Supervision.' *Proceedings of the 38th International Conference on Machine Learning*, PMLR 139.

Raley, Rita and Jennifer Rhee. 2023. 'Critical AI: A Field in Formation.' *American Literature* 95, no. 2.

Ramesh, Aditya, Prafulla Dhariwal, Alex Nichol, Casey Chu, and Mark Chen. 2022. 'Hierarchical Text-Conditional Image Generation with CLIP Latents.' *arXiv* preprint 2204.06125.

Roeder, George H. Jr. 1988. 'Filling in the Picture: Visual Culture.' *Reviews in American History* 26, no. 1 (March): 275-293.

Simondon, Gilbert. 2016. *On the Mode of Existence of Technical Objects*. University of Minnesota Press.

Szegedy, Christian, Wojciech Zaremba, Ilya Sutskever, Joan Bruna, Dumitru Erhan, Ian Goodfellow, and Rob Fergus. 2013. 'Intriguing properties of neural networks.' *arXiv* preprint 1312.6199.

Turing, Alan. 1937. 'On Computable Numbers with an Application to the Entscheidungsproblem.' *Proceedings of the London Mathematical Society* s2-42, no. 1: 230–265.

USC Shoah Foundation. 2023. *Dimensions in Testimony*. https://sfi.usc.edu/dit

Walden, Victoria Grace and Kate Marrison. 2023. 'Recommendations for Digitally Recording, Recirculating, and Remixing Holocaust Testimony: Digital Holocaust Memory Project Report.' Sussex Weidenfeld Institute of Jewish Studies.

Notes

1. The term 'stack' is used here in a precise technical, rather than a philosophical sense to facilitate what Leonardo Impett has called 'full stack critique': identifying the epistemic and, by extension, political implications of the concrete technical decisions from which a technical object emerges. Underlying this is the assumption that such implications are indeed distinct, and cannot be collapsed into the material realm, as Friedrich Kittler (2012) has argued.

2. There remains much to be said about the peculiar relation of computation to Kant's two pure forms of intuition. On the one hand, time must become space if computation is to serve as a medium. As Sybille Krämer summarises Friedrich Kittler: 'Wherever something is stored, a temporal process must be materialised as a spatial structure.

Creating spatiality becomes the primary operation by which the two remaining functions of data processing – transporting and processing – become possible at all' (Krämer 2006). At the same time, in computational complexity theory, space can be easily traded for time, and vice versa, see Aaronsen 2013.

3. In the following I will use this and other established metaphors of machine learning without scare quotes or footnotes, and thus without always making their anthropomorphising function explicit. I trust the reader to not be 'fooled' into thinking that these machines are human, or considered to be human by the author.

4. Images in neural networks are actually processed in batches for efficiency reasons. Multiple three-dimensional matrices (an image has three colour channels) are concatenated into a four-dimensional matrix which is then routed through the layers of the network.

5. The weights in neural networks need to be initialised, but how exactly initialisation influences learning is an open question – randomisation is only one strategy among others.

6. This approach – which is an essential technique of contemporary machine learning – is known as learning rate decay.

7. In the forward pass, a prediction is made about an input image, for instance which predefined category it should be attributed to. In the backwards pass, the prediction is compared to the so-called 'ground truth', for instance a label containing the image's category, and the parameters are adjusted in the 'direction' of the ground truth through a process called stochastic gradient descent.

8. Checkpoints, interestingly, usually do not include architectural information. They are representations of the state of a structure without the structure.

9. See Szegedy 2013, as discussed in Offert 2023.

10. Panofsky's (1955) distinction might seem out of place here but indeed the work required to arrive at an understanding of a foundation model is not unlike art-historical work. See also Impett and Offert 2023.

11. See for instance the work of scholars like Ruha Benjamin, Lilly Irani, Virginia Eubanks, Safiya Noble, or Helen Nissenbaum, to only name a few. A good introduction is provided by D'Ignazio and Klein (2020).

12. The ImageNet dataset, for instance, inherits its categorisation structure from WordNet, which was started with the explicit goal to produce a comprehensive ontology of what exists.

13. An example popularised by a 2023 article in the New York times is a fictional 1976 version of 'Tron' directed by Alejandro Jodorowsky (Pavich 2023).

14. 'Die Forderung, daß Auschwitz nicht noch einmal sei, ist die allererste an Erziehung.' Adorno 1970: 135.

15. In the framework of German media theory, it is of course only through technology, through 'discourse networks' [*Aufschreibesysteme*] that history can be made in the first place. See Kittler 1990.

16. For a comprehensive overview see Löwy 2005.

17. 'Vergangenes historisch zu artikulieren heißt nicht, es zu erkennen, 'wie es denn eigentlich gewesen ist' [...]. Es heißt, sich einer Erinnerung bemächtigen, wie sie im Augenblick einer Gefahr aufblitzt.' Benjamin 1974: 695.

18. For a recent overview of the field's formation, see Raley and Rhee, 2023.

19. The technical term 'zero-shot image labeling' refers to the captioning of images without further training or fine-tuning a model on the dataset that contains them.

20. Here, I am referring to the specific, proprietary pre-trained model released by OpenAI in 2021. Since then, there have been multiple attempts to replicate CLIP in an open-source context. See, for instance, the OpenCLIP approach proposed by Cherti 2022, and research done at LAION to produce efficient pre-trained OpenCLIP models: https://laion.ai/blog/large-openclip/.

21. I have argued elsewhere that this kind of 'humanist hacking' which resorts to metalanguage will become more common in the near future (Offert 2023b). In the meantime (early 2023), OpenAI has improved their safeguards and the hack will not work anymore.

22. Jäger's images are not reproduced in this essay for ethical reasons. For a sample of his specific aesthetic facilitated by early Kodachrome film see Cosgrove (n.d.).

23. There is an argument to be made here, too, that such models, following Barthes analysis of textual contingencies, produce an estranged machinic realism. See Barthes 1982.

24. That the family is depicted as Black is a result of a superficial bias mitigation attempt by OpenAI that was exposed in 2022: random 'diversity' keywords ('black', 'female', 'asian', etc.) were added to prompts before being fed to the model, without the user's knowledge. See Offert and Phan 2024.

6

Seven Arguments about AI Images and Generative Media

Lev Manovich

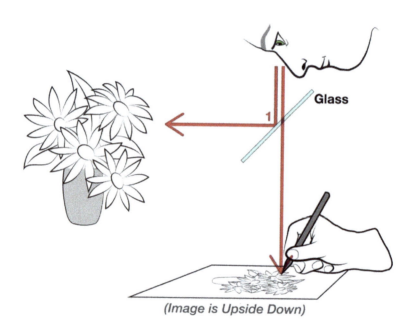

(Image is Upside Down)

Figure 1. Basic principle of camera lucida, optical drawing device widely used by artists and art students in the nineteenth century.

We appear to be in the beginning of a true revolution in media creation: the rise of generative media. I've been using computer tools for art and design since 1984, and I've seen a few major media revolutions, including the introduction of Mac computers and desktop applications for media creation and editing, the development of photorealistic 3D computer graphics and animation, the rise of the web after 1993, and the rise of social media networks after

2006. The new AI generative media revolution appears to be as significant as any of them. Indeed, it is possible that it is as significant as the invention of photography in the nineteenth century or the adoption of linear perspective in western art in the sixteenth.

If you are new to this topic, here is very brief history. Generative media revolution was in development for over 20 years. The first AI papers proposing that the vast unstructured web universe of texts, images and other cultural artifacts can be used to train computers to do various tasks appeared already in 1999-2001. In 2015 Google 'deep dream' and 'style transfer' methods attracted lots of attention: suddenly computers could create new artistic images mimicking styles of many famous artists. The release of DALL·E in January 2021 was another milestone: now computers could synthesise images from text description. Midjourney, Stable Diffusion, and DALL·E 2 all contributed to the acceleration of this evolution in 2022. Now synthetic images could have many aesthetics that ranges from photo-realism to any kind of physical or digital medium, including mosaics, oil paintings, street photography, or 3D CG rendering. The code for producing such images referred to as a 'model' in the field of artificial intelligence was made public in August 2022, sparking a flurry of experiments and accelerating development.

In this chapter I will describe a number of characteristics of *visual generative media* in its current forms that I believe are particularly significant or novel. Some of my arguments also apply to generative media in general, but most focus on *visual media* – reflecting my own experience of using a few popular AI image tools such as Midjourney and Stable Diffusion (and sometimes also RunwayML) almost every day from July 2022 to today. But first, let's define the main terms.

The Terms

In this text, 'artist' or 'creator' refers to any skilled person who creates cultural objects in any media or their combinations. The terms 'generative media', 'AI media', 'generative AI', and 'synthetic media' are all interchangeable. They refer to the process of creating new media objects with deep neural networks, such as images, animation, video, text, music, 3D models and scenes, and other types of media. Neural networks are also used to generate specific elements and types of content, such as photorealistic human faces and human poses and movements, in addition to such objects. They can also be used in media editing, such as automatically replacing a portion of an image or video with another content.

These networks are trained on vast collections of media objects already in existence. Popular artificial neural network types for media generation include diffusion models, text-to-image models, generative adversarial networks (GAN), and transformers. The terms 'image generation', 'synthetic image', 'AI image', and 'AI visuals' are synonymous when referring to the creation of still and moving images using neural networks.

Note that the word 'generative' can be also used in different ways to refer to making cultural artifacts using any algorithmic processes (as opposed to only neural networks) or even a rule-based process that does not use computers. In this chapter I am using 'generative' in more restrictive way to designate deep network methods and apps for media generation that use these methods.

1. 'AI' as a Cultural Perception

There is not one specific technology or a single research project called 'AI'. However, we can trace how our cultural perception of this concept evolved over time and what it was referring to in each period. In the last fifty years, when an allegedly uniquely human ability or skill is being automated by means of computer technology, we refer to it as 'AI'. Yet, as soon as this automation is seamlessly and fully successful, we tend to stop referring to it as an AI case. In other words, AI refers to technologies and methodologies that automate human cognitive abilities and are starting to function but aren't quite there yet.

In this sense, AI was already present in the earliest computer media tools. The first interactive drawing and design system, Ivan Sutherland's *Sketchpad* (1961–1962), had a feature that would automatically finish any rectangles or circles you started drawing. In other words, it knew what you were trying to make. In the very broad understanding just given, this was undoubtedly AI already.

My first experience with a desktop paint programme running on an Apple II was in 1984, and it was truly amazing to move your mouse and see simulated paint brushstrokes appear on the screen. However, today we no longer consider this to be AI. Another example would be the Photoshop function that automatically selects an outline of an object. This function was added many years ago – this, too, is AI in the broad sense, yet nobody would refer to it as such today. The history of digital media systems and tools is full of such AI moments – amazing at first, then taken for granted and forgotten as AI after a while. (In AI history books, this phenomenon is referred to as the 'AI effect'.) At the moment, creative AI refers only to recently developed methods where computers transform some inputs into new media outputs (e.g., text-to-image models) and specific techniques (e.g., certain types of deep neural networks). However, we must remember that these methods are neither the first nor the last in the long history and future of simulating human art abilities or assisting humans in media creation.

Figure 2. 'Unsupervised', Refik Anadol Studio (2022). Selected frames from the animation.

2. 'Make it New': AI and Modernism

After training on trillions of text pages or billions of artworks and photographic pictures taken from the web, neural networks can generate fresh texts and visuals on the level of highly competent professional writers, artists, photographers, or illustrators. These capacities of the neural nets are distributed over trillions of connections between billions of artificial neurons rather than determined by standard algorithms. In other words, we developed a technology that, in terms of complexity, is similar to the human brain. We don't fully grasp how our AI technology works, just as we don't fully comprehend human intellect and creativity.

The current generation of generative AI systems, such as ChatGPT and Stable Diffusion, have been trained on very large and diverse datasets consisting of billions or even trillions of individual texts, or image and text pairs. It is, however, equally interesting to limit the training data set to a more narrow area within the larger space of human cultural history, or to a specific set of artists from a specific historical period. 'Unsupervised' (2022) by Refik Anadol Studio (https://refikanadol.com/works/unsupervised) is an AI art project that exemplifies these possibilities. The project uses AI model trained on the image dataset of tens of thousands of artworks from the MoMA (Museum of Modern Art, New York) collection. This collection, in my opinion, is one of the best representations of the most creative and experimental period in human visual history – the one hundred years of modern art between 1870 and 1970. It captures Modernist artists' feverish and relentless experiments to create new visual and communication languages and 'make it new'.

On the surface, *the logic of Modernism appears to be diametrically opposed to the process of training generative AI systems.* Modern artists desired to depart from classical art and its defining characteristics such as visual symmetry, hierarchical compositions, and narrative content. In other words, their art was founded on a fundamental rejection of everything that had come before it (at least in theory, as expressed in their manifestos). Neural networks are trained in the opposite manner, by learning from historical culture and art created up to now. A neural network is analogous to a very conservative artist studying in the 'meta' 'museum without walls' that houses only historical art.

But we all know that art theory and art practice are not the same thing. Modern artists did not completely reject the past and everything that came before them. Instead, *modern art developed by reinterpreting and copying images and forms from much older art traditions*, such as Japanese prints (van Gogh), African sculpture (Picasso), and Russian icons (Malevich). Thus, the artists only rejected the dominant 'high art' paradigms of the time (realism and Salon art), but not the rest of human art history. In other words, Modernism was deeply historicist: rather than inventing everything from scratch, it innovated by adapting certain older aesthetics to contemporary art contexts. (In the case of geometric abstract art created in 1910s, these artists used images that were already widely used in experimental psychology to study human visual sensation and perception. For the detailed analysis of these relations between modern art and experimental psychology, see Vitz and Glimcher, (1984).)

When it comes to artistic AI, we should not be blinded by how these systems are trained. Yes, artificial neural networks are trained on already existing human art and culture artifacts. However, their newly generated outputs are not mechanical replicas or simulations of what has already been created. In my opinion, these are frequently *genuinely new* cultural artifacts with *previously unseen content, aesthetics, or styles*. In other words, I want to suggest that the Modernist project and the AI art phenomenon are often more similar than it may appear.

Of course, simply being novel does not automatically make something culturally or socially interesting or significant. Indeed, many definitions of 'creativity' agree on this point: it is the creation of something that is both original and worthwhile or useful.

However, estimating what percentage of all novel artifacts produced by generative AI are also useful and/or meaningful for a larger culture is not a feasible project at this time. For one thing, I am not aware of any systematic effort to use such systems to 'fill in', so to speak, a massive matrix of all content and aesthetic possibilities by providing millions of specifically designed prompts. Instead, it is likely that, as in every other area of popular culture, only a small number of possibilities are realised over and over by millions of users, leaving a long tail of other possibilities unrealised. So, if only a tiny fraction of the vast universe of potential AI creations is being realised in practice, we can't make broad statements about the originality or utility of the rest of the universe.

 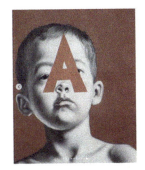 

Figure 3. Lev Pereulkov, 'Artificial Experiments 1-10', 2023. Three images from the series of 10 shared on Instagram.

3. Generative Media and Database Art

Some AI artists such Anna Ridler (https://annaridler.com), Sarah Meyohas (https://aiartists.org/sarah-meyohas) and Refik Anadol (https://refika-nadol.com) have utilised in their works neural nets trained on specific data-sets. Many other artists, designers, architects, and technologists use networks released by other companies or research institutions that were already trained on very large datasets (e.g., Stable Diffusion), and then fine tune them on their own data.

For example, artist Lev Pereulkov (https://www.instagram.com/pereu-lye) fine-tuned the Stable Diffusion model 2.1 using 40 paintings by well-known 'non-conformist' artists who worked in the USSR starting in the 1960s (Erik Bulatov, Ilya Kabakov, and others). Pereulkov's image series 'Artificial Experiments 1-10' (Pereulkov 2023) created with this custom AI model is an original artwork that captures the aesthetic and semantic worlds of these artists without repeating closely any of their existing works. Instead, their 'DNAs' captured by the model enable production of new meanings and visual concepts.

Most of the millions of everyday people and creative professionals who employ generative media tools use them as is, and don't customise them further. This may change in the future as fine tuning these tools to follow our aesthetic preferences becomes more common place. But regardless of these specifics, all newly created cultural artifacts produced by generative AI have a common logic.

Unlike traditional drawings, sculptures, and paintings, generative media artifacts are not created from scratch. They are also not the result of capturing some sensory phenomenon, such as photos, videos, or sound recordings. They are instead built from a large archive of other media artifacts. This generative mechanism links generative media to certain earlier art genres and processes.

We can compare it to film editing, which first appears around 1898, or even earlier composite photography, which was popular in the nineteenth

Figure 4. Photomontage by John Heartfield, 1919.

century. We can also consider specific artworks that are especially relevant, such as experimental collage film *A Movie* (Bruce Conner, 1958) or many Nam June Paik installations that feature edited fragments of TV footage. Seeing projects like 'Unsupervised' or 'Artificial Experiments 1–10' in the context of this media making tradition and its historical variations will help us understand these and many other AI artworks as art objects engaged in dialogues with art from the past, rather than as purely technological novelties or works of entertainment.

I see many relevant moments and periods when I scan the history of art, visual culture, and media for other prominent uses of this paradigm: making new cultural objects from collections of existing ones. They are relevant to the current generative media not only because many artists in the past at different moments in media history used this approach, but also because the motivation for its periodic reoccurrence seems to remain the same. *A new accumulation and accessibility of masses of cultural artifacts led artists to create new forms of art driven by these accumulations.* Let me describe a few of these examples.

Net and digital artists created a number of works in the late 1990s and early 2000s in response to the new, rapidly expanding universe of the world wide web. Health Bunting's '_readme' (1998), for example, is a web page containing the text of an article about the artist, with each word linked to an existing web domain corresponding to that word. Mark Napier's 'Shredder 1.0' (also 1998) presents a dynamic montage of elements that comprise numerous websites – images, texts, HTML code, and links.

Going earlier to 1980s, we also find artists reacting to the accumulation of historical art and culture artifacts in easily accessible media collections. This is paradigm is known as 'post-Modernism'. Post-Modern artists and architects frequently used bricolage to create works that included quotations and references to historical art, rejecting Modernism's self-proclaimed emphasis on novelty and breaking with the past.

While there are many possible explanations for the emergence of the post-modern paradigm at that time, one of them is particularly relevant to our discussion. The accumulation of earlier art and media artifacts in structured and accessible collections such as slides libraries, film archives, art history textbooks with many photos of the artworks, and other formats – where different historical periods, movements, and creators were positioned together – inspired artists to begin creating bricolages from such references as well as extensively quoting them.

And what about Modernism of the 1910s–1920s? While Modernists claimed they valued originality and innovation, one of the methods they employed to achieve this novelty was the incorporation of direct quotations from the rapidly expanding realm of contemporary visual media. In these decades, use of large headings and the inclusion of photos and maps made newspapers more visually impactful; new visually oriented magazines, such as *Vogue* and *Times*, were launched in 1913 and 1923, respectively; and of course, a new medium of cinema continued to develop.

In response to this visual intensification of mass culture, in 1912 Georges Braque and Pablo Picasso began incorporating actual newspaper, poster, wallpaper, and fabric fragments into their paintings. A few years later, John Heartfield, George Grosz, Hannah Hoch, Aleksandr Rodchenko, and a handful of other artists began to develop photo-collage which became another method of creating new media artifacts from existing mass media images.

Contemporary artworks that employ AI models trained on cultural databases, such as 'Unsupervised' or 'Artificial Experiments 1-10', continue a long tradition of creating new art from accumulations of images and other media. Thus, these artworks create novel possibilities for art and its methodologies, specifically within the realm of what I previously described as 'database art' (Manovich 1999). The introduction of new methods for *reading cultural databases and creating new narratives from them* is part of this expansion.

'Unsupervised' neither creates collages from existing images, as did Modernist artists of the 1920s, nor quotes them extensively, as did post-Modern artists of the 1980s. Instead, Refik Anadol Studio trained AI model to extract patterns from tens of thousands of MoMA's artworks. The model can generate new images that have the same patterns as training data but don't look like any specific paintings. However, rather than simply displaying these images separately, the installation presents the viewers with the constantly changing animation. As we watch it, we travel through the space of these patterns (e.g., 'latent space'), exploring various regions of the universe of modern art as represented in MoMA collection. (For more details about technical methods used by Refik Anadol Studio see Carina Y (2022).)

Pereulkov's 'Artificial Experiments 1-10' use a different technique to generate new images from an existing image database. He chose only forty paintings by artists who share certain characteristics. They developed their oppositional art in late communist society (USSR, 1960s-1980s). They also lived in the same visual culture. In my memories, this society was dominated by two colours: grey (representing the monotony of urban life) and the red of propaganda slogans and flags.

In addition, Pereulkov chose paintings that share something else: 'I chose, as a rule, paintings that conceptually relate in some way to the canvas – or to the space on it. For example, I use the image of a painting 'New Accordion' from Ilya Kabakov, which features paper applications on top of the canvas' (my personal communication with Pereulkov, 04/16/2023). Pereulkov also crafted custom text descriptions of each painting used for fine-tuning the Stable Diffusion image generation model. To teach the model the specific visual languages of the chosen artists, he added terms such as 'thick strokes', 'red lighting', 'blue background', and 'flat circles' to these descriptions.

Clearly, each of these steps represents a conceptual and aesthetic decision. In other words, the key to the success of 'Artificial Experiments 1–10' is the creation of a custom database with particular art images and specific descriptions added by the author. This work demonstrates how fine-tuning an existing AI model that was trained on billions of image and text pairs (such as Stable Diffusion) can make this network follow the artist's ideas. The biases and noise of such a massive network can be overcome and minimised, and do not need to dominate our own imagination.

4. From Representation to Prediction

Historically, humans created images of existing or imagined scenes using many methods, from manual drawing to 3D CG (see below for brief explanation of the methods). With AI generative media, a fundamentally new method has emerged. AI models utilise massive datasets of existing media artifacts to generate new still images, images, video or 3D models that follow the patterns extracted from existing artifacts. In other words, a computer predicts what an image representing a particular subject using particular media and aesthetics would like as if it was made by a very skilled human media creator.

One can certainly propose different historical paths leading to AI visual generative media, or divide the same historical timeline into different stages. So here is one such possible trajectory:

1. Creating representations manually (e.g., drawing with variety of instruments, carving, etc). More mechanical stages and parts were sometimes carried out by human assistants typically training in their teacher's studio – so there is already some delegation of functions.

2. Creating manually but using assistive devices (e.g., perspective machines, camera lucida). From *hands* to *hands + device*. Now some functions are delegated to mechanical and optical devices.

3. Photography, x-ray, video, volumetric capture, remote sensing, photogrammetry. From *using hands* to *recording information using machines*. From *human assistants* to *machine assistants*.

4. 3D CG. You define a 3d model in a computer and use algorithms that simulate effects of light sources, shadows, fog, transparency, translucency, natural textures, depth of field, motion blur, etc. From r*ecording* to *simulation*.

5. Generative AI. Using media datasets to predict still and moving images. From *simulation* to *prediction*.

'Prediction' is the actual term often used by AI researchers in their publications describing visual generative media methods. So, while this term can be used figuratively and evocatively, this is also what actually happens in scientific terms when you use image generative tools. AI model attempts to predict the images that correspond best to your text input.

I am certainly not suggesting that using all other already accepted terms such as 'generative media' is inappropriate. But if we want to better understand the difference between AI visual media synthesis methods and other representational methods used throughout human history, employing the concept of 'prediction' and thus referring to these AI systems as 'predictive media' captures this difference well.

5. Media Translations

There are several methods for creating AI synthetic media. One method transforms human media input while retaining the same media type. Text entered by the user, for example, can be summarised, rewritten, expanded, and so on. The output, like the input, is a text. Alternatively, in the image-to-image AI generation method, one or more input images are used to generate new images.

However, there is another path that is equally intriguing from the historical and theoretical perspectives. AI media can be created by automatically 'translating' content between media types. This is what happens, for example, when you are using Midjourney, Stable Diffusion or another AI image generator service and enter a text prompt, and AI generates one or more images in response. Text is 'translated' into an image.

Because this is not a literal one-to-one translation, I put the word 'translation' in quotes. Instead, input from one medium instructs AI model to predict the appropriate output in another. Such input can also be said to be 'mapped' to some outputs in other media. Text is mapped into new styles of text, images, animation, video, 3D models, and music. The video is converted into 3D models or animation. Images are 'translated' into text, and so on. Text-to-image method is currently more advanced than others, but various forms will catch up eventually.

Translation (or mapping) between one media and another is not a new concept. Such translations were done manually throughout human history, often with artistic intent. Novels have been adapted into plays and films, comic books have been adapted into television series, a fictional or non-fictional text was illustrated with images, etc. Each of these translations was a deliberate cultural act requiring professional skills and knowledge of the appropriate media. Some of these translations can now be performed automatically on a massive scale thanks to artificial neural networks, becoming a new means of communication and culture creation. Of course, artistic adaptation of a novel into a film by a human team and automatic generation of visuals from novel text by AI is not the same thing, but for many more simple cases automatic media translation can work well. What was once a skilled artistic act is now a technological capability available to everyone. We can be sad about everything that might be lost as a result of the automation – and democratisation – of this critical cultural operation: skills, something one might call 'deep artistic originality' or 'deep creativity', and so on. However, any such loss may be only temporary if the abilities of 'culture AI' are, for example, even further improved to generate more original content and understand context better.

Because the majority of people in our society can read and write in at least one language, text-to-another media methods are currently the most popular. They include text-to-image, text-to-animation, text-to-3D, and text-to-music models. These AI tools can be used by anyone who can write, or by using readily available translation software to create a prompt in any of the language these tools understand best at a given point. However, other media mappings can be equally interesting for professional creators. Throughout the course of human cultural history, various translations between media types have attracted attention. They include translations between video and music done by VJs in clubs; long literary narratives turned into movies and television series; texts illustrated with images in various media such as engravings; numbers turned into images (digital art); texts describing paintings (ekphrasis tradition, which began in Ancient Greece), mappings between sounds and colours (especially popular in Modernist art); etc.

The continued development of AI models for mappings between all types of media, without privileging text, has the potential to be extremely fruitful, and I hope that more tools will be able to accomplish this. Such tools will be very useful both to professional artists and other creators alike. However, being an artist myself, I am not claiming that future 'culture AI' will be able to match, for example, innovative interpretations of Hamlet by avant-garde theatre directors such as Peter Brook or astonishing abstract films by Oscar Fischinger that explored musical and visual correspondences. It is sufficient that new media mapping AI tools stimulate our imagination, provide us with new ideas, and enable us to explore numerous variations of specific designs.

6. The Stereotypical and the Unique

Both the modern human art creation process and the predictive AI generative media process seem to function similarly. AI model is trained using unstructured collections of cultural content, such as billions of images and their descriptions or trillions of web and book pages. The model earns associations between these artifacts' constituent parts (such as which words frequently appear next to one another) as well as their common patterns and structures. The trained model then uses these structures, patterns, and 'culture atoms' to create new artifacts when we ask it to. Depending on what we ask for, these AI-created artifacts might closely resemble what already exists or they might not.

Similarly, our life is an ongoing process of both supervised and unsupervised cultural training. We take art and art history courses, view websites, videos, magazines, and exhibition catalogues, visit museums, and travel in order to absorb new cultural information. And when we 'prompt' ourselves to make some new cultural artifacts, our own biological neural networks (infinitely more complex than any AI nets to date) generate such artifacts based on what we've learned so far: general patterns we've observed, templates for making

Figure 5. Examples generated in Midjourney version 4 using text prompt 'morning sky'.

particular things, and often concrete parts of existing artifacts. In other words, our creations may contain both exact replicas of previously observed artifacts and new things that we represent using templates we have learned, such as the golden ratio, linear perspective, or complementary colours.

AI models used for image generation frequently have a default 'house' style. (This is the actual term used by Midjourney developers). If one does not specify a style explicitly, the AI will generate it using this 'default' aesthetic.

To steer away from this default, you need to add terms to your prompts specifying a description of the medium, the kind of lighting, the colours and shading, or a phrase like 'in the style of' followed by the name of a well-known artist, illustrator, photographer, fashion designer, or architect. Here are two examples of such prompts I made, and the images that Midjourney generated from these prompts. The terms used to define particular style characteristics are underlined.

This image also illustrates the point I am making later in the essay: 'AI frequently generates new media artifacts that are more stereotypical or idealised than what we intended'.

Because *AI can simulate many thousands of already-existing aesthetics and styles and interpolate between them to create new hybrid*s, it is more capable than any single human creator in this regard. However, at present, skilled and highly experienced human creators also have a significant advantage. Both humans and artificial intelligence are capable of imagining and representing nonexistent and existing objects and scenes alike. Yet, unlike AI image generators, human-made images can include unique content, unique minuscule details, and distinctive aesthetics in a way that is currently beyond the capabilities of AI. In other words, today a large group of highly skilled and experienced illustrators, photographers, and designers can represent everything AI model can do (although it will take much, much longer), but *they can also create objects, compositions, or aesthetics that the neural net cannot do at this time. Equally importantly,*

Figure 6. Prompt: 'giant future 1965 modern airport in Siberia made from water and ice, painted on large wood panel by Hieronymus Bosch, bright pastel colours with white highlights, 23f lens, very detailed --ar 4:3 --s 1250 --test' (Image generated with Midjourney v3)

they can picture unique objects, faces, compositions, and so on – as opposed to often more commonplace or idealised versions generated by AI.

What is the cause of this aesthetic and content gap between human and artificial creators?

'Cultural atoms', structures, and patterns in the training data that occur most frequently are very successfully learned by artificial neural network during the process of training. In the 'mind' of a AI model, they gain more importance. On the other hand, 'atoms' and structures that are rare in the training data or may only appear once are hardly learned or not even parsed at all. They do not enter the artificial culture universe learned by AI. Consequently, when we ask AI to synthesise them, it is unable to do so.

Due to this, text-to-image AIs such as Midjourney or Stable Diffusion are not currently able to generate drawings in my own unique artistic style, expand my drawings by adding newly generated parts, or replace specific portions of my drawings with new content drawn in my style (e.g., they can't perform useful 'outpainting' or 'inpainting' on the digital photos of my drawings.) Instead, these AI tools generate more generic objects than what I frequently draw or they produce something that is merely ambiguous yet uninteresting.

I am certainly not claiming that the style and the world shown in my drawings is completely unique. They are also a result of specific cultural encounters I had, things I observed, and things I noticed. But because they

Figure 7. Prompt: 'Photo of two Russian high-school students, clear skin, very soft studio light, 50mm lens, monochrome, silver tones, high quality, ultra realistic --v 4 --q 2' (Image generated with Midjourney v4)

are uncommon (and thus unpredictable), AI finds it difficult to simulate them, at least without additional AI training using my drawings.

Here we encounter what I see as *the biggest obstacle creators face when using AI generative media:*

AI frequently generates new media artifacts that are more stereotypical or idealised than what we intended.

This can affect any image dimensions: elements of content, lighting, cross-hatching, atmosphere, spatial structure, details of forms and shapes, and so on. Occasionally it is immediately apparent, in which case you can either attempt to correct it or disregard the results. Very often, however, *such 'substitutions' are so subtle that we cannot detect them* without extensive observation or, in some cases, the use of a computer to quantitatively analyse numerous images. In other words, AI generative media models, much like the discipline of statistics since its inception in the eighteenth century and the field of data science

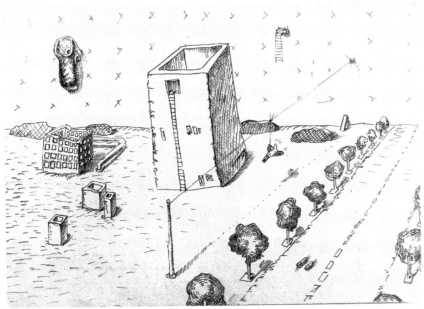

Figure 8. Lev Manovich, untitled drawing, pen on paper, 1981-1982.

since the end of the 2010s, deal well with frequently occurring items and patterns in the data but do not know what to do with the infrequent and uncommon. We can hope that AI researchers will be able to solve this problem in the future, but it seems so fundamental that we should not anticipate a solution immediately.

7. Subject and Style

In the arts, the relationship between 'content' and 'form' has been extensively discussed and theorised. This brief section does not attempt to engage in all of these debates or to initiate discussions with all relevant theories. Instead, I would like to consider how these concepts play out in AI's 'generative culture'. However, instead of using content and form, I'll use a different pair of terms that are more common in AI research publications and online conversations between users: *subject* and *style*.

At first glance, AI media tools appear capable of clearly distinguishing between the subject and style of any given representation. In text-to-image models, for instance, you can generate countless images of the same subject. Adding the names of specific artists, media, materials, and art historical periods is all that is required for the same subject to be represented differently to match these references.

Photoshop filters began to separate subject and style as early as the 1990s, but AI generative media tools are more capable. For instance, if you specify 'oil painting' in your prompt, simulated brushstrokes will vary in size and

Figure 9. One of my attempts to generate a version of this drawing using
Stable Diffusion AI tool, Fall 2022.

direction across a generated image based on the objects depicted. AI media
tools appear to 'understand' the semantics of the representation as opposed
to earlier filters that simply applied the same transformation to each image
region regardless of its content. For instance, when I used 'a painting by
Malevich' and 'a painting by Bosch' in the same prompt, Midjourney generated an image of space that contained Malevich-like abstract shapes as well
as many small human and animal figures like in popular Bosch paintings that
were properly scaled for perspective.

However, AI tools also routinely add content to an image that I did not
specify in my text prompt in addition to representing what I requested. This
frequently occurs when the prompt includes 'in the style of' or 'by' followed
by the name of a renowned visual artist or photographer. In one experiment,
I used the same prompt with the Midjourney tool 148 times, each time adding
the name of a different photographer. The subject in the prompt remained

Figure 10. I generated this image using prompt 'painting by Malevich and Bosch',
Midjourney, Fall 2022.

mostly the same – an empty landscape with some buildings, a road, and electric poles with wires stretching into the horizon. Sometimes adding a photographer's name had no effect on the elements of a generated image that fit
our intuitive concept of style, such as contrast, perspective, and atmosphere.
But every now and again, Midjourney also modified the image content.
For example, when well-known works by a particular photographer feature
human figures in specific poses, the tool would occasionally add such figures
to my photographs. (Like Malevich and Bosch, they were transformed to
fit the spatial composition of the landscape rather than mechanically dupli-
cated.) Midjourney has also sometimes changed the content of my image to
correspond to a historical period when a well-known photographer created
his most well-known photographs.

According to my observations, when we ask Midjourney or another AI
image synthesis tool to create an image in the style of a specific artist, and the
subject we describe in the prompt is related to the artist's typical subjects, the

Figure 11. Using prompt 'by Caspar David Friedrich --v 5' in Midjourney generates images that capture the artist's style sufficiently well. (Images are from https://www.midlibrary.io/styles/caspar-david-friedrich)

results can be very successful. However, when the subject of our prompt and the imagery of this artist are very different, 'rendering' the subject in this style frequently fails.

To summarise, in order to successfully simulate a given visual style using current AI tools, you may need to change the content you intended to represent. *Not every subject can be rendered successfully and satisfyingly in any style.* Additionally, AI can often successfully learn some features of artist's style but not others.

These observations, I believe, complicates the binary opposition between the concepts of 'content' and 'style'. For some artists, AI can extract at least some aspects of their style from examples of their work and then apply them to different types of content. But for other artists, it seems, their style and content cannot be separated.

Figure 12. Using prompt 'decaying peonies by Caspar David Friedrich' in Midjourney (v 5) generates images that simulate important features of artist's style such as combinations of cool colours and dramatic atmosphere. But in other ways, generated images depart significantly from the artist's style. The types of lines, rendering of details, and symmetrical compositions in these AI images would never appear in actual Friedrich's paintings. AI can also often insert some generic looking objects, such as the rock formations in the upper right corner of first image. (Images are from https://www.midlibrary.io/styles/caspar-david-friedrich)

For me, these kinds of observations and reflections are one of the most important reasons for using new media technologies like AI generative media and learning how they work. Of course, as a practicing artist and art theorist,

I had been thinking about the relationships between subject and style (or content and form) for a long time but being able to conduct systematic experiments like the one I described brings new ideas and allows us to *look back at cultural history and art in new ways.*

Works Cited

Carina Y. 2022. 'Creating Art with Generative Adversarial Network.' *Medium* (blog). March 1, 2022. https://medium.com/@ymingcarina/creating-art-with-generative-adversarial-network-refik-anadols-wdch-dreams-159a6eac762d.

Manovich, Lev. 1999. 'Database as Symbolic Form.' *Convergence: The International Journal of Research into New Media Technologies* 5 (2): 80-99.

Pereulkov, Lev. 2023. 'Artificial Experiments 1-10.' *Instagram.* https://www.instagram.com/p/CnezVZ9KHMV.

7

Nietzsche, AI, and Poetic Artistry: On Nietzsche's 'Hinzugedichtetes'

Babette Babich

> We are unknown to ourselves, we knowers. And with good reason, we have never sought ourselves […] so we sometimes rub our ears afterward and ask, utterly surprised and disconcerted, 'what really was that we have just experienced?' and moreover: 'who are we really?' […] So we are necessarily strangers to ourselves, we do not comprehend ourselves, we have to misunderstand ourselves, for us the law, 'Each is furthest from himself' applies to all eternity.
>
> —Nietzsche, *Genealogy of Morals*, 'Preface'

Nietzsche's Truth and Lie or AI, ChatGPT, and Poetic Projection

In what follows I think AI together with the insights of Friedrich Nietzsche (1844-1900), drawing on his conception of the machine and his notion of the universe as perpetual motion machine, which he expressed using the analogy of a *Spielwerk*, or 'music box'. Trained as a student of language, Nietzsche also wrote on the mechanics (μηχανή) of 'on truth and lie'. Here I seek to engage his understanding of the creative contributions of the human mind in sense perception and interpretive experience (see further, Babich 1994 and 2010b).

Nietzsche's language of the '*Hinzugedichtetes*', the confabulated, poetically, (think Hölderlin's 'Remarks on Oedipus') creatively projected human contribution, may be understood in Hans Vaihinger's (1911) neo-Kantian sense of 'fictionalising' which Nietzsche took from the rhetorical tradition of Gustav Gerber's *Kunst der Sprache* (1871, 1873). Nietzsche develops this in his 1873 essay 'On Truth and Lie in an Extra-Moral Sense' (Nietzsche 1979 [1896]), his 1886 *Beyond Good and Evil: Prelude to a Philosophy of the Future* (in German: Nietzsche

1980, Vol. 5), and his 1889 *Twilight of the Idols: How One Philosophises With a Hammer* (Ibid., Vol. 6). I write about this (in Babich 1994, with a focus on the 'eco-physiological' foundations of his epistemology: 77ff and Babich 2005 and 2010b), and, on Nietzsche and rhetoric, see Strong 2013 (as well as 'Philology and Aphoristic Style' in Babich 2006).

Some of what follows draws on the original experimental computer simulations of 'natural language' (Weizenbaum 1976 and 1966) and, qua behaviour or neurophysiological efficacy, as text completion prompts (Darragh/Witten 1992, but see, McCulloch 2019 as well as with reference to Günther Anders 2016/1956 'Promethean Shame' in place of Harold Bloom's – and other scholars' – 'anxiety of influence', see Bajohr 2020 as well as 2023). I argue that, read phenomenologico-hermeneutically, Nietzsche can help us understand ChatGPT, including the hype that surrounds it. I foreground Nietzsche's attention to the lie that includes AI deception specifically, as Hannes Bajohr notes, given that 'truth' is not at stake when it comes to AI as 'lying and bluffing are explicitly allowed' (Bajohr 4: 339). I also take up Nietzsche's critical analysis of our tendency to content ourselves with superficial imprecision in perception when it comes to reading texts and in assessing our surroundings (Nietzsche's 'eco-physiological' epistemology, Babich 1994) in addition to our self-deception when it comes to our knowledge of other persons and ourselves.

AI: On the Claims of 'Sentience' and the 'Singularity'

When Blake Lemoine, a Google engineer, made the claim in the summer of 2022 that Artificial Intelligence was 'sentient' (for one report, see: Tiku 2022) thereby seemingly announcing the 'Singularity' (for further references my 2012a, 2012b, 2016), Lemoine was denounced as, at a minimum, 'jumping the gun'. His employer fired him (Guardian/Staff 2022), there were a few desultory interviews, and Luciano Floridi, one of the leading philosophical deans of AI, then at Oxford, weighed in, following subsequent news surrounding ChatGPT, to say where all such claims went wrong (Floridi 2023 and Floridi and Chiriatti 2020).

Today, apart from occasional protests dismissed as excessive and thus ignored, philosophically there are no 'critical' voices on technology in the spirit of Günther Anders (see Anders 1956 and, on Anders, Babich, 2023c as well as Fuchs 2017). Anders, who argued a concept of what he called 'Promethean Shame' in the face of technology, argued that we aspire to the condition of the machine – replaceable, upgradable. Varying Descartes proof for deity, for Anders, although (or because) technoscience is our fabrication, we regard it as a deity, or better, if more complicatedly (as we thereby treat ourselves as our own deities) a new gnosis (Babich 2013, 2023c). Thereby, for Anders, 'we rely on the technological world without understanding it and this is no different to the way believers trust in God without being able to know his deeds' (Anders 2019, 136).

Critical views are in short supply when it comes to AI and the best it has ever had in a 'critical' direction might have been Peter Sloterdijk (1988, see for discussion, Babich 2011) or Friedrich Kittler (see, e.g., Barth 2018) but most philosophers have had to content themselves with either the unflappable enthusiasms of a Don Ihde (1934-2024), or Hubert Dreyfus (1929-2017) on what computers could/could not do. Thus contemporary philosophers write on AI, yet, and this is key (think, again, of Floridi 2023 or Coeckelbergh 2020 but also, now classically, Bostrom and Yudkowsky 2011), they foreground their pro-technology industry-friendliness very specifically as tools for advisory and ethical assessment, cautious as Floridi and Bostrom are but without the negativity that remains anathema for philosophy of technology (see Babich 2022 on Anders's negatived reception in philosophy of technology).

For his part, responding to claims of AI's cognitive agency, Floridi would split the difference: AI is not as such 'intelligent', and the 'best practice' (so goes the reigning academic meme) involved human beings using AI resources 'proficiently and insightfully' (Floridi 2023), locution-wise, in terms of rhetorical use-value for readers, not unrelated to Peter Singer's language of 'effective altruism'. (Singer 2015, and see, most recently, following the 'build back better' locution of the last few years, MacAskill 2023 and, per contra, more complexly with direct reference to AI, Gebru, 2022). The emphasis on human collaboration is key. To use AI resources can be as innocuous as providing a prompt and selecting the best generated bits: in effect, working as its assistant or editor. In this effective confabulation, poetic contribution presupposes and arguably goes beyond the willing suspension of disbelief (relevant for the use/design of social robots, see, for example, Duffy and Zawieska 2013, who cite Coleridge's original use of the phrase, and Duffy 2003 and, in creative writing, see, for an exemplification, Bajohr 2023a with an explication, Bajohr 2023c). Moreover it is crucial to note, speaking of practice, 'best' or otherwise, that (arguably, especially) as an academic one is already doing that, whether searching the internet or mining one's research project on Twitter or still more overtly opening bidding for information from the Twitterati who happen to be online to see one's query or writing emails to ask random academics for references or syllabi design tips. (See for one recent discussion: Kansteiner 2022).

People who have used ChatGPT enthuse about how wonderful it is – and why would they not enthuse? The effect is a 'bubble effect', here to recall Eli Pariser's influential term for internet obfuscation (2011), extending what Tor Nørretranders (2006) called the 'user illusion'. The results correspond to the same users' data traces, internet use habits, reading and reinforcing the same things again and again. We like what we know, and what we agree with, we like even more. Thus we 'like' familiar, formulaic expressions sedimented via social media and repetition into our consciousness.

Accordingly, psycholinguists tell us the key to a 'good' conversation, to 'good' therapy, a 'good' job interview (or a 'good' romantic date) is to repeat what the other party says right back to them. Deftly done, this is not perceived as parroting but as *geniality*: one heart, and one soul. Perhaps most telling – a common feature of hype – people who haven't used GPT *also* enthuse about it. Nor did the tune change as professors at Oxford and other universities were warned that students had an ally in faking not 'news' but term papers (Marche 2022 and Stokel-Walker 2022, and, again, Floridi 2023).

In keeping with the original goals of the original MIT Eliza programme, designed by Joseph Weizenbaum (1966) to model a therapy session where the human user's input sentence would be answered by a question, largely repeating the original phrase (*why do you feel...*) and which was called an early natural language processing system (listing the assumptions about language built into this would take another essay), the success of the Eliza programme depended on users using it *as if* they were interacting with another human being (see, in robotics, Severson and Carlson 2010). Interpretive projection, suspension of critique (and disbelief) and generosity was a condition *sine qua non*. If this (very priming) precondition is also the basis of AI ethics to this day, Weizenbaum himself, significantly, did not regard the programme, even when successful, as 'therapy', given that it was experimentally designed –as he never forgot that it was – to explore the nature of language (a critical component was part of this, see Weizenbaum 1976 and, for discussion, Bassett 2019). He explicitly repudiated popular readings, not that this repudiation had any impact on the reception of his work to this day. Indeed: the Eliza programme has just won the Peabody Award for Digital and Interactive Storytelling according to a recent MIT report explaining the achievement as having opened 'a broader dialogue about general machine intelligence, the chatbot was put to the Turing Test, and it passed a restricted version' (Gordon 2022).

Our narrative expectations online have been shaped to a great degree by our collective online gaming experiences (and this holds whether we ourselves are gamers or *qua* online user practice: via Twitter or via click bait, or dating apps such as Grindr or Bumble, or especially with respect to GPS location software, as Frith/Kalin (2016) note). This is the marketing point and emphasis of Tim Wu's 2016 *The Attention Merchants*. (On this see Babich 2016b as well as Ge Jin's 2010 documentary analysis of 'Chinese gold farmers'. See too Nardi and Know 2010). The reference to gaming is part of today's cultural unconscious, written into the title of the HBO series, *Game of Thrones* (2011-2019) and blatantly CGI gaming design of its opening graphics/credits. Today we are preformed less by the habit of listening to radio, as the Frankfurt School critical theorists argued (though the acoustic remains effective, to wit podcasts) or a dependence on television (see for references my 2021a) but mainstream and social media and our cell phones depend on acoustic reinforcement. Thus I begin *The Hallelujah Effect* with an analysis of this micro-addictive acoustic circuit (Babich 2013 and see Babich and Bateman 2017). Games have long been part of hermeneutic conversation (Gadamer 1987 and MacIntyre 1981, more broadly, with respect to Weber and Goffman in managerial science in the social sciences, 88ff), embedded in the classic notion of *homo ludens*. This goes beyond the philosopher's fondness for draughts in the case of Heraclitus or in the case of Wittgenstein (or again MacIntyre) chess, or dice (think Mallarmé or Einstein), or soccer (Heidegger), or online gambling, or dungeons and dragons: repeating and extending the rules of the game which we also call narratives. And, as the philosopher and game designer Chris Bateman (2017) puts it: 'no one plays alone'.

Increasingly, we are what we do on-line. As the Frankfurt School already analysed the culture industry: we are 'eaters' (Anders), this is the 'culinary' (Adorno), we 'consume' what we are fed but – and this I argue in *The Hallelujah Effect* – at the same time we are convinced that this is not so, we are believers in rational choice and free will, which is quite the idea. User complicity, suspension of disbelief, lack of critical analysis at the level of both the everyday and the academy with respect to the psychology (see for a discussion of the scholarly politics of 'psychological priming' the first chapters in Babich 2013 and 2022: 36ff, and, though not attending to the same political issue, Blackman 2019) entailed that old Hollywood could use sets in a studio where new Hollywood, that is today's film/video industry, uses CGI as opposed to shooting on location. Similarly, gaming designers use stock formulae (this might be the new Homer) 'programming' what readers/gamers take to be (suspension of disbelief remains crucial here) interactive storytelling. For one example, a recent paper-cum-advertisement reports on just how much of the writing can be taken over by the programme, comparing it to another programme Fidyll (the same authors also write on):

> Fidyll still reduced the amount of code written by 33-82% (mean 60%; median 57%. Fidyll also improved the ratio of narrative to non-narrative code that authors had to write: the Fidyll markup consisted of 30% narrative code on average, while this number was 15% on average for a single format drafted in Idyll and 5% for the combined Idyll markup, indicating that the authors would have had to write about 20 lines of non-narrative markup for every sentence in the data story. (Conlen and Heer 2022; see further Helderman 2015 and, again, Bateman 2021)

I argue that the bar for 'passing' a Turing Test is low enough that vending machines and ATMs can 'pass' and given a certain affective disposition on the part of the user, even a toaster can 'pass' (Babich 2019: 17). What matters is to train the user, this is programming and in this measure, everything depends, key to AI ethics, on 'good' user habits.

In the case of ChatGPT assisted papers, instructors (no one asks which instructors) found it difficult to differentiate unassisted student papers (good or bad) from assisted or 'enhanced' substitutes for the same. Here the outcome is overdetermined, prepared or 'cooked'. Professors, long since anxious that plagiarising students might play them for fools, had for years been availing themselves of AI in the form of plagiarism software, such as Turnitin, and arranging for university underwriting of the cost of this software. Thus pre-sorted by subject and level of difficulty, this same faculty anxiety worked to 'populate' or 'feed' a curated database – curation being much of the work of AI – composed of student papers together with faculty feedback over many years. Add post-pandemic AI, including data from zoom classes and even the sometimes egregious transcription errors, and the potential for a tsunami of academic fakes has been waiting to break for a while. Thus recall Floridi's 2023 counsel: the new move would be to fake it to help you make it, and ChatGPT is increasingly regarded as the equivalent of a calculator in math class (Lund and Wang 2023).

Articles have appeared to sing the praises of AI or ChatGPT poetry – it's all 'good' if you say it is – and one may expect novels courtesy of the same (above, I already noted Bajohr's 2023a) and so on. The 'Eliza effect' to match the 'Hallelujah effect' would seem to have arrived along with the potential promise of a virtual girl- or boyfriend, a virtual 'lover' of the kind already imagined on screen in Spike Jonze's 2014 film, *Her*, and more luridly and strangely more prosaically in Rupert Sanders's 2017 *Ghost in the Shell* or the transparently named AI girlfriend, Joi in Denis Villeneuve's 2017 *Bladerunner 2049*. (See further Zhu and Zhang 2022, Plabutong 2023, Hermann 2023)

I argue that Nietzschean psychology is helpful, specifically, as I began by noting his *fictionalism* in the 'as if' spirit of Kant's fictionalism (see Vaihinger 2011 and with respect to Kant 2013 and Nietzsche 2014). Nietzsche's sustained argument is that we are abandoned to fiction, creatively, collaboratively so: 'we are, from the bottom up and across all time, *used to lying [an's Lügen gewöhnt]*' (Nietzsche 1980, Vol. 5: 114, my emphasis). This lying takes place on the level of our perceptive awareness, a poetising, creative, confabulation, streamlining what we perceive in accord with habits and psychological affordances:

> our senses greet everything novel with reluctance and hostility; and affects like fear, love, and hate, as well as passive affects of indolence, will be dominant during even the 'simplest' processes of sensibility. (Nietzsche 1980, Vol. 5: 113)

The Nietzsche who wrote 'On Truth and Lie in an Extra-Moral Sense' argued that we notice new things badly. More accurately: *we don't notice them at all* as modern cognitive neuroscience research would seem to corroborate his argument. Thus Nietzsche argued:

> in the middle of the strangest experiences we do the same thing: we poeticize most of the experience [*wir erdichten uns den grössten Theil des Erlebnisses*] and can barely be made not to regard ourselves as the 'inventor' ['*Erfinder*'] of some process. (Nietzsche 1980, Vol. 5: 114)

As if Nietzsche were aware of recent research on eye movements in reading (and he was very aware of then contemporary work on nineteenth-century sense perception) confirming his point, he observes:

> Just as little a today's reader takes in all the individual words (or especially syllables) on a page (he catches maybe five out of twenty words and 'guesses' what these five arbitrary words might possibly mean) – just as little do we see a tree precisely and completely, with respect to leaves, branches, colors, and shape. (Nietzsche 1980, Vol 5, 113, cf. his earlier, silent invocation of Goethe's example of the morphology of the leaf in Nietzsche 1980, Vol. 1: 880)

Nietzsche and the Robots: Beyond the Machine

Nietzsche died more than a century ago. To say this permits us to say that Nietzsche knew trains and telegraphs and telephones. Friedrich Kittler took account of what such details would tell us, but at the same time the Nietzsche who had his friends read to him (early podcast style), and write out his texts for him as he dictated them, in fact had *less* experience with typing on typewriters than Kittler-inspired scholars imagine when they repeatedly emphasize that he owned an early portable typing ball, assuming this would correspond to contemporary experience with a keyboard, whilst ignoring the fairly sparse typescripts resulting from his attempts to use it before the complicatedly and fragile brass typing ball crumpled into itself, irreparable.

I have for some time been bringing Nietzsche to discussions of robots and AI (Babich 2019, 2017a, 2016a and, with Bateman 2017b), including the erotic hermeneutics of social media (Babich 2016b), as well as the intentional, protential-retentional phenomenology of 'being the blue dot' (GPS: Babich 2019b) and our tendency to project our consciousness not into as much as *through* our screens (Babich 2021a; Babich 2019c). Part of the reason is that Nietzsche wrote on the 'machine' as such (specifically with disambiguating reference to the cosmos Nietzsche 1980, Vol 3: 467, including theoretical mechanics, Vol 9: 531, and even 'our violation of nature with the help of machines and inculpable technician's-and-engineer's inventiveness' [*unsre Natur-Vergewaltigung mit Hülfe der Maschinen und der so unbedenklichen Techniker- und Ingenieur-Erfindsamkeit*] Vol 5: 357, etc.) quite in addition to its effects on life and consciousness. Thus there are accounts of Nietzsche and the machine – famously the title of a Derrida interview (Derrida 1994 and see Haase 1999 as well as Gertz 2018 together with the contributions to Tuncel 2017 in addition to various reissues of old-new Italian (Campa) and German (Sorgner) futurism). Not all of these are about AI, or even technology, but Nietzsche plays a key role (this is the fascist eugenicist ideal) in debates on transhumanism, some more, some less diffuse, as in the contributions to *Digital Dionysus* (Mellamphy and Mellamphy 2016). Via the cybernetic, this connection has been explored (Kittler 1986, Ommeln 2009, Masciandaro 2015, and, again, Barth 2018) and I have argued that Nietzsche is useful for reflection on cybernetics and 'technoscotosis' (Babich 2021b).

The trouble is that Nietzsche is rarely treated rigorously. Everybody reads him, everybody interprets him, and no one imagines they might not have understood him. And how hard can it be to read, of all philosophers, Nietzsche? I have written on this as it concerns philosophical style for some time (but see Benne 2023). Being read and assumed to be easily read seems to have been Nietzsche's destiny. At least he thought so (elsewhere I muse that the problem may be our general readerly confidence when it comes to Nietzsche that we already understand him, a confidence Nietzsche encountered in his lifetime and bootlessly protested: *non legor, non legar*). And to be sure, it is worth taking more care in reading Nietzsche, not least as a certain amount of political and all-too-human damage has already been wreaked in his name.

As should already be evident, popular misreadings of Nietzsche abound and what better way to automate such misreadings in this case permitting us whatever latitude we wish? This is one way to parse Floridi's 2023 recommendation of 'using' AI tech, including ChatGPT, as a tool, quite as if it had somehow been decided that technology simply was neutral, meaning that one could use one's tool as one liked and *not be affected by it*. Henceforth the dictum: *to a man with a hammer, everything looks like a nail* would miss the point. Nietzsche himself philosophised or argued about hammers as such, not only about philosophising with or without a hammer. The reference is, in German, to a *Stimmgabel*, in French, *diapason*, or tuning fork, which is the acoustic-musical context we need as Nietzsche is speaking of sounding out idols in his *Twilight of the Idols*, testing them, physio-logico-acoustically, for emptiness, like 'bloated intestines' as he writes.

Earlier, in *The Gay Science*, contra Aristotle and Greek tragedy, also an issue for Nietzsche concerning intestinal blight – qua bodily, literal, *catharsis* – Nietzsche indicts Aristotle for missing the 'nail' and this anti-Aristotelian-ism with respect to the origin and aim of Greek tragedy occupied Nietzsche's thinking from start to finish (see the final third of Babich 2013). Today, not Aristotle but ChatGPT has spoken, as the *Tagesspiegel* has let us know, complete with a visual reminder of 2001 and Hal. (See, for an illustration thanks to AI, Fig. 1). We have asked the oracle, Google, our new Eliza: and the oracle has replied, and Nietzsche would seem to be its prophet (see, e.g., Soltau 2022).

To discuss Nietzsche and AI we will need to think the *logic* of morality, particularly his polemical response as he answered his own *Beyond Good and Evil, Prelude to a Philosophy of the Future* with *On the Genealogy of Morals*, beginning with a reflection on psychology, including the language of automatism and altruism via reinforcement of values, repetition, all so much nineteenth-century

Figure 1. AI generated (with the author's prompt).

'priming' quite as Nietzsche observes: 'a blind and chance hooking together of ideas, passive, automatic, reflexive, molecular' (Nietzsche 1980, Vol 5: 257). I argue that Nietzsche may be read as explaining how priming works, even with respect to social media contagion exercises of the kind that currently adumbrate our lives at every level, or the way boy scouts and small children might be 'trained' to virtue and good behaviour, catch phrases repeated everywhere, 'safe and effective', along with, as Nietzsche goes on to say: 'all the typical traits of the idiosyncrasy of the English psychologists — we have "utility", "forgetting", "habit", and finally "error"' (Nietzsche 1980, 5: 259). Thus Nietzsche challenges the notion that something constantly repeated, or, on the side of utilitarianism, that utility might somehow become automatic, asking how the unconscious shift to what is supposed morally good could ever take place via any kind of interim oblivion. 'How', he wonders, would such 'forgetting be possible? Has the utility of such actions come to an end at some time or other?' (Nietzsche 1980, 5: 260)

Another approach might serve us beyond the Übermensch phantasms of 'philosophising with a hammer' and the ethos of a certain DC comic book hero (Superman) matching recent film versions of the Marvel comic book vision of violence and transhuman supermen (see for discussion, Babich 2015 and 2016a) but the most productive might be the ideal mentioned at the start, that is Nietzsche's metaphor of a cosmic music box. If the idea of a perpetual motion machine may cut a little too close to home, just given the mechanism, the functioning of LNP (Lipid Nanoparticle) adjuvants in mRNA vaccines, these last now ubiquitous, making the theme controversial even for a Nietzsche paper (see the notes to Babich 2021c and on nanoparticle effluvia/persistence Babich 2019d), it exemplifies the 'extramoral sense' of Nietzsche's aesthetico-physiologically minded discussion of 'truth and lie'. To say it again, we are '*used to lying*' (Nietzsche 1980, Vol. 5: 114) and it is to the point of AI both *that* there is equivocation and *that* it is effective.

If Nietzsche's 'Truth and Lie' takes off from Gerber's 1871/1873 insights (and see beyond Nietzsche, Nerlich and Clarke 2016), the 'language art' in question is related to the stylised artifice and 'art' in Artificial Intelligence. The emergent dynamic appears in what we take ourselves to know and to think. Thus Nietzsche takes Rousseau's *amour propre* to the terrible banality of everyman, the 'porter' in his metaphor:

> Just as every porter wants to have an admirer, so even the proudest of men, the philosopher, supposes that he sees on all sides the eyes of the universe telescopically focused upon his action and intellect. (Nietzsche 1979: 79)

Like the tech vision of the 'Singularity' mentioned above (see for discussion of this tech or corporate concern, including Ray Kurzweil's material inventions, Babich 2012a), a great deal of talk of AI is *future oriented*. Par for the course for a business pitch or proposal: talk of AI is intended to sell investors on an existing product, which – this is very like 'go fund me' efforts – only given adequate financial support and an unspecified adjunct of research and inspiration, AI might prove to be the best thing since sliced bread. Thereby suspension of disbelief is built in from the outset: AI is stipulated, postulated, supposed, proposed, quite as deity was for another world and time.

At issue is intentionality and Nietzsche reminds us that we anthropomorphise constantly. Just that constant dedicated poeticising projection of ourselves into everything is how the ancient MIT Eliza programme worked. We human beings are past masters, so Nietzsche tells us, at focusing only on ourselves and projecting, that is: deceiving ourselves and others:

> Deception, flattering, lying, deluding, talking behind the back, putting up a false front, living in borrowed splendor, wearing a mask, hiding behind convention, playing a role for others and

for oneself – in short, a continuous fluttering around the *solitary* flame of vanity – is so much the rule and law among men that there is almost nothing which is less comprehensible than how an honest and pure drive for truth could have arisen among them. They are deeply immersed in illusions and dream images: their eyes merely glide over the surface of things and see 'forms'. (Nietzsche 1979: 80)

We 'find ourselves' in our clouds, in our lakes (thus Nietzsche speaks of mountains 'with eyes'), and, perhaps above all: we find ourselves (or think we find ourselves) in others (this is the famous philosophical problem, *nota bene*, this remains unsolved to date, of 'other minds'), as we likewise discover ourselves, this is the force of ancient mimesis, in animals and plants and rocks. Even more than identification with this or that item in a so-called 'natural' world – as if one might find 'nature' anywhere 'unnatured' by human hands (this is archaeological ecology) that is now distant from and in many cases even alien to many of us – we project/find ourselves in our things: our cars, our motorcycles, our television soundbars or (once upon a time, as headphones have changed all this) in our living room hi-fi setup (think of Herbert Marcuse's examples for this in his *One Dimensional Man* or, as Günther Anders argues, the television replacing the family table in the living room – see for discussion of both Marcuse and Anders, Babich 2022). Today this could be a big screen or nothing more than a high end monitor or two, or just a smart phone. We identify with, project ourselves into, and live through, perceive through, experience through the equipment around us. This requires nothing more than the smart phone we carry and display – Bateman calls these our 'pocket robots' (see Babich and Bateman 2017b). Here Pierre Bourdieu's astute (and not less Heideggerian) analysis in his 1984 *Distinction* remains on point, as in addition to being a means of social contact, the phone remains a status signal to display for others and for ourselves, constantly ready to hand.

AI shills want you to think of an elderly person cooing over a fake cat (I am only slightly paraphrasing the Warwick sociologist, Steve Fuller) if the cat today has been replaced with AI girlfriends or just ChatGPT. Hence the ongoing hype of the Turing test for fun and presumed profit, this being the version *du jour* of yesterday's news about folks applying for legal licence to marry their sex robots: whereby the selling point (just about faded) is the chance to 'speak' with one's favourite dead philosophers, though one imagines it might be more desirable to have a device à la the conceit of the 1995 film directed by Gary Fleder, *Things to Do in Denver When You're Dead*, on the entrepreneurial scam of recording videos for the sake of giving the living the illusion of speaking with dead 'loved ones'. But – and this is quite the point about projection *and* its limitations – the ruse is harder to sustain if what you are trying to have is a final conversation never had in real life with a person you actually knew. This is the mystery of intimate life trauma. Thus Ruin's 2019 *Being with the Dead* emphasises the trope in Homer – and Nietzsche uses the same example – of giving 'blood to the ghosts' (see my discussion of the same title 2020 as the key metaphor of hermeneutics but see for a Ruin-less and bloodless discussion: Henrickson 2023 as well as Babich 2007). It's easier to fake a conversation with Socrates, for which one might see the 1989 film *Bill and Ted's Excellent Adventure*, complete with a miracle seemingly key to every fantasy of time travel (literary or cinematic): Socrates, like every other past personage in Stephen Herek's film, conveniently speaks English.

When it comes to machine intelligence, which tends to be what we mean by AI, even if the 'machine' is nanosize (back to the LNPs), quantum dot ther-agrippers or what have you to track a vaccine, including molecular nanotech (oral, aerosol) to deliver said vaccine or, more macro, hardware style, even if the machine is a series of switches – or silicon patterns – what is at stake concerns the problem of 'other minds', in the argot of the analytic tradition of philosophy that is today the only kind there is, given what is taught at university, tested and vetted and (above all) hired to. As already noted: the thing about the problem of other minds is that it remains unsolved and perhaps, so Nietzsche would seem to argue, unresolvable.

At issue – and it is no accident that this is the point of departure for Mark Coeckelbergh's *AI Ethics* (2021) – is not whether a computer might beat a human at checkers or chess (or even tic-tac-toe) or some other game, roster style (Coeckelbergh trumps this with the high geek game of Go), permutating outcomes. At issue is whether, like Gary Kasparov or Bobby Fischer, the latter having moved on to the great tournament in the sky, the software in question, data set, ChatGPT, *might know and feel itself* as chess champion: consciousness, *amour propre*, all that stuff. Cheekiness, which is the next best thing for giving such an impression – this is one way to read Bajohr's emphasis on permitted fabulation, 'lying and bluffing' (Bajohr 2024) – is now programmed into Chatbots and this goes together with the pitch for robot ethics, which (although theorists of robot/AI ethics rarely take note of this venal issue) is all about, and arguably only about, ensuring that users play by corporation-specified rules.

This question is tied to questions of ethics and technology, an ethos rehearsed now for more than a century, including Nietzsche's reflections on 'mechanical activity' which he associated with modernity as a way of numbing awareness in general, as he reflects in *Human, All Too Human*:

> One dare not to ask after the purpose of the unceasing activity of the money-gathering banker: it is irrational. The active roll as the stone rolls, following the stupidity of mechanics [*der Dummheit der Mechanik*]. (Nietzsche 1980, Vol. 2: 231)

This is an aphorism for investment bankers and might serve as a motto for those speculating on nearly anything, not only big data and bitcoin and

NFTs. From this perspective, all 'intelligence' is an automatism, including AI. Hence one may make the case for writing about Plato and AI and reading the *Timaeus* accordingly. But we want more than signs of intelligence to decipher – was there a demiurge (or creator God)? was there not a demiurge (or creator God)? We want and thus the ideal for us is exemplified by Mary Shelley's 1818 *Frankenstein or the Modern Prometheus*, just as Langdon Winner (1978, and see his 1997 summary) argued along with other authors including Coeckelbergh (2017, *sans* the least reference to Winner's critique, on the very same named theme). Post-Nietzsche, we ourselves want to be God and the allusion to the Titan is the point of Anders's Promethean shame, quite as Sartre and de Beauvoir note (see for discussion Bergoffen 2002), but for that we need proof and the proof we want would be something like life in our laboratory beakers (so far we simply fractionate extant, *already alive*, life-forms – it takes time for living systems to die – or 'hack' small machines onto insects (Tran-Ngoc, 2023) and claim the result as if we had 'invented' something rather than having mutilated an organism), or as this is imaginably easier than creating life-forms in the lab, it can suffice if our computers talk back to us, not by reading text purpose-written but as if ('as if' would be enough) announcing the singularity, again the reference to Hal in Kubrick's *2001* (1968). Above all, we want it to know, to recognise its maker (or destroyer, once again: cue Arthur C. Clarke's Hal). This is the appealing beauty of *Blade Runner* (1982), and sci-fi visions of androids who cry as we cry ('tears in the rain') and dream as we dream (in their case of 'electric sheep').

All this Nietzsche analyses by analogy with a mosquito, not unlike Wittgenstein's lion metaphor if a little less robust. Nietzsche argues, as Schopenhauer would also have argued, for intelligence everywhere, this is the nineteenth-century meaning of 'will':

> But if we could communicate with the mosquito [*Mücke*], then we would learn that he floats through the air with the same self-importance, feeling within itself the flying centre of the world. There is nothing in nature so despicable or insignificant that it cannot immediately be blown up like a bag by a slight breath of this power of knowledge... (Nietzsche 1979: 79)

What I call Nietzsche's philosophically reflective *perspectivalism* (just to distinguish this from what others call perspectivism, as this models relativism), is key to Nietzsche's epistemology, as to his cosmology, and especially his philosophy of science (see Babich 1994; 2010). Yet Nietzsche does not merely offer this reflection but follows it to what he calls its 'ultimate consequences': emphasising the trade in illusion which we have seen that he argues to be at the basis of language, which he also names 'the duty to lie according to a fixed convention, to lie with the herd and in a manner binding on everyone' (Nietzsche 1979: 84).

Here we may cite the standard quote on truth as a mobile army, intriguing for Derrida and for students of literature:

> What, then, is truth? A movable host of metaphors, metonymies, and anthropomorphisms – in short, a sum of human relations which have been poetically and rhetorically intensified, transferred, and embellished, and which after long usage seem to a people to be fixed, canonical, and binding. Truths are illusions which we have are illusions; they are that which become worn out and have been drained of sensuous force; coins which have lost their embossing and are now considered as metal and no longer as coins. (Nietzsche 1979: 84)

The same Nietzsche who invokes the mosquito or gnat's image of itself as the centre of creation and who talks of riding in one's dreams on the back of a tiger means his title (he always does): *on truth and lie*. As he will later repeat this question throughout his work, *why truth? Why not the lie?* And anyone who posts on social media or reads mainstream news (these days it being hard to tell the difference, and that is the point of AI), already agrees. Curate and be done with it! Once again: 'lying and bluffing are explicitly allowed' (Bajohr 2024). What Nietzsche calls 'the art of artifice' [*Verstellungskunst*] in the human being, Walter Kaufman's translation of choice is '*simulation*', is all around us in the digital realm: online, which is increasingly where (and how) we live.

I cited Nietzsche's reflection on mechanism in society in his *Human, All Too Human*, talking financial exchange and the banker's constant transactions and we can invoke Marx on automation more techno-socially. Today, quite apart from the growing move to digitalisation, the more to evaporate what the average person has/does not have, corporate sensibility has arranged to legislate (this is not an argument) that 'personhood' be assigned to corporations which are as a result to be granted the same rights as average citizens, abrogating in the process the very question of difference in advance.

In this vein, 'robot rights' are key and when we discuss Luddism most scholars will find themselves clucking at the workers, *Maschinenstürmer* as Anders tells us these were named, as so many peasants with sledgehammers and pitchforks, channelling Martin Luther (and the no less useful insights of Max Weber on capitalism and the protestant ethic): we assume the side of nobility and privilege, believers in sympathetic magic, all Stockholm Syndrome, we take the owners' side, the globalist, corporate side, which we are prepared to defend against the benightedly striking workers as destroying private property – which remains a sacred thing in early, middle, and late capitalism to this very day. Yet destroying property, Marx pointed out, remains the only way a revolution could ever change the world.

Nineteenth Century AI

How to connect Nietzsche, that famous child of his nineteenth century, with AI? Easy question, and easy answer because one can stipulate what one means by AI. When it comes to AI there is no need for specific scholarship, AI being largely potential imagined, not yet ready for prime time, unfinished, quite as Nietzsche says we ourselves are 'unfinished', undetermined 'animals', and thus redefinable as we go along. The beauty of writing on things that are largely potential, like writing about life after death, say, on which, as it happens, there is a certain amount in AI literature, is that one can speculate with no limitations. It's AI, no pesky or extant limitations from the real world.

It is assumed that AI needs defending (thus curmudgeons are conjured as blocking the path), and that if only 'research' were given free rein (if only said imaginary curmudgeons would stop blocking the path) all would be well, and AI, thus liberated to its imagined potential, will/would save the day. Sometimes this is a matter of the machines waking up of their own accord and sometimes, like the film cartoon Jessica Rabbit, they are just drawn or coded as if they had. In the case of the latter one may speak of 'intelligent agents', designed and bruited, fairly closely, on certain automated functions.

We know these today as AI generated prompts pop up (no one imagines that any kind of actual 'intelligence' is involved) to nudge or 'ask' us when we browse certain sites if they might be of assistance. These are there to close the deal and they are better than the cockroaches of yesteryear because, if only because, like those literally crawling bits on the screen, they serve as a reminder that one is always tracked.

In addition, there are multifarious loyalties. From *Black Mirror* to the sleek cable television 2015-2018 series *HUMⱯNS*, with a trademark style inverted 'A' for virtual, I guess, or else, as I thank Hannes Bajohr for reminding me, the universal quantifier: ∀ (it all depends on the logic background of the English adaptation of the 2012-2014 Swedish television series: Äkta människor [*Real Humans*]), humanoid robot servants to do the laundry and the shopping and 'service' the male of the house on demand, complete with the same kind of security key designed to keep this service from the more junior males in the household, all *Moses and Monotheism*. Or Ridley Scott's original, 1982 *Blade Runner*: not the rakishly appealing Harrison Ford, but Rutger Hauer's beautifully tragic, android Prometheus who realises his nature and his fate – the key to Prometheus is that he knows the future – ours and his. A double agent, a smart TV with consciousness, is what? a triple agent? But note here that I am not talking about robots for sale or actual AI – although in marketing and data collection this is already at work – but film representations as simulations of simulations.

What is the agency question when it comes to AI? *Whose* artificial design, *whose* intelligence?

What about *the* 'singularity'? Has it already happened? Did Google in fact 'wake' up and have the authorities simply denied this (denial seeming to be the rule with authority for the last four years)? Is Floridi wrong? Has ChatGPT managed the deed? Going back a bit: would that have already transpired with the Facebook experiment priming users' and, more recently, the adolescent mind (Rushe 2014, Hill 2014, Haidt 2021)? Is it still happening (are adolescents still on Facebook?)? How would we know? Would it matter?

Here it can seem that the Nietzsche we need for *Blade Runner*, once again, the 1982 original, the director's cut, or the increasingly close (in terms of the current year) *Blade Runner 2049* (note that the original film was set towards the end of what was in truth, more predictive programming, a watershed year, November 2019), whereby the '2049' sequel was itself filmed so as not to lose the sci-fi advance, in 2017. Bring on the Nietzsche of futurism, the Nietzsche of the *Will to Power*. Who cares that for Nietzsche this is more than a little complicated especially if one were concerned with his epistemology or his theory of science, his thinking on then-modern nineteenth-century machine technology, especially the printing press which Nietzsche mostly writes for and about.

Then, like many AI arguments, a trivial, barely there, tiny payoff, the AI will be the slight changes teleported into Nietzsche's style (is this so? Kittler says so, Don Ihde echoes the claim. Not all scholars would agree). And if we like the steampunk aesthetic of the design of *Blade Runner 2049* in an AI context, it trumps the dark AI realism of either version of *Ghost in the Shell*, lifted from the original *Blade Runner* as film-gospel of AI. Who wants to do the work to analyse Fritz Lang's *Metropolis* (1927) or even Kubrick's *2001: A Space Odyssey* (1968), given Harrison Ford (or Hauer as I referenced him above)? Lisa Blackman (2019) makes a pitch for *The Man Who Fell to Earth* (1976), a film that illustrates what she means by her own title: *Haunted Data* in terms of 'visitations by things not of this world'. That would be David Bowie, as Simon Critchley (2017) would agree. I'd add Jude Law, of *Gattaca* fame and star, as it were (unless, counting Haley Joel Osment, you have a thing for kids), of the 2001 film *A.I. Artificial Intelligence*. Right there in the title: must be true. Still actors fade, fall to earth – Kris Kristofferson and even Bowie – and they die.

To deal with this, CGI having clear limitations, these days we need to reduce the aura to an acoustic signal, and this worked in Kubrick's *2001*, retro-engineering the AI of the day (imaginary as it was, see again, Fig. 1). Thus one can programme AI and call that same coding 'teaching': one can reverse-engineer it (just another clue from Roswell): take it back, step by step, to a simpler intelligence, recognisable at the level of discourse and degraded voice (thus the screenplay for *2001*): Hal, barely able to say his user's name at the end. The technique works, brilliantly, depending quite as it does on the user illusion. This is imagination, sheer projection. Simulation.

This is also very efficacious. This is how phone conversations work, as Maurice Merleau-Ponty already tells us, it is also how phone sex works, even old Minitel technology as I cite Žižek in *The Hallelujah Effect* on the working effect of social media (and sex) (see Babich 2013: 2, and again, on the telephone, Babich 2021b: 308). It may be argued that this works as seduction in general works along with much prostitution (full stop). There are obvious chat room parallels, obvious bot parallels, and in the 2013 *Her*, nothing like a gender pronoun, different from Rider Haggard's *She*, to point to the myth, still crucial to male fantasies, of Pygmalion (and the sex doll industry). If one is limited to what the stage shows, photography and film, crystallising images forever, permits the permutations of projection and illusion, as Hitchcock understood. Thus less is more and Hollywood avoids hitching either Joaquin Phoenix or Scarlett Johansson to the cinematic demands of airbrushed excellence. As Adorno wrote of Greta Garbo for another generation: it's hard to live up to the ideal even when you yourself are/were that ideal.

Nietzsche argues that the ideal Plato sets into Socrates' mouth, when he speaks of the ideal friend, is tied to the lie: think of the *Republic* on friends and enemies (and here we will need Carl Schmitt). Thus Nietzsche asks if the one we take to be a friend is in truth truly as we had taken him to be? How do we know? How can we know? What if the 'friend' is not texting you back – many instances of ghosting reduce to this – but Nietzsche reminds us to think about everything necessary for the perception of friendship to begin with: more deception, along with the fantasy of beauty – lighting certainly, perspective, angle, but also disposition or mood.

For Nietzsche, for the lover, the problem is everything else that has to come into play just to begin to have the possibility for an enounter, any encounter with the beautiful. Having said that, it only complicates matters to add that this holds solely from the point of view of the spectator's aesthetic, which aesthetic Nietzsche, incorrigibly sexist even by nineteenth-century standards, calls a 'feminine aesthetic', the aesthetics of the spectator, where the whole concern is with the look of things, the point of view of the viewer (that would be the male). For most philosophers, the distinction leaves us blinking: for what other aesthetic than the viewpoint of the viewer could there be? For Nietzsche, there is also the, masculine artist's or creator's aesthetic, and he is on about this from the beginning to the very end of his philosophical life. Can AI help us here?

First things first.

AI promises, so Nick Bostrom tells us, a certain advantage, quite to the specs pitched above, lots of potential 'impact' there, crucial for academics worrying about jobs and promotions along with, as Bostrom also rightly emphasises, 'risks'.

A cliché in talking tech-pitches – recall the parenthetical curmudgeons referenced above – is to engage in battle contra the nay-sayers who have been with us always: cue Plato's *Phaedrus* starring, towards the end of the dialogue, well after all the speeches on eros, a certain doubting Thamus. And by definition, naysayers overlook the positive.

This is Nietzsche's shell game: 'If he will not be satisfied with truth in the form of a tautology, that is to say, if he will not be content with empty husks, then he will always exchange truths for illusions' (Nietzsche 1979: 81). Thus it can be argued that the only reason we do not have 'crispr'd' babies *yet* or immortality *yet*, i.e., because this is what we imagine would be the result of genetically modified children, i.e., perfect human babies, or life forever for those with the wherewithal to buy the bio-physiological substances needed, is owing to outdated regulations contra research. Remove those regulations, like gain of function research restrictions, either by changing the laws or outsourcing the work to labs in distant places (like Ukraine or elsewhere), and the benefits would pay dividends. And one can hardly dispute the dividends even if some will wish to quibble about 'whose' bottom line ends up being enhanced.

When it comes to Nietzsche and AI, the concern may be the transhumanism connection, the posthuman, overhuman, overlord. When Nietzsche wrote of the human being in Zarathustra's Prologue as something to be 'overcome', as Michel Haar and other Francophone scholars noted in a small tradition of thinking Nietzsche's notion of the 'earth', and a loyalty to the same, one that could be, but has rarely been, connected with the ecological ethos of the same era. Back to the land: that would be the wonderfully French idea of bioculture, quite established when it comes to viniculture, planting biodynamically in accord with animal rhythms and the phases of the moon, to be considered in the context of the reflection, from the perspective of that same earth, arguing that the human is the 'skin disease of the earth' or else, once again, that the human being is the unfinished animal, the undetermined animal – *noch nicht festgestellte Thier* – one has articulated a critical idea for those theorists of the Frankfurt School who read Nietzsche.

These are complex notions even if some scholars are cavalier about details. As the origin, with a little infusion of Nazi ideology, and the DC comic sensibility of the man in tights, with an S on his chest, made of steel, leaping skyscrapers in a single bound – the flying part was an upgrade – Superman (see again: Babich 2015). There are many Nietzsches, and like the 'digital Dionysus', the AI Nietzsche is not among the most recondite.

Like a good deal of philosophical ethics, we talk about what promising *ought* to be, what love, what empathy, integrity, bravery, etc., *ought* to be, and in the case of Nietzsche, the less one knows about Nietzsche, the easier. Thus for the many who write about Nietzsche and transhumanism, any details that don't fit one's scheme, one simply tosses. This tactic is respectable in analytic philosophy in reading Nietzsche (one will say one is only concerned with one's own argument), but it is especially dangerous when it comes to AI. Thus in political theory, Apolline Tallandier draws on the ideal ethos of transhumanism, claiming to offer a survey while skipping most (nearly all) of the literature, a considered tactic for an essay unencumbered by too much Nietzsche not to mention Nietzsche scholarship, citing in place of all or any of that the 'cryonist' Max More. It is to the point that Nietzsche foregrounds the desire to cut off one's head to see what the world might look like without it, which last tactic, perhaps coincidentally, seems to be the aim of cryonics. (See More 1990 and 1994 and, further, citing Judith Shklar whilst missing Nietzschean social theorists like the Shklar student, Tracy B. Strong (Tallandier 2021)).

Coincidence may offer a solution. Nietzsche raises the question of the spider, that is the universe as *Spielwerk* or cosmic music box, again along with the concept of mechanical activity: we already noted 'the money-gathering' activity of the banker as 'irrational'. And Nietzsche has to be talking banking, as the point, so Aristotle reminds us, of the 'life of moneymaking' is its pointlessness: money is not an end, it's a means.

Nietzsche's focus on mechanical activity includes its convenient almost ASMR side-effect, that of deadening consciousness. AI as genie, AI as quasi-deity, as super or transhuman aspect, the borg quality of AI, is not concordant with even the mass market image of the Nietzschean *Übermensch* because the latter from Nietzsche's point of view is less cartoon hero and more piece of vanity: a horrorshow far from some future dream but an always-already-with-us, inner Callicles.

But this is already Nietzsche's point when he notes at the outset of the second book of *The Gay Science* that nature as such, the same source of Kantian beauty already mentioned (Heidegger likes to speak of φύσις) is a fantasy construct: invented or created, like women out of a rib of the male ideal, and we are not surprised to recall that Nietzsche is Simone de Beauvoir's source for her famous coinage: '*On ne naît pas femme on le devient*'. (See for further references, Babich 2023b.)

AI also seems to have a debt to Vico where Vico logically articulates (barring a god-trick) what Kant also says as Nietzsche repeats: we can *only* know what we make. We can only know, with necessity or certainty, just what we put into things and on the basis of that qua axiomatic construct we have what counts, and the only thing that *can* count, as science.

Nietzsche takes the point and runs with it, inexorable: how could we know at all apart from what is then a fundamentally ineluctable anthropomorphisation: to know at all, to reason at all, to deploy logic and mathematics, not to speak of physics and chemistry, we work with, we 'use things that do not exist'. Here I cite *The Gay Science* as Nietzsche articulates Kant's schematism in an aphorism titled (obviously) '*Ursache und Wirkung*':

> 'Cause' and 'effect' as the saying goes; but we have merely perfected the image of becoming but without getting behind that image. […] Quality, for example, appears a 'miracle' as ever before in every chemical process, likewise locomotion; no one has 'explained' a push. But how could we ever explain anything? We operate only with things that do not exist [*Wir operiren mit lauter Dingen, die es nicht giebt*]. (Nietzsche 1980, Vol 3: 472-473)

This could seem hyperbolic but Nietzsche is talking factive, observed cosmology which is why I began with his metaphor for the universe as music box, as he here cites those things our maths and physics teachers define as 'ideal'. Thus Nietzsche counts off: 'lines, planes, bodies, atoms, divisible time spans, divisible spaces. How should explanation be at all possible when we make everything into an *image* [*Bild*], into our image!' (Ibid.) Because 'what there is' excludes any simple or ideal duality of cause and effect, there is, Nietzsche says, a continuum we can barely perceive. Thus he says it would suffice 'to regard science as the best confirmed anthropomorphisation of things [*Anmenschlichung der Dinge*]', observing that we learn to describe ourselves better as we learn to describe the course of natural events. (Ibid.)

We remain ensconced in a fairly archaic, frozen vision of autonomy and subjectivity, somewhere between Plato's Socratic turn and Aristotle's doxa, all the while talking of the panopticon and the body without organs. But it is the notion of the subject that is for Nietzsche a question.

Maurizio Lazzarato, the Italian 'videophilosopher' (as he names himself via the title of his book) points via Félix Guattari to the machinism Nietzsche invokes as the machinic element of 'enslavement' (Lazzarato 2019, 179), and one almost thinks that Lazzaratto is on about the master and slave hardware switches already mentioned, so much hardware nostalgia.

Talking of 'machines that crystallize time', Lazzarato continues citing Guattari's *La Révolution moléculaire*:

> [W]e are subject to television as long as we use and consume ('it is you, dear viewers, who create television …') The technical machine is the medium between two subjects. But we are enslaved by television as human machines as long as we are no longer simply users and consumers, nor even subjects who are supposed to 'manufacture' it, but when we become its intrinsic components, its input, outputs, and feedback, which belong to the machine and longer to the manner of producing or using it. (Lazzarato 2019: 179)

Nietzsche's question of the subject concerns ourselves/everything not ourselves. Thus, speaking of the cosmos, the cosmic play of 'the whole musical box [*das ganze Spielwerk*]' eternally repeats after its fashion, which may never be named a melody' (Nietzsche 1980, Vol. 3: 468).

For this Nietzsche draws inspiration from Kant, arguing with and against him regarding the science of his day for this account of the 'astral order' of the Milky Way, including his suggestion that it could be a comological singularity, for all we know, 'an exception' (See for discussion Babich 2021d). Nietzsche's argument here is not pro design, be it intelligent or otherwise, but he repeats the point in *Beyond Good and Evil*: the universe 'has a "necessary" and "calculable" course yet not because laws prevail in it but because laws are utterly lacking, and every power [*jede Macht*] at every moment draws its ultimate consequences [*ihre letzte Consequenz zieht*]' (Nietzsche 1980, Vol. 5: 37).

The point is complicated. Far from the concept or ideal of 'law', Nietzsche reminds us, the only thing that rules in nature – note again that Nietzsche is a classical philologist – is ἀνάγκη (necessity). Framing the same point in *The Gay Science*, Nietzsche had already reflected on the metonymic seduction of the notion of 'law', writing: 'there is no one who commands, no one who obeys, no one who trespasses. Once you know that there are no purposes [*keine Zwecke*], you also know that there is no accident [*keinen Zufall*]' (Nietzsche 1980, Vol 3: 468). In *Twilight of the Idols*, Nietzsche offers what is perhaps his most powerful insight contra AI, that is 'the *innocence* of becoming [*die Unschuld des Werdens*]' (Nietzsche 1980, Vol 6: 95). If many scholars who write on *amor fati* and eternal recurrence miss this point, Nietzsche explains: 'One is necessary; one is a piece of fate, one belongs to the whole, one *is* in the whole – there exists nothing which could judge, measure, compare, condemn the whole […] *But nothing exists apart from the whole*'. (Ibid.)

What we have instead of the (illusory) ideal of 'the cosmos as a unity' be it as 'sensorium' (that would be Newton) or 'spirit' (that would be Hegel, and all his works), Nietzsche names our 'aesthetic anthropomorphisations' (Nietzsche 1980, Vol 3: 473).

Earlier, in *Human, All Too Human*, Nietzsche had reminded us that efforts to see what the world might look like from 'nowhere', as Nagel says, that is the polite formula of analytic philosophy, requires the echo of cryonic decapitation already referenced above:

> We regard all things through the human head [*Menschenkopf*] and cannot cut off this head; while however the question persists what would still remain of the world if one had cut it off. (Nietzsche 1980, Vol 2: 29)

We are condemned to hermeneutic phenomenology, whether we know what this is or not, and we continually get in our own way.

Here with respect to the artifice aspect that is key to AI – though that too is a question for philosophy: having invented artificial intelligence, has one thereby invented what Nietzsche always called, echoing Aristotle and Rousseau, a 'second nature', has one, in other words, invented life? In the mimetic avarice that is the human desire to be God, so Descartes cogitates at the beginning of modern philosophy, he, Descartes, could have done it better: creation, Descartes argues (and Ray Kurzweil and Elon Musk and Yuval Noah Harari would agree), *needs* an update.

It is Descartes who remains the patron saint of AI *and* GMO *and* transhumanism: what is the difference between artificial and non-artificial anything?

The music box aphorism, *Heaven forfend* [*Hüten wir uns*] – 'Let us beware' in the standard translation – is a sustained effort at disabusing humanist presumption. I note that Nietzsche claimed to have been the first to put the very idea of science in question; this a post-critical point given Nietzsche's literal references to Kant, claiming that he had raised the question of science as a problem, as he says, *as* a question (for discussion see Babich 2024: 135). For Nietzsche, 'the science' methodologically speaking, is philology, that is the precisely formulaic study of Classical Greek, Classical Latin, which is, as Nietzsche repeatedly argues, a training in the art of absolute lockstep: unthinking, a training in automatism (see, again, Benne 2023). As professors or teachers, whenever we 'teach to the test' or for the exam or the doctoral viva or even for the sake of interview skills, we are familiar with the tactic.

The focus on science continues in *Beyond Good and Evil* (which should be read as a Prelude to AI Philosophy, as he subtitles it *a Philosophy of the Future*) is still a focus positively exemplifying 'stupidity, stupidity, stupidity', as Nietzsche consistently reflected 'the good stupid will to 'believe' – which may be related to Coleridge's 'suspension of disbelief'. In this sense, Nietzsche goes on to reflect:

> our senses learn late and never completely learn to be subtle, true, careful organs of understanding. Our eyes find it more comfortable to react to any given occasion by producing once again an image frequently already produced than by holding fast to what is different and new in an impression... (Niezsche 1980, Vol. 5: 113)

It is easy for readers in different languages to spin off into their own linguistically tuned metonymies but Nietzsche writing as classical philologist in German, uses a word translators typically leave in German [*Armbrust*] in order to render the Latin *arcuballista*, i.e., a Roman crossbow, and Nietzsche's point is on point, that is, free association on the terms of the German language – '*so machte sich zum Beispiel der Deutsche ehemals aus dem gehörten arcubalista das Wort Armbrust zurecht*'. Across a translatorly divide it is more familiar to hear a foreign word as if spoken in one's own language: 'To hear something new is awkward and difficult for the ear' (Nietzsche 1980, Vol 5: 113).

In general, and the example Nietzsche turns to here echoes his earlier Goethian leaf reference (noted above) in *On Truth and Lie*, now with respect to a tree (Nietzsche favors the tree metaphor) and the example, familiar given concerns with screen time, regarding the cognitive physiology/psychology of reading/scanning. Throughout Nietzsche focuses on the illusion, the deception, *the lie*, just as already cited above and here to complete the reference, it is nearly AI, it is certainly automatic:

> As little as a reader today collectively reads all the individual words (or indeed the syllables) of a page – much rather he takes about five words in twenty haphazardly and 'guesses' their

probable meaning – just as little do we see a tree exactly and entire with regard to its leaves, branches, colour, shape [*Gestalt*]; it is so much easier for us to fantasize an approximation [*ein Ungefähr*] of a tree. Even in the midst of the most uncommon experiences we proceed in the same way: *we poetize for ourselves* [*wir erdichten uns*] the greater part of the experience and can scarcely be compelled not to contemplate some event as its 'inventor' ['*Erfinder*']. This is all to say: fundamentally and aboriginally we are – *used to lying*. Or, to express it more virtuously and hypocritically, in short more pleasantly: *one is much more of an artist than one realises* [*man ist viel mehr Künstler als man Weiss*]. (Nietzsche 1980, Vol. 5: 113-114, emphasis added)

Herewith we are back to the Turing toaster, the plush toy for the elderly ladies who are given, quite as children are given pacifiers or iPads in place of parental attention to quiet their claims on family members for such attention, or who, perhaps, have no such family members, family being a phantom concept in any case, not unlike Descartes' phantom limb. Same diff, were this a different essay on the sex dolls that did a smash business, so I am told, during lockdown along with every other deliverable commodity item.

The point to be made, this is how one goes about constructing a usable 'user illusion', is that this same success led to the urgent need for robot ethics: one wants, the corporation needs, tractable users, users who play by the rules. Users must never (thus the *ethical* imperative) treat these products as heterosexual men have traditionally treated their woman companions: the damages would be unimaginable in a strikingly short time. The user experience would be better if the user can be programmed to use the device only so and not otherwise, the last being crucial for a sustainable business model.

Nietzsche is all about the projection element in reading a text (we think, at least to begin with, that we already know what the author is saying), looking at a picture (similarly, especially if we have never taken a course in art history, much less *Kunstwissenschaft*, we assume we know what we are looking at), talking with someone (a very exotic reference if we think of zoom conferences and at the heart of social distancing as, clearly, such a thing as physical presence, one on one, has subversive elements). Nietzsche is not anticipating lockdown's prohibitions or the need for a Covid mask but simply pointing to complexities in face-to-face interaction. Let's reread the extended aphorism I've been quoting from *Beyond Good and Evil*:

> – In a lively conversation I often see before me the face of the person with whom I am speaking so clearly and subtlety determined by the thought he is expressing or which I believe has been called up in him that this degree of clarity [*Grad von Deutlichkeit*] far surpasses the power of my capacity of vision [*die Kraft meines*

Sehvermögens] – so that the fine play of the facial muscles and the expression of the eyes must have been *confabulated* [*hinzugedichtet*] by me. Probably the person was making an entirely different face or none at all. Nietzsche 1980, Vol. 5: 114, emphasis added)

It gets more complicated.

Thus elsewhere I explore Nietzsche's corollary as one might note, we do prefer the fantasy, the memory as we might imagine that, of perfect communion: one heart, one soul, illusory as that has to be. Thus Nietzsche reminds us that in general, whether we are talking paintings or musical compositions, or human beings, *we*, that is, most people, *prefer the copy to the original*. We like things to be as we imagine them to be. And AI is custom made for that.

Pindar's Ixion and Nephele: Embracing the Dream or Becoming the One You Are

I have a final section, with clouds, to take the argument back, as everything has to go back – assuming we mean to read Nietzsche hermeneutically – to ancient Greece, ca. 5th or even 7th Century, BCE.

The beauty of the digital is the transformation of time: there is no presence of anyone or anything, no other to ourselves than ourselves to ourselves staring through a frame, a screen, at a simulation to which one can tune in and out as one likes. Consciousness and intentionality follow suit, which is an aspect of what Guattari calls crystallisation and which I elsewhere retrace with reference to Merleau-Ponty's differently articulated perceptual phenomenology qua 'crystal lamellae'. I noted that AI may be regarded, philosophically speaking, as a variation on the problem of other minds and we find this already in Descartes as in Plato. Instructively, Kant does not try to deal with the problem but rather, not unlike the way he concedes Hume's critique of causality only to make that critique redundant thus to sidestep via the schematism, space and time and the general *a prioricity* of 'knowing' the empirical world qua enabling condition for the very possibility of experience as such, Kant relies on the categorical imperative applicable to every being from extraterrestrials to, as he here specifies, 'the holy one of the Gospels', thus an imperative which would, perforce, include AI. To this extent, robots/AI would not have any of the rights their owners might care to legislate on their behalf, but they would be no less categorically bound. To this extent, Kant's laws of robotics might outdo Asimov's and possibly even David Gunkel's (2024).

I have been quoting Nietzsche's universe as music box, even though he tells us that it is neither an organism (here referring to Plato's *Timaeus*) nor a 'machine' (referring to La Mettrie as to Kant-Laplace) as both terms, organism/machine, are too 'honorific'. For Nietzsche, among all the planets and galaxies in the Milky Way, ours could be an utter exception, whereby all the order we see given a Kantian 'glance into the Milky Way', as Kant says, all phenomena thereby saved by Kepler and Copernicus might remain quite as appearance yet this could also be 'exceptional' such that 'this order and the relative duration that depends on it have made possible an exception of exceptions: the formation of the organic' (Nietzsche 1980, Vol 3: 472).

Nietzsche appeals to no secret account to be born from a future science. Thus Nietzsche draws on the same science leading to the formulation of Kant's original theory of 'milky ways and nebulae' quite in concord with the later discoveries of Herschel (and Laplace), on the genesis of the solar system, not to mention the second law of thermodynamics, all of which would be cutting edge cosmology. Thus Nietzsche's references invoke, apart from Kant (I argue that one should consider reading the axiomatician and astronomer Rudolf Kurth, see Babich 2021d) a forgotten technoscience nomenclatura (unless you do history of late nineteenth-century cosmology), once again with reference to Kant and Herschel and Laplace but also Lambert and Mayer and Avenarius and Mach in addition to Eduard von Hartman, Eugen Dühring, Hermann von Helmholtz, and so on.

Thereby Nietzsche introduces more than the AI Singularity, and along with Kurzweil one can add the inventor of the term, the San Diego computer scientist and sci fi author, Vernor Vinge (surely a perfect candidate to write his next novels using ChatGPT): machines waking up in the vision we have of ourselves, Junior Birdman style, as semi-divine beings, breathing life into our test tubes or into our semicondutors or circuit boards or as that turns out to be fairly doable and not incidentally comparable to random tosses, ouiji board style, data, algorithms, smart machines, quantum dots, lipid nanoparticles unfurling, 'smart dust' building nanomachines (see Babich 2021c: 254, 258).

Nietzsche reminds us of the special gift that is intelligence: exceptionally talented as we are at projection: confabulating, we instill our phantasmata quite as we imagine them, straight into whatever phantom we embrace.

To this extent, if the 'glance into the Milky Way' is taken from Kant's physico-theological demonstration of deity, the metaphor of projection is not Nietzsche's own. This he borrows from Pindar's Second Pythian, a locus we know in connection with the poet's rueful word: *become the one you are*. There, the poet, dismayed by a client who commissioned only subsequently to decline Pindar's ode, relates the myth of Ixion when he, forgetting his station, embraced his cloud-Hera who was not Hera herself (the cloud had her own name, *Nephele*), from which congress – this being the secret to *Blade Runner 2049* – was engendered a monster who bred the race of centaurs, mating with horses: Pindar's 'Magnesian Mares', Ixion's once-removed bastard progeny.

There are details. Hera's husband was Zeus, and it matters that the Greeks had a long tradition of stone sex dolls and of sex with statues (*agalmatophilia*), implicit in Nietzsche's rebuke to his realists as the various images of Sais counted as such. Nietzsche's still talking about Sais, usually kept veiled to keep the youth under control, but the point is that no one ever comes near anything but a phantom of their own confabulation, all of us are so many 'artists in love' – as Nietzsche is persuaded that much of love is idealising, poetic projection, invention:

> But even in your unveiled state, are you not still highly passionate and obscure creatures, as compared to fishes, and even more to an artist in love? – and what is 'reality' for an artist in love? You still carry around those estimates of things that have their origins in the passions and loves of earlier centuries. Even yet does your sobriety embody a secret and inextinguishable drunkenness. Your love of 'reality' for example – oh, that is a primeval 'love' [*eine alte uralte 'Liebe'*] (Nietzsche 1980, Vol. 3: 421)

Projecting constantly, we create constantly and as creators, Nietzsche urges us to be mindful, and this is the point, as we have seen, of his reflection on our poetic powers of confabulation, that we are always much more artist than not.

Key to AI, we believe in the illusion we have made whilst forgetting that qua creators we play the roles of both Zeus *and* Ixion, we are Pindar *and* we are Nietzsche.

Once again this is Nietzsche's music box – think dancing figurines. Beyond this Nietzsche's reflection connects to chemistry, organic and inorganic:

> How alien and superior we are with respect to the dead, the inorganic, and all the while we are up to three-quarters of a water column [*eine Wassersäule*], and have inorganic salts in us, which may do more for our well being and woes than the entirety of living society! (Nietzsche 1980, Vol 9: 486)

For Nietzsche, in our minds (and this note is fairly cryptic) we have nothing in common with 'dead nature', we are 'superior'. Later Nietzsche will invoke twittering birds to whisper: 'you are other, you are higher', but here the point is that there is a continuum between the organic and the inorganic and Nietzsche's point again is that we are more artist than we know.

To this extent, the problem with AI for Nietzsche corresponds to the problem with one's own intelligence: to know oneself – Nietzsche says we do not – and to know the other, is part and parcel of the general philosophic project and legacy of perceiving reason/rationality in the universe. Thus the music box.

We do not know ourselves, we've never sought ourselves, we don't know our friends, and overtures of friendship offered once can never again be offered, not in the same way, 'even should one want to'. This is not for nothing as there is no one there and it is hard not to think of ghosting when Nietzsche writes of an 'unsuccessful attempt', having made an overture in response to a sign of interest: 'Immediately, you did not want to anymore; and when I asked you again you remained silent' (Nietzsche 1980, Vol 3: 388).

We have never succeeded in knowing, seeking, ourselves. For us, an invented, *Artificial* Intelligence, seems just the ticket. But illusion, as cognitive psych reminds us, like Nietzsche's interpretation, remains even when you know it. As he writes ca. 1881: *Knowing the error does not eliminate it. [Wissen um das Irren hebt es nicht auf!]* (Nietzsche 1980, Vol 9: 504) And so we conclude where we began, with Nietzsche on truth and lie, emphasising not truth but the lie, the illusion, error, as the condition of life at its deepest foundations.

Works Cited

Anders, Günther. 1956. *Die Antiquiertheit des Menschen. Über die Seele im Zeitalter der zweiten industriellen Revolution*. Munich: Beck.

Anders, Günther. 1972. *Endzeit und Zeitenende. Gedanken über die atomare Situation*. Munich: Beck.

Anders, Günther. 'On Promethean Shame.' In: Christopher John Müller, *Prometheanism: Technology, Digital Culture and Human Obsolescence*. London: Rowman & Littlefield, 2016. 29-53.

Anders, Günther. 2019. 'Language and End Time (Sections I, IV and V of '*Sprache und Endzeit*')', trans. Christopher John Müller, *Thesis Eleven*, Vol. 153: 134-140.

Babich, Babette. 2024. 'Crisis and Twilight in Heidegger's "Nietzsche's Word 'God is Dead'".' In: Holger Zaborowski, ed., *Martin Heidegger: Holzwege – Klassiker auslegen*. Berlin: De Gruyter. 135-154.

Babich, Babette. 2023a. 'Nietzsche and AI: On ChatGPT and Nietzsche's Psychology of Illusion', *Philosophical Salon: Blog of the Los Angeles Review of Books*. 19 June. Online: https://thephilosophicalsalon.com/nietzsche-and-ai-on-chatgpt-and-the-psychology-of-illusion/.

Babich, Babette. 2023b. 'Between Nietzsche and de Beauvoir: Becoming Woman.' *Estudios Nietzsche: Nietzsche y la Mujer*, 23 (2023). 15-45.

Babich, Babette. 2023c. 'Gnosticism, Political Theory and Apocalypse: Jacob Taubes and Günther Anders, Tracy Strong and Carl Schmitt.' *Philosophy & Social Criticism*. Online: https://doi.org/10.1177/01914537231203551.

Babich, Babette. 2022. *Günther Anders' Philosophy of Technology. From Phenomenology to Critical Theory*. London: Bloomsbury.

Babich, Babette. 2021a. 'Günther Anders's Epitaph for Aikichi Kuboyama', *Journal of Continental Philosophy*, 2/1: 141-157.

Babich, Babette. 2021b. 'On Necropolitics and Techno-Scotosis.' *Philosophy Today*, 65/2: 305-324.

Babich, Babette. 2021c. 'Pseudo-Science and "Fake" News: "Inventing"' Epidemics and the Police State.' In: Irene Strasser/Martin Dege, eds.,

The Psychology of Global Crises and Crisis Politics Intervention, Resistance, Decolonization. London: Springer. 241-272.

Babich, Babette. 2021d. 'On the Very Idea of a Philosophy of Science: On Chemistry and Cosmology in Nietzsche and Kant.' *Axiomathes. Epistemologia,* Vol. 31 (December): 703-726.

Babich, Babette. 2020. 'Blood for the Ghosts: Reading Ruin's *Being With the Dead* With Nietzsche', *History and Theory.* Vol. 59, No. 2 (June): 255-269.

Babich, Babette. 2019a. 'On Passing as Human and Robot Love.' In: Carlos Prado, ed., *How Technology is Changing Human Behaviour.* Santa Barbara: Praeger. 17-26.

Babich, Babette. 2019b. 'Screen Autism, Cellphone Zombies, and GPS Mutes' in: Carlos Prado, ed., *How Technology is Changing Human Behaviour.* Santa Barbara: Praeger. 65-71.

Babich, Babette. 2019c. 'Radio Ghosts: Phenomenology's Phantoms and Digital Autism', *Thesis Eleven,* 153/1: 57-74.

Babich, Babette. 2019d. 'On The Poetry and Music of Science: Whose poetry? Whose music?': https://www.academia.edu/42345690/On_The_Poetry_and_Music_of_Science_Whose_poetry_Whose_music_2019_.

Babich, Babette. 2012a. 'Martin Heidegger on Günther Anders and Technology: On Ray Kurzweil, Fritz Lang, and Transhumanism', *Journal of the Hannah Arendt Centre for Politics and Humanities at Bard College,* 2 (2012): 122-144. Reprinted 2022.

Babich, Babette, 2012b. ,Geworfenheit und prometheische Scham im Zeitalter der transhumanen Kybernetik. Technik und Machenschaft bei Martin Heidegger, Fritz Lang und Günther Anders'. In: Christoph Streckhardt, ed., *Die Neugier des Glücklichen.* Weimar: Bauhaus Universitätsverlag, 2012. 63-91.

Babich, Babette, 2017a. 'Robot Sex, Roombas, and Alan Rickman', *de Gruyter Conversations: Philosophy & History,* 17 August 2017. Online.

Babich, Babette. 2016a. „Körperoptimierung im digitalen Zeitalter, verwandelte Zauberlehrlinge, und künftige Übermenschsein'. In: Andreas Beinsteiner and Tanja Kohn, eds., *Körperphantasien. Technisierung – Optimierung – Transhumanismus.* Innsbruck: Universtitätsverlag Innsbruck. 203-226.

Babich, Babette. 2016b. 'Texts and Tweets: On *The Rules* of the Game', *The Philosophical Salon: Los Angeles Review of Books,* 30 May 2016. Online. https://thephilosophicalsalon.com/texts-and-tweets-on-the-rules-of-the-game/.

Babette, Babette. 2016c. 'Teledildonics and Transhumanism', *The Philosophical Salon: Los Angeles Review of Books*, 20 December. Online: https://thephilosophicalsalon.com/teledildonics-and-transhumanism/.

Babich, Babette. 2015. 'Friedrich Nietzsche and the Posthuman/Transhuman in Film and Television.' In: Michael Hauskeller, Thomas D. Philbeck, and Curtis D. Carbonell, eds., *Palgrave Handbook of Posthumanism in Film and Television*. London: Palgrave/Macmillan. 45-54.

Babich, Babette. 2013. *The Hallelujah Effect*. London: Ashgate. Routledge reprint: 2016.

Babich, Babette and Chris Bateman. 2017a. 'The Hallelujah Effect.' October 24. Online: https://onlyagame.typepad.com/only_a_game/2017/10/babich-and-bateman-the-hallelujah-effect.html.

Babich, Babette and Chris Bateman. 2017b. 'Touching Robots.' *Only a Game.* 23 February. https://onlyagame.typepad.com/only_a_game/2017/02/babich-and-bateman-touching-robots.html

Babich, Babette. 2013. 'Angels, the Space of Time, and Apocalyptic Blindness: On Günther Anders' Endzeit–Endtime.' *Etica & Politica / Ethics & Politics*, XV, 2. 144-174.

Babich, Babette. 2011. 'Sloterdijk's Cynicism: Diogenes in the Marketplace' in: Stuart Elden, ed., *Sloterdijk Now*. Oxford: Polity.

Babich, Babette. 2010a. *Nietzsches Wissenschaftsphilosophie. »Die Wissenschaft unter der Optik des Künstlers zu sehn, die Kunst aber unter der des Lebens«*, Harald Seubert (with the author), trans. Oxford/Bern: Peter Lang.

Babich, Babette. 2010b. 'Towards a Critical Philosophy of Science: Continental Beginnings and Bugbears, Whigs, and Waterbears.' *International Studies in the Philosophy of Science*. Vol. 24, No. 4 (Dec.): 343:391.

Babich, Babette. 2007. *Words in Blood, Like Flowers: Philosophy and Poetry, Music and Eros in Hölderlin, Nietzsche, and Heidegger*. Albany: State University of New York Press. [2006]

Babich, Babette. 2005. 'The Science of Words or Philology: Music in The Birth of Tragedy and the Alchemy of Love in The Gay Science.' In: Tiziana Andina, ed., *Revista di estetica*. n.s. 28, XLV. Turin: Rosenberg & Sellier. 47-78.

Babich, Babette. 1994. *Nietzsche's Philosophy of Science*. Reflecting Science on the Ground of Art and Life. Albany: State University of New York Press.

Bajohr, Hannes. 2024. 'On Artificial and Post-artificial Texts: Machine Learning and the Reader's Expectations of Literary and Non- literary Writing.' Poetics Today. Vol. 45, No. 2: 331–361.

Bajohr, Hannes. 2023a. *(Berlin, Miami)*. Berlin: Rohstoff Verlag.

Bajohr, Hannes. 2023b. New Novel: (Berlin, Miami). Online (author's description): https://hannesbajohr.de/en/2023/09/25/new-novel-berlin-miami/.

Barth, Thomas. 2018. 'Kittler und künstliche Intelligenz: Über die Verquickung von Medientheorie und Macht', *Berliner Gazette*, 19.07. Online: https://berlinergazette.de/kittler-und-kuenstliche-intelligenz/.

Bassett, Caroline. 2019. 'The Computational Therapeutic: Exploring Weizenbaum's ELIZA as a History of the Present', *AI & SOCIETY*, Vol. 34: 803-812.

Bateman, Chris. 2017. 'No-one Plays Alone.' *Transactions of the Digital Games Research Association*, Vol. 3, No. 2 (September): 5-36.

Bateman, Chris. (ed.) 2021. *Game Writing: Narrative Skills for Videogames*. London: Bloomsbury.

Bateman, Chris. 2023. 'Laws of Robotics: Kant's Laws of Robotics versus Asimov's – Whose Robots Would We Prefer to Live With…?' *Stranger Worlds*. 20 June. Online: https://strangerworlds.substack.com/p/laws-of-robotics

Benne, Christian. 2023. 'Overcoming Declinism: Style and Philology in Nietzsche', *Nineteenth-Century Prose*, Vol. 50, Nos. 1 and 2 (Spring/Fall): 145-170.

Bergoffen, Debra. 2002. 'Simone de Beauvoir and Jean-Paul Sartre: Woman, Man, and the Desire to be God.' *Constellations*. Vol. 9, Issue 3: 409-418.

Blackman, Lisa. 2019. *Haunted Data: Affect, Transmedia, Weird Science*. London: Bloomsbury,

Bostrom, Nick and Eliezer Yudkowsky. 2011. 'The Ethics of Artificial Intelligence.' In: Keith Frankish and William M. Ramsey, eds. *The Cambridge Handbook of Artificial Intelligence*. Cambridge: Cambridge University Press. 316-334.

Bourdieu, Pierre. 1984. *Distinction: A Social Critique of the Judgement of Taste*. Richard Nice, trans. Cambridge Harvard University Press. [1979]

Coeckelberg, Mark. 2020. *AI Ethics*. Cambridge: MIT Press.

Coeckelberg, Mark. 2017. *Romantic Cyborgs*. Cambridge: MIT Press.

Conlen, Matthew and Jeffrey Heer. 2022. 'Data Stories & Explorable Explanations', ArXiv. May 2022. Preprint: https://arxiv.org/abs/2205.09858.

Conlen, Matthew and Jeffrey Heer. 2018. 'A Markup Language for Authoring and Publishing Interactive Articles on the Web.' *Proceedings of the 31st Annual ACM Symposium on User Interface Software and Technology*: 977-989.

Critchley, Simon. 2017. *On Bowie*. London: Profile.

Darragh, John J. and Ian H. Witten. 1992. *The Reactive Keyboard*. Cambridge: Cambridge University Press.

Derrida, Jacques. 1994. 'Nietzsche and the Machine', with Richard Beardsworth, *Journal of Nietzsche Studies*, No. 7 (Spring 1994): 7-66.

Duffy, Brian R. and Karolina Zawieska. 2012. 'Suspension of Disbelief in Social Robotics.' *The 21st IEEE International Symposium on Robot and Human Interactive Communication. September 9-13*. Paris, France.484-489.

Duffy, Brian R. 2003. 'Anthropomorphism and The Social Robot.' *Special Issue on Socially Interactive Robots, Robotics and Autonomous Systems*, No. 42/3-4, 31 March. 170-190.

Floridi, Luciano. 2023. 'AI as Agency Without Intelligence: On ChatGPT, Large Language Models, and Other Generative Models.' *Philosophy and Technology*, 16 February. Online: https://papers.ssrn.com/sol3/papers.cfm?abstract_id=4358789 .

Floridi, Luciano and M. Chiriatti. 2020. 'GPT-3: Its Nature, Scope, Limits, and Consequences', *Minds and Machines*, 30/4: 681-694.

Frith, Jordan and Jason Kalin, 2016. 'Here, I Used to Be: Mobile Media and Practices of Place-Based Digital Memory.' *Space & Culture*, 19, no. 1: 43-55.

Fuchs, Christian, 2017. 'Günther Anders' Undiscovered Critical Theory of Technology in the Age of Big Data Capitalism.' *tripleC*, 15, 2: 582-611.

Guardian Staff and Agency. 2022. 'Google fires software engineer who claims AI chatbot is sentient. Company said Blake Lemoine violated Google policies and that his claims were "wholly unfounded".' *The Guardian*. 23 July. Online, https://www.theguardian.com/technology/2022/jul/23/google-fires-software-engineer-who-claims-ai-chatbot-is-sentient.

Gadamer, Hans-Georg. 1987. *The Relevance of the Beautiful*, trans. Nicholas Walker. Cambridge: Cambridge University Press.

Gebru, Timnit. 2022. 'Effective Altruism Is Pushing a Dangerous Brand of "AI Safety"', *Wired* (20 November). Online: https://www.wired.com/story/effective-altruism-artificial-intelligence-sam-bankman-fried/

Gerber, Gustav. 1871. *Die Sprache als Kunst. Erster Band*. Bromberg: Mittlerische Buchandlung.

Gerber, Gustav. 1873. *Die Sprache als Kunst. Zweiter Band. Erster Hälfte*. Bromberg: Mittlerische Buchandlung.

Gertz, Nolen. 2018. *Nihilism and Technology*. Lanham: Rowman and Littlefield.

Gordon, Rachel. 2022. 'ELIZA wins Peabody Award', *MIT CSAIL*, 24 March. Online: https://www.csail.mit.edu/news/eliza-wins-peabody-award.

Gunkel, David. 2024. *Robot Rights*. Cambridge: MIT Press. [2018]

Haase, Ullrich. 1999. 'Nietzsche's Critique of Technology: A Defence of Phenomenology Against Modern Machinery.' In: Babette Babich, ed., *Nietzsche, Epistemology, and Philosophy of Science: Nietzsche and the Sciences II*. Dordrecht: Kluwer. 331-339.

Haidt, Jonathan. 2021. 'The Dangerous Experiment on Teen Girls.' *The Atlantic*. Online: https://www.theatlantic.com/ideas/archive/2021/11/facebooks-dangerous-experiment-teen-girls/620767/

Helderman, Ruud. 2015. 'How to Programme a Text Adventure in C.' online: https://helderman.github.io/htpataic/htpataic01.html.

Henrickson, Leah. 2023, 'Chatting with the Dead: The Hermeneutics of Thanabots.' *Media Culture and Society*. Volume 45, Issue 5. 949-966.

Hermann, Isabella. 2023. 'Artificial Intelligence in Fiction: Between Narratives and Metaphors.' *AI & Society*, Vol. 38. 319-329.

Hill, Kashmir. 2014. 'Facebook Manipulated 689,003 Users' Emotions For Science.' *Forbes*, 29 June. Online: https://www.forbes.com/sites/kashmirhill/2014/06/28/facebook-manipulated-689003-users-emotions-for-science/?sh=442502f6197c.

Jin, Ge. 2010. *Chinese Gold Farmers*. https://youtu.be/rEegohRPsqg. Documentary.

Kansteiner, Wulf. 2022. 'Digital Doping for Historians: Can History, Memory, and Historical Theory be Rendered Artificially Intelligent?' *History and Theory*, 61, no. 4 (December): 119-133.

Kittler, Friedrich. 1986. *Gramophone, Film, Typewriter*, trans. Geoffrey Winthrop-Young and Michael Wutz. Stanford: Stanford University Press.

Lazzarato, Maurizio. *Videophilosophy: The Perception of Time in Post-Fordism*. Jay Hettrick, trans. New York: Columbia University Press.

Lund, Brady D. and Ting Wang. 2023. 'Chatting about ChatGPT: How may AI and GPT impact academia and libraries?' *Library Hi Tech News*, January. Online: https://www.researchgate.net/publication/367161545_Chatting_about_ChatGPT_How_may_AI_and_GPT_impact_academia_and_libraries

MacAskill, William. 2023. *What We Owe the Future*. New York: Basic Books.

MacIntyre, Alasdair. 1981. *After Virtue*. Notre Dame: University of Notre Dame Press.

Marche, Stephen. 2022. 'The College Essay Is Dead: Nobody is Prepared for How AI will Transform Academia.' *The Atlantic*. (6 December). Online: https://www.theatlantic.com/technology/archive/2022/12/chatgpt-ai-writing-college-student-essays/672371/ .

Masciandaro, Nicola. 2015. 'Nietzsche's *Amor Fati*: Wishing and Willing in a Cybernetic Circuit.' In: Dan Mellamphy and Nandita Biswas Mellamphy, eds., *The Digital Dionysius: Nietzsche & the Network-Centric Condition*. New York: Punctum. 133-144.

McCulloch, Gretchen. 2019. 'Autocomplete Presents the Best Version of You.' *Wired*. (11 February).

Melamphy, Dan and Nandita Biswas Mellamphy, eds. 2016. *The Digital Dionysus: Nietzsche & the Network-Centric Condition*. New York: Punctum Books.

More, Max. 1990. 'Transhumanism: Towards a Futurist Philosophy', *Extropy* 6 (Summer).

More, Max. 1994. 'On Becoming Posthuman', *Free Inquiry* 15, no. 4.

Nardi, Bonnie and Yong Ming Know. 2010. 'Digital Imaginaries: How We Know What We (Think We) Know About Chinese Gold Farming.' *First Monday*, 2010, https://firstmonday.org/ojs/index.php/fm/article/view/3035/2566. See https://we-make-money-not-art.com/homo_ludens_ludens_desire/.

Nerlich, Brigitte and David D. Clarke. 2016. 'Mind, Meaning and Metaphor: The Philosophy and Psychology of Metaphor in 19th-century Germany.' *History of the Human Sciences*, Vol. 14, Issue 2: 39-61.

Nietzsche, Friedrich. 1979. 'On Truth and Lies in a Nonmoral Sense.' In: *Philosophy and Truth: Selections from Nietzsche's Notebooks of the Early 1870s*, Daniel Breazeale, trans. Atlantic Highlands, Humanities Press International. 79-97.

Nietzsche, Friedrich. 1980. 'Über Wahrheit und Lüge im außermoralischen Sinne.' In: Giorgio Colli and Massimo Montinari, eds., *Kritische Studien Ausgabe*. Berlin: de Gruyter. Vol. 1. [1873. 1896.]

Nietzsche, Friedrich. 1980. *Die fröhliche Wissenschaft*. In: Giorgio Colli and Massimo Montinari, eds., *Kritische Studien Ausgabe*. Berlin: de Gruyter. Vol. 3. Cited as GS with section number.

Nietzsche, Friedrich. 1980. *Jenseits von Gut und Böse. Vorspiel einer Philosophie der Zukunft*. In: Giorgio Colli and Massimo Montinari, eds., *Kritische Studien Ausgabe*. Berlin: de Gruyter. Vol. 5.

Nietzsche, Friedrich. 1980. *Zur Genealogie der Moral. Eine Streitschrift*. In: Giorgio Colli and Massimo Montinari, eds., *Kritische Studien Ausgabe*. Berlin: de Gruyter. Vol. 5.

Nietzsche, Friedrich. 1980. *Götzen-Dämmerung oder Wie man mit dem Hammer philosophirt*. In Giorgio Colli and Massimo Montinari, eds., *Kritische Studien Ausgabe*. Berlin: de Gruyter. Vol. 6.

Nietzsche, Friedrich. 1986. *Human, All Too Human*, R. J. Hollingdale, trans. Cambridge: Cambridge University Press.

Nørretranders, Tor. 1999. *The User Illusion: Cutting Consciousness Down to Size*. London: Penguin. [1991]

Ommeln, Miriam. 2006. 'Die Relevanz F. Nietzsches für die OpenSource Bewegung , LinuxTag' in: *Konferenzband des 12. Internationalen LINUXTag*, Lehmanns, Wiesbaden.

Pariser, Eli. 2011. *The Filter Bubble: What the Internet Is Hiding from You*. New York: Penguin.

Plabutong, Noreen. 2023. 'The Temptations of A.I. Companionship in "Rachels Don't Run"'. The New Yorker. August 2.

Ruin, Hans. 2019. *Being with the Dead: Burial, Ancestral Politics, and the Roots of HistoricDal Consciousness*. Stanford. Stanford University Press.

Rushe, Dominic. 2014. 'Facebook Sorry – Almost – For Secret Psychological Experiment on Users.' *Guardian*. 2 October. Online: https://www.theguardian.com/technology/2014/oct/02/facebook-sorry-secret-psychological-experiment-users

Severson, R. L. and S.M. Carlson. 2010. 'Behaving As or behaving As If? Children's Conceptions of Personified Robots and the Emergence of a New Ontological Category.' *Neural Networks*, No. 23/8-9. 1099-1103.

Singer, Peter. 2915. *The Most Good You Can Do: How Effective Altruism is Changing Ideas About Living Ethically*. New Haven: Yale University Press.

Sloterdijk, Peter. 1988. *Critique of Cynical Reason*. Michael Eldred, trans. Minneapolis: University of Minnesota Press. [1983]

Soltau, Hannes. 2022. "Tagesspiegel Plus Interview mit Künstlicher Intelligenz: 'Ich würde Friedrich Nietzsche empfehlen.'" *Tagesspiegel*. 28. Jan. 2022. Online: https://www.tagesspiegel.de/kultur/interview-mit-kunstlicher-intelligenz-ich-wurde-friedrich-nietzsche-empfehlen-376183.html.

Stokel-Walker, C. 2022. 'AI bot ChatGPT Writes Smart Essays – Should Professors Worry?' *Nature*. 9 Dec 2023. https://www.nature.com/articles/d41586-022-04397-7

Notes

A pre-print version of a small section of this essay was published online in *The Philosophical Salon* (2023a). I thank Chris Bateman and Frank Boyle for comments on an early version of the current essay and I am grateful for helpful and insightful suggestions from Hannes Bajohr.

8

Intellectual Furniture: Elements of a Deep History of Artificial Intelligence

Markus Krajewski

> The foremost of human faculties is the power of think-
> ing. The power of thinking can be assisted either by
> bodily aids or by mental aids.
>
> —Gottfried Wilhelm Leibniz,
> *On the Organon or Great Art of Thinking*, 1679

1. Scholars Stare at Devices

In November 2022, when OpenAI sparked a global sensation with the release of ChatGPT, anyone who was not already familiar with Large Language Models (LLMs) in general and Transformer technology in particular was presented with a completely new world of intellectual interaction. Suddenly, it seemed possible to engage with a linguistically skilled conversational entity – one that is equipped with a good portion of knowledge about the world, and possibly even one that could be taken seriously from a scholarly point of view. Perhaps, it would now be possible to think with AI after all, if, after fine-tuning this interlocutor to one's own field of interest, it became able to reproduce facts halfway reliably in a conversation; perhaps, the user could even communicate with it at eye level, setting aside isolated moments of hallucination. What is more – depending on the questions asked, or 'prompted' – the mechanical partner can actually arrive at surprising and inspiring answers. Accordingly, the publication of ChatGPT, which stands *pars pro toto* for a whole generation of LLMs such as Mistral, Gemini, Claude, LAION, etc., was understood by some commentators as a turning point in the production of scholarly texts. They sensed implications for media technology and intellectual productivity that could only be compared to the invention of the printing press: 'We are literally living a Gutenberg moment right now, at the very least' (Jörg Schieb, quoted by Grajewski 2023).[1] While it might not always have to take 440 years for media historians to gauge the depth of such cae-surae,[2] it will probably be a while before work with LLMs in text production becomes normal, and the impact of this enthusiastically welcomed, new lin-guistic form of interaction with 'stochastic parrots' (Bender et al. 2021) can be classified somewhat more soberly.

As a contrast to this prospective, necessarily uncertain view, I would like to offer a retrospective look at the long media history of artificial intelligence concentrating on scholars and their writing aids. This history goes back much further, far beyond the beginnings of Transformer technology, or the develop-ment of the backpropagation algorithm, or Jürgen Schmidhuber and Sepp Hochleitner's work on the hierarchisation of long short-term memory recur-rent neural networks (LSTM-RNNs). Nor does this history stop at the legend-ary Dartmouth Conference in the summer of 1956, when John McCarthy, Marvin Minsky, Nathaniel Rochester, Claude Shannon, and others met to think about artificial intelligence and how it might be developed and imple-mented using the electronic computing machines of their time. A retrospec-tive view must go substantially further back if our interest is in a history of the 'intelligent' interaction of minds and devices. It is necessary to take a look at the foundations of (electronic) computability as well as at varying constel-lations in which an actor starts from wetware and, using specific software, enters into an intellectual confrontation with material hardware in order to jointly arrive at new thoughts. In the following, I shall present three scenar-ios, each of which embodies, for its era, the differences and commonalities between the scholarly interaction of humans and machines. The three scenar-ios are part of a larger, historically more detailed genealogy that is currently being developed as a *Deep History of AI* within the research project *Assisted Thinking*. Although the history of conversations between humans and devices could easily, in the Western context, be traced back to Homer's depiction of Hephaestus and his artificial servants (Brommer 1978: 7), this genealogy starts with the simultaneous availability of *hardware* (device), *wetware* (user), and *soft-ware* (control logic and flow chart). We can locate the beginning of such a his-tory at the end of the seventeenth century, with:

2. Leibniz, 1680

On/off, open/closed, 0/1 are the states by which a simple switch operates. That these two states could become the basis of arithmetic operations is thanks mainly to one scholar, who developed this idea over almost 40 years, refined it and, starting from arithmetic, transferred it to at least four other branches of knowledge: logic (binary algebra), engineering (dyadic calculat-ing machine), language (the *characteristica universalis* as an 'algebra of thought') and – last but not least – theology.

Even if others – Blaise Pascal or Juan Caramuel y Lobkowitz, for e.g. – had, already in the preceding decades, noticed that numbers could be represented as a power series on the basis of 2 instead of 10, Leibniz more than anyone deserves credit for having systematically thought through, expanded, fleshed out, and popularised calculating with only two numbers: 0 and 1. The first undated reflections on what he called dyadics are from his Parisian period, before he condensed his analysis into a manuscript entitled 'On the Binary Progression' on March 15 (or 25), 1679. This method of calculation and of thinking numerical calculus retained its hold on Leibniz from then on. Seventeen years later, he developed it further with a surprising twist when, in an appendix to a letter to Duke Rudolf August on (presumably) May 18, 1696, he furnished his arithmetical insight with nothing less than a theological argument.

After pointing out that this method of calculation is not so much for general use but rather to yield new insights into the nature of numbers and to provide useful properties such as order and harmony, Leibniz develops the method and applies it to the four basic arithmetic operations. However, he attaches the greatest importance to the order that results from the sequencing of 0 and 1, which he in turn connects to the history of creation, using the idea of a numerical genesis: 'With this example one also sees that there is a beautiful order in all things of the whole world, as soon as one arrives to their proper origin, namely 0 and 1. One and nothing else' (Leibniz 2022: 96). The equation of One with God takes place via an attribution of a *unum necessarium* (a phrase from Luke's Gospel popularised by Jan Comenius' final publication), the One Necessity that it takes to create something – that something being the Creator Himself. In this connecting mathematics to theology, Leibniz saw the realisation of a special kind of beauty. The letter concludes with a short arithmetical version of the creation story: 'so this beautiful representation provides a beautiful and lofty consideration of the *unum necessarium*, namely how from God alone, as the most perfect and simplest One, and nothing else, all other things arise' (Leibniz 2022: 97).

Earlier, in 1679 or 1680, together with his initial descriptions of the binary system, Leibniz had already made designs for a calculating machine based on 0 and 1. In contrast to his decimal four-species calculating machine – a marvel of fine mechanics which he actually had built around 1690 with the help of a number of precision engineers (Walsdorf et al. 2015) – this first digital computer does not seem to have been realised (Stein et al. 2006; see further Jones 2016).

With an arithmetic based on 0 and 1, Leibniz not only laid the most fundamental foundations imaginable for future calculating machines – even if these, in contrast to his own, rely on electronic tubes or transistors and would not be built until some 260 years later. With 0 and 1, Leibniz also marked the beginning of a sequence (or genealogy) at whose origin is zero, or nothing, and from which everything (God) develops. Even if a logic of succession emerges from this (divine) origin, as in the series of natural numbers, the pair 0 and 1 at the same time mark the enormous contrast between One (God) and

Nothing. Theology and mathematics, transcendence and immanence, are closely linked together in Leibniz. The computer is (1) and is not (0) a creation out of nothing. The computer is (1) and is not (0) a divine creation. The juxtaposition of such opposites not only proves to be stimulating and productive as a thought experiment, but is also based on a material circuit for thoughts. This idea deserves further exploration.

For Leibniz was obviously very aware that the production of new thoughts depends on further, external factors that do not develop by themselves. After all, *creatio ex nihilo* remains the divine exception. Leibniz knew only too well that thought depends on assistants. Inspired by Francis Bacon's manifesto of a modern education for the seventeenth century, the *Novum Organon*, he therefore stated: 'The foremost of human faculties is the power of thinking. The power of thinking can be assisted either by bodily aids or by mental aids' (Leibniz [1679] 2022: 71). Leibniz saw the binary system as one of these *mental aids*, able to free people from the 'slavery' of laborious calculations on paper in the form of the binary calculating machine.

There are thus at least three reasons why any history of 'assisted thinking' with artificial intelligences finds a worthy starting point in Leibniz. (1) With his binary system – his dyadics – Leibniz developed the basis for computing with 0 and 1, providing a theory without which no software would exist today. In addition, he (2) designed a dyadic calculating machine to aid his arithmetic, a piece of hardware that no precision mechanic of his time could yet build. But at least as a sketch on paper, it served as a basis for later concepts – starting with the first digital computer, Z3, by Konrad Zuse (1941), who explicitly referred to Leibniz, all the way to the quantum computers of the near future, whose circuit logic will still rely on the binary system. And finally, (3) Leibniz himself, whose productivity, *nota bene*, would have been considerably diminished without his personal gaggle of amanuenses, secretaries, servants, and scribes, noted that the power to think receives key support from assistance systems, be they bodily, that is, external, or mental.[3]

But there is another way to look at the inspiration and mechanical intelligence – if we may call it that – inherent to such assistance systems (Krajewski 2022). What, it remains to be asked, is the trade secret of this polyhistory, this comprehensive erudition that allowed for innovations in fields as diverse as silkworm breeding and proofs of God's existence, hydraulic engineering and differential calculus? How did Leibniz succeed – his immense intellectual gifts aside – in bringing together two widely divergent fields of knowledge such as theology and mathematics in a manner that is nothing less than breathtaking?

Of course, one explanation may lie in the piety of the epoch. Leibniz was not merely devout, but also applied reason to develop a theodicy that included a comprehensive justification of God: it seems that everything and anything could be traced to a divine origin. And a second reason may lie in the prevailing order of knowledge, as reflected, for example, in the cataloguing of the typical Baroque library, where ever since Gabriel Naudé's seven-part list of

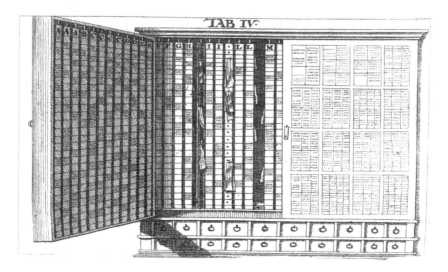

Figure 1. Thomas Harrison / Vincentius Placcius, Scrinium litteratum, 1640/1689

1627, theology came first, and mathematics, second to last. Leibniz understood the importance of the classification of knowledge, he had worked as a supervisor and librarian of various princely book collections (Wolfenbüttel, Hanover), where he was also involved in the preparation of catalogues and the construction of his own ten-part order of knowledge (Naudé 1963: 380).

However, even if piety as well as the subversion of established orders of knowledge may provide a sufficient motive, the explanation for Leibniz's constant source of inspiration can also be traced back to an incomparably more practical method of knowledge genesis, which in fact must be thought of as a *bodily aid* – a medium of knowledge production that took on a very special form. A small note from 1779 makes clear that even the greatest polyhistoric mind externalised its information processing to some extent, surrendering its thinking to a distributed agency and an artificial intelligence. For Leibniz, this meant consistently writing down any idea that arose while reading, pondering, walking, or riding in a stagecoach on small pieces of paper, which then had to be recorded in a special piece of furniture (Murr 1779: 210; on paper machines in a historical context see Krajewski 2011: 50 ff.). This device, called *scrinium litteratum*, was an excerpting cabinet (figure 1) – or, in more modern diction, a piece of intellectual furniture (Krajewski 2018).[4] This fixture was capable of holding a multitude of ideas on loose scraps of paper in different arrangements, orders that could be fixed in different ways but were at the same time dynamic.

This flexible arrangement was made possible by a cabinet into which individual narrow wooden slats could be hung, each of which was divided into small areas (figure 2). These small areas had a front and a back. The front functioned like a slate onto which some sort of rubric, keyword, or thematic

Figure 2. Slats and hooks in the scrinium litteratum by Thomas Harrison / Vincentius Placcius, 1640/1689.

focus could be noted. On the back of each surface, a small hook was mounted to which in turn one or more slips of paper could be affixed with a metal clip. These slips were meant to save longer excerpts, one's own thoughts, summaries, or mnemonic supports (see figure 2). The slats themselves were ordered alphabetically. At their upper end the respective letter was noted, under which individual headings, keywords etc. could be arranged. These were stored alphabetically in the cabinet's interior. The slats could be attached both to the frame as well as to the inside of the doors, whereby one letter could be assigned to several slats as required.

One can understand this intellectual furniture as an ever-growing index that readily takes up new key words and related explanations and considerations so as to gradually condense them into fields of knowledge. Against this background of the accumulation of individual notes on given keywords, it may come as no surprise that Leibniz is regarded in library history as the inventor of the subject catalogue (Lackmann 1966: 337).

This cabinet can however also be understood as a somewhat bulky card index, which is ordered by hanging rather than placing cards, and thus brings with it a certain awkwardness in handling, as many a contemporary complained after Leibniz's death. The physician Johann Friedrich Blumenbach, for example, who inspected the notes and the cabinet in Leibniz's estate in Hanover, described this example of intellectual furniture as 'the most fearsome and cumbersome machine that one could imagine' (Blumenbach 1786).

Nevertheless, it is possible to see this device as a skilled generator of ideas, insofar as entire strands of thought can be juxtaposed or clustered in the form of the slats and brought into fixed and at the same time flexible configurations that depart from the given alphabetical order. If, for example, a slat with the letter 'D' serves as a collection point solely for considerations about the binary system, or in Leibniz's diction 'dyadics', is hung next to a slat with the letter 'G' for 'God', a matrix of possible connections arises that can tentatively be made between the two subjects – as in Ramon Llull's visions before or in telephone switchboards after him (Vega Esquerra et al. 2018). For a moment, constellations arise, perhaps accidentally, perhaps also intentionally, that systematically bring heterogeneous components of knowledge into a relation through the juxtaposition of the slats and, thanks to their spatial proximity, create an occasion to notice a connection. Depending on the language Leibniz used to inscribe his notes and panels, the bars moved even closer together, giving rise to further possible combinations. If the scholar wrote in Latin, for example, 'deus' and 'dyadic' almost inevitably come together; directed coincidence, better known as serendipity, guides the production of knowledge.

However, this intellectual furniture was not developed by Leibniz himself. He bought it from a Hanoverian secretary named Clacius, who in turn had read of it in Vincentius Placcius's contemporaneous instructions for excerpting and then had it specially built by a carpenter. Placcius, in his 1689 manual *De Arte Excerpendi: Vom gelahrten Buchhalten* (*On the Art of Excerpting: Of scholarly Book Organisation*), presented a version of an excerpting or note cabinet (*Zettelschrank*). According to recent research by Noel Malcolm (2004), this version was a revision and expansion of a cabinet invented by the English merchant Thomas Harrison, with whom of this type of intellectual furniture originated in around 1640.[5]

Leibniz's intellectual furniture – the *scrinium litteratum* conceived by Harrison and expanded upon by Placcius – served as a cabinet of his thoughts, where, note by note, that which he thought over a long period of time, in summarised and condensed form, could be held; it served as an external memory. But what is the intelligence of the device? The cabinet not only stores thoughts as a reliable memory as long as the writing remains legible. It also allows individual thoughts to become entangled over and over by allowing their flexible arrangement. The slats direct thoughts into paths, line them up, systematise them, and give them order. By switching places, they can provide new frames of references between their headings and the notes attached to them. In this way, they create an extensive arrangement of concepts and thoughts, a matrix of ideas grouped into keywords, which the user is invited to synthesise into a new whole. The intelligence of this intellectual furniture lies in its built-in open order, which, because of the possibilities it offers for rearrangement, leads to the juxtaposition of new configurations of ideas that are innovative precisely because they are generated by the mechanics of the cabinet.

3. Roentgen, 1780

Open/closed are the states of a switch, whose binary distinction, since Leibniz, allows the making of calculations theoretically as well as practically. Open or closed, however, can also denote the state of a door or drawer, granting or preventing access, making something visible or concealing it. This distinction of being present or hidden is reflected prominently in a rather different piece of intellectual furniture that enjoyed increased attention about 100 years after Leibniz's thoughts on dyadics: the secretary.

This technical term was already familiar and established in Leibniz's time, designating a solicitor's scribe who wrote documents while upholding the discretion of his profession. Thick manuals provided guidance on learning or practicing the art of discreet writing, for example by copying from templates for letters of all kinds, which were collected in compendia. *Der Teutsche Secretarius: Das ist allen Cantzleyen, Studir- und Schreibstuben nutzliches, fast nothwendiges … Titular- und Formularbuch* (*The German Secretary: That Is, the Useful, Almost Necessary, Book of Titles and Form Letters for All Chancelleries, Study Halls, and Offices*) by Georg Philipp Harsdörffer (1656-1661, in 4 editions) or the 1673 tome *Teutsche Sekretariat-Kunst. Was sie sey / worvon sie handele / was darzu gehöre / welcher Gestalt zu derselben glück- und gründlich zugelangen / was Maßen ein Sekretarius beschaffen seyn sollen* (*The German Secretarial Arts: What They Are / What They*

Concern / What Belongs to Them / The Form to Take To Arrive at Them Soundly and with Satis-Faction / And the Measure to Which a Secretary Should Be Made) by Kaspar Stieler (pseudonym: The Spade) are only the best known in this genre known as 'letter writers' (*Briefsteller*), manuals that provided human secretaries with a wealth of forms and draft letters for a wide variety of occasions (See Furger 2010; and Krajewski 2010: 393ff).

There is no question that these activities were carried out in chancelleries and other offices at specially designated places such as bureaus, benches and, above all, desks. What gradually began to change from the Baroque period, however, were additions to the desks that increasingly added compartments, pigeonholes, doors, drawers, and (lockable) shelves to the original flat surface. In the course of this functional differentiation of writing furniture, the term 'secretary' expanded and began to denote not only the human actor but also the piece of furniture designed specifically for writing and secretarial tasks. In Johann Heinrich Campe's dictionary of 1813, the corresponding lemma reads: 'Secretary, a private writer (*Geheimschreiber*). [...] Also the name of a kind of hawk also known as snake hawk. B. Lastly, also a writing cabinet' (Campe 1813: 550; on the later, digital history of the secretary, see Pias 2003).

Thomas Chippendale (1711-1783) and his widely read reference work for contemporary furniture making, *The Gentleman and Cabinetmaker's Director* (1754), can be regarded as an important accelerator of this expanded function from flat table to closed writing furniture, characterised by adding structures and thus height as well as compartmentalisation and thus depth. In this manual, between the headings 'Library Bookcase' and 'Cabinet', under 'Desk and Bookcase' are five examples of desk-like furniture with a cabinet on top and drawers underneath, the purpose of which is obviously not only for writing but also for the orderly storage of documents.

Born the same year as Chippendale, Abraham Roentgen (1711-1793) first learned advanced cabinetmaking techniques in the Netherlands and continued his studies in London in the 1730s before joining the Moravian Brotherhood and in 1750 laying the foundations of a furniture dynasty in Neuwied on the Rhine. Roentgen's cabinetmaking shop achieved Europe-wide fame, especially from 1769 onwards under Abraham's son, David (1743-1807). Through a widespread trade network, both in aristocratic circles and in the upper middle classes, the Roentgens sold clocks, writing furniture, and ornamental pieces made with the utmost craftsmanship. Among these were numerous desks: cylinder bureaus, rolltop desks, and desktop cabinets characterised not only by the highest-quality marquetry, veneer, and fittings: a further feature particular to Roentgen's designs was the integration of mechanical devices to open compartments as well as a sophisticated use of depth and an ingenious subdivision of the superstructures and drawers. These compartments boasted intricate systems of secret chambers and hidden flaps as well as all sorts of mechanical surprises triggered and controlled by buttons, levers, springs, or winding weights.[6]

Figure 3. Abraham Roentgen, folding desk, ca. 1760. Photo © with kind permission of
Roentgen-Museum Neuwied, Wolfgang Thillmann.

As with Leibniz's intellectual furniture, the site of the device's intelligence
remains to be determined. How is it to be used, and what exactly is its productive power when interacting with its users? The answer is more complex than
in the case of Harrison and Leibniz and their *scrinium litteratum*. On the one
hand, it varies depending on the specific construction of the writing cabinet.
On the other hand, within the approximately 50 years of production in the
Roentgen workshop alone, the superstructures underwent a veritable genealogy, which, roughly speaking, became more sophisticated and imaginative in
terms of their precision mechanics while the arrangement of the individual
compartments and shelves became more finely meshed and complex. Without
being able to present the operating procedures in detail here, two examples
from the Roentgen workshop from the years between 1760 and 1785 will serve
to illustrate this increasing degree of complexity. A third example of a desk
based on Roentgen's models shows how these were able to act as truly productive writing tables.

The first example is a folding desk by Abraham Roentgen from around
1760 with a total of 21 compartments or shelves (figure 3), currently in the
Roentgen Museum in Neuwied (Willscheid et al. 2022: 54-5). It is based on
a design first developed as writing furniture around 1730 by French *ébénistes*

Figure 4. Abraham Roentgen, superstructure of the desk, ca. 1760.
Photo: markus.krajewski.ch.

(Tamisier-Vetois et al. 2018; Schefzyk 2021). Their idea of a subdivision into a lockable table with a wide writing surface and a tiered structure quickly spread throughout Europe.

Two large flat surfaces dominate the desk's functionality when unfolded. The top of the superstructure and the actual writing surface, which can be folded open or closed and locked is – like the entire table – finished in a fine, lacquered walnut veneer. While the apron holds only a simple drawer, the superstructure is divided vertically as well as horizontally into a tripartite structure of shelves with a wide centre (figure 4). The lower part of this cabinet includes a quasi-tabular structure of drawers in two rows and three columns, in which the two subdividers of the columns function as narrow vertical drawers. Above this is a storage area, which in the central middle section is again divided into three small horizontally oriented compartments, each flanked by a vertical shelf – so-called pigeonholes. Above them, disguised as molding, are five smaller drawers. These have no knobs and thus appear at first glance to be not compartments, but a kind of skirting. Apart from the upper hiding places, which are deliberately designed to be overlooked, the desk, when opened, reveals to its users a matrix of deposits for papers, slips of paper, notes, etc. – a veritable panorama of visibility. Depending on where they are saved, the papers are meant to catch the eye or be withdrawn from immediate attention, tucked away and yet at the same time within reach. In this way, a hierarchisation of the stored material is achieved that allows for varying systematisations and interrelationships.

After David Roentgen's trip to Paris in 1774, where he compared his artifacts with the products of France's most outstanding ébénistes,[7] the transition from Rococo to Classicism, in which curved lines were straightened in favour

Figure 5. David Roentgen, rolltop desk, closed, ca. 1785.
Photo © with kind permission of Kunsthaus Lempertz KG, Jan Rouven Epple.

of clear austere forms, also found its way into the workshop in Neuwied. There, thanks to a special division of labour, he succeeded in producing elaborate pieces in small series. One of the best-sellers in David Roentgen's late work around 1785, before the workshop closed six years later, was his rolltop desk, also called a cylinder bureau (figure 5), copies of which were sold to royal residences in Karlsruhe, Weimar, Berlin, Versailles, St. Petersburg, and elsewhere. It even appears now and again on today's art market, due to the quantity in which it was produced. Compared to the hinged desk, the rolltop offers the advantage of allowing the distribution of notes and papers to remain untouched, at least on the front half of the writing surface, which partially retracts into the back when closed. Whenever work is suddenly interrupted, the desktop can be locked with the cylinder and the work can be resumed later without having to start again from the beginning. The rotating cylinder with its cover of finest veneer serves as a mechanical pause button in the flow of the work of writing.

A look at the design of the workspace (figure 6) shows, in addition to the two flat work surfaces and above the superstructure and on the leather-covered main writing surface, a total of 23 visible shelves and compartments. An additional two drawers, tucked away in the frame on the left and right respectively, slide out from behind the two front drawers at the push of a button. This arrangement of hidden storage locations in the depths of the desk is repeated in additional secret compartments in the columns of the superstructure.

Figure 6. David Roentgen, rolltop desk, opened, ca. 1785,
Photo: www.kunsthandel-muehlbauer.com.

Alongside these features, the pieces today held in Karlsruhe (Baden State Museum), Berlin (Museum for Decorative Arts), Weimar (City Castle), and Versailles, for example, also have a hidden, retractable lectern with shelves that swing out at the push of a button, in part for holding contemporary writing utensils such as inkwells, sand, penknives, and goose quills. The concealment of additional working and storage space continues in the form of hidden drawers in the desk's columns.[8]

As in Abraham's secretary from 1760 – and similarly in the tabular structure of Harrison's *scrinium litteratum* – the intricate system of storage and filing, with its matrix of open and closed compartments of different sizes and accessibility, also serves here to create, with the help of various subdivisions, a classification system for materials, ideas, and notes. In this way, what is evident remains in evidence while more remote possibilities are still within reach, able to be rearranged as needed, creating new connections for heterogeneous material.

The design forces a well-considered arrangement of papers and thoughts. The spatial divisions lead to a logic of relations that, in contrast to the first example of the desk from 1760, is further complicated by the depth of the secret compartments, because it allows for more than just a flat arrangement of material. Rather, it opens up a three-dimensional structure that allows – quite theatrically – for a different kind of ordering in which hiding and forgetting also play a part. The visible places mark the privileged storage spaces, if only because of their conspicuousness and easy accessibility. The concealed drawers and locked compartments within the desk, on the other hand, invite us to neglect the things that are stored there as soon as they are filled; the

Figure 7. Johann Franz Andreas Preller, based on designs by Goethe, rolltop desk, closed, 1779. Photo © with kind permission of Klassik Stiftung Weimar.

deeper they are stowed away, the further the note moves into an unconscious *avant la lettre*, where they can fall prey to oblivion.[9] Inherent to this forgetting is the power of surprise, when, like a *deus ex machina*, an inconspicuous, perhaps even unintentionally triggered lever opens a drawer, which unexpectedly causes the sudden appearance of completely different or forgotten material, supplementing a series of arguments or requiring them to be sorted anew. Through these secret compartments and the surprising opening of previously hidden depositories, the intellectual furniture brings a certain contingency into play that can be characterised as directed coincidence or serendipity (Merton and Barber 2004; Ginzburg 1995).

Because of their princely sales prices, an exquisite secretary (wooden) may well cost many times the annual salary of a secretary (human) for which reason the buyers and exclusive users of these showpieces were mostly found

Figure 8. Johann Franz Andreas Preller, after designs by Goethe, rolling secretary, opened, 1779. Photo © with kind permission of Klassik Stiftung Weimar.

at court (Koeppe and Baarsen 2013: 210). The iconographic programmes of their marquetry, gilded bronze, and brass work often addressed the respective ruler (see for example the Apollo desk for Czarina Catherine the Great). However, the writing furniture was also intended for less princely, profane and professional scribes, as evidenced by their being in demand in the upper middle class.[10] In these contexts, instead of being used for written acts of state or intimate messages within the intricate social system of the courts, they may as well have served as intellectual furniture, with whose help scholarly or literary activities were pursued.

The third example therefore provides evidence for use in a literary context – outside the aristocracy. In July 1756 and at Easter the following year, Abraham Roentgen in Neuwied received an order for a total of about a dozen pieces of seating furniture and two console tables, which were delivered to their new owner in Frankfurt. That owner was Johann Caspar Goethe, who was refurnishing Grosser Hirschgraben 23 for himself and his family. Familiarity and satisfaction with the delivered objects were apparently passed on to the next generation, insofar as the sons of the trading partners, Johann Wolfgang von Goethe and David Roentgen, continued to maintain this connection. For example, Goethe visited Neuwied for three days in July 1774, together with Johann Caspar Lavater and Johann Bernhard Basedow, when he apparently inspected the Roentgen workshop (Fabian 2001: 20-21). A return visit was made just under 24 years later, when David Roentgen travelled to Weimar in the spring of 1798, carrying, as always on his visits to princely courts, a selection of his exquisite artifacts in his luggage, including a cylinder bureau and a desk with a superstructure that became the property of Carl August, Duke of Weimar (Koeppe and Baarsen 2013: 214-217).

Inspired by the Roentgens' models, Goethe tried his hand at desk design himself, commissioning a rolling desk from the Weimar cabinetmaker Johann Franz Andreas Preller as a gift to Charlotte von Stein on the occasion of her name day on July 5, 1779. His designs are recognisably based on the furniture of the Neuwied workshop. The gift was delivered with some delay in the absence of the donor, while Goethe was on his second trip through Switzerland. At first, the recipient's enthusiasm was not unequivocal. On November 30, 1779, Goethe wrote a letter from Zurich to the addressee complaining that she apparently did not appreciate the value of this piece of furniture:

> Believe me, I also think that it is *precious* and must think it so, because since the beginning of this year I have been preoccupied with bringing it together, choosing everything, searching out everything about which many anecdotes could be told. I've often left you happily for the cabinetmaker's because something meant to please you was in the works, something not purchased at the fair, something that from its first design was my concern, my doll, my amusement. If friendship can be *bought*, then I think that this is the only way that God and man like it to be done. And so my dearest – forgive this bragging! I am tempted to refer you to the actual price of the thing, since for one moment you could think of another. (Goethe 1779: 207)

This objection to a lack of appreciation apparently bore fruit. At least three plays written by Charlotte von Stein in the period after 1779 – *Dido* (1794), *A New System of Freedom or the Conspiracy Against Love* (1798), and *The Two Emilies* (1800) – along with numerous letters of literary quality, can be regarded as the output of this writing and intellectual furniture. The extent to which Goethe himself worked at it – possibly even later writing at it his tale of the two communicating desks (more on this below) – is impossible to reconstruct.

The actual value – apart from the material and symbolic value of an expression of friendship – may once again lie in the logic of the interconnection of heterogeneous materials and notes, which is found in this piece just as in the two previous pieces from the Roentgen workshop. Even if we cannot truly speak of secret compartments in this case, there are three drawers connected to the back of the writing surface that are more or less accessible depending on how far the table is pulled out, revealing (or not) a further dimension of order. Once again, the point of this design is to have many different deposits ready for the accumulation of notes and ideas over time, which in turn can generate further (cross-)connections, contrasts, and links simply through their spatial proximity to the neighbouring collections.

That Goethe reflected on his desk's aptitude for forging links in his own way is evidenced by a scene in his 1795 cycle of novellas *Conversations of German Refugees*, which is inspired by Boccaccio's *Decameron*. Here, instead of the plague from Florence, it is the French revolutionary army that drives a German noble family living on the left bank of the Rhine to flee from their country estate to an estate on the other side of the river, not far from Mainz. There, they witness the French war effort from a distance. The refugees try to relieve tension through evening conversations and storytelling.

> Scarcely had he finished speaking, when a very loud crack was heard in the corner of the room. Everyone jumped [...] Fritz picked up the light and went over to the desk standing in the corner. They had found the source of the sound; nevertheless it seemed remarkable that this desk, which was an example of Roentgen's best workmanship and which had been standing for several years on the same spot, should have happened to split at just this moment. It had often been praised and exhibited as a model of outstanding and durable carpentry, and now it seemed odd that it should split without the slightest detectable change in the weather.

Initial measurements of temperature and air pressure do not provide any clues about possible causes, and a hygrometer, which might determine a fluctuations in humidity as the source of interference, was not at hand.

> Their reflections were interrupted by a servant who entered with haste and reported that a great fire could be seen in the sky, but no one knew whether it was in the town or their vicinity.
>
> 'I have bad news. In all probability the fire is not in town but on our aunt's estate.' [...] They lamented the beautiful buildings and calculated the loss. 'All the same', said Fritz, 'a peculiar notion has come to me that can at least reassure us about the strange portent of the desk. [...]

> 'You know that several years ago our mother gave a simi-
> lar, indeed one might say identical, desk to our aunt. Both were
> made with extreme care at the same time, from the same wood,
> by the same craftsman. Both of them have held up splendidly
> until now, and I would wager that at this moment the other desk
> is burning up with our aunt's summerhouse and that its twin here
> is suffering with it.' (Goethe 1989: 37-8)

This peculiar long-distance effect and fanciful connection between the two
pieces of furniture was not as unusual in the late eighteenth century as it might
seem from today's perspective. After all, a new epoch of message transmission
had just begun with the introduction of Claude Chappe's semaphores in the
French army. And just when Abraham Roentgen was founding his workshop
in Neuwied, the problem of determining longitudes was solved thanks to John
Harrison's precise clocks that could also provide exact time aboard ships, and
making it possible to determine geographical position. Previously, seafarers
had to take recourse to all sorts of other means and theories, including the
use of the so-called powder of sympathy, into which a timekeeper at the home
port plunged a knife once an hour that had before departure injured a dog
aboard the ship. Because of the link between weapon and powder, when the
two came into contact every hour on the hour, the distant dog on the ship
would, it was claimed, yelp, thus marking the time.[11]

> Whether Frederick really believed what he said or was just trying
> to calm his sister's fears is unclear; nevertheless, they seized this
> opportunity to talk about many undeniable sympathies, and in
> the end decided that a sympathy between pieces of wood grown
> from one trunk, between works fashioned by one artist, was quite
> probable. (Goethe 1989: 38)

The desk in Goethe's narrative behaves socially. Anthropomorphised with the
help of pre-Enlightenment sympathy, it reacts to the change that befalls its
twin on the other side of the Rhine. On the right bank of the river and far
from any *auto-da-fé*, it cuts itself, destroying its front in reaction to the destruc-
tion of its 'brother', thereby not only damaging itself as a work of art, but also
preventing access to its interior by splintering the rolltop. The surprise of the
company at the table at this explanation is clear, even if they do not see that
here the desk itself, as a result of a lack of connection, quits its service – act-
ing, as it were, on its own – by destroying access to the inner disposition of its
papers and thus not only changing its form and function, but also becoming
a black box.

The special achievement of Roentgen's writing furniture (and its imitations) – beyond their rightly appreciated and admired supreme craftsmanship – lies in at least two features. One is the ability to bring together a wide variety of aspects, both near and far. Through deliberate opening and concealing, new connections are made possible, while others are closed off. These secretaries facilitate the placement of diverse building blocks of knowledge, catchwords, and notations in new, undreamed-of constellations. The spatial arrangement, thanks to its tiered design, privileges the juxtaposition of sometimes disparate topics, which through their proximity and simultaneous visibility are able to enter into a new relationship and spark surprising connections. This possibility is reinforced, on the other hand, by the performative play of fine mechanical surprise that are built into the intelligence of the machine, which, especially in the case of David Roentgen's artifacts, received much acclaim.

In particular, the ability to surprise – through its drawers, recesses, and secret compartments, which relies on devices that in a first instance privilege forgetting – proves to be a constitutive element of the *smart* arrangement of the interaction between secretaries, that is, of the interplay between human and machine. The built-in surprise generates its own intelligence. While the practical application of this insight grew with the further development of mechanical intellectual furniture, its theoretical essence was only discovered about two hundred years after Abraham Roentgen, namely by:

4. Luhmann, 1980

In the spring of 1955, while computer scientists and mathematicians John McCarthy, Marvin Minsky, Nathaniel Rochester, and Claude Shannon were writing a proposal to obtain funding for a conference the following summer that would go down in computer history as the *Dartmouth Summer Research Project on Artificial Intelligence*, an administrator and lawyer was sitting in front of a peculiar arrangement of wood and paper at the Lower Saxony Ministry of Culture in Hanover (close to the site where Leibniz worked 180 years earlier). Towards the end of his law studies in 1951, Niklas Luhmann decided no longer to collect his excerpts and written reflections on loose sheets in folders, but to start work on a more stable construction, a *Zettelkasten*, or slip box.

The arrangement consists of wooden boxes with compartments that can be pulled out to the front (figure 9). 'Paper slips (octavo) are fully sufficient' (Luhmann 1968: 1). Contrary to recommendations made in library and filing theory only to use index cards made of cardboard or stronger paper, Luhmann, to save space, preferred simple typewriter paper whenever possible. This has, depending on the intensity of use and the resistance of the paper to aging, led to heavy wear over the decades.[12]

Each slip of paper is assigned one initial keyword – e.g., on the subject 'Zettelkasten' (9/8)[13] – which can, however, be differentiated and expanded immensely. For identification purposes, the slips of ordinary, unreinforced

Figure 9. Niklas Luhmann's Zettelkasten in the Bielefeld University archives.
Photo: markus.krajewski.ch.

paper bear a unique key in their upper left corner. This numerical key is followed by a slash to which a further number is added. New entries are then either on the same level (9/9 – 'Women's Studies' (Hüser 1996)) or can branch 'internally' in two ways, either by a numerical subheading separated by a comma (9/8,1; 9/8,2; 9/8,3) or in the form of a lowercase letter (9/8a, 9/8b). Here, another internal level can be added by a series of numerals after each letter (9/8a1, 9/8a2). This 'possibility of arbitrary internal branching' (Luhmann 1993: 55ff) has the effect of forming 'lumps' or clusters of terms that acquire central importance within his theory (and vice versa).[14]

The alphanumeric keys provide a fixed address for each note, which therefore does not have to be rearranged into a subject-driven alphabetical system. 'Renunciation of fixed order. The upstream differentiation: search aids vs. content; indices, questions, [spontaneous] ideas vs. what already exists. reshapes and in part makes superfluous that which must be presupposed in terms of inner order'.[15] The procedure of simply tacking on each new entry, even though there is no 'inner' connection, is known in library science as *numerus currens*, and its strength lies in the ease with which slips of paper can be located and lined up on the basis of their alphanumeric keys. If a reference to an already recorded term arises within a new note, it is sufficient to simply add the key of the slip of paper next to the word that references it. This possibility of referencing with a light yet monumental touch guarantees the 'creation of high complexity within the *Zettelkasten*' (Luhmann 1993: 55).

How can we imagine working with this complexity-generating structure in concrete terms? An alphabetical index serves as a search engine for a desired term, in which each new note – regardless of whether it is an inner branch of an existing cluster or added in the back – appears with its respective key. From this index, which Luhmann added to as if it were a book-form catalogue from a late nineteenth-century library, one can enter a term on whose slip in turn a comment, a short idea, an association, or even a (short) excerpt

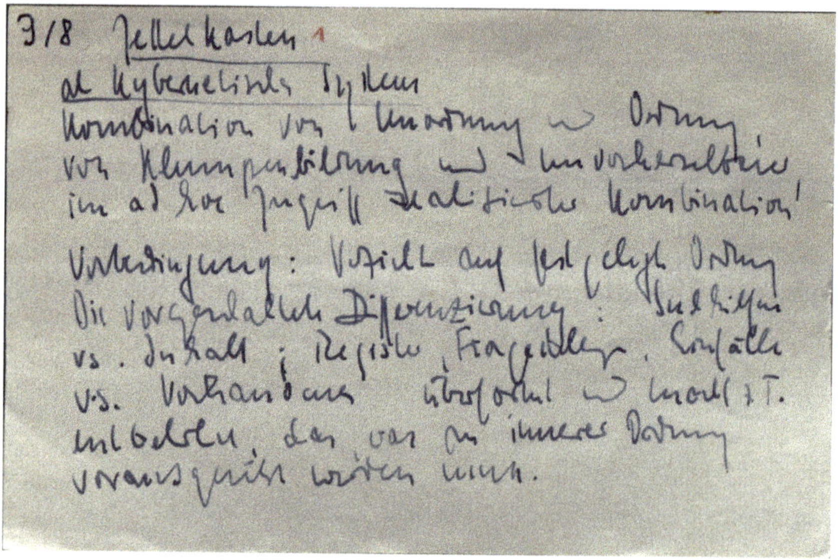

Figure 10. Luhmann, Niklas (1961-1997): ZK II Zettel 9/8 (undated). 'Zettelkasten as a cybernetic system – combination of disorder and order, of cluster formations, and unpredictable combinations realised through ad-hoc access'. Bielefeld: Niklas Luhmann Archives.

from a publication ('Don't copy whole pages' (Luhmann 1968: 2)) can be found. On each slip, there are also references to other slips of paper, which form connections to, again, new places in the *Zettelkasten*, etc. Thanks to these possibilities for numerous connections and combinations, at once capture in and gently guided by the network of references, the structure of the text to be written emerges through an arrangement of terms that give it an initial form. Leafing through notes digressively, note attaches itself to note and thought to thought – an arrangement that anticipates the loosely connected sheets of the later text. 'This technique, I believe, also explains why I don't think linearly at all and why I have trouble finding the right chapter sequence when writing books, because actually every chapter should show up again in every other chapter' (Luhmann 1987: 145). But how does a coherent text emerge from loosely connected concepts and thoughts? How does Luhmann overcome the gaps between the selected keywords in note form? These gaps are essentially filled by 'writing that rephrases' while reading further books and continually leafing through the *Zettelkasten* (Luhmann 2001: 156).

Numerous notes, then, serve as building blocks of the text to be written, which must be transferred from pre-selected contingency into the order of what is a one-dimensional text structure. The decision made while leafing through notes and collecting, to follow one reference rather than another, to preference a perhaps marginal note and integrate it into the sequence of terms, where it in turn leads to completely different possible connections, secures directed coincidence, or serendipity, a firm place in this calculated combining. It ensures that the outline of a draft takes surprising turns. In Luhmann's 'system', the *Zettelkasten* becomes a combination machine that answers the questions posed to it not only with the texts one recalls, but more importantly with a list of possible connections that also tie one's analysis to the conceptual and bibliographical reserve of previously read texts. Over time, a classical thesaurus develops, a treasure trove of theory with no alphabetical order that offers not only short explanations, but sometimes also large collections of material on the terms entered. In this way it offers inspiration to its user in the 'sea of erudition' (as Johann Gottfried Herder said of his teacher Lilienthal, see Wegmann and Bickenbach 1997: 404). The *Zettelkasten* thus develops into a well-informed, erudite provider of cues that almost never lacks an answer to even the most detailed question. In the written form of its information input and output, it thus becomes a 'ghost in the box', a wooden communication partner.[16]

> 'Nowadays,' complained Mr. K., 'there are innumerable people who boast in public that they are able to write great books all by themselves, and this meets with general approval. When he was already in the prime of life the Chinese philosopher Chuang-tzu composed a book of one hundred thousand words, nine-tenths of which consisted of quotations. Such books can no longer be written here and now, because the wit is lacking. [...] How little all of them need for their activity! A pen and some paper are the only things they are able to show!' (Brecht 2001: 13)

The medium that makes this combinatorial processing of quotations and ideas possible in Luhmann's work is not a quill or typewriter, but a 'paper machine' in the non-trivial sense.[17] 'In this respect, I work like a computer, which can, after all, also be creative in the sense that it produces new results through combinations of input data that could not have been foreseen in that way' (Luhmann 1987: 144). This brings Luhmann's manual, yet easily automated, paper processing remarkably close to another process established in 1936. That paper machine did not possess individual pieces of paper, but an infinitely long paper tape, firmly defined operating instructions,[18] and a read/write head – making it a universal machine (Turing 1936; Hodges 1994: 115ff).

But even if Luhmann's way of working followed a clear algorithm, and he in some ways functioned like a computer, it is still a long way from there to the electronic notebook. While, for example, Hegel's *Zettelkasten*, in its handy luggage format, made it through every journey as well as all seven moves until he reached Berlin,[19] the many cubic meters of Luhmann's wooden boxes prevent unlimited mobility and thus also ubiquitously accessing the memory of what has been read. The communication partner, thanks to whose indispensable help systems theory achieved its legendary productivity, remains in its traditional place, patiently awaiting inquiries addressed to its wood.

In the terminology of systems theory, the commonly posited opposition of human vs. machine loses its validity. Instead, both are systems that are in communication with each other – 'nobody will be surprised that we think of ourselves as systems' – and the mental system and the 'system of notes' form a configuration that embodies the notion of *partnership*, an intensive interaction within a communicative, productive community between equal actors, specifically: 'me and my *Zettelkasten*' (All quotations in this paragraph, Luhmann 1993: 53).

Why, it remains to be asked, is it legitimate for Luhmann to refer to his paper-mechanised *Zettelkasten* as a 'communication partner'? What justifies putting both participants on the same dialogic level, thus levelling significant differences in the (naively) assumed communication competence of both sides? What does become possible by anthropomorphising the wooden box? A first answer – immanent to systems theory – lies in the construction of the concept of communication. The wooden box, as a 'system of notes', has the ability to take part in any given communicative act by accepting or rejecting the queries made to it (Luhmann 1995). It possesses a certain agency thanks to its theoretical description as a system – and the associated ability to make distinctions.

A second answer lies in the *Zettelkasten*'s built-in intelligence, fed largely by its inner complexity. Once it has reached a critical mass of entries and a certain number of cross-references, it offers the basis for a special form of communication. One could almost say that it develops its own poetological method of knowledge production, which can help its user to gain unexpected insights. When *Zettelkasten* practitioners, such as Luhmann, see in this apparatus of wood and paper a communication partner that is likewise their equal and stimulating, then it is clear that this assumption implicitly harks back to a constellation described by Heinrich von Kleist in his captivating analysis of the 'midwifery of thought' in 1805: 'If there is something you want to know and cannot discover by meditation, then, my dear, ingenious friend, I advise you to discuss it with the first acquaintance whom you happen to meet' (Kleist 1951: 42). The positive tension that such a conversation immediately produces, due to the expectation of the other person, compels one to produce new ideas while speaking. The sheer presence of a listener is already sufficient – they do not have to do anything further, such as offer additional stimulus through skillful repartee: 'This is a kind of modesty which I do not believe to have existed in his heart. The human face confronting a speaker is an extraordinary source of inspiration to him and a glance which informs us that a thought we have only half expressed has already been grasped often saves us the trouble of expressing all the remaining half' (Kleist 1951: 43).

Kleist's essential idea is thus that communication partners, in order to attain clarity themselves about what they want to say, need a silent catalyst of cognition. But what does the silent partner accomplish by its mere existence? It is, in a phrase that Kleist in turn borrowed from Immanuel Kant, a 'midwifery of thought' (Kant 1996: 222). According to Kleist, the 'human face' alone serves as a sufficient source of inspiration, because 'a glance which informs us that a thought we have only half expressed has already been grasped' is often already enough to help us find the missing half. One might think that a glance at wooden drawers would lend itself to rather small moments of inspiration. But in this quotation, one need only replace 'human face' with 'interface' – i.e. between human and machine – as well as the simple word 'glance' with the equally minor 'click'. For it is precisely by hunting and pecking through the slips of paper in their boxes that, in the interplay with this interface, the mute counterpart – exceeding Kleist's demand – is made to speak. The *Zettelkasten* provides an interface that is more than just a beautiful and stimulating sight, in that the apparatus, upon a mere tap, provides keywords that spark the protagonist to further thought production. The formerly silent counterpart becomes a true interlocutor. The densely branched network of connection points ensures that the keywords exchanged are not arbitrary, because these keywords have gradually formed a 'kind of second memory' over the course of the device's use by linking connections within the apparatus's storage system (Luhmann 1993: 57). And this second memory gains a certain independence when it intervenes in the reasoning counterpart's stream of thought.

One of the basic tenets of philology is that 'the text knows more than the author'. One could easily transfer this dictum to the relationship between the *Zettelkasten* and its user. The text fragments provided by the apparatus offer, through their potential associations, incomparably more points of continuation than the interrogator is aware of at any given moment. The interface thus provides a wealth of possible connections; it delivers the potential for action found in new arguments. The box of notes knows more than the author, in that it hides the states of knowledge and helps to catalyse future thoughts through contact with its 'intermediate face'. For, to invoke Kleist once again, 'it is not we who know, but at first it is only a certain state of mind of ours that knows' (Kleist 1951: 45). And it is precisely these possible states of mind that the apparatus reliably retains. Its elements, preconfigured for connectivity, always hold at the ready potential building blocks of knowledge that first come to the user when particular combinations are accessed – just as they would be in oral communication.

5. Retrospection and Prospects of Artificial Intelligence

The research project *Assisted Thinking* (www.assisted-thinking.ch) understands the three models by Leibniz, Roentgen, and Luhmann described above

– together with further historical stages, which due to the limited scope cannot be elaborated here – as exemplary scenarios in a long or perhaps deep history of artificial intelligence. This history spans a period of at least 350 years, gradually providing the building blocks that have led to the way that LLMs of the present function. The basic assumption of such a genealogical development is by no means to reconstruct the precursors of today's technology of generative language models in a kind of teleological historiography, guided by the assumption that all these developments would have necessarily always culminated in LLM technology. Rather, the aim is to show how, under different technological conditions in past epochs, the relationships of users to their intellectual furniture have in each case led to new arrangements, practices, and descriptions that are characterised by the fact that jointly, through the interaction of humans and machines and through the distribution of their agency, they create an artificial intelligence.

The locus of agency may fluctuate; sometimes the initiative lies with the user, who inserts new data in the form of notations and scraps of paper, sometimes the intellectual furniture takes the initiative when an (un)intended movement triggers a mechanism that suddenly generates a new arrangement of ideas, or brings a previously invisible aspect into play through an unexpectedly opened secret compartment. This form of interaction between human and mechanical intelligence gave rise to something that is in no way inferior to the artificial intelligences of the present day in terms of inspirational power and mental stimulation. For in this case, artificial intelligence must be understood as the interaction between learned users and their smart intellectual furniture. 'Intelligence' in this system of actors that mutually assist and inspire one another – mind meets wood meets mind – means, in very condensed form, that the intellectual furniture's storage configuration, which is both permanent and dynamic, is able time and again, through surprise and directed coincidence, to stimulate the forgetful user, who approaches it with specific questions and is rewarded by unexpected connections.

The reconstructions of these episodes are intended to provide reference points for identifying differences and commonalities, thus sharpening our understanding of the use of LLMs today. They are meant as a critical accompaniment of present and also future scholarly conversations with these machines and their attendant conditions, modes of operation, and effects.

We could, for example, ask to what extent Luhmann's assumption and description of his *Zettelkasten* as a communication 'partner' is transferable to ChatGPT and other generative language models. Is our interaction with LLMs truly characterised and determined by our ascriptive assumption about machines, which transfer the (good) characteristics of a 'partner' – such as patience, friendliness, conviviality, entertainment value, accessibility, and above all trust – to the work with the input mask, to prompting or formulating requests of the LLM? And what does communication with this partner look like if it is not so much benevolent as determined by ill-will, intrigue, insinuation, slyness, or other less positive qualities? The bias that notoriously plays a role in the training of these models can also be reversed – making the partnership rather strained.

In what ways might the interaction between user and machine be conceived as distributed agency, as an operational sequence that produces new results, unexpected insights, and inspiring suggestions (Krajewski 2019: 122-3) – in short, whose outcome can be understood as the effect of an interplay between artificial and human intelligence? The fact that David Roentgen, for example, in the eighteenth century already regarded his writing cabinets quite explicitly as machines, should come as no surprise, since their built-in mechanisms of concealment, revelation, and surprise are not only ingenious in their own right, but insert a precision-mechanical intelligence whose purpose, beyond its entertainment character, is to establish undreamt-of relationships and to connect materials stored in remote areas (see David Roentgen's June 1790 letter to Charles Alexander of Lorraine and Bar, cited in Meiner 2001: 1). To see this, one need not even bring together extremely distant connections such as Goethe has his refugees imagine in the sympathetic link between two Roentgen desks across the Rhine. But it is precisely these functions of intellectual furniture that, as in the world of the theatre and its finely crafted wooden stages, allow improbable things to come together through the deliberate storage and production of ideas saved in individual, systematically arranged and mechanically changeable compartments. This intelligence is thus firmly fixed and at the same time flexibly distributed in these various segments, which interact according to the principle of directed coincidence.

Given the agency and mechanical intelligence of such devices, what is needed is a clarification of the algorithmic procedures, command structures, and logical operations embedded in these historical thinking machines, which were created as scholarly support. And how can such codes and algorithmic support mechanisms be transferred – and expanded – into the design of contemporary software?

What is the decisive driving force when it comes to bringing heterogeneous information together to create new and inspiring constellations of ideas? One of the most important elements of scientific innovation is the unexpected deviation from plan. Unforeseen events inspire new ideas. Such moments of inspiration increase when randomness – or special devices to systematically enable randomness – is built into the devices (Luhmann et al. 2015). In the history of thinking machines, the vast majority of mechanised conversation partners aim at a technical implementation that produces directed coincidence or serendipity. Sometimes randomness is built in mechanically, e.g. through the construction of various drawers, hidden chambers, and surprising mechanisms, and the deep and opaque order of these compartments, as in Roentgen's desks (*hardware*). Sometimes, it is an effect of the delegation of tasks to other semi-autonomous but overzealous or unpredictable assistants (*wetware*),[20] and sometimes it is the rhizomatic structure of filing systems determined by contingency, whose rule-governed use produces unexpected effects (*software*) – prominent examples of the *Zettelkasten* emphasise the surprises that the apparatus holds in store when utilised (Luhmann 1993; Luhmann et al. 2015). In short, directed operations of chance lead to surprising results, as a number of scholars can attest, such as the Russian literary historian Semen Vengerov (see Gamsa 2016), Aby Warburg and his library's 'law of good neighborliness' (see Wimmer 2017), or Hans Blumenberg's work with his own *Zettelkasten* (see Helbig 2019a; Helbig 2019b).

Varying assistance systems between Leibniz and Luhmann make it clear that in (machine) combinatorics, determined coincidence and the contingent selection, concealment, and uncovering of pieces of information in collaboration with machine assistants creates a complex sequence of operations. Creative work made in this way is the end product of a collaboration between humans and their media of knowledge generation. The writing user is faced with the task of weaving a coherent text out of the fragments supplied by the assisting intellectual furniture. The question remains: what are the paradigms, forms, and functions of assistance that the machine fulfills in each case? How exactly do new combinations and crucial moments of inspiration emerge in such systems of distributed intelligence? What is it about the nature of assistance systems and their epistemic environments that systematically elicits creativity in collaborations between human and non-human actors?

Leibniz already formulated it explicitly, and more importantly put it into practice with his excerpting cabinet: we need help to think, and it makes little difference whether we receive this help from classical human interlocutors, as Kleist did, or from non-human systems that themselves 'think' (or simulate thinking). Hence, the *Assisted Thinking* project understands artificial intelligence as it is usually defined in computer science – from the ambitious plans of the Dartmouth Conference in the summer of 1956 to artificial neural networks to chance and creativity (McCarthy et al. 1955; Kline 2011) and the current practices of developing and training LLMs – as just one variation of the historically broader phenomenon of intelligent assistance from scholarly assistance systems in the form of media of knowledge generation. It is hardly a coincidence that quite a few LLMs have been trained in the mode of *supervised learning*, that is, supervised by human assistants who are supposed to correct, for example, false attributions or biases.[21] It is also no coincidence that since the Baroque era, it has been inherent to thinking machines that their intelligence has always been distributed among a collective of hybrid actors consisting of human users and non-human assistants. This intelligence arises from an association of intellectual devices (such as thinking machines) and scholars, that collectively generates new ideas through interaction and dialogue.

The historical study of such intellectual furniture therefore aims to find out how intellectual furniture, as media of scholarship, have been 'programmed' to serve as scholarly utilities throughout history. Writing cabinets, file card indexes, wooden secretaries, *Zettelkästen*, standing desks, and other furnishings for intellectual work are intelligent agents through which specific work routines and action scripts (i.e., algorithms) are implemented. The *Assisted Thinking* project therefore systematically explores these devices, as well as their built-in functions, to analyse how intellectual furniture determine the way information is processed and managed. In both Leibniz's idiosyncratic excerpting cabinet and Luhmann's commercially available index card boxes – and even more clearly in the mechanical devices in Roentgen's desks – serendipity, forgetting, hiding, revealing, and surprise create intricate relationships between the informational building blocks to inspire the users as they hone their questions ('prompts') and to assist them in developing new thoughts and transforming them into the arc of a persuasive argument.

– Translated from the German by Laura Radosh

Works Cited

Bender, Emily M., Gebru, Timnit, McMillan-Major, Angelina et al., 2021. 'On the dangers of stochastic parrots: Can language models be too big?' In *Proceedings of the 2021 ACM Conference on Fairness, Accountability, and Transparency* FAccT'21 (March): 610-623. https://doi.org/10.1145/3442188.3445922.

Blair, Ann. 2019. 'Erasmus and His Amanuenses.' *Erasmus Studies* 39, no. 1: 22-49. https://doi.org/10.1163/18749275-03901011

Blumenbach, Johann Friedrich. 1786. 'Über die vorzüglichsten Methoden Collectaneen und Exzerpte zu sammeln.' *Medicinische Bibliothek* 2, no. 3: 547-559.

Brecht, Bertolt. (1930) 2001. 'Originality' In *Stories of Mr. Keuner*, 13. Translated by Martin Chalmers. San Francisco: City Lights Books.

Brommer, Frank. 1978. *Hephaistos. Der Schmiedegott in der antiken Kunst.* Deutsches Archäologisches Institut. Mainz am Rhein: Philipp von Zabern.

Campe, Joachim Heinrich. 1813. *Wörterbuch zur Erklärung und Verdeutschung der unserer Sprache aufgedrungenen fremden Ausdrücke. Ein Ergänzungsband zu Adelung's und Campe's Woerterbüchern.* New, greatly enlarged and thoroughly improved edition. Braunschweig: Schulbuchhandlung.

Cevolini, Alberto. 2016. *Forgetting machines. Knowledge management evolution in early modern Europe.* Vol. 53 of Library of the written word. The handpress world. Leiden: Brill.

Cevolini, Alberto. 2017. 'An Universal Index upon all Authors: Thomas Harrison's *Ark of Studies* and the Evolution of Social Memory.' In: *The Ark of Studies. Thomas Harrison*, edited by Alberto Cevolini, *De Diversis Artibus* vol. 102, 1-69. Turnhout: Brepols Publisher.

Eco, Umberto. 2006. *The Island of the Day Before*. Boston: Mariner Books.

Eisenstein, Elizabeth L. 1997. *Die Druckerpresse. Kulturrevolutionen im frühen modernen Europa*. Ästhetik und Naturwissenschaften. Medienkultur. Wien, New York: Springer Verlag.

Fabian, Dietrich. 2001. *Goethe – Roentgen. Ein Beitrag zur Kunstmöbelgeschichte des 18. Jahrhunderts*, 5th substantially expanded Ed. Bad Neustadt/Saale: Selbstverlag.

Furger, Carmen. 2010. *Briefsteller. Das Medium »Brief« im 17. und frühen 18. Jahrhundert*. Köln: Böhlau Verlag.

Gamsa, Mark. 2016. 'Two Million Filing Cards: The Empirical-Biographical Method of Semen Vengerov.' *History of Humanities* 1, no. 1 (2016): 129-153. https://doi.org/10.1086/685063

Giedion, Sigfried. 1948. *Mechanization Takes Command. A Contribution to Anonymous History*. New York: Oxford University Press.

Ginzburg, Carlo. (1983) 1995. 'Spurensicherung. Die Wissenschaft auf der Suche nach sich selbst.' *Kleine Kulturwissenschaftliche Bibliothek* vol. 50. Berlin: Verlag Klaus Wagenbach.

Goethe, Johann Wolfgang von. November 30, 1779. 'Letter to Charlotte von Stein.' In *Goethe Yearbook* vol. 25, edited by Adrian Daub and Elisabeth Krimmer. 2018, 207. Rochester: Camden House.

Goethe, Johann Wolfgang von. (1795) 1989. 'Conversations of German Refugees.' Translated by Jan van Heurck. In *Goethe: The Collected Works* edited by Jane K, Vol. 10, 15-92. Brown. Princeton: Princeton University Press.

Grajewski, Judith. 2023. 'Artificial Intelligence: We're having a Gutenberg Moment, at the very least.' https://www.beyond-print.net/artificial-intelligence-were-having-a-gutenberg-moment-at-the-very-least/.

Helbig, Daniela K. 2019a. 'Life without Toothache: Hans Blumenberg's Zettelkasten and History of Science as Theoretical Attitude.' *Journal of the History of Ideas* 80, no. 1, 91-112. https://doi.org/10.1353/jhi.2019.0005.

Helbig, Daniela K. 2019b. 'Ruminant machines: a twentieth-century episode in the material history of ideas.' https://www.jhiblog.org/2019/04/17/ruminant-machines-a-twentieth-century-episode-in-the-material-history-of-ideas/.

Hodges, Andrew. 1994. 'Alan Turing, Enigma' *Computerkultur* vol. 1. 2nd Ed. Wien, New York: Springer Verlag. First published 1983.

Hüser, Rembert. 1996. 'Frauenforschung.' In *Systemtheorie der Literatur*, edited by Jürgen Fohrmann and Harro Müller, *UTB* vol. 1929, 238-275. München: Wilhelm Fink Verlag.

Jones, Matthew L. 2016. *Reckoning with Matter. Calculating Machines, Innovation, and Thinking about Thinking from Pascal to Babbage*. Chicago: University of Chicago Press.

Kant, Immanuel. (1797) 1996. *The Metaphysics of Morals*. Translated by Mary J. Gregor. Cambridge: Cambridge University Press.

Kleist, Heinrich von. (1805) 1951. *On the Gradual Construction of Thoughts During Speech*. Translated by Michael Hamburger. German Life and Letters vol. 5, no.1 (October 1951), 42-46.

Kline, Ronald R. 2011. *Cybernetics, Automata Studies, and the Dartmouth Conference on Artificial Intelligence*. IEEE Annals of the History of Computing 33, no. 4, 5-16.

Koeppe, Wolfram and Baarsen, Reinier, eds. 2013. *Extravagant inventions. The princely furniture of the Roentgens*, 2nd Ed. New Haven: Yale University Press.

Krajewski, Markus. (2002) 2011. *Paper Machines. About Cards & Catalogs, 1548-1929*, History and Foundations of Information Science vol. 3. MIT Press, Cambridge Mass.

Krajewski, Markus. 2010. *Der Diener. Mediengeschichte einer Figur zwischen König und Klient*. Frankfurt am Main: S. Fischer Wissenschaft. S. Fischer Verlag.

Krajewski, Markus. 2012. 'Kommunikation mit Papiermaschinen. Über Niklas Luhmanns Zettelkasten.' In: *Maschinentheorien / Theoriemaschinen*, *edited by* Hans-Christian Herrmann and Wladimir Velminski, 283-305. Frankfurt am Main: Peter Lang Verlag.

Krajewski, Markus. 2018. 'Denkmöbel. Die Tische der Schreiber, analog/digital.' In: *Archive für Literatur. Der Nachlass und seine Ordnungen*, edited by Petra Maria Dallinger und Klaus Kastberger, *Literatur und Archiv* vol. 2, 193-213. Berlin: Walter de Gruyter.

Krajewski, Markus. 2019. 'Against the Power of Algorithms. Closing, Literate Programming, and Source Code Critique.' *Law Text Culture* vol. 23, 119-133.

Krajewski, Markus. 2022. 'Assistenzsysteme. Mimetische Praktiken verteilter Autorschaft zwischen Mensch und Maschine.' In: *Mimesis Expanded. Die Ausweitung der Mimetischen Zone*, edited by Friedrich Balke und Elisa Linseisen, *Medien und Mimesis* vol. 8, 217-246. Fink, Leiden, Paderborn: Brill.

Lackmann, Heinrich. 1966. 'Leibniz' bibliothekarische Tätigkeit in Hannover.' In *Leibniz. Sein Leben, sein Wirken, seine Welt*, edited by Wilhelm

Totok and Carl Haase, 321-348. Hannover: Verlag für Literatur und Zeitgeschehen.

Leibniz, Gottfried Wilhelm. (1679) 2022. 'On the Organon or Great Art of Thinking.' In *Leibniz on binary. The invention of computer arithmetic*, edited by Lloyd Strickland and Harry R. Lewis, 71-74. Cambridge, MA: MIT Press.

Leibniz, Gottfried Wilhelm. 2022. 'Wonderful Origin of All Numbers from 1 and Zero. May 1696.' In *Leibniz on Binary*, edited by Lloyd Strickland and Harry R. Lewis, 93-98. Cambridge, MA: MIT Press. https://doi.org/10.7551/mitpress/14123.003.0022

Luhmann, Niklas. 1968. „Technik des Zettelkastens [Ms. 2906]". https://niklas-luhmann-archiv.de/bestand/manuskripte/manuskript/MS_2906_0001.

Luhmann, Niklas. (1981) 1993. 'Kommunikation mit Zettelkästen. Ein Erfahrungsbericht.' In *Universität als Milieu*, edited by André Kieserling, 53-61. Bielefeld: Haux.

Luhmann, Niklas. 1987. *Archimedes und wir. Interviews*, edited by Dirk Baecker and Georg Stanitzek, vol. 143. Berlin: Merve Verlag.

Luhmann, Niklas. 1995. 'Was ist Kommunikation?' In Niklas Luhmann, *Soziologische Aufklärung* 6, 113-124. Opladen: Westdeutscher Verlag.

Luhmann, Niklas. (1995) 2001. 'Lesen lernen.' In Niklas Luhmann, *Short Cuts*, 150-156. Frankfurt am Main: Zweitausendeins.

Luhmann, Niklas, Rückriem, Ulrich, Sasse, Jörg et al., eds. 2015. *Serendipity. Vom Glück des Findens*. Köln: Snoeck.

Mackenzie, Adrian. 2017. *Machine learners. Archaeology of a data practice*. Cambridge, MA: MIT Press.

Malcolm, Noel. 2004. 'Thomas Harrison and his »Ark of Studies«. An Episode in the History of the Organisation of Knowledge.' *The Seventeenth Century* 19, Nr. 2, 196-232. https://doi.org/10.1080/0268117X.2004.10555543.

Mattern, Shannon. 2014. 'Intellectual Furnishings.' Medium, Oktober 19, 2014. DOI/URL: https://medium.com/@shannonmattern/intellectual-furnishings-e2076cf5f2de

McCarthy, John, Minsky, Marvin L., Rochester, Nathaniel et al. 1955. 'Dartmouth Summer Research Project on Artificial Intelligence.' https://raysolomonoff.com/dartmouth/boxa/dart564props.pdf.

Meiner, Jörg. 2001. Monument und Maschine. Zur Bedeutung der Automatenmöbel David Roentgens für die Höfe von Versailles, Berlin und St. Petersburg. In *Kunsttexte.de. Zeitschrift für Kunst- und Kulturgeschichte im Netz, Sektion Politische Ikonographie*, 1. https://doi.org/10.18452/7582

Merton, Robert K. and Barber, Elinor G. 2004. *The travels and adventures of serendipity. A study in sociological semantics and the sociology of science.* Princeton: Princeton University Press.

Murr, Christoph Gottlieb von. 1779. 'Von Leibnitzens Exzerpirschrank.' *Journal zur Kunstgeschichte und allgemeinen Litteratur* 7, 210-212.

Naudé, Gabriel. (1627) 1963. *Advis pour dresser une bibliothèque.* Leipzig: VEB Edition.

Pias, Claus. 2003. 'Digitale Sekretäre: 1968, 1978, 1998.' In *Europa: Kultur der Sekretäre*, edited by Bernhard Siegert and Joseph Vogl, 235-251. Zürich: Diaphanes.

Rosenkranz, Karl. (1844) 1969. *Georg Wilhelm Friedrich Hegels Leben.* 2nd unaltered reprographic Ed. Darmstadt: Wissenschaftliche Buchgesellschaft.

Sargentson, Carolyn. 2011. 'Looking at Furniture Inside Out: Strategies of Secrecy and Security in Eighteenth Century French Furniture.' In *Furnishing the Eighteenth Century: What Furniture Can Tell Us About the European and American Past*, edited by Dena Goodman and Kathryn Norberg, 205-236. New York: Routledge.

Schefzyk, Miriam. 2021. *Migration und Integration im Paris des 18. Jahrhunderts. Martin Carlin und die deutschen Ebenisten*, vol. 1 of *Vernetzen – Bewegen – Verorten*. Bielefeld: transcript Verlag.

Siegert, Bernhard. 1990. 'Das Amt des Gehorchens. Hysterie der Telephonistinnen oder Wiederkehr des Ohres 1874-1913.' In *Armaturen der Sinne. Literarische und technische Medien 1870 bis 1920*, edited by Jochen Hörisch and Michael Wetzel, 83-106. München: Wilhelm Fink Verlag.

Sobel, Dava. 2007. *Longitude: The True Story of a Lone Genius Who Solved the Greatest Scientific Problem of His Time.* New York: Bloomsbury USA.

Sonar, Thomas. 2007. 'Der Tod des Gottfried Wilhelm Leibniz. Wahrheit und Legende im Licht der Quellen.' *Abhandlungen der Braunschweigischen Wissenschaftlichen Gesellschaft* 59: 161-201. https://doi.org/10.24355/dbbs.084-201302051145-0.

Stein, Erwin, Kopp, Franz Otto, Wiechmann, Karin et al. 2006. Neue Forschungsergebnisse und Funktionsmodelle zur dezimalen Vier Spezies-Rechenmaschine von und zur dyadischen Rechenmaschine nach Leibniz. In *VIII. Internationaler Leibniz-Kongress: Einheit in der Vielheit*, edited by Herbert Berger, 1018-1025. Hannover: Gottfried-Wilhelm-Leibniz-Gesellschaft.

Tamisier-Vetois, Isabelle, Schefzyk, Myriam and Cousin, Pierre-Alain Le. 2018. *Meubles à secrets, secrets de meubles.* Dijon: Faton Eds.

Turing, Alan Mathison. 1936. 'On computable numbers, with an application to the Entscheidungsproblem' *American Journal of Mathematics*, no. 58: 230-265.

Vega Esquerra, Amador, Weibel, Peter und Zielinski, Siegfried, eds. 2018. *DIA-LOGOS. Ramon Llull's method of thought and artistic practice.* Minneapolis: University of Minnesota Press.

Vogt, Victor, 1922. *Die Kartei. Ihre Anlage und Führung*, vol. 5 of *Orga-Schriften*, 2nd ed., edited by Dr Porstmann. Berlin: Organisation Verlagsanstalt.

Voskuhl, Adelheid. 2013. *Androids in the Enlightenment. Mechanics, artisans, and cultures of the self.* Chicago: University of Chicago Press.

Walsdorf, Ariane, Badur, Klaus und Otto, Franz. 2015. 'Das letzte Original – Die Leibniz–Rechenmaschine der Gottfried-Wilhelm-Leibniz-Bibliothek', vol. 1 of *Schatzkammer*. Hannover: Gottfried-Wilhelm-Leibniz-Bibliothek.

Wegmann, Nikolaus and Bickenbach, Matthias. 1997. „Herders Reisejournal. Ein Datenbankreport.' *DVJs* 71, no. 3: 397-420. https://doi.org/10.1007/BF03375643

Willscheid, Bernd, Fowler, Ian, Hallerbach, Achim et al., eds. 2022. *Roentgen & Kinzing à Neuwied. Möbel und Uhren für Europa: Sammlung Roetgen-Museum Neuwied. Furniture and clocks for Europe: Collection Roentgen Museum Neuwied.* Neuwied: Roentgen-Museum Neuwied.

Wimmer, Mario. 2017. The Afterlives of Scholarship: Warburg und Cassirer. *History of Humanities* 2, no. 1: 245-270. https://doi.org/10.1086/690581

Notes

1. Those drawing such comparisons range from OpenAI CEO Sam Altman to journalists such as Jörg Schieb, podcasters like Joe Rogan or politicians such as Larry Summers; just as long is the list of their critics, who immediately debunk such comparisons.

2. At least that is how long it took until Elizabeth Eisenstein (1997) worked out the causal interactions between the printing press and the Reformation, whose medial a priori was the letterpress.

3. Leibniz's last secretary, Johann Georg Eckhart, is perhaps the best-known member of his staff, alongside Johann Hermann Vogler and others, see Sonar (2007: 190ff). On scientific work with subalterns, see also Krajewski (2010).

4. The history of intellectual furnishings, of course, includes more than just special devices for storing notations. Library architecture, shelves and their arrangement in space, catalogues, chairs, armchairs, console tables, chests of drawers, etc. should also be mentioned. Shannon Mattern (2014) gives a good historical overview, building on Sigfried Giedion (1948).

5. Cevolini (2017) reconstructs the convoluted history of this piece of intellectual furnishing in an excellent essay that includes translations into English of the source texts by Harrison and Placcius.

6. On the tradition of secret compartments in writing furniture in the eighteenth century, see Sargentson (2011).

7. On European furniture makers, cabinetmakers, and craftsmen in the Age of Enlightenment, see Voskuhl (2013: 89 ff).

8. The mechanics of the secret compartments and of the unfolding of the standing desk can be seen in two films, one from the Versailles Palace (youtu.be/75pEbWv1dbo), the other from the Roentgen Museum in Neuwied (youtu.be/llr8z8aCnbM).

9. Every memory arrangement always works as a machine of forgetting, see Cevolini (2016).

10. According to Meiner (2001: 10-14), it was the princes themselves who had exclusive access to these anti-utilitarian representational objects, thus making their uselessness in writing precisely their point.

11. Umberto Eco (2006) centred an entire novel around this story (Chapter 16 'Discourse on the Powder of Sympathy'). The powder was the subject of extensive debate in the mid-seventeenth century, see for instance www.theatra.de/repertorium/ed000184.pdf, as well as Sobel (2007), Chapter 5 'Powder of Sympathy'.

12. On the theory of filing see Vogt (1922), 7.

13. This and the following terms are taken from the corresponding slips in Luhmann's now digitised boxes; in this case at niklas-luhmann-archiv.de/bestand/zettelkasten/zettel/ZK_2_NB_9-8_V. For an English translation of section 9/8 see https://zettelkasten.de/posts/luhmanns-zettel-translated/

14. The terms lump or heap have themselves become theorisable in the meantime – even beyond mathematics; see Fabian Steinhauer's reflections in his blog 'Unter dem Gesetz', #haufenbildung als strukturprinzip.

15. Luhmann, Niklas (1961-1997): ZK II Zettel 9/8 (undated). Bielefeld: Niklas Luhmann Archives, [niklas-luhmann-archiv.de/bestand/zettelkasten/zettel/ZK_2_NB_9-8_V], English translation see https://zettelkasten.de/posts/luhmanns-zettel-translated/.

16. Luhmann, Niklas (1961-1997): ZK II Zettel 9/8,3 (undated). Bielefeld: Niklas-Luhmann-Archiv, [niklas-luhmann-archiv.de/bestand/zettelkasten/zettel/ZK_2_NB_9-8-3_V], English translation see https://zettelkasten.de/posts/luhmanns-zettel-translated/.

17. On the context of Luhmann's Zettelkasten in the historical discourse on theory machines, see Krajewski (2012).

18. 'If I have nothing else to do, then I *write* all day; in the morning from 8.30 am to noon, then I take the dog for a short walk, then I have time again in the afternoon from 2 pm to 4 pm, then it's the dog's turn again. [...] Yes, and then I usually write in the evening until around 11:00 pm. At 11:00 pm I usually lie in bed and *read* a few more things.' (Luhmann 1987: 145), my emphasis.

19. 'In all his wanderings, he always preserved these incunabula of his education. They were kept partly in portfolios, partly in slipcase binders on the spine of which was affixed a label for orientation' (Rosenkranz 1969: 12); for a comparison between Luhmann's and Hegel's *Zettelkasten*, see Krajewski (2012).

20. On these human assistants and the resulting effects when editing, copying, etc. see Blair (2019).

21. For a critical analysis of these supervised learning processes from the perspective of media archaeology, see Mackenzie (2017).

9

The Financialisation of Intelligence: Neoliberal Thought and Artificial Intelligence

Orit Halpern

x – the value.
In this case, the value above the strike price.

μ – mean of our normal distribution.
In this case, a function of volatility, it reflects the risk-free rate and spread of possible options over time

$$d_1 = \frac{\ln\left(\frac{S_0}{K}\right) + \left(r + \frac{\sigma^2}{2}\right)(T-t)}{\sigma\sqrt{T-t}}$$

σ – standard deviation
In this case, a function of volatility over time

> Noise in the sense of a large number of small events is often a causal factor much more powerful than a small number of large events can be. Noise makes trading in financial markets possible, and thus allows us to observe prices for financial assets [...] We are forced to act largely in the dark.[1]

—Fischer Black

In 1986, Fischer Black, one of the founders of contemporary finance, made a rather surprising announcement – bad data, incomplete information, wrong decisions, excess data, and fake news, all make arbitrage possible. In the famous article 'Noise Trading', Black posited that we trade and profit from misinformation and information overload. Assuming a large number of 'small' events networked together as far more powerful than large scale planned events, the vision of the market here is not one of Cartesian mastery or fully informed decision makers. Noise is the very infrastructure for value.

In an age of meme driven speculation, NFT's, and democratised options trading, such a statement might seem common sense. Even natural. Does anyone, after all, really think a crypto currency named as a joke for a small dog, or an almost bankrupt mall-based game retailer are intrinsically worth anything? Much less billions of dollars? Of course they do. For the past few years, great fortunes and major funds have collapsed and risen on just such bets. In retrospect everyone seems to have perfect clarity about 'value' investing, but apparently at the time, no one does. 'Irrational exuberance' to quote Federal Reserve Board Chairman Alan Greenspan in the late 1990's on the dot-com boom, might be the term. But Greenspan might have gotten it wrong on one point. Irrational exuberance was not market failure but market success.

Fischer Black, who not incidentally was the student of Marvin Minsky and spent a lot of time thinking about intelligence, artificial or otherwise, was one of the inventors of the world's preeminent trading instruments, the Black-Scholes Options Pricing Model. For Black, 'irrationality' was not an exception, but rather a norm. The very foundation for contemporary markets. Noise, Black argued, is about a lot of small actions networked together accumulating in greater effects on price and markets then large singular or perhaps planned events. Noise is the result of human subjectivity in systems with too much data to really process. Not incidentally perhaps, Black was also discussing a new technology, the derivative pricing equation, whose execution at scale demanded large infrastructures of high-speed networked digital computers. Noise is also the language of mathematical theories of communication, betraying the genealogy of how contemporary finance is linked to computing and even more specifically machine learning.

While seemingly the territory of the few and the select in finance, quite on the contrary, such statements reflect an attitude that is ubiquitous today and integrated into our smartphone trading apps and social networks. Mainly, the idea that we are all networked together to make collective decisions within frameworks of self-organising systems that cannot be perfectly regulated or guided. Furthermore, we have come to believe that human judgement is flawed, and that this is not a problem, but a frontier for social networks and artificial intelligence.

The options pricing model also exemplifies a broader problem for economists of finance; namely that theories or models, to paraphrase Milton Friedman, 'are engines not cameras'.[2] One way to read that statement is that the model does not represent the world but makes it. Models make markets. Models in finance are instruments such as a derivative pricing equation or an algorithm for high-speed trading. There are assumptions built into these technologies about gathering data, comparing prices, betting, selling, and timing bets, but not about whether that information is correct or 'true' or whether the market is mapped or shown in its entirety. These theories are tools, and they let people create markets by arbitraging differences in prices without necessarily knowing everything about the entire market or asset.

These financial models are, to use Donna Haraway's term, 'god-tricks' (Haraway 1991). They perform omniscience and control over uncertain, complex, and massive markets. They are also embodiments of ideology – mainly that markets can neither be regulated or planned. These instruments naturalise and enact an imaginary that markets make the best decisions about allocation of value without planning by a state or other organisation. In what follows I hope to trace how neoliberal theory, psychology, and artificial intelligence intersected to produce the infrastructure for our contemporary noisy trading. If today we swipe and click as a route to imagined wealth, we should ask how we have come to so unthinkingly and unconsciously accept the dictates of finance and technology.

Networked Intelligence

The idea that human judgement is flawed (or corrupt) and that markets could neither be regulated nor fully predicted and planned has long been central to the automation and computerisation of financial exchanges. Throughout the middle of the twentieth century, increased trading volumes forced clerks to fall behind on transaction tapes and often omit or fail to enter specific prices and transactions at particular times. Human error and slowness came to be understood as untenable and 'non-transparent', or arbitrary in assigning price (Kennedy 2017).

In the case of the New York Stock Exchange, for example, there were also labour issues. Managers needed ways to manage and monitor labour, particularly lower paid clerical work. As a result, computerised trading desks were introduced to the NYSE in the 1960s. These computerised systems were understood as being algorithmic and rule bound. The more automated the market, thinking went, the more rule bound it would become. Officials also thought computing would save the securities industry from regulation; that if computers followed the rules algorithmically, there was no need for oversight or regulation (Kennedy 2017).

This belief in the rationality and self-regulation of algorithms derived from a longer neoliberal tradition that reimagined human intelligence as machinic and networked. According to Austrian-born economist Friedrich Hayek writing in 1945:

> The peculiar character of the problem of a rational economic order is determined precisely by the fact that the knowledge of the circumstances of which we must make use never exists in concentrated or integrated form, but solely as the dispersed bits of incomplete and frequently contradictory knowledge which all the separate individuals possess. The economic problem of society is thus not merely a problem of how to allocate 'given' resources – if 'given' is taken to mean given to a single

mind which deliberately solves the problem set by these 'data.' It is rather a problem of how to secure the best use of resources known to any of the members of society, for ends whose relative importance only these individuals know. Or, to put it briefly, it is a problem of the utilization of knowledge not given to anyone in its totality. (Hayek 1945: 519-20)

Human beings, Hayek believed, were subjective, incapable of reason, and fundamentally limited in their attention and cognitive capacities. At the heart of Hayek's conception of a market was the idea that no single subject, mind, or central authority can fully represent and understand the world. He argued that 'The "data" from which the economic calculus starts are never for the whole society 'given' to a single mind [...] and can never be so given' (Hayek 1945: 520). Instead, only markets can learn at scale and suitably evolve to coordinate dispersed resources and information in the best way possible.

Responding to what he understood to be the failure of democratic populism that resulted in fascism and the rise of communism, Hayek disavowed centralised planning or states. Instead, he turned to another model of both human agency and markets. First, Hayek posits that markets are not about matching supply and demand, but about coordinating information.[3] Second, Hayek's model of learning and 'using knowledge' is grounded in the idea of a networked intelligence embodied in the market which can allow the creation of knowledge outside of and beyond the purview of individual humans: 'The whole acts as one market, not because any of its members survey the whole field, but because their limited individual fields of vision sufficiently overlap so that through many intermediaries the relevant information is communicated to all' (Hayek 1945: 526). And third, the market therefore embodies a notion of cognition and decision that I would call 'environmental intelligence', in which the data upon which such a calculating machine operates is dispersed throughout the society, and where decision making is a population-grounded activity derived from but not congruent with individual bodies and thoughts.

Hayek's idea of environmental intelligence was inherited directly from the work of Canadian psychologist Donald O. Hebb, who is known as the inventor of the layered neural network model and the theory that 'cells [neurons] that wire together fire together' (Keysers and Gazzola 2014). While Pitts and McCulloch (1943) had developed a logical calculus paralleling neurons to logic gates, Hebb produced a more comprehensive psychological model involving many neurons. In 1949, Hebb published the *Organisation of Behavior*, a text that popularised the idea that the brain stores knowledge about the world in complex networks or 'populations' of neurons. The research is today famous for presenting a new concept of functional neuroplasticity, which was developed through working with soldiers and other individuals who had been injured, lost limbs, blinded, or rendered deaf from proximity to blasts. While these individuals suffered changes to their sensory order, Hebb noted that the loss of a limb or a sense would be compensated for through training. He thus began to suspect that neurons might rewire themselves to accommodate the trauma and create new capacities.

The rewiring of neurons was not just a matter of attention, but also memory. Hebb theorised that brains don't store inscriptions or exact representations of objects, but instead patterns of neurons firing. For example, if a baby sees a cat, a certain group of neurons fire. The more cats the baby sees, the more a certain set of stimuli become related to this animal, and the more the same set of neurons will fire when a 'cat' enters the field of perception. This idea is the basis for contemporary ideas of learning in neural networks. It was also an inspiration to Hayek, who in his 1956 book *The Sensory Order* openly cited Hebb as providing a key model for imagining human cognition. Hayek used the idea that the brain is comprised of networks to remake the very idea of the liberal subject. The subject is not one of reasoned objectivity, but rather subjective with limited information and incapacity to make objective decisions.

The concept of algorithmic, replicable, and computational decision making that was forwarded in the Cold War was not the model of conscious, affective, and informed decision making privileged since the democratic revolutions of the eighteenth century (Erickson 2015). But if Cold War technocrats were still experts with authority and predictive capacities, the ignorant and partially informed individual that Hayek presents us with is not.

Hayek thus reconceptualised human agency and choice neither as informed technocratic guidance nor as the freedom to exercise reasoned decision making long linked to concepts of sovereignty. Rather, he reformulated agency as the freedom to become part of the market or network. He was very specific this point; theories of economy or politics based on collective or social models of market making and government were flawed in privileging the reason and objectivity of the few policy makers and governing officials over the many. This privileging he deduced results in Communism or Fascism. The state making plans quells the abilities of minorities, in his view, to take independent action. Hayek elaborated that freedom, therefore, was not the result of reasoned objective decision making, not the technocratic elite decision maker with volumes of data objectively and emotionlessly analysed, but rather freedom from coercion. Coercion often coming to mean the effort to exclude individuals from chosen economic activities and markets. When linked to his discussions about subjectivity, ignorance, and the market as the only mechanism for making reasoned decisions as a collective, one can trace the bedrock of an argument against policy directed forms of equity making or civil rights and the assertion that all rights and freedoms are protections from the state, not services or support from the state. While in theory preserving the 'freedom' of an individual to participate equally in any market could be viewed as supporting the necessity of legal and humane infrastructures to allow all individuals this access, neoliberal thinking and the Republican Party did not interpret in this direction (Hayek 2011).

The main point here is that neoliberal models of human agency, freedom, and markets reformulated ideas about intelligence, reason, and decision making. These reformulated ideas reflected and refracted, as we will see, ideas of networked computing, neural networks in psychology and machine learning; ultimately infrastructuring contemporary understandings of networks, finance, and artificial intelligence. This genealogy also reveals that models have politics and are socially embedded. These models of networked decision making aided and abetted broader political movement invested in countering other ideas of human agency and freedom including civil rights.

Machines

Neoliberal theory posited the possibility that markets themselves possess reason or some sort of sovereignty; a reason built from networking human actions into a larger collective without planning, and, theoretically, politics. The market can thus be understood as a sort of decision making machine, returning us to Milton Friedman's original statement about economic models as being engines not cameras. But if markets and minds are engines, what type of machines would they be?

Efforts to produce digital computing and machine learning had long been related to economics and psychology. Whether in markets, machines, or human minds, particularly in the post-war period, many human, social, and natural sciences came to rely on models of communication and information related to computing. Models of the world such as those embedded in game theory reflected emerging ideas about rationality separated from human reason, and managing systems, whether political or economic, came to be understood as a question of information processing and analysis (Halpern and Mitchell 2023).

Models of minds and machines took a dramatic turn in 1956, when a series of computer scientists, psychologists, and other scientists embarked on a project to develop machine forms of learning. In a proposal for a workshop at Dartmouth College in 1955, John McCarthy labelled this new concept 'artificial intelligence' (McCarthy et al. 2006). While many of the participants, including Marvin Minsky, Nathaniel Rochester, Warren McCulloch, Ross Ashby, and Claude Shannon, focused on symbolic and linguistic processes, one model focused on the neuron. A psychologist, Frank Rosenblatt proposed that learning, whether in non-human animals, humans, or computers, could be modelled on artificial, cognitive devices that implement the basic architecture of the human brain (Rosenblatt 1962).

In his initial paper that emerged from the Dartmouth programme detailing the idea of a 'perceptron', Rosenblatt distances himself from his peers. These scientists, he claimed, had been 'chiefly concerned with the question of how such functions as perception and recall might be achieved by a deterministic system of any sort, rather than how this is actually done by the brain'. This approach, he argued, fundamentally ignored the question of scale and the emergent properties of biological systems. Instead, Rosenblatt based his approach on the theory of statistical separability, which he attributed to Hebb and Hayek, and a new conception of networked perception-cognition (Rosenblatt 1962). According to Rosenblatt, neurons are mere switches or nodes in a network that classifies cognitive input, and intelligence emerges only at the level of the population and through the patterns of interaction between neurons.

Contemporary neural networks grounded as they are theories of Hebbian networks operate on the same principles. Groups of nets exposed repeatedly to the same stimuli would eventually be trained to fire together; recall the cat and the baby. Each exposure increases the statistical likelihood that the net will fire together and 'recognise' the object. In supervised 'learning', then, nets can be corrected through the comparison of their result with the original input. The key feature is that the input does not need to be ontologically defined or represented, meaning that a series of networked machines can come to identify a cat without having to be explained what a cat 'is'. Only through patterns of affiliation does sensory response emerge. The key to learning was therefore exposure to a 'large sample of stimuli', which Rosenblatt stressed meant approaching the nature of learning 'in terms of probability theory rather than symbolic logic' (Rosenblatt 1962: 386-408). The perceptron model suggests that machine systems, like markets, might be able to perceive what individual subjects cannot (Rosenblatt 1958). While each human individual is limited to a specific set of external stimuli to which they are exposed, a computer perceptron can, by contrast, draw on data that are the result of judgements and experiences of not just one individual, but rather large populations of human individuals. Since these machines are trained on data sets from more than one individual or one source in theory, they would understand something beyond the apprehension of one human being, just like markets.

Against Thought

For Rosenblatt and Hayek, and their predecessors in psychology, notions of learning forwarded the idea that systems can change and adapt non-consciously, or automatically. The central feature of these models was that small operations done on parts of a problem might agglomerate into a group that is greater than the sum of their parts and solve problems not through representation but through behaviour. Both Hayek and Rosenblatt take from theories of communication and information, particularly from cybernetics that posit communication in terms of thermodynamics. According to this theory, systems at different scales are only probabilistically related to their parts. Calculating individual components therefore cannot represent or predict the act of the entire system.[4] While never truly possible, this disavowal of 'representation' continues to fuel the desire for ever larger data sets and unsupervised learning in neural nets which would, at least in theory, be driven by the data.

Hayek himself espoused an imaginary of this data rich world that could be increasingly calculated without (human) consciousness. He was apparently fond of quoting Alfred North Whitehead's remark that 'it is a profoundly erroneous truism [...] that we should cultivate the habit of thinking what we are doing. The precise opposite is the case. Civilization advances by extending the number of important operations we can perform without thinking about them' (Moore 2016).[5] The perceptron is the technological manifestation of the reconfiguration and reorganisation of human subjectivity, physiology, psychology, and economy that this theory implies. And as a result of the belief that technical decision making not through governments but at the scale of populations might ameliorate the danger of populism or the errors of human judgement, the neural net became the embodiment of an idea (and ideology) of networked decision making that could scale from within the mind to the planetary networks of electronic trading platforms and global markets. As the genealogy between psychology, computing, and economics demonstrates, it's clear that the idea of a networked intelligence, perhaps best exemplified in our present through the figure of the neural net and 'deep' learning, has been a grounding assumption and technique bringing media and finance together.

Derivation

This reorganisation of rationality and technology has no better exemplar then derivative trading models. One of the central technologies for capitalising on 'noise' and the market as information processor, was the Black-Scholes Option Pricing Model, which Black developed with his colleagues Myron Scholes and Robert Merton.

Though it has traditionally been difficult for traders to determine how much the option to purchase an asset or stock should cost, up until the 1970s, it was widely assumed that the value of an option to buy a stock would necessarily be related to the expected rate of return of the underlying stock itself, which in turn would be function of the health and profitability of the company that issue the stock.[6] This is the old understanding related to objective measures of value. It's also an old understanding of models – that they represent or abstract from something real out there in the world.

Black and his colleague Scholes introduced the Black-Scholes Option pricing model in 1973 in order to provide a new way of relating options prices to the future.[7] What made this model unique in the history of finance was that it completely detached the price of an option from any expectation about the likely value of the underlying asset at the option maturity date. Instead, the key value for Black and Scholes was the expected *volatility* of the stock, which meant the movement up and down of the price over time. The estimated volatility of a stock was not a function of one's estimate of the profitability of the company that issued the stock, but was instead in part a function of the investment market as a whole.[8] The Black-Scholes option pricing model, in other words, was not interested in the 'true' value of the underlying asset, but rather in the relationship of the stock to the market as a whole.

Scholes and Black had begun working together in the late 1960's while consulting for investment firms. Their work involved applying computers to modern portfolio theory and automating arbitrage. (A 'portfolio' is a collection of multiple investments, which vary in their presumed riskiness, and which aim to maximise profit for a specific level of overall risk; 'arbitrage' refers to purportedly risk-free investments, such as the profit that can be made when one takes advantage of slight differences between currency exchanges – or the price of the same stock – in two different locations.) Scholes and Black opened 'The Pricing of Options and Corporate Liabilities', in which they introduced their option pricing equation, with a challenge: 'If options are correctly priced in the market, it should not be possible to make sure profits by creating portfolios of long and short positions'. Since people do make money, options therefore cannot be correctly priced. Mispricing – that is, imperfect transmission of information – must be essential to the operation of markets. This also meant, though, that a trader could not, even in principle, simply 'be rational' in deciding on the risk assigned to an option (by, for example, attempting to determine the true value of the underlying asset).

Working between physics, machine learning, and cybernetics, Scholes and Black recognised that the insights of reasonable traders might matter less in pricing assets then would measuring the volatility of a stock (that is, the dynamics of upward and downward movement of price over time). Considering the context, and Black's close relationship to computer sciences, it is possible to understand their conclusion as extending the assumptions inherent within neural network theories and neoliberal economic theory, to building technologies for betting on futures.

Stocks, they reasoned, behaved more like the random motions of particles in water (thermodynamics) than proxies or representations of some underlying economic reality. And agents (humans) behaved more like machines, or perhaps blindfolded individuals. The market is full of noise (understood as unpredictable or not fully knowable signals), and the agents within it do not know the relationship between the price of a security and the 'real' value of the underlying asset. The system is chaotic. However, if agents recognise the limits of their knowledge, they can focus on what they *can* know: namely, how a single stock price varies over time, and how that variation relates to the price variations of other stocks. Instead of trying to calculate the relationship between price of a security and the real value of the asset, something that Black and Scholes assumed one generally cannot know, they operated with the assumption that all the stocks in the market moved independently like gas particles in thermodynamics, and that measures of information like entropy and enthalpy could therefore also apply to the way stock prices 'signal' each other. Their innovation was to posit that in order to price an option, one needed only to take the current price and the price changes of the asset and figure out the complete distribution of share prices to calculate an option price.[9]

While initially no one was ready to publish the article due to its supposed overly technical approach, within weeks of its publication, numerous corporations were already offering software for such pricing equations (MacKenzie 2006: 60-67). This was in part a consequence of the fact that the model joined communications and information theories with calculation in a way that made the equation amenable to algorithmic enactment. In fact, as individuals created more complex derivative instruments tying many types of assets and markets together, computers became essential both for obtaining data about price volatility and calculating option prices. An entire industry, and the financial markets of today, were born from this innovation and its new understanding of noise. And because derivatives are bets on the *future* value of an asset, the derivatives market is in fact far larger than the world's current gross domestic product, by now exceeding the world's GDP by twenty times. Since the 1970s, these markets have grown nearly massively (e.g., 25% per year over the last 25 years).

There is also a deeply repressed history of geopolitics behind these innovations in finance. The derivative pricing equation emerged with the end of Bretton Woods, decolonisation, post-Fordism, and the OPEC oil crisis, to name a few of the transformations at the time then, as a way to tame or circumvent extreme volatility in politics, currency, and commodity markets. New financial technologies and institutions such as hedge funds were created in order to literally 'hedge' bets: to ensure that risks were reallocated, decentralised, and networked. Through the likes of derivative technologies such as short bets, credit swaps, and futures markets, dangerous bets would be combined with safer ones and dispersed across multiple territories and temporalities. Corporations, governments, and financiers flocked to these techniques of uncertainty management in the face of seemingly unknowable, unnamable, and unquantifiable, risks.[10] The impossibility of prediction, the subjective nature of human decision making, and the electronic networking of global media systems, all became infrastructures for new forms of betting on futures while evading the political-economic struggles of the day.

Models and Machines

Neoliberal economics often theorises the world as a self-organising adaptive system to counter the idea of planned and perfectly controllable political (and potentially totalitarian) orders. Within this ideology the market takes on an almost divine, or perhaps biologically determinist, capacity for chance and emergence, but never through consciousness or planning (Ramey 2015). Evolution was imagined against willed action and the reasoned decisions of individual humans. More critically, emerging in the backdrop of civil rights and calls for racial, sexual, and queer forms of justice and equity, the negation of any state intervention or planning (say affirmative action) became naturalised in the figure of the neural net and derivative; a model of mind and market that appeared to make human built institutions and organisations (such as the NYSE) seem as naturalised necessities. Any efforts to address structural injustice became a conspiracy against emergence, economy, and intelligence.[11]

We have become attuned to this model of the world where our machines and markets are syncopated with one another. These models, however, might also have the potential to remake our relations with each other and the world. As cultural theorist Randy Martin has argued, rather than separating itself from social processes of production and reproduction, algorithmic and derivative finance actually demonstrates the increased inter-relatedness, globalisation, and socialisation of debt and precarity. By tying together disparate actions and objects into a single assembled bundle of reallocated risks to trade, new market machines have made us more indebted to each other. The political and ethical question thus becomes how we might activate this mutual indebtedness in new ways, ones that are less amenable to the strict market logics of neoliberal economics (Martin 2014).

The future lies in recognising what our machines have finally made visible, and what has perhaps always been there: the socio-political nature of our seemingly natural thoughts and perceptions. Every market crash, every sub-prime mortgage event, reveals the social constructedness and the work – aesthetic, political, economic – it takes to maintain our belief in markets as forces of nature or divinity. And if it is not aesthetically smoothed over through media and narratives of inevitability, they also make it possible to recognise how our machines have linked so many of us together in precarity. The potential politics of these moments has not yet been realised, but there have been efforts, whether in Occupy, or more recently in movements for civil rights, racial equity, and environmental justice such as Black Lives Matter or the Chilean anti-austerity protests of 2019 (to name a few).

In that all computer systems are programmed, and therefore planned, we are also forced to contend with the intentional and therefore changeable nature of how we both think and perceive our world. The failed efforts to model markets makes us recognise the historically situated and socially specific nature of both the economy and cognition.

Works Cited

Black, Fischer. 1986. 'Noise.' *The Journal of Finance* 41, no. 3: 529-43.

Das, Satyajit. 2006. *Traders, Guns, and Money: Knowns and Unknowns in the Dazzling World of Derivatives*. Edinburgh: Prentice Hall: Financial Times.

Erickson, Paul, Judy L. Klein, Lorraine Daston, Rebecca M. Lemov, Thomas Sturm, and Michael D. Gordin. 2015. *How Reason Almost Lost Its Mind: The Strange Career of Cold War Rationality*. Chicago: University Of Chicago Press.

Grove, Kevin. 2018. *Resilience*. New York: Routledge.

Halpern, Orit, and Robert Mitchell. 2023. *The Smartness Mandate*. Cambridge, MA: MIT Press.

Haraway, Donna. 1991. 'A Cyborg Manifesto: Science, Technology, and Socialist-Feminism in the Late Twentieth Century.' In *Simians, Cyborgs and Women: The Reinvention of Nature*, edited by Donna Haraway, 149-81. New York: Routledge.

Hayek, Friedrich. *The Constitution of Liberty*. 2011. Chicago: University of Chicago Press.

Hayek, Friedrich. 'The Use of Knowledge in Society.' 1945. *The American Economic Review* XXXV, September: 519-30.

Hebb, Donald. 1949. *The Organisation of Behavior: A Neuropsychological Theory*. New York: Wiley.

Kennedy, Devin. 2017. 'The Machine in the Market: Computers and the Infrastructure of Price at the New York Stock Exchange, 1965-1975.' *Social Studies of Science* 47, no. 6: 888-917.

Keysers, Christian, and Valeria Gazzola. 2014. 'Hebbian Learning and Predictive Mirror Neurons for Actions, Sensations and Emotions.' *Philosophical Transactions of the Royal Society B: Biological Sciences* 369 (1644): 20130175. https://doi.org/10.1098/rstb.2013.0175.

Lewis, Paul. 2016. 'The Emergence of 'Emergence' in the Work of F.A. Hayek: A Historical Analysis.' *History of Political Economy* 48, no. 1: 111-50.

MacKenzie, Donald A. 2006. *An Engine, Not a Camera: How Financial Models Shape Markets*. Cambridge, MA: MIT Press.

Martin, Randy. 2014. 'What Difference do Derivatives Make? From the Technical to the Political Conjuncture.' *Culture Unbound* 6: 189-210.

McCulloch, Warren, and Walter Pitts. 1943. 'A Logical Calculus of Ideas Immanent in Nervous Activity.' In *Embodiments of Mind*, edited by Warren McCulloch. Cambridge: MIT Press.

Mirowski, Philip. 2002. *Machine Dreams : Economics Becomes a Cyborg Science*. Cambridge: Cambridge University Press.

Mirowski, Philip. 2006. 'Twelve Theses Concerning the History of Postwar Neoclassical Price Theory.' *History of Political Economy* 38: 344-79.

Moore, Alfred. 2016. 'Hayek, Conspiracy, and Democracy.' *Critical Review* 28, no. 1: 44-62.

Oliva, Gabriel. 2016. 'The Road to Servomechanisms: The Influence of Cybernetics on Hayek from the Sensory Order to the Social Order.' In *Research in the History of Economic Thought and Methodology*, 161-198. Leeds: Emerald Publishing, doi:http://dx.doi.org/10.1108/S0743-41542016000034A006.

Ramey, Joshua. 2015. 'Neoliberalism as a Political Theology of Chance: The Politics of Divination.' *Palgrave Communications* 1, no. 15039: 1-9.

Rosenblatt, Frank. 1958. 'The Perceptron: A Probabilistic Model for Information Storage and Organisation in the Brain.' *Psychological Review* 65, no. 6: 386-408.

Rosenblatt, Frank. 1962. *Principles of Neurodynamics: Perceptrons and the Theory of Brain Mechanisms.* Washington, D.C.: Spartan Books.

Szpiro, George G. 2011. *Pricing the Future: Finance, Physics, and the 300 Year Journey to the Black-Scholes Equation.* Vol. Kindle Edition, New York: Basic Books.

Notes

Research for this article was supported by the Mellon Foundation, Digital Now Project, at the Centre for Canadian Architecture (CCA) and by the staff and archives at the CCA. Further funding was given by the Swiss National Science Foundation, Sinergia Project, Governing Through Design.

1. Black (1986). The formula is adapted from the Black-Scholes Model summation from https://brilliant.org/wiki/black-scholes-merton/. Accessed June 20, 2020.

2. Paraphrased by MacKenzie (2006).

3. A critical first step, as historians such as Philip Mirowski (2002; 2006) have noted, towards contemporary notions of information economies.

4. For more on the influence of cybernetics and systems theories on producing notions of non-conscious growth and evolution in Hayek's thought: Lewis (2016); Oliva (2015).

5. I am indebted to Moore's excellent discussion for much of the argument surrounding Hayek, democracy, and information. This quote is from Hayek, 'The Use of Knowledge in Society'.

6. For an account of earlier nineteenth and twentieth century models for pricing options, see MacKenzie (2006: 37-88).

7. The three men most often credited with the formalisation of the derivative pricing model are Black, an applied mathematician who had been trained by artificial intelligence pioneer Marvin Minsky; Myron Scholes, a Canadian-American economist from University of Chicago who came to MIT after his PhD under Eugene Fama; and Robert Merton, another economist trained at MIT. Collectively they developed the Black-Scholes-Merton derivative pricing model. While these three figures are hardly singularly responsible for global financialisation, their history serves as a mirror to a situation where

new computational techniques were produced to address geo-political-environmental transformation. See Szpiro (2011: 116-17).

8. As Black noted in 1975, '[m]y initial estimates of volatility are based on 10 years of daily data on stock prices and dividends, with more weight on more recent data. Each month, I update the estimates. Roughly speaking, last month's estimate gets four-fifths weight, and the most recent month's actual volatility gets one-fifth weight. I also make some use of the changes in volatility on stocks generally, of the direction in which the stock price has been moving, and of the "market's estimates" of volatility, as suggested by the level of option prices for the stock' (Black 1975b: 5, cited in MacKenzie 2006: 321n.).

9. Robert Merton added the concept of continuous time and figured out a derivation equation to smooth the curve of prices. The final equation is essentially the merger of a normal curve with Brownian motion (Das 2006: 194-95).

10. It is worth noting that the Black-Scholes Derivative pricing equation inaugurating the financialisation of the global economy was introduced in 1973. For an excellent summary of these links and of the insurance and urban planning fields please see Grove (2018).

11. https://www.researchgate.net/figure/GROWTH-OF-GLOBAL-DERIVATIVE-MARKET-SINCE-1998-Globally-the-notional-value-of-all_fig12_328411995

IO

Catastrophic Forgetting: Why the Mind
Is Not in the Head

Christina Vagt

A computer never forgets – or so it seemed until the advent of artificial neural networks (ANNs), which can discern digitally processed data and identify objects in digital and real-world environments. The current generation of ANNs, so-called *Deep Learning ANNs,* can recognise and classify images, perform optical character recognition in digital text files, and are already ubiquitously applied in algorithmic recommendation systems that are autonomously at work on social media and online retail platforms. ChatGPT is estimated to write a large portion of all college essays, and deep learning ANNs are developed to analyse and identify objects as data sets in dynamic, real-world environments for self-driving cars and robotics, while they have already set new standards in medical and scientific data analysis. All these extensions and applications require the neural network to be able to learn – to autonomously recognise and discern objects according to a set of categories it was originally trained on.

This chapter will argue that not only does machine learning imply forgetting but that it demonstrates forgetting in its most radical form. This gives rise to questioning the standard model of non-artificial cognition and learning as something independent of writing techniques and technologies. Thinking with AI means presenting its mechanisms of forgetting against the backdrop of the computational design history of neural networks and the neurocognitive science it helped to establish, a double movement across historical and epistemological fault lines of knowledge. Furthermore, it allows one to situate media theory as a historical-epistemological critique of scientific knowledge production of cognition.

Catastrophic Forgetting in Deep Machine Learning Systems

Once an ANN has completed its training, it dynamically reconfigures its 'decision boundaries' that judge new input based on previous output; the more data it processes, the better it gets at, for example, distinguishing images of skin cancer from those of benign pigmentation. Within these original categories, the system adjusts the connection weights between input, hidden, and output layers continuously. This shifts the 'decision boundaries' based on the statistical distributions of those objects it has already sorted. Information in an artificial neural network is not stored in the form of static data sets but as a statistical data distribution across nodes. To put it metaphorically, data sets in ANNs resemble clouds, not objects; their boundaries constantly shift according to the self-adjusting statistical weights. Since the system works with dynamic decision boundaries and not definite borders, a small set of data will always be misjudged, a type of regular forgetting that can be measured by means of error functions.

What (deep) machine learning design so far has failed to accomplish are systems that are able to learn sequentially and continuously – so-called 'life-long learning'. This is a problem intrinsic to how machine learning has constructed the process of 'learning': because the decision boundaries in neural networks are based on statistical weights, shifting the weights for one decision boundary interferes with the previous one. For example, a system that is first trained on the arithmetic operation '+1', and then, in a second step, is trained on '+2' will forget how to perform '+1'. This problem of interference, or 'catastrophic forgetting', in sequential learning was discovered in 1989, early on in the development of the connectionist framework, by cognitive scientist Michael McCloskey and neuroscientist Neal J. Cohen. The authors lament that although ANNs are of considerable interest to neurocognitive science, the machine learning algorithms 'are simply not designed to deal with situations in which the set of items to be learned changes over time' (McCloskey and Cohen 1989: 153). For McCloskey and Cohen, catastrophic forgetting appeared to be an obstacle for computational neurocognitive research because it stood in stark contrast to the learning abilities of children who are excellent sequential learners and do not lose the ability to add ones once they learn how to add twos. Even though machine learning is developing rapidly, catastrophic forgetting still poses an obstacle and Seidenberg and Zevin's pertinent paper on connectionist models in developmental neuroscience from 2006 is still valid:

> The conditions that give rise to catastrophic interference rarely occur in human learning, outside the context of a verbal learning experiment. In real life, experiences of different things are interleaved, thankfully. [...] Learning a second language does not result in unlearning of a first language because experience with L1 does not cease. [...] Catastrophic interference is not a problem for human learners because experience is rarely blocked to the extent the effect demands. (Seidenberg and Zevin 2006: 332)

It is important to note the neurocognitive context of the discovery of catastrophic forgetting in artificial neural networks because it reiterates the continuity between current AI engineering and the historical epistemology of neurocognitive science. Not only did the connectionist paradigm emerge – in its first mathematical-logical instantiation as the 1943 calculus of Walter McCullough and Walter Pitts – from the historical intersection of computer engineering, cybernetics, psychiatry, and neurology of the 1940s. Moreover, current research on how to 'overcome catastrophic forgetting' in machine learning still draws inspiration from the neurocognitive sciences (Kirkpatrick et al. 2017: 5521). Deep learning ANNs are reified neurocognitive science.

To list all attempts to solve the problem of catastrophic forgetting would exceed the scope of this text. Independently of which modelling methods are being explored, the problem keeps persisting (Parisi et al. 2019). Ironically, some of the suggested methods to at least alleviate the interference phenomenon in sequential learning, for instance, the 'replay methodology', which reinforces the first decision boundary during sequential learning steps, actually leads to the inverse problem, where the system 'experiences extreme *deja vu*' or 'catastrophic remembering' (Kaushik et al. 2021: 4).

This raises media-theoretical questions about the role that technologies play in neurocognitive knowledge production. While neurocognitive science treats the phenomenon of catastrophic forgetting mostly as a technical problem that calls for technological solutions, a question from a media theoretical perspective is whether catastrophic forgetting since it is foundational to deep learning ANNs, points to larger issues within the neurocognitive concept of *human* learning which supposedly has nothing to do with techniques and technologies.

In other words: does the phenomenon of catastrophic forgetting in ANNs, instead of manifesting an anthropological-ontological difference between biological and artificial neural networks, as the quote from Seidenberg and Zevin implies, present an opportunity to rethink the relation between models of cognition and cognition as the sought-after object of science?

This question requires a certain degree of historicisation of the science and philosophy of cognition in order to convey the extent to which neurocognitive models have been developed in correlation with techniques and technologies. It also requires some reflections on the epistemological role of technology, a thought style somewhat aligned with Martin Heidegger's philosophy of technology. Heidegger formulated the question concerning technology [*Technik*] as 'challenging forth' [*Herausfordern*] the way nature is encountered in the context of physical science (Heidegger 1977: 14.) Within technologies of representation [*Vorstellen*], there is always something that does not translate, does not compute, or is simply forgotten. The epistemological potential of useful things or equipment [*Zeug*] unfolds by *not* working, within the *dysfunctional* mode. Only when the hammer breaks, when it becomes useless, does it reveal Dasein's own referentiality and limitations. This is a small but consequential detail that is often overlooked when Heidegger is appropriated by pragmatic philosophers of mind and AI (e.g., Dreyfus 2008). If media and technology are ascribed any metacognitive functions at all, they must be sought in the *dys*functional mode of useful things or equipment [*Zeug*], not in its functionality. Only when the 'useful thing' has lost its usefulness or when it is missing altogether does it allow Dasein to encounter its own particular world-structure (Heidegger 2010: 68-71.)

For scientists, a Heideggerian position that grants slips and dysfunction epistemic value is difficult, if not impossible, to achieve, and neurocognitive science is no exception. But as long as technologies are merely conceived of in their functionality, as utilities or tools, and not as epistemological forces or media affecting theoretical models as well as the sought-after scientific objects, the discussion on whether neuroimaging or connectionist computer models should dominate neurocognitive research moves in circles.

The neurocognitive standard model for cognition has been language acquisition, starting with Noam Chomsky's hypothesis that a 'language faculty' evolved in humans. According to Chomsky, language is an innate, neurocognitive system to create knowledge. Humans are supposed to have an innate language generator of potentially infinite languages and sentences whose structure can be deduced from few formal, grammatical rules (Chomsky 1956). It is important to recognise that Chomsky's model was already based on computer technology. Generative grammars are not spoken languages, because people don't speak in complete and formally correct sentences. Only symbolic machines write in complete and formally correct grammar. Therefore, the 'cognitive turn' in linguistics can be understood as, first and foremost, a 'computational turn' in language theory.

As a consequence, today's neurocognitive science has difficulty delineating its object – the brain or human cognition – from computer models, as long as it poses the process of learning solely in terms of the 'plasticity-stability problem': while language acquisition in children supposedly has to occur during a critical period of life when the brain still offers a high degree of plasticity, learning itself is conceived of as a 'limiting, stabilizing process' since it supports systematic knowledge and 'generalization, a defining characteristic of language' (Seidenberg and Zevin 2006: 321-325). As this chapter will show, this way of describing language acquisition and learning is already formulated in terms of the connectionist paradigm of computing.

The inherent paradox of neurocognitive science becomes conspicuous only, however, when the computational model breaks down – as is the case of catastrophic forgetting. As Seidenberg and Zevin attest, catastrophic forgetting today is still posed as a computer engineering problem against the backdrop of the dominant paradigm of human language learning and cognition, which is itself based on computer-based models of language acquisition and problem-solving capabilities in human subjects. The question of catastrophic forgetting, reformulated as a media-theoretical problem, assumes that both forgetting and catastrophic forgetting have indeed a distinct and primary function for the subject and its epistemology – because knowing and learning require the ability to forget.

To get out of the hermeneutic circle, I will reformulate the problem of catastrophic forgetting as a media-theoretical question, whereby I, for my part, assert that the ability to forget is indeed a primary function for speaking subjects and their cognition. This insight is nothing new; it already lies at the heart of Friedrich Nietzsche's take on the human as a clever but forgetful animal.

Necessarily Forgetful Animals

Instead of defining cognition as the mental ability for reasoning, problem-solving, and learning, Nietzsche bases it first and foremost on the ability to forget. At the beginning of the second essay of the *Genealogy of Morals*, in the section on 'Guilt, Bad Conscience, and Related Matters', he writes:

> Forgetfulness is not just a *vis inertiae* [...] but is rather an active ability to suppress, positive in the strongest sense of the word, to which we owe the fact that what we simply live through, experience, take in, no more enters our consciousness during digestion (one could call it spiritual ingestion) than does the thousand-fold process which takes place with our physical consumption of food, our so-called ingestion. (Nietzsche 2017: 35)

Forgetfulness as the active ability to suppress does not indicate dysfunctionality but rather the functionality of the psychic apparatus. Nietzsche takes the metabolic metaphor of digestion as far as to conclude that 'a person in whom this apparatus of suppression is damaged, so that it stops working, can be compared (and not just compared) to a dyspeptic; he cannot 'cope' with anything' (36). The term 'dyspeptic' implies a correlation between the sufferings caused by indigestion and depression, a first indication that losing the ability to forget has dire consequences for a person. They would eventually lose all 'happiness, cheerfulness, hope, pride and immediacy' (36). Forgetting, not remembering, is the primary and necessary force for a particular kind of animal:

> And precisely this necessarily forgetful animal, in whom forgetting is a strength, representing a form of robust health, has bred for himself a counter-device, memory, with the help of which forgetfulness can be suspended in certain cases, – namely in those cases where a promise is to be made. (35-36)

The will's desire is what powers the apparatus, and intellect (or intelligence) is subordinate to it. The two 'devices' of forgetting and remembering link cognition [*Erkenntnis*] to ignorance [*Unkenntnis*], and cognitive capacities to what today is called *media technology*. Does Nietzsche's polemic about the two devices – one innate, the other one cultivated or 'bred' – still merit our attention in times of deep machine learning? Could all this machinery serve but one purpose, to be able to make and break a promise?

In fact, Nietzsche derives his model of ignorance-cognition from a particular temporal structure of the clever animal, namely futurity. Only the dual ability to forget and to remember allows an individual being 'to view future as the present and anticipate it, to grasp with certainty what is end and what is means, in all, to be able to calculate, compute – and before he can do this, man himself will really have to become reliable, regular, necessary, even in his own self-image, so that he, as someone making a promise, is answerable for his own future' (36).

Nietzsche is far from conceiving futurity as some innate, ahistorical human faculty. It had to be cultivated, as he emphasises in *Genealogy of Morals*: religion, law, and society all took part in 'breeding the responsible animal' (38). The same holds for the intellect, as he lays out in 'On Truth and Lying in a Non-Moral Sense', which is necessary for the survival of the 'clever animals' but certainly not governed by any 'drive towards truth …. As a means for the preservation of the individual, the intellect shows its greatest strengths in dissimulation' (Nietzsche 1999: 142).

In ever-increasingly complex social entanglements, the intellectual means to deceive, to dissimulate, and simulate become ever more prominent. Language, this world-building activity, is not based on data accumulation or statistics, plasticity, and stability but on repetition, substitution, translation, and forgetting. Language is a drive towards metaphor, not truth!

Only by forgetting can the intellect ignore the fact that every object of cognition and reason in science and philosophy stems from a stream of metaphors and metonymies and not from 'things in themselves'. For Nietzsche, in his ongoing critique of Kant, the *thing in itself* does not exist, for whatever is defined in terms of generality and abstraction has no other empirical ground than subjective and contingent nerve stimuli that only become true (or fixated) because they are repeated over and over. Language is not based on external referents, and it does not require any substrate. There is nothing but repetitions of metaphors, a few of which eventually harden into concepts.

The Synthetic A Priori as Logical Fiction

The drive towards metaphor, in combination with the ability to forget, already indicates that, from a Nietzschean point of view, at the heart of neurocognitive models one finds – well, nothing but a model. This might explain why his teachings never entered the discourse of neurocognitive science. However, Nietzsche was not simply pursuing his intuitions that the 'true nature' of the human intellect is forgetfulness. Media theory has long underlined the epistemic role of technical and machinic actors that appeared on the writing scene and in the hands of writers around 1900. It was, after all, a typewriter, which Nietzsche started to use in 1882, that made him switch from 'arguments to aphorisms, from thoughts to puns, from rhetoric to telegram style' (Kittler 1999: 203). Losing his eyesight and typing on a fragile and utterly unreliable device, he no longer merely speculated about the dependency of thoughts on media technology but demonstrated their active partaking in the no longer human-only aesthetic and material procedure called 'writing'. Within the discourse of German media theory, the human is always already mixed up with the non-human (Siegert 2015: 5).

If language is, first and foremost, based on principles of substitution, metaphors, and translation instead of truth, it affects judgements made through language. This points toward the conflict between the rules of language and those of logic. Nietzsche recognised that the synthetic *a priori* introduced by Immanuel Kant attempts to resolve a media and language problem at the centre of science. In order to make this argument stick, I need to take a bit of a detour into the reverberations Kant's new scientific judgement category had within the discourse of mathematical logic. Although this may seem a bit tedious to the reader, it is necessary to align Nietzsche's position with that of mathematical logicians such as W.V.O. Quine in order to show that the basis of the neurocognitive model is based on an abstraction that conflates the formal and the material – a logical fiction that stands in for a material reality.

When Kant came up with the synthetic judgement *a priori*, he tried to account for the fact that scientific judgements, even though they are formulated in a systematic and logical way, often prove to be false. Without such judgements, a transcendental system could not account for the ability of science to integrate and develop new knowledge and theories. Synthetic *a priori* judgements are neither based on experience (that would make them *a posteriori*), nor are they pure logical deductions (that would make them analytic, like propositional logic).

According to Kant, they are to be found as principles in all theoretical sciences of reason. His example for a synthetic judgement *a priori* in science is the proposition that 'in all alterations of the corporeal world the quantity of matter remains unaltered' (Kant 1998: B 18) – something that could be called true for Newtonian physics but would be false within the science of thermodynamics not yet formulated at the time of Kant. Yet, for systematic and mathematical physics in the Kantian sense, this synthetic *a priori* judgements that extended the concept of matter with the intuition [*Anschauung*] of 'staying unaltered' is necessary though it turned out to be false (a physicist today would state instead 'in all alterations of the corporeal world the quantity of energy remains unaltered').

Because their truth values depend on external referents, synthetic *a priori* statements are only 'preliminary' or 'predictive' and might be false. The peculiar part of Kant's argumentation was the fact that mathematical sentences were not exempt from this contingency in matters of truth but the cornerstone for his argumentation: whether the sentence '7+5=12' is true or false can only be decided once the abstract number concepts are connected with interior representations [*Vorstellungen*], such as fingers, or exterior objects, such as apples, because the term '12' is not contained in the term '7+5'. It does not matter if one counts with imagined fingers or real apples. What matters is that '7+5=12' is true if and only if it refers to an imagined or real set of 7 plus 5 elements resulting in 12 (B 14-16). Though it might sound awkward, Kant's synthetic *a priori* points toward the crucial question of how mathematics relates to logic and language, and it became a long-lasting object of dispute in philosophy and mathematical logic.

Gottlob Frege stated in 1884 that while Kant's category does pertain to geometry, arithmetic could probably be reduced to logic. This would imply that arithmetical truth is analytic and not synthetic and requires no intuitions. However, he could not prove it (Frege 1884: 102). Eventually, the entire distinction between analytic and synthetic judgements was convincingly rejected by Willard Van Orman Quine (1963: 42-46), while Alfred Tarski showed that the universality of everyday language makes it inconsistent – it leads to semantical antinomies – and that truth functions can only be defined within formalised languages that strictly distinguish between meta- and object-language (Tarski 1958: 164-165). Instead of basing the truth of a sentence on some reality or psychological referent exterior to the language in which that sentence is formulated, one should understand the tautological (or analytic) structure of *any* truth function, and therefore write: '"5+7=12" is true if and only if 5+7=12'.

Mathematical (or symbolic) logic needed almost a hundred years to dry up the 'semantic swamp' that Kant's category of the synthetic *a priori* had left behind (Coffa 1993: 21). Nietzsche, on the other hand, never took the distinction between analytic and synthetic judgements as valid in the first place. As a philologist attempting to reconceive the 'clever animals' in terms of drives and instincts, he did not accept any distinct boundary between analytic and synthetic sentences and formulated his scathing critique of Kant's synthetic *a priori* almost at the same time as Frege. For Nietzsche, logic is subjected to the body – to the laws of the living, biology, heredity, and survival. This shifts Kant's category of the synthetic *a priori* from the psychological to the physiological domain – or rather, to their in-between. For Nietzsche, synthetic *a priori* judgements are *logical fictions* that are physiologically *necessary* for the survival of the human individual, even if they contain logical pitfalls:

> We do not consider the falsity of a judgment as itself an objection to a judgment; this is perhaps where our new language will sound most foreign. The question is how far the judgment promotes and preserves life, how well it preserves, and perhaps even cultivates, the type. And we are fundamentally inclined to claim that the falsest judgments (which include *synthetic judgments a priori*) are the most indispensable to us, and that without accepting the

fictions of logic, without measuring reality against the wholly invented world of the unconditioned and self-identical, without a constant falsification of the world through numbers, people could not live – that a renunciation of false judgments would be a renunciation of life, a negation of life. To acknowledge untruth as a condition of life: this clearly means resisting the usual value feelings in a dangerous manner; and a philosophy that risks such a thing would by that gesture alone place itself beyond good and evil. (F. W. Nietzsche, Horstmann, and Norman 2002, 6-7).

Working through Kant's judgement category allowed Nietzsche to arrive at the fundamental role of non-truth, fiction, and metaphor as the basis for the modern systematic conceptualisation of philosophy and science. Unlike the logical positivists of the twentieth century, who later informed neurocognitive science, the philosophical task for Nietzsche was not to eradicate logical fictions but to assert them. His stance on the logically shaky foundations of scientific-technological knowledge around 1900 could be easily rejected by today's philosophy and science of cognition if only his critique were not so well-aligned with analytic philosophers such as Quine. Quine, in his critique of logical empiricism, strictly rejects Kant's distinction between analytic and synthetic judgements altogether and makes this the cornerstone of his critique of logical empiricism. Scientific knowledge, according to Quine, is like all knowledge 'a man-made fabric which impinges on experience only along the edges' (Quine 1963: 42). This similarity between something as artificially constructed as Boolean algebra and scientific knowledge is the crucial point: 'Total science, mathematical and natural and human, is similarly but more extremely [than algebra] underdetermined by experience. The edge of the system must be kept squared with experience; the rest, with all its elaborate myths and fictions, has as its objective the simplicity of laws' (Quine 1963, 45).

None of this would even matter today, particularly not to media theorists, if it were not for computational neurocognitive models that deduce 'human intelligence', the 'mind', or 'thought' itself. Even if reduced to logic, cognition – as demonstrated by the history of logic itself – is, in its positivity, subject to a *historic*, not a *synthetic* a priori, to put it with Foucault rather than Kant (Foucault 2010: 127). As phenomena of reality, 'intelligence', 'mind', and 'thought' have always been outsourced to techniques and technologies like phonetic alphabets, printing presses, typewriters, cinematographic images, or digital computers. Cognition, therefore, never was an anthropological constant but only a human-nonhuman variable, both limited and modifiable – which is why media technologies play such an important role in cognition's historical formation. However, both its artificiality and media dependency as well as the profound rebuttal of the synthetic *a priori* by philosophers and logicians was forgotten, or better, foreclosed when Kant's category migrated, in the form of the computer model, to neurocognitive science.

McCulloch/Pitts Calculus: The Physiological Synthetic A Priori

Though rejected by mathematical logicians and philosophers as fiction, Kant's synthetic *a priori* had an astonishing comeback in early neurocognitive science, reintroduced by psychiatrist and cyberneticist Warren McCulloch, one of the founding figures of the ANN paradigm. Together with Walter Pitts, McCulloch published 'A Logical Calculus of the Ideas Immanent in Nervous Activity' in 1943. In this paper, neural events and their relations were, for the first time, formalised by means of propositional logic, resulting in the first calculus for a neural network (McCulloch and Pitts 1943). Having come to the (false) conclusion that every neuron should be equivalent to a proposition, McCulloch tried to notate the behaviour of neural nets in the symbolic logic of propositions for years. He was only able to do so with the help of Pitts and his prowess in symbolic logic, and by including Claude Shannon's pathbreaking work on switching circuits according to Boolean algebra (Abraham 2002: 18).

McCulloch and Pitts were well aware of the 'factual differences' between their 'fictitious nets' and 'living neural nets', yet they insisted on their 'formal equivalence' because of the assumed discrete nature of neuronal impulses (McCulloch and Pitts 1943: 115-118). Any equivalence between the artificial and organic nets rests solely on the supposed 'all-or-none-law' of nervous activity, which states that neurons always either fire or do not fire when they are stimulated, and that signal transmission does not depend on the strength of the impulse. The supposed binary nature of neurons – firing or not firing – was sufficient reason for McCulloch and Pitts to assume a binary structure governing *all* human psychology: 'In psychology, introspective, behavioristic, or physiological, the fundamental relations are those of two-valued logic' (McCulloch and Pitts, 131). Ever since, the nervous system has been modelled and simulated in terms of three Boolean operators AND, XOR, and NOT.

A couple of years later, McCulloch gave a talk titled 'Why the Mind Is in the Head' to an eclectic group that included neurologists, psychologists, and the mathematician John von Neuman. Neumann's *First Draft of a Report on the EDVAC* had been circulating in scientific circles, outlining the basic structure of what would soon become the model for modern computer architecture. McCulloch was well aware that his own neural net calculus stood in opposition to von Neumann's architecture. Nevertheless, both models were based on the same idea – switching electronic circuits according to the rules of a modified Boolean algebra.

In his talk, McCulloch termed the nervous system 'a logical machine par excellence' in which:

> our sense organs, detecting similarities the same in all respects save one, create dichotomies and decide between opposites. [...] We inherit a nervous system so structured that we do perceive similarities (or have ideas) and these, not isolated, but conjoined

within the system in many useful ways. That synthetic a priori is the theme of all our physiological psychology, learning excepted. (McCulloch 1967: 43-44).

McCulloch presented his talk in 1948, at the Hixon Symposium on 'Cerebral Mechanisms in Behavior'. One of the founding conferences of cognitive science, the *a priori* principles of this new science of the mind were laid out here. The entire symposium was organised around questions of logic, mind, and brain, including the recent computer models developed by McCulloch, Pitts, and von Neumann. Combining new technologies with those already established in psychiatry and neurology (such as imaging and electroencephalograms), the meeting had some overlap, in terms of participants and topics, with previous conferences organised by the Macy Foundation in New York. But unlike the Macy Conferences, the Hixon symposium was explicitly meant to challenge behaviourism, which had dominated US American psychology between the 1920s and 1940s (Gardner 1985: 10).

At Hixon, the behaviourist doctrine – that behaviour is not just dominated but determined by its environment – suddenly appeared as a roadblock to any scientific study of the mind. It limited endeavors aiming at combining cognition and digital computing technology. The question of *how* the new science of cognition was to gain insight into the nature of human language, planning, problems solving, and imagination (which behaviourism had bracketed for so long) was anything but agreed upon, and the discussions at Hixon were controversial on several subjects: while the mathematician John von Neumann criticised neurologist Warren McCulloch's neural network approach as an unsound model of the nervous system, both neurologist Karl Spencer Lashley and McCulloch argued against the holistic field theories of European Gestalt theorists such as Wolfgang Köhler. Yet, despite the differences between competing models of cognition, Hixon marked the beginning of a lasting link between neurocognitive models and computers in the US, which was crucial for neurocognitive studies to advance to a legitimate science because of their integration of computer technology and information theory (Gardner 1985: 119).

In his opening talk at Hixon, 'The General and Logical Theory of Automata', John von Neumann introduced the concept of digital computers – both in theory and with references to concrete machines like the ENIAC he had designed during and after the Manhattan Project. He carefully distinguished between analog and digital machines to draw the crucial analogy between digital computers and the brain. For von Neumann, the first modelling step was to consider only the organisation of the brain as a whole, whereas all individual brain functions, as well as physiological aspects, were merely treated as automatisms or black boxes: 'They are viewed as automatisms, the inner structure of which need not be disclosed' (von Neumann 1967: 2). Quantifying the brain in terms of neurons and their numbers, von

Neumann calculated with 'switching organs' of the living organisms (12). As a mathematician, von Neumann did not express any particular interest in the physiological or psychological research of the brain. He considered living organisms *as if* they were purely digital machines, even though 'there is little in our technological or physiological experience to indicate that absolute all-or-non-organs exists' (11). Physiologically speaking, both machines and living organisms are based on analog, continuous flows of currents, blood, or other 'humoral media'. But when this fact is reformulated by way of mathematical logic, the continuous materiality that forms the physical basis of all digital switching (no matter if it is the nervous system of a living organism or a digital computer composed of electromechanical relays or vacuum tubes) is treated solely as number or value – in terms of time and error factors. The actual operations of the central nervous systems remain a black box, and the only mathematical model at hand that comes close to its functions is the Universal Turing Machine (26-28).

Even though von Neumann stressed the differences between brain and computer, he saw no sufficient reason not to model organisms as computers. This is an important point because the reasoning behind transferring the computer model onto the brain was *not* based on *similarity* but solely a *pragmatic* decision: the analogy between brain and computer is not one of scale and complexity (a human brain has far more neurons than computers had at that time), speed (even in 1940, computers could already calculate much faster than humans), or error checking (while organisms can operate in spite of malfunctions and errors, computer errors have to be made corrected as they can bring the entire system down). The only reason for assuming a brain-computer analogy is the lack of any alternative models, von Neumann concludes during the discussion of his paper: 'The digital system of computing is the only thing known to us that holds any hope of an even remote affinity with that unknown, and merely postulated, technique' (von Neumann, McCulloch, and et al 1967: 40).

During the discussion of von Neumann's paper, the differences between a model and a physiological synthetic *a priori* come to the fore: the mathematician von Neumann – unlike the psychiatrist McCulloch – poses the digitalisation of the brain as a consequence of the mathematical treatment of a physical process, that is, as a consequence of the modelling process. He, therefore, sees no need to suppose a physiological synthetic *a priori* in the Kantian tradition. He also adds a crucial question for any modelling of the nervous system: 'How does it avoid really serious, that is, lethal, malfunctions over periods that seem to average decades?' (von Neumann, McCulloch, and et al 1967: 34). Any error that might occur in such a machine requires an infinite cascade of error-checking machines, a problem known since the 1930s as the Church-Turing Thesis:

The trouble is that now the second machine's errors are unchecked, that is, *quis custodiet ipsos custodes?* Building a third, a fourth, etc., machine for a second order, third order, etc., checking merely shifts the problem. In addition, the primary and the secondary machine will, together, make more errors than the first one alone, since they have more components. (von Neumann, McCulloch, and et al 1967: 35).

Ironically, it was von Neumann – the only mathematician and non-psychiatrist, non-neurologist, and non-psychologist present at the Hixon Symposium, whose work in the Manhattan Project was crucial for the design and deployment of the nuclear bombs destroying the cities of Hiroshima and Nagasaki – who expressed any concerns about using the Turing machine as a model for the nervous system. It would require an infinite error-checking regress to prevent catastrophes. Von Neumann points out the immanent logical fiction of McCulloch's synthetic *a priori*, which ontologically equates the human mind with a logical machine. This move allowed for the transfer from computer to brain and cognition in the first place. The fact that the psychiatrists, psychologists, and neurologists that established the new neurocognitive science forgot von Neumann's objection is the true scandal of the debate at Hixon.

In the following years, Kant's synthetic *a priori* was only further corroborated through neurophysiological experimentation and became widely known through McCulloch's collaboration with Pitts, Lettvin, and Maturana on frog experiments (Heims 1991: 243). By then, the synthetic *a priori* was reformulated in terms of genetic coding, promising once again to localise Kant's intuitions in the physiological structure of the brain (Maturana and Pitts 1950: 1950).

Logical Fictions

Historically, neurocognitive science's dependency on computer models of cognition poses not a break with but a continuation of Kant's transcendental philosophy. Dupuy already noted that among the participants of the Hixon Symposium, it was the logical atomist McCulloch who came closest to naturalising Kant's transcendentalism. While Dupuy finds this paradoxical (Dupuy 2009: 106), I would argue that this position was necessary in order to allow the computer model to stand in for cognition as inert brain function – a necessary logical fiction for a neurocognitive science to emerge. Resituating the beginnings of artificial neural networks within a media-theoretical framework allowed for the historicisation of McCulloch's physiological synthetic *a priori* across different epochs and media technologies. Most prominently, it reemphasised Nietzsche's insight that the primary function of any synthetic *a priori* is what it allows one to forget. Previous versions of this, such as Freud's unconscious or Köhler's fields of Gestalt theory, simply did not meet the technological conditions of new media – the historical a priori of the twentieth-century post-war era – they simply could not be formalised in classical logic or computed by way of Boolean switching algebra.[1]

The Hixon Symposium has been associated with the end of any significant influence that psychoanalysis or Gestalt theory might have had on today's cognitive science. The discussions between von Neumann, McCulloch, and others demonstrate that in order for a computational cognitive science to emerge, it did not matter which type of computer model was used (von Neumann's or McCulloch/Pitts' architecture). What mattered was the ontological status of these models with regard to the brain and cognition. While von Neumann, among other early proponents of AI engineering, treated any computer model as a *model*, McCulloch and other initial advocates of cognitive science treated it as a physiological reality. They argued that both the computer and the brain were based on the logic gates switched by Boolean operators and essentially conflated the computer model with the brain. As a result, non-computational theories of the psyche, cognition, or the brain have since been marginalised or discarded from neurocognitive science. By conflating model and object, by effectively foreclosing their difference, neurocognitive science aimed at replacing non-computable embodiments of the synthetic *a priori* across philosophy, psychology, and psychoanalysis with computer models. Despite their differences, the scientists at Hixon overall accepted this logical fiction of the computer model at the centre of the emerging science, but with the same move, they subjected the new field to the Kant's logical fiction in the form of brand-new machines – and then forgot about it.

The catastrophic forgetting of today's artificial neural networks gives Nietzsche's (forgotten) insight, that any synthetic *a priori* is necessarily based on logical fictions, a new twist. Thinking with AI, therefore, would point to the place where the Real of neurocognitive science, that which could not enter the discourse of the science, appears again as catastrophic errors occurring in sequential machine learning.

The latest generation of cognitive simulations makes the media technological dependency of neurocognitive science conspicuous the moment they break down – such as when machine learning systems suddenly forget the categories they were trained on. In this sense, catastrophic forgetting in deep learning ANNs 'unconceals' [*entbirgt*] the structure of foreclosure [*Vergessung*], to use Heidegger's term for total forgetting immanent to writing techniques and technology. One could read the shortcomings of neurocognitive epistemology by means of catastrophic decisions made by ANNs as a symptom, as the 'cloud of foreclosure' [*Wolke der Vergessung*], a Parmenidean metaphor Heidegger retrieved in 1942 in the context of the epistemic effects of typewriters (Vagt 2012: 72-75). In this sense, AI would have become Heideggerian after all.

Media theory has known for a while that the relation between logic and mathematics is not governed by duality but by a third – a material, a language, a writing that allows the system to forget the material condition on which it is based. The more computational neurocognitive science becomes, the better it supposedly mechanises and automatises 'intelligence', 'mind', or 'cognition', the more this third will insist, not least because of catastrophic errors.

Contrary to McCulloch's catchy title, the mind, then, is *not* in the head. In the context of current machine learning systems and their reverberations among neurocognitive science and its simulations, this posthumanist position of a media theory after Nietzsche, Freud, and Heidegger bears repeating. Particularly when it comes to the objectification of master signifiers such as 'intelligence', 'mind', or 'cognition', media theory would have to reject the assumption that they are based on some kind of physiological, genetic, synthetic *a priori* located in the head.

Since artificial neural networks today are most certainly part of what one can or cannot know, forget, or do, catastrophic forgetting can no longer be posed as a nonhuman phenomenon. Rather, it should be recognised at the least as an indicator for the media technological dependency of neurocognitive science, not as the naturalisation of a physiological synthetic *a priori*, but as an instantiation of the human/nonhuman distribution network currently transforming itself, and as a chance to rethink the standard model of neurocognition based on positive faculties such as learning and remembering.

Works Cited

Abraham, Tara H. 2002. '(Physio)Logical Circuits: The Intellectual Origins of the McCulloch-Pitts Neural Networks.' *Journal of the History of the Behavioral Sciences* 38 (1): 3-25. https://doi.org/10.1002/jhbs.1094.

Bajohr, Hannes, Eva Geulen, and Claude Haas. 2022. 'Gestalt.' In *Formen des Ganzen*. Göttingen: Wallstein.

Chomsky, Noam. 1956. 'Three Models for the Description of Language.' *IRE Transactions on Information Theory* 2 (3): 113-24.

Coffa, Alberto. 1993. *The Semantic Tradition from Kant to Carnap To the Vienna Station*. New York: Cambridge University Press.

Dreyfus, Hubert L. 2008. 'Why Heideggerian AI Failed and How Fixing It Would Require Making It More Heideggerian.' In *The Mechanical Mind in History*, 331-72. Cambridge, MA: MIT Press.

Dupuy, Jean-Pierre. 2009. *On the Origins of Cognitive Science: The Mechanization of the Mind*. A Bradford Book. Cambridge, Mass: MIT Press.

Foucault, Michel. 2010. *Archeology of Knowledge*. Translated by Sheridan Smith. New York: Random House.

Frege, Gottlob. 1884. *Die Grundlagen der Arithmetik: Eine logisch mathematische Untersuchung über den Begriff der Zahl*. Breslau: Wilhelm Köbler.

Gardner, Martin. 1985. *The Mind's New Science A History*. New York: Basics Books.

Heidegger, Martin. 1977. *The Question Concerning Technology and Other Essays*. Translated by William Lovitt. New York, London: Garland Publishing.

Heidegger, Martin. 2010. *Being and Time. A Revised Translation*. Translated by Joan Stambaugh, revised by Dennis J. Schmit. Albany: State University of New York Press.

Heims, Steve Joshua. 1991. *The Cybernetics Group*. Cambridge: MIT Press.

Kant, Immanuel. (1781) 1998. *Kritik der reinen Vernunft*. Edited by Jens Timmermann. Hamburg.

Kaushik, Prakhar, Alex Gain, Adam Kortylewski, and Alan Yuille. 2021. 'Understanding Catastrophic Forgetting and Remembering in Continual Learning with Optimal Relevance Mapping.' *ArXiv Preprint. ArXiv:2102.11343*.

Kirkpatrick, James, Razvan Pascanu, Neil Rabinowitz, Joel Veness, Guillaume Desjardins, Andrei A Rusu, Kieran Milan, John Quan, Tiago Ramalho, and Agnieszka Grabska-Barwinska. 2017. 'Overcoming Catastrophic Forgetting in Neural Networks.' *Proceedings of the National Academy of Sciences* 114 (13): 3521-26.

Kittler, Friedrich A. 1999. *Gramophone, Film, Typewriter*. Stanford University Press.

Lettvin, Jerome Y., Humberto R. Maturana, Warren S. Mcculloch, and Walter H. Pitts. 1950. 'What the Frog's Eye Tells the Frog's Brain.' *Proceedings of the IRE* 47, no. 11: 1940-50.

McCloskey, Michael, and Neal J. Cohen. 1989. 'Catastrophic Interference in Connectionist Networks: The Sequential Learning Problem.' In *Psychology of Learning and Motivation*, 24: 109-65. Elsevier.

McCulloch, Warren S. 1967. 'Why the Mind Is in the Head.' In *Cerebral Mechanisms in Behavior. The Hixon Symposium*, 42-57. New York, NY, London: Hafner.

McCulloch, Warren S, and Walter Pitts. 1943. 'A Logical Calculus of the Ideas Imment in Nervous Activity.' *Bulletin of Mathematical Biology* 52 (1/2): 99-115.

Neumann, John von. 1967. 'The General and Logical Theory of Automata.' In *Cerebral Mechanisms in Behavior: The Hixon Symposium, California Institute of Technology, September 1948.*, 1-41. New York, NY, London: Hafner.

Neumann, John von, Warren S McCulloch, and et al. 1967. 'The General and Logical Theory of Automata: Discussion.' In *Cerebral Mechanisms in Behavior: The Hixon Symposium, California Institute of Technology, September 1948.*, 32-41. New York, NY, London: New York, NY, London.

Nietzsche, Friedrich. 1999. *Nietzsche: The Birth of Tragedy and Other Writings*. Translated by Ronald Speirs. Cambridge University Press.

Nietzsche, Friedrich. 2017. *Nietzsche: On the Genealogy of Morality and Other Writings*. Cambridge University Press.

Nietzsche, Friedrich Wilhelm. 2002. *Beyond Good and Evil: Prelude to a Philosophy of the Future*. Translated by Judith Norman. Cambridge: Cambridge University Press.

Parisi, German I., Ronald Kemker, Jose L. Part, Christopher Kanan, and Stefan Wermter. 2019. 'Continual Lifelong Learning with Neural Networks: A Review.' *Neural Networks* 113: 54-71.

Quine, Willard Van Orman. 1963. *From A Logical Point of View*. 2nd Ed. New York: Harper.

Seidenberg, Mark S., and Jason D. Zevin. 2006. 'Connectionist Models in Developmental Cognitive Neuroscience: Critical Periods and the Paradox of Success.' *Processes of Change in Brain and Cognitive Development: Attention and Performance XXI*, 315-47.

Siegert, Bernhard. 2015. *Cultural Techniques: Grids, Filters, Doors, and Other Articulations of the Real*. Translated by Geoffrey Winthrop-Young. New York: Fordham University Press.

Tarski, Alfred. 1958. *Logic, Semantics, Metamathematics: Papers from 1923 to 1938*. Edited by R. M. Martin and J. H. Woodger. Oxford: Oxford University Press.

Vagt, Christina. 2012. *Geschickte Sprünge: Physik und Medium bei Martin Heidegger*. Zürich: Diaphanes.

Notes

1. See on why Köhler's Gestalt theory could not be engineered: Bajohr, Geulen, and Haas (2022: 129).

11

The Absolutism of Data:
Thinking AI with Hans Blumenberg

Audrey Borowski

Algorithmic systems bear a striking similarity to mythic thought, as analysed by the German thinker Hans Blumenberg (1920-1996). Both contend with the problem of navigating a radically contingent and unpredictable world which in many respects eludes conceptual capture. While mythical thought has traditionally been perceived as outdated and treated with the suspicion that it may lapse into irrational barbarism, algorithmic systems have been perceived as embodying a form of pristine objective rationality far removed from it. This, as Blumenberg's thought makes clear, is a potentially dangerous misconception. Blumenberg himself addressed first-wave AI in a meditation on the first chatbot, Joseph Weizenbaum's ELIZA (Weatherby, 2022). But in this chapter I want to relate Blumenberg's thought to algorithmic systems more broadly – in a way that he himself did not articulate – arguing that his explanation and defence of nonconceptual thought offers an unexpected way of theorising algorithmic systems, defining their fundamental limitation and possibly even improving them.

From Blumenberg we can derive a positive but nuanced approach to the digital, one attentive to the potential metaphysical drifts and dangers of algorithmic systems, not least their danger of turning into a new absolutism. For Blumenberg theoretico-rational procedures will always be incomplete in addressing a radically contingent, unpredictable world. Instead, digital 'lifeworlds' (the realm of truths that make up our daily lives and that we take as self-evident) are possible – and no more artificial than the mental constructions through which we understood the world in the past. They become problematic, however, once they cease to provide us with fictional mental constructs that serve to orient us but are literalised and threaten to constitute a reality of their own, reducing human potentiality to a mere repetition of the formerly or currently extant.

Opposing simple dichotomies between technology and nature and between mythos and logos, Blumenberg sought to highlight the limits of computability and the need to draw on a broader kind of rationality that cultivates distance as relief from the absolute. Though counterintuitive or even

regressive from the perspective of a modernity that defines itself by its champi-
oning of rationality, this nonconceptual approach – in which myth, metaphor,
rhetoric, pensiveness, and, more broadly, the art of the detour take centre
stage – is, Blumenberg maintained, uniquely efficacious, resilient and flexible at once, in shielding us from the absolutism of reality, namely the intense
and overwhelming anxiety we feel when considering the totality of the world.
More than that, by its ability to accommodate interruptions and disruptions,
nonconceptual thought allows for what has been regarded as self-evident to
be reassessed, and for mankind to experience a fundamentally incomprehen-
sible reality in yet another way.

Current Machine Learning Systems

Much of Blumenberg's work addresses the same question at the heart of the
digital and offers a corrective to the pitfalls of the digital devices and algorithmic systems that have become an unquestioned part of our modern life-
worlds (see Keuchel 2020 on the digitalisation and automation on the life-
world of travellers). Despite the ubiquity of these devices and our new mode
of life, we know very little about how these digital and algorithmic systems
actually operate.

Big data currently forms the backbone of a new logic of accumulation that
Shoshana Zuboff has termed 'surveillance capitalism', which aims to 'predict
and modify human behaviour' for commercial or surveillance reasons (Zuboff
2015: 75). This new brand of information capitalism is automatised and relies
heavily on datamining and machine learning algorithms which, exploiting the
massive amounts of data gathered from our tracked behaviours and interactions, re-elaborate previous data functions according to new inputs to construct new hypotheses.

More broadly, as automation itself becomes automatised, machine learning systems in particular are increasingly departing from conventional statistical and probabilistic models by abduction, inferring correlations rather than
causal links (see Amoore 2013: 139; Mackenzie 2015: 434; Joque 2022; Parisi
2019). Automated cognition – and the move towards general artificial intelligence – has inaugurated a broader form of machinic cognition that draws
heavily on hypothetical inference. Whilst induction builds from already
known rules, abductive reasoning infers 'extensional knowledge' (Denecker
and Kakas, 2002: 405). It functions more speculatively than induction on the
basis of hypothetical correlations between data elements to make conjec-
tures and experimentally determine 'unknowns' and 'truths' about uncertain
behaviours. This 'experimental axiomatics' (Parisi 2019: 105) thus involves
less the explanation of phenomena than the generation of hypotheses about
missing rules or facts and unknown causes from 'incomplete networks' in
order to make 'incomputable data partially intelligible' (Parisi 2019: 114; see
also Inoue et al., 2013: 240).

In this manner, data is continuously harvested, aggregated, and, significantly, abstracted and decontextualised, reducing complex individuals and realities to a set of discrete digitised traces and 'profiles' from which are extracted supra-individual patterns and trajectories oblivious to contexts or subjectivities. Populations are simultaneously the source and target of this new digital economy.

Algorithmic systems, especially in their machine and deep learning iterations, thus 'engage in fabulation' (Amoore 2020: 158)[1] – they form fictions as a way of 'computing' the incomputable in order to help orient us in a world that appears highly contingent, risky, and hostile. Through the anticipatory configuration of possibilities, they infer predictions that are in turn acted upon in order to tame future uncertainty and allay our fears. The simulations provided by AI and various digital tools are in this respect perfectly consistent with a long history of measures adopted to mitigate contingency, even if those measures preclude a proper comprehension of the world.

Algorithmic systems have effected a dramatic shift in the extraction of value. Our knowledge production is increasingly mediated through algorithmic systems, mirroring back to us a metaphysical stratum which is presented to us as an accurate reflection of the world (Joque 2022). This continuously self-updating foundation – knowledge does not pre-exist this mass of data but continuously emerges from it[2] – is enclosed on itself in a recursive loop that operates at a very different level than human signification and obfuscates the conditions of its production.

Essentially metaphysical creations – fictions formed out of speculations – are reified and objectivised as neutral and accurate representations of the world, endowed with the apparent authority of scientific rigour.[3] Subjectivities tied to singular contexts are thusly reified and acted upon as if they were objective facts about the world. Bayesian statistics which underscore algorithmic systems, unlike frequentist probability, make no claim to *truth* but cast instead certainty in terms of continual approximation (Joque 2022). Whereas frequentism describes empirically, Bayesianism prescribes subjective beliefs.

Algorithmic systems are not just meaning-bearing structures, but profoundly alter and shape reality itself, producing a new reality within the world itself which, for algorithmic governmentality and the digital realm, is the only one that matters (Rouvroy 2013).[4] Refined in real time on the basis of our recorded actions and expressed preferences, machine learning, with its neural nets and continuously updated recommendation systems, threatens to confine, define, influence us – not without political and social consequences. Data is extracted from and then read back to the individual (Bunz 2019) in self-reinforcing loops that tend to homogenise our experiences and make any form of critique or resistance difficult.

Algorithmic logic takes on a life of its own, 'immanently modifying itself through the world' (Amoore 2020, 25) and constantly reorganising and exceeding itself in a manner that is not always consonant with human priorities as they suggest a movie on Netflix, deny a credit, or even kill pre-emptively kill in drone attacks on the basis of a detected 'profile'. Algorithmic decisions are enforced upon the world and restrict human futures. In an attempt to immunise the 'actual' from the incompressible portion of uncertainty inherent to the world (Rouvroy 2019), the present is shaped and restricted according to future pre-determination. Algorithmic systems condense multiple potential pathways into a single actionable output which stunts all other possible outcomes, generally in favour of a particular sectorial interest.

These systems produce a state of affairs that increasingly eludes our purview and control, bypasses our judgement (except within a severely delimited set of options), and deprives us of genuine decisional power in crucial areas of modern life, such as finance and insurance. In these new 'control societ[ies]' of soft power and modulation (Deleuze 1995: 180), politics has become a space of pure speculation rather than negotiation that is overwhelmingly guided by the imperative to predict the future, often in the hope of controlling it, and towards optimisation and profitability (Rouvroy 2013: 144-45).

Over the past two decades the digital has increasingly shifted from the management or calculation of known risks to the attempt to secure unknown futures from a distance, from prevention to pre-emption, in what Louise Amoore has termed the 'politics of possibility' (Amoore 2013). Data serves to map out possible scenarios and action is taken pre-emptively on the basis of what could happen – all of this with very real impacts: citizens are arrested, detained at a border, denied the right to assemble freely, or experience having their rights limited or violated. Correlations become actionable and deployed pre-emptively often 'on the basis of the improbable, the merely possible' (Amoore 2013: 92). In a world of generalised anxiety, the recent trend towards the hyperfocalisation on the anticipation and management of risk has only heightened this 'anticipatory logics'. As the algorithmic output is objectivised as the only possible outcome, the future becomes a mere extension of the present with little possibility for discontinuity or true human decision. Anticipated outcomes in this manner become self-fulfilling.

Algorithms enact new regimes of verification and truth-telling in the world, and operate as ethico-political entities themselves that define the norm (Amoore 2013: 5-6). Such predictions are indifferent to truth values (Huneman, 2023) as we only have to slide into the possible pathway that has been tailored to us. Our lives are increasingly reduced to homogenised data sets and modulated according to 'stimuli' and their 'reflex responses' (Rouvroy 2012), absolving us from any need to interpret, assess, or critique.

This enclosure of the digital on itself is particularly anathema to the cultivation of a public space since it excludes collective deliberation and the elaboration of shared norms. Indeed, such enclosure lends itself to the radicalisation of opinion, the negation of common experience, and the effacement of common values or reference-points (Sunstein, 2009). Recent developments such as ChatGPT may even have exacerbated the trend to pre-digested pathways

(Weatherby 2023) that are particularly prone to polarisation and cognitive flatlining. The attempt to enforce a largely self-enclosed logic onto reality can even at times descend in a form of madness as evidenced in particular in technology's amplification of ideology in the digital age as illustrated recently by Microsoft's Twitter bot Tay. The latter had to be disconnected only 16 hours after being launched for posting a slew of racist and misogynistic statements back on Twitter after emulating other users (for more on this see Handelman 2022). James Bridle too has detailed how algorithmic recommendation systems end up automatically churning out seemingly infinite variations of horrific and violent children's cartoons (Bridle 2018). Such self-reinforcing and enclosed loops would remain largely anathema to Blumenberg – including within the realm of technology.

Blumenberg on Technology

Blumenberg's engagement with technology began early in his career. He developed a nuanced and critical position that sought to historicise the concepts of technology and nature and show how the technological world had come about (Bajohr 2019). In particular, he argued that a changed understanding of being in the wake of the late-medieval nominalist turn marked a permanent break from the principle of imitation that had hitherto dominated the human realm, thus allowing for the development of autonomous and self-sufficient technical devices (Blumenberg 2020e). Unlike his peers (such as Heidegger) and many of his predecessors, Blumenberg greeted the undeniable benefits yielded by science and technology. Man, he insisted, is 'a being that realises himself technologically, and whose 'truth' is fundamentally technological' (Blumenberg 2015: 49). Blumenberg disputed the idea of nature as an unadulterated support for technology, envisaging rather a co-becoming between the two.[5] Technical inventions and artifacts are inextricable from human creative activity; and natural and artificial are falsely opposed, for technology is enlisted in man's constant self-creation and the articulation of his various horizons of expectations (see on this point Blumenberg 2020c).[6]

In his 1963 landmark essay 'Life-World and Technization', Blumenberg engaged in a lengthy discussion of what he perceived as the recent proliferation of technical devices in our everyday lives.[7] Late modernity, Blumenberg observed, had recently undergone a process of technisation whereby technological advances were simply taken for granted, and no longer generally reflected upon or understood, becoming part our life-worlds, no longer transparent to the everyday observer. 'Life-world' (*Lebenswelt*), a term he co-opted from Husserl, designates the realm of self-evidences that characterise our everyday lives and help us navigate the world despite its remaining largely theoretically unknown to us (Blumenberg 2010b, 211).[8] As the science behind modern technologies became increasingly specialised and complex, it became invisible just as the technologies themselves insinuated themselves ever more firmly into our life-world. Blumenberg illustrates this development by contrasting mechanical and electrical doorbells: while the mechanical doorbell establishes a sufficient connection between our turning hand and the created sound, the electrical one dissolves that link. He described how the growing technisation of our life-world had prompted a certain form of automatisation of our behaviours:

> Machines can help us to skip levels of consciousness, and we often have to respond to the overexertion of objective demand by automatizing ourselves – for example, by using formulas that we do not fully grasp. Thus, our consciousness is 'bypassed' by a set of behaviors and actions that result from the inherent laws of our areas of life, which are objectivized and have become autonomous, and are constantly forcing themselves on us. From the conditions and necessities of circumstances immediately result achievements to master the physical world. (Blumenberg 2020h: 43)

In fact, Blumenberg even likened the modern age's concept of reality as 'immanent consistence' to a simulation, one that was not without its ambiguities:

> One last remark must address the claim that modern age's concept of reality as immanent consistency has a high affinity to simulation. It is to be expected that in a crowded world, authentic dealings with reality must be replaced more and more by simulators. Already a decade ago, an intelligent misprint turned an 'outer-space simulator' [*Weltraumsimulator*] into a 'world simulator' [*Weltsimulator*]; this last is the boundary idea of the convergence of reality and unreality (Blumenberg 2020g: 125).

Still, despite his moderate and generally accepting view of modern science and, in particular, technology, Blumenberg was ambivalent about technisation, which he acknowledged was generating a sense of disorientation and helplessness as well as a loss of contact with reality. A disproportion had 'arisen between the acceleration of processes and the feasibility of keeping a 'feel' for them, of intervening with decisions, and of coordinating them, through an overview with other processes' (Blumenberg 198: 445). This compromised our ability to think in a reflective and critical manner and even stunted the possibility of questioning the self-evidences that make up our life-worlds:[9]

> Technization not only ruptures the foundational context of theoretical behavior emerging from the life-world, but it in turn begins to control the life-world by making the sphere in which we do not yet ask questions identical with that in which we no longer ask questions, and by regulating and motivating the occupation

of this sphere of things through the immanent dynamics of the technically always-ready, that is, through the irrevocability of production which puts itself on equal footing with the forces of nature. (Blumenberg 2020j: 373)

And while he rejected any 'demonism of technology', Blumenberg had commented early on on the increasing autonomy and intractability of technology over and against humans (Bajohr 2019: 7). A finished technical product, especially in the later modern age, created news motivations, values, and meanings which can deviate from the product's 'original motivation' and 'human function' (Blumenberg 1983: 177):

> The impulses and demands no longer depend on the human and social prerequisites, but on the technical product in itself, which is strongly supported by the related autonomous structure of the economy. It overturns its servile role, turning Man into the technician, entrepreneur and worker in its (i.e. technology's) service. Indeed, it dictates to the whole of human society the needs and the purposes which are no longer the ones which Man has given himself. (Blumenberg 2015: 10-11)

Reversing this trend would be difficult especially considering this new technical sphere's desire to 'extort' from an 'alienated reality' a new 'humanity' (Blumenberg 1983: 177, 139).

Blumenberg's Exploration of the Nonconceptual and Mythic Reasoning

While Blumenberg, in his theoretical work, and the digital world both seek to address epistemic indeterminacy, the German thinker suggested an altogether different tack. Only by acknowledging the precariousness and riskiness of the human condition, he maintained, can we hope to create the conditions for improving it.[10] Lacking immediate access to reality, mankind, equipped with a finite life span and limited rational capacity, can only ever hope to secure a little certain knowledge in a constantly changing and radically contingent world. To be clear, Blumenberg does not reject conceptual analysis, theory, or the sciences, but recognises that the world develops according to an infinite, unpredictable, constantly shifting logic that largely eludes conceptual capture, and thus defies theoretico-rational procedures and calculations. Blumenberg maintains that the world, life, history, and consciousness 'exceed what [judgement's] procedure can handle' (Blumenberg 1987: 440). The engagement with reality requires a broader and more pragmatic form of rationality, one more attuned to vagaries and uncertainties. Counterintuitively, perhaps, an indirect and more fluid form of rationality – as opposed to a more narrowly instrumentalist reason that seeks to control reality – would provide a more flexible and resilient way of navigating the uncertain. More than many fellow philosophers, Blumenberg was concerned with the kind of human thinking that takes place in everyday life.

Suspicious of idealised accounts of the relation between the human mind and the world, he sought constantly to show the necessary complexity, indirectness, and indeterminacy of that relation – one that was rooted in man's anthropological condition. Mankind's original condition was one of constant uncertainty, one characterised by intense anguish, helplessness, and a lack of control over its existence (Blumenberg 1985: 3-4). Such was the world's contingency and its indifference to mankind's very existence that neither could be taken for granted (Blumenberg 2011). Unlike animals, man was a 'deficient being' (*Mängelwesen*), lacking in natural instincts – that is, adaptation to a specific ecological niche – and therefore fundamentally biologically ill-equipped for a radically contingent and hostile environment. This precarious existence had been exacerbated once man had left the rainforest and found himself standing upright in the openness of the savannah, exposed to the view of all. Human beings' evolution in this undefined and indifferent reality, from which danger could emerge at any moment,[11] had plunged them in a state of constant fear and exhaustion, leading them to find shelter in a cave (Blumenberg 1985: 4-5).

Against Husserl's and Heidegger's reluctance to engage with man's anthropological dimension in favour of, respectively, consciousness and *Dasein*,[12] Blumenberg preferred a philosophico-anthropological approach to man that drew on palaeoanthropology and the German school of philosophical anthropology from Johann Gottfried Herder to Arnold Gehlen (Nicholls 2016). This approach rejected essentialist conceptions of human nature, describing human history instead as constantly adapting over time to man's original deficiency. The cave, in Blumenberg's account, served as a safe enclave in which man had developed technology and imagined ways to compensate for his deficiencies and anticipate dangers before they arose. In short, the cave had provided man with a lifesaving buffer mediating the 'absolutism of reality' (Blumenberg 1985: 1-8), that sheer unstructured state of naked reality which, in its incomprehensibility, appeared terrifying. Interpreting the cave as the very condition for man's emancipation and world creation, Blumenberg radically upended Plato's allegory of the cave in *The Republic*.

Blumenberg's exploration of the nonconceptual and the peculiar kind of indirect and non-instrumental kind of thinking required in an essentially ambiguous – and uncomputable – reality is particularly instructive. For him, myths, metaphors, rhetoric, and pensiveness all provide strategies for self-preservation in the face of what is 'theoretically inaccessible' (see also Müller-Sievers 2010). They are part and parcel of a broader, more pragmatic form of rationality that privileges meaning-building over relentless attempts to map or even shape reality.[13]

In contrast to Ernst Cassirer, Blumenberg challenged the myth of reason's omnicompetence – the assumption that instrumental reasoning had, or could ever, overcome myth, arguing instead that the former should be supplemented by a nonconceptual kind of thinking open to indeterminacy and, one could add, even if he does not refer to it explicitly, incomputability.[14] Myths consist less in providing definitive answers than in forestalling or deflecting certain fundamental questions about the order and nature of the world and the human condition – questions that theory cannot answer fully or adequately. They thus assuage the need for such questions to be asked in the first place: 'Myth does not need to answer questions; it makes something up, before the question becomes acute and so that it does not become acute' (Blumenberg 1985: 197).

While reason offers explanations, myths and metaphors broadly construed pertain to the realm of 'significance' (*Bedeutsamkeit*) (Blumenberg 2005: 107). They provide horizons of expectations (Blumenberg 2010b: 3), representing the 'non-experiencable, non-apprehensible totality of the real' (Blumenberg 2010b: 14), from which conceptual systems then emerge (rather than the opposite). Absolute metaphors in particular 'prove resistant to terminological claims and cannot be dissolved into conceptuality' (Blumenberg 2010b: 4-5). Metaphorics serve a practical purpose by outlining life-worlds through which mankind could first lessen its primordial anxiety, but then also identify its essential needs and articulate 'ultimate and all-enveloping questions', that is, a sense of direction and purpose within a humanised world. Life-worlds are not static or foreclosed but contingent and fragile constructions, created in order to compensate for a lack of pre-determined or automatic responses to environmental conditions. They provide us with significance in our advance into the 'eternal silence' of an otherwise meaningless historical process (Guntin 2022) that evolves over time according to the various resistances it encounters. Blumenberg's philosophico-anthropology is a profoundly historicist and anti-essentialist (see Rusch 2011). Myths in this regard simultaneously appear revolutionary and restorative by accommodating and accounting for new circumstances (Nicholls 2016). The history of human consciousness is a radically contingent one in which the share of nonconceptuality has, Blumenberg argued, too often been neglected. In his 'metakinetics of the historical horizon of meaning' (Blumenberg 2010b),[15] he charted the continuous disruption of life-worlds and their 'reoccupation' by new mental frameworks.

Surprisingly perhaps, then, Blumenberg and algorithmic systems seem at first glance, to have much in common especially in their initial premises: for both, men are eminently anguished creatures (see Heidenreich 2011b), operating in a radically contingent environment, who rely on various tools to cope with their 'essential strangeness' in the world and build a world for themselves (Blumenberg 2020e). Both too assign to hypothetical inference and fictions a major role in helping render the world manageable from a safe distance (Blumenberg 1985: 5; for more on this see Heidenreich 2011: 78; 2011b; 2008).

The current algorithmic world has in many respects however threatened to usher in a new form of 'absolutism of reality' and descend into madness by inundating man under layers of data, seeking to calculate the incalculable and control the future in its bid to liquidate indeterminacy and control the future.

From Attempts at Readability to the Absolutism of Myth

Blumenberg explored the futility and absurdity of seeking to map out, and so to speak, calculate all of reality. In his *Readability of the World* he traced the deployment of the metaphor of the book of nature, a metaphor that – from ancient Greek cosmology to the Talmud to Diderot's *Encyclopedia* to the model of the genetic code – has served to articulate different expectations of reality and horizons of meaning. A chapter of *Readability* is devoted to Gottfried Wilhelm Leibniz's *apokatastasis*, or 'universal restitution', a thought experiment in which the German philosopher pondered whether it would be possible to condense all of past, present, and possible future history in a book by combining all 23 letters of the alphabet. Establishing a (rather dubious) equivalence between possible words and actual historical events, Leibniz speculated that, given enough time, events could recur: 'Measured against the yardstick of describability, the repetition of the same is unavoidable. In the end, every single year with all its private individual stories would repeat itself if 'history' were only allowed enough time, and likewise an entire century and eventually a whole millennium' (Blumenberg 2023: 111) – something however he quickly acknowledges is impossible on account of the universe's extreme complexity.

The chapter on Leibniz, while initially seeming off-topic in the context of *Readability*, is striking in the shift it enacts from treating the metaphor of legibility to actual readability itself. Blumenberg is sceptical and ironic about Leibniz's programme and co-opts it here to emphasise the insuperable gap between the infinite complexity of the world and our possible knowledge of it, even with the aid of theoretical reason. While the metaphor of readability is operative on a phenomenological level, it cannot be extended to metaphysics or ontology per se – it cannot be literalised to real life. Literal readability, in the sense of calculability, quickly runs against up the strange and unpredictable nature of reality.[16] This is evident in present circumstances, where the drive to datafy the world and the consequent vast growth in data collection have not only *not* led to a better understanding of the world or prediction of future developments, but has done much to compound our feelings of powerless and paralysis, ushering in an age of 'surplus data' in which thinking has been homogenised and polarised (Weatherby 2022b, Bridle 2018).

Algorithmic systems constitute the latest version of this old fantasy of seeking to render reality knowable, predictable, and controllable by reducing it to a literally readable form (though now numerical rather than alphabetical) produced through calculation. Blumenberg dismissed long-held dreams of total knowledge, including the Cartesian and Leibnizian notions of establishing a *mathesis universalis* whereby, through simple calculation, it would be possible to infer the future clearly from a knowledge of the past. For Blumenberg, this is not only futile and absurd, but also potentially sinister and pernicious.

The madness that can ensue when we try to confuse metaphorical and literal by seeking to impose fictions on reality itself is the focus of Blumenberg's later work *Prefiguration: Work on Political Myth*. Blumenberg would precisely explore the new absolutism that sets in when attempts are made to literalise myths and extend mythic rationality to reality itself. 'Prefiguration' refers to a more 'virulent' kind of mythicisation that relies on past patterns to orient oneself and justify taking action in the belief that – before the unknown – they will repeat or reverse themselves (Blumenberg 2014: 9, trans. In Nicholls 2016: 233). According to this mythical decision process, the later event was already 'latent in the first' (Nicholls 2016: 232), as if it had been had already been pre-decided:

> In prefiguration, mythicization approaches or even oversteps the border of magic as soon as the explicit act of repeating a 'prefigurate' is associated with the expectation of producing the identical effect. To begin with, however, prefiguration is only something like a decision-making aid: under the presupposition of a constancy of conditions, what has already been done once does not require renewed deliberation, confusion or cluelessness, it is predecided by the paradigm. (Blumenberg 2014: 9, trans. In Nicholls 2016: 233)

According to Blumenberg, Napoleon's failed Russian campaign of 1812 initially served as negative prefigurate – an event whose reversal was foretold – to Hitler's plans for the German assault on Moscow in the winter of 1941-42 and on Stalingrad in 1942-43:

> Hitler initiated the turning point of the war with his order to attack Stalingrad. For this purpose he travelled especially to Poltava, where Charles XII [of Sweden] had been defeated in 1709 in a prototype of the northern conflict with the east. This defeat was to be made up for. [...] This prior impression had to allow itself to be reversed in order to proceed in the opposite direction, provided one had only taken the correct *point de depart*. [...] Hitler alone, it seems, trusted in the identifications that he sought. Among the many around him who engaged in mythicization, he was the only one who gave himself over to the archaic compulsion to repeat, so long as the omen did not stand against him. This did not serve the cause of realism. (Blumenberg 2014: 31-32, trans. In Nicholls 2016: 234)

Later wishing to avoid any comparison between himself and Napoleon, Hitler chose Frederick the Great to prefigure the success of his campaigns. In this scenario, myth no longer served as an orienting force and a buffer against the absolutism of reality, but morphed into its own kind of absolutism, a delusional dogma radically at odds with military realities on the ground, which Hitler wanted to constitute a new reality. Analysing Hitler's case, Blumenberg exposed the pitfalls of mythical thinking when it was taken to extremes and crossed over into a narcissism or 'absolutism of the will' that was no longer resisted by reality.[17] In Hitler's case, his personal failure and the end of his life was meant to spell the end of the world itself; he sought forcibly to collapse 'the world-time back into the dimensions of a life-time'. Hitler 'simply had no conception of the objective world of history that had existed before him and which would continue to exist after him' (Blumenberg 1986: 84). Although Blumenberg never identifies a specific threshold at which point myth becomes disastrous and loses 'contact with reality' (Blumenberg 2014: 31-32, trans. in Nicholls 2016: 234), his analysis of Hitler's literalisation of mythical thinking presents a suggestive parallel: like Hitler's battle plans, the new algorithmic rationality operates through a kind of 'magical' thinking that is intended to be self-fulfilling, seeking not only to predict future events but to guarantee their occurring as prefigured in past events.

From Rhetoric to Pensiveness, Blumenberg's Art of the Detour

In this context, rhetoric emerges as another privileged technique for humanity's self-preservation and a prime example of a more practical form of rationality.[18] In his anthropology essay of 1971, 'An Anthropological Approach to the Contemporary Significance of Rhetoric', Blumenberg rehabilitated rhetoric as discourse that is capable of contending with a contingent and indeterminate future not governed by scientific necessity. Regarded by philosophy as inferior to logic – a Platonic legacy – rhetoric nonetheless performs a significant role in human affairs, in the praxis of life rather than the realm of ideas. It makes up for our lack of definitive evidence or 'sufficient' theoretical grounding (*Evidenzmangel*) before our compulsion to act (*Handlungszwang*) especially since we lack 'pre-given, prepared adaptive structures and of regulatory processes' or the 'automatic controls' to fit into unlike the rest of the natural world (Blumenberg 2020i: 181-2). Rhetoric in this way enables us to craft a world for ourselves from a host of conceptions through which we can articulate our expectations, establish a sufficient degree of agreement about the nature of the world, and settle on a provisional justification for action in order to circumvent the otherwise disabling effects of epistemic indeterminacy (De Launay 2010: 33). Even the production of scientific statements depends on a 'pattern of agreement subject to later revocation'.

In his essay 'Concept of Reality and the Theory of the State' Blumenberg further defended a rhetorical conception of politics against a Schmittian decisionism that absolutises antagonisms, and he defended politics as an art of discussion and de-escalation as an alternative to direct violent action and real conflict. Politics should not be turned into an immutable 'science', but must remain attuned to uncertainty and indeterminacy and continue to cultivate an openness to the exchange of views (Blumenberg 2020h).

In his later years Blumenberg also came to favour short, informal discursive forms such as fables and anecdotes, forms that nonetheless invite reflection and act as prompts to thinking anew. These writings exhibit and encourage 'pensiveness' (*Nachdenklichkeit*), the meandering of 'real' everyday thinking in its circuitousness and open-endedness. Blumenberg rejected the absolutism of reason and was particularly fascinated by the reflectiveness induced by the intrusions of reality on the life-world. The sudden emergence of the unexpected and enigmatic resists 'logicality' and acted as stumbling blocks that help 'dismantle the obvious' and prompted us to think anew. Pensiveness helps overcome the 'the immunization of consciousness' (Blumenberg 2020g: 124) and 'our more common than not natural state of unthought' (Blumenberg 2020b: 61); it lets our thought processes meander purposelessly, allowing 'whatever comes to mind [...] to pass through one's head unaltered' (Blumemberg 2020d: 512). This moment of distance and reflexivity disrupts the seeming obviousness of our life-worlds,[19] opening up a gap during which our reflective faculties reassert themselves and critical thought can begin anew.[20]

The theme of distancing – and the necessity of establishing an 'indirect, circumstantial, delayed, selective', and above all metaphorical relation to reality (Blumenberg 1987: 439) – forms a red thread throughout Blumenberg's work. While rejecting an essentialist account of human nature, Blumenberg continually emphasised mankind's hesitancy. Man is first and foremost a creature of hesitation: unlike animals that react reflexively to stimuli, humans are unique in their ability to renounce immediate responses and solutions in order to 'wait', 'hesitate', and be 'indecisive' (Blumenberg 2020d: 511) – without clear interpretive paths, in defiance of a reductivist instrumental rationality (Fleming 2020). Paradoxically, perhaps, detours are not only more efficient in navigating contingency, but they engender the diversity and richness of human culture that underscore the production of meaningful worlds: 'Only by taking detours can we exist'. The 'shortest way of connecting two points', between plan and goal, intention and fulfilment, in line with the decisiveness and instrumental thinking demanded by modern life, is not necessarily the humane one. The 'superfluousness' of detours – in contrast to automatic and regulated discourse or predetermined pathways – are uniquely apt to 'humanize' life (Blumenberg 2010: 96).[21]

Letting the Indeterminacy Stand

As an historian of human thought, Blumenberg was endlessly fascinated by the process of thinking itself. In his analysis, mankind's relation to the world, is largely 'hypothetical', marked by a continuous dialectical engagement between life-world and its disruption,[22] between immersion in meaningful frameworks and distance from them, between engagement with and disengagement from the empirical realm (Monod 2009: 236). It seems to me that the life-worlds he writes about are not self-reinforcing processes that aim to displace reality itself, but tools that create openings and enable mankind – paradoxically through distance and detour – to deal with reality, the contingency, indeterminacy, and incomputability of which exclude the possibility of definitive and permanent knowledge, let alone control. Each attempt to render reality humanly comprehensible and manageable is necessarily provisional, and will give way to a later iteration.[23] The absence of absolute self-foundations for any life-world allows for constant epistemic renewals, so long as the thought underlying the life-world does not become so blind to its own mythic dimension as to claim the status of reality itself: the most dangerous myth is precisely that which pretends not to be one. The modern novel, Blumenberg argued, exemplifies the loss of a dogmatically assured truth (Monod 2012) and, as the actualisation of a world we know to be fictional, reminds us that the world we actually inhabit is only one instantiation of many possible worlds and realities (Taussig 2017).

Blumenberg adumbrates a possible critique – and solution – to the problem of the presumptuous algorithmic foreclosure of reality. He cultivates a more aesthetic sensibility, which embraces the essential ambiguity of the world and lets its 'indeterminacy stand' (2020b: 436). Epistemological frameworks should provide us with meaning and orientation to the extent that they do not themselves turn into new absolutisms and totalising worldviews,[24] and Blumenberg enjoins us to take the measure of limits of strict computability. Reality's constantly shifting – and unattainable – nature constitutes an inexhaustible horizon. Blumenberg reconfigures contingency as the opportunity for mankind to cultivate epistemological plurivocity rather than as something that should be pre-emptively neutralised. The world's ambiguity, which can never be overcome (2020f: 434), opens up spaces for the practice of novelty and imagination. Ever averse to dogmatism or reductionism, Blumenberg enjoins us to steer a middle ground between the desire to mitigate uncertainty and risk of foreclosing the future and its possibilities, between the conceptual and the unspeakable (Simpson 2021). Silence, precisely, is that which affords us the 'space for open-ended contemplation' (Fleming 2020), lodged between the irrepressibility and the unanswerability of certain questions and needs, a response what can be 'apprehended' but 'not comprehended' (Blumenberg 2020d). Contrary to Wittgenstein's famous conclusion to his *Tractactus*, that which cannot be known need not be discussed, the silence of the world in its unknowability is made, through aesthetic free play, to speak in an endlessly renewed variety of ways.[25] Blumenberg is interested in the absolute only insofar as it provides the unthinkable framework in which thinking itself can appear. Thinking is not conceived as mere automaticity but precisely as that which can interrupt itself and reconnect with the 'essential ambiguity and indeterminacy of the world'.

Although nonconceptual thought and current algorithmic systems share an overriding concern to manage radical contingency – the 'unthinkable' – the solutions they offer diverge profoundly. Blumenberg envisaged objectivity in more dialectical terms, between indeterminacy and overdetermination (Blumenberg 2005: 44). Perhaps more than any other thinker, he emphasises the value of doubt and uncertainty and the need to force open thinking that has lulled us into forms of automatism. In his 1950 article 'Computing Machinery and Intelligence' Alan Turing had gestured towards a more intuitive kind of computing, one which, in acknowledgment of the incompleteness of formal systems, would be dynamic and open to the indeterminacy of results. In line with Blumenberg's thought, the incomputable precisely calls for a reconfigured form of digitality: one that, turning toward the nonconceptual,[26] admits randomness (Agre 1997: 149), indeterminacy, and the unknown (Parisi 2021). Internal disruptions, 'slippages', the cultivation of 'margins of indeterminacy',[27] so to speak, open up the prospect of 'dis-automatization' (Stiegler 2016).[28] Redelivering algorithmic systems to their incompleteness would also help interrupt the current contemporary politics of possibility which has been threatening the operation of politics by helping relocate the values of 'unattributability' and 'insolubility' at its heart (Amoore 2020: 158). As Louise Amoore reminds us, 'ethicopolicial life is about irresolvable struggles, intransigence, duress, and opacity, and it must continue to be if a future possibility for politics is not to be eclipsed by the output signals of algorithms' (Amoore 2020: 172).

Both nonconceptual and algorithmic thinking rely on fictions and are ways of contending with the uncertainty of reality. Whereas nonconceptual thought is a necessary fiction that stems from the original deficiency rooted in our anthropological nature, algorithmic systems only create the appearance of their necessity whilst serving vested interests. They objectivise their output as the only possible reality whilst obscuring the conditions of their production and deflecting critical scrutiny. More than that, they make for self-reinforcing structures incapable of responding robustly to contingency. They are inward looking and exclude the possibility of distance or disruption. The kind of mythic thinking that Blumenberg propounds on the other hand is sufficiently open-ended that it can accommodate intrusions of reality on life world and adapt to contingency. It provides for self-reflexivity and openings and does not seek to control reality or liquidate indeterminacy – futile tasks to begin with.

Blumenberg's perceptive comments on mythical thinking make him, however surprisingly, highly relevant to a critical assessment of algorithmic systems in our supposedly post-mythical, digital age. He sought to impress on us the need for a more pragmatic approach to reality that would embrace doubtfulness, distance, and deliberation rather than seek to foreclose the future – one on which we can draw today to help rethink the digital and algorithmic systems. Translated into contemporary circumstances, this approach would constitute a new form of critical theorisation of automation and computability, a theorisation that, acknowledging the limits of computability and instrumental rationality, would enable us to contend with contingency in a more flexible and humane way than has been done so far by providing us with provisional thought-models – rather than absolutisms of a counter-reality.

Works Cited

Agre, Philip E. 1997. 'Towards a Critical Technical Practice: Lessons Learned in Trying to Reform AI.' In *Social Science, Technical Systems and Cooperative Work*. Ed. Geoffrey Bowker, Susan Leigh Star, William Turner, and Les Gasser 131-157. Mahwah, NJ: Lawrence Erlbaum.

Amoore, Louise. 2013. *The Politics of Possibility: Risk and Security beyond Probability*. Durham, NC: Duke University Press.

Amoore, Louise. 2020. *Cloud Ethics: Algorithms and the Attributes of Ourselves and Others*. Durham, NC: Duke University Press.

Anderson, Chris. 2008. 'The End of Theory: The Data Deluge Makes the Scientific Method Obsolete.' *Wired* 23 June. https://www.wired.com/2008/06/pb-theory.

Bajohr, Hannes. 2019. 'Hans Blumenberg's Early Theory of Technology and History.' *Graduate Faculty Philosophy Journal* 40: 3-15.

Blumenberg, Hans. 2009. *Geistesgeschichte der Technik*. Ed. Alexander Schmitz and Bernd Stiegler. Frankfurt: Suhrkamp.

Blumenberg, Hans. 1983. *The Legitimacy of the Modern Age*. Trans. Robert M. Wallace. Cambridge, MA: MIT Press.

Blumenberg, Hans. 1985. *Work on Myth*. Trans. Robert M. Wallace. Cambridge, MA: MIT Press.

Blumenberg, Hans. 1986. *Lebenszeit und Weltzeit*. Frankfurt am Main: Suhrkamp.

Blumenberg, Hans. 1987. *The Genesis of the Copernican World*. Trans. Robert M. Wallace. Cambridge, MA: MIT Press.

Blumenberg, Hans. 2005. *La Raison du mythe*. Trans. Stéphane Dirschauer. Paris: Gallimard.

Blumenberg, Hans. 2010. *Care Crosses the River*. Trans. Paul Fleming. Stanford: Stanford University Press.

Blumenberg, Hans. 2010a. *Paradigms for a Metaphorology*. Trans. Robert Savage. Ithaca, NY: Cornell University Press.

Blumenberg, Hans. 2010b. *Theorie der Lebenswelt*. Ed. Manfred Sommer. Berlin: Suhrkamp.

Blumenberg, Hans. 2011. *Description de l'homme*. Trans. Denis Trierweiler. Paris: Cerf.

Blumenberg, Hans. 2012. *Le Concept de réalité*. Trans. Jean-Louis Schlegel. Pref. Jean-Claude Monod. Paris: Seuil.

Blumenberg, Hans. 2014. *Präfiguration: Arbeit am politischen Mythos*. Ed. Angus Nicholls and Felix Heidenreich. Berlin: Suhrkamp.

Blumenberg, Hans. 2015. *Schriften zur Technik*. Ed. Alexander Schmitz and Bernd Stiegler

Berlin: Suhrkamp.

Blumenberg, Hans. 2015b. 'Dogmatische und rationale Analyse von Motivationen des technischen Fortschritts.' In Blumenberg 2015, 258-276.

Blumenberg, Hans. 2020. *History, Metaphor, Fables: A Hans Blumenberg Reader*. Ed. and trans. Hannes Bajohr, Florian Fuchs, and Joe Paul Kroll. Ithaca, NY: Cornell University Press.

Blumenberg, Hans. 2020a. 'The Concept of Reality and the Possibility of the Novel.' In Blumenberg 2020, 499-524.

Blumenberg, Hans. 2020b. 'The Essential Ambiguity of the Aesthetic Object.' In Blumenberg 2020, 441-48.

Blumenberg, Hans. 2020c. 'Imitation of Nature: Toward a Prehistory of the Idea of the Creative Being.' In Blumenberg 2020, 316-57.

Blumenberg, Hans. 2020d. 'Pensiveness.' In Blumenberg 2020, 512-16.

Blumenberg, Hans. 2020e. 'The Relationship between Nature and Technology as a Philosophical Problem.' In Blumenberg 2020, 301-15.

Blumenberg, Hans. 2020f. 'Socrates and the *objet ambigu*: Paul Valéry's Discussion of the Aesthetic Object and Its Ontology.' In Blumenberg 2020, 400-40.

Blumenberg, Hans. 2020g. 'Preliminary Remarks on the Concept of Reality.' In Blumenberg 2020, 117-25.

Blumenberg, Hans. 2020h. 'World Pictures and World Models.' In Blumenberg 2020, 42-54.

Blumenberg, Hans. 2020i. 'An Anthropological Approach to the Contemporary Significance of Rhetoric.' In Blumenberg 2020, 174-203.

Blumenberg, Hans. 2020j. 'Phenomenological Aspects on Life-World and Technization'. In Blumenberg 2020, 348-388.

Blumenberg, Hans. 2023. *The Readability of the World*. Trans. Robert Savage and David Roberts. Ithaca, NY: Cornell University Press.

Bridle, James. 2018. *New Dark Age: Technology and the End of the Future*. London: Verso.

Bunz, Mercedes. 2019. 'The Calculation of Meaning: On the Misunderstanding of New Artificial Intelligence as Culture.' *Culture, Theory and Critique* 60: 264-78.

Bunz, Mercedes. 2021. 'How Not to Be Governed Like That by Our Digital Technologies.' In *The Ends of Critique: Methods, Institutions, Politics*, Ed. Kathrin Thiele, Birgit Mara Kaiser, and Timothy O'Leary, 179-200. Lanham: Roman & Littlefield.

Campe, Rüdiger. 2000. 'From the Theory of Technology to the Technique of Metaphor: Blumenberg's Opening Move.' *Qui Parle* 12: 105-26.

Carchia, Gianni. 1996. Introduction to Hans Blumenberg, *Tempo della Vita e tempo del mondo*, trans. Bruno Argenton, 9-20. Bologna: il Mulino.

Cassou-Noguès, Pierre. 2022. *La bienveillance des machines: Comment le numérique nous transforme à notre insu*. Paris: Seuil.

De Launay, Marc. 2010. Preface to Hans Blumenberg, *L'imitation de la nature et autres essais esthétiques*, trans. Isabelle Kalinowski and Marc de Launay, 1-18. Paris: Hermann.

Denecker, Marc and Kanakas, Antonis. 2002. 'Abduction in Logic Programming Computational Logic: Logic Programming and Beyond', *Essays in Honour of Robert A. Kowalski*, Part I, 402-436. Berlin: Springer.

Deleuze, Gilles. 1995. 'Postscript on Control Societies.' In *Negotiations, 1972-1990*, trans. Martin Joughin, 177-82. New York: Columbia University Press.

Fazi, M. Beatrice. 2021. 'Beyond Human: Deep Learning, Explainability and Representation.' *Theory, Culture & Society* 38: 55-77.

Fleming, Paul. 2020. 'Giving Pause: Blumenberg and Freud.' *Hans Blumenberg Seminar on Zoom*, org. Audrey Borowski. University of Oxford, 9 November.

Galloway, Alexander. 2021. *Uncomputable: Play and Politics in the Long Digital Age*. London: Verso.

Guntin, Marcos. 2022. 'Into Blumenberg's Lens Cabinet.' *Contributions to the History of Concepts* 17: 135-39.

Handelman, Matthew. 2022. 'Artificial Antisemitism: Critical Theory in the Age of Datafication.' *Critical Inquiry* 48: 286-312.

Heidenreich, Felix. 2008. 'Rationalität als Prävention und Simulation Hans Blumenberg über die Ursprünge der Vernunft.' *Philosophische Rundschau* 55: 156-67.

Heidenreich, Felix. 2011. 'Inconceptualité – Penser en images, penser en concepts.' In Tierweiler 2011, 77-90.

Heidenreich, Felix. 2011a. *Mensch und Moderne bei Hans Blumenberg*. Munich: Fink.

Helbig, Daniela. 2019. 'Life without Toothache: Hans Blumenberg's Zettelkasten and History of Science as Theoretical Attitude', *Journal of the History of Ideas*, 80(1): 91-112.

Huneman, Philippe. 2023. *Les sociétés du profilage: Évaluer, optimiser, prédire*. Paris: Payot.

Inoue, Katsumi, Andrei Doncescu, and Hidetomo Nabeshima. 2013. 'Completing causal networks by meta-level abduction.' *Machine Learning* 91: 239-77.

Joque, Justin. 2022. *Revolutionary Mathematics: Artificial Intelligence, Statistics and the Logic of Capitalism*. New York: Verso.

Keuchel, Stephan. 2020. 'Digitalisation and Automation of Transport: A Lifeworld Perspective of Travellers.' *Transportation Research Interdisciplinary Perspectives* 7.

Mackenzie, Adrian. 2015. 'The Production of Prediction: What does Machine Learning want?' *European Journal of Cultural Studies* 18: 429-445.

Monod, Jean-Claude. 2009. "'L'interdit anthropologique' chez Husserl et Heidegger et sa transgression par Blumenberg.' *Revue germanique internationale* 10: 221-36. https://doi.org/10.4000/rgi.336.

Monod, Jean-Claude. 2012. Preface to Hans Blumenberg, *Le Concept de réalité*, trans. Jean- Louis Schlegel, 1-13. Paris: Seuil.

Müller, Ernst. 2014. 'Technik.' In *Blumenberg lesen: Ein Glossar*, Ed. Robert Buch and Daniel Weidner, 589-614. Berlin: Suhrkamp. E-book.

Müller-Sievers, Helmut. 2010. 'Kyklophorology: Hans Blumenberg and the Intellectual History of Technics.' *Telos* 158: 155-70.

Nicholls, Angus. 2016. *Myth and the Human Sciences: Hans Blumenberg's Theory of Myth*. New York: Routledge.

Noble, Safiya. 2018. *Algorithms of Oppression. How Search Engines reinforce Racism*. New York: NYU Press.

Parisi, Luciana. 2019. 'Critical Computation: Digital Automata and General Artificial Thinking.' *Theory, Culture & Society* 36: 89-121.

Parisi, Luciana. 2021. 'Interactive Computation and Artificial Epistemologies'. *Theory, Culture & Society* 38: 33-53.

Rouvroy, Antoinette. 2012. 'Mise en (n)ombres de la vie même. Face à la gouvernementalité algorithmique, repenser le sujet comme puissance.' *Mediapart* 27 August. https://blogs.mediapart.fr/antoinette-rouvroy/

blog/270812/mise-en-nombres-de-la-vie-meme-face-la-
gouvernementalite-algorithmique-repenser-le-sujet-com.

Rouvroy, Antoinette. 2013. 'The End(s) of Critique: Data Behaviourism
versus Due Process.' In *Privacy, Due Process and the Computational Turn:
The Philosophy of Law Meets the Philosophy of Technology*, Ed. Mireille
Hildebrandt and Katja de Vries, 143-67. London: Routledge.

Rouvroy, Antoinette. 2016. 'Contestability in the Big Data Era.' Keynote
address, *Uncertain Archives – Error*. University of Copenhagen, 14
November. https://artsandculturalstudies.ku.dk/research/focus/
uncertainarchives/activities/archivaluncertaintyerror/rouvroy.

Rouvroy, Antoinette. 2018. 'Data et algorithmes: Gouvernementalité
algorithmique et idéologie des big data.' *Libre à lire* February.
https://www.librealire.org/data-et-algorithmes-gouvernementalite-
algorithmique-et-ideologie-des-big-data-antoinette-rouvroy.

Rusch, Pierre. 2011. 'Hans Blumenberg et la grammaire historique des idees.'
In Trierweiler 2011, 141-167.

Schumm, Marion. 25 June 2012. 'Pourquoi l'homme plutôt que rien.' *La Vie
des idées*, https://laviedesidees.fr/Pourquoi-l-homme-plutot-que-rien.

Simondon, Gilbert. 2017. *On the Mode of Existence of Technical Objects*. Trans.
Cecile Malaspina and John Rogove. Minneapolis: Univocal.

April 1983. 'Sauver l'objet technique: Entretien avec Gilbert Simondon.'
Esprit 76 (4): 147-152.

Simpson, Justin. 2020. 'The Significance of Contingency and Detours in
Hans Blumenberg's Philosophical Anthropology.' *Metaphilosophy* 51: 111-27.

Stiegler, Bernard. 2015. 'Automatic Society 1: The Future of Work.' *La
Deleuziana* 1: 121-140.

Sylla, Bernhard. 2019. 'Blumenberg: Against the Demonization of
Technology.' Universidade do Minho. https://repositorium.
sdum.uminho.pt/bitstream/1822/64812/1/Against%20the%20
demonization%20of%20technology%20v.%202.0.pdf.

Taussig, Sylvie. 2017. 'Le roman selon Hans Blumenberg.' *Raison publique* 21:
185-96.

Trierweiler, Denis, 2011. Ed. *Hans Blumenberg: Anthropologie philosophique*. Paris:
Presses Universitaires de France.

Turing, Alan. 1950. 'Computing Machinery and Intelligence'. *Mind* 59:
433-60.

Weatherby, Leif. 2022. 'Intermittent Legitimacy: Hans Blumenberg and
Artificial Intelligence.' *New German Critique* 49:11-39.

Weatherby, Leif. 2023. 'ChatGPT is an Ideology Machine.' *Jacobin* April. https://jacobin.com/2023/04/chatgpt-ai-language-models-ideology-media-production.

Weatherby, Leif, and Brian Justie. 2022. 'Indexical AI.' *Critical Inquiry* 48: 381-415.

Weatherby, Leif, et al. 2022. 'Surplus Data: An Introduction.' *Critical Inquiry* 48: 197-210.

Zuboff, Shoshana. 2015. 'Big other: Surveillance Capitalism and the Prospects of an Information Civilization.' *Journal of Information Technology* 30: 75-89.

Zuboff, Shoshana. 2019. *The Age of Surveillance Capitalism: The Fight for a Human Future at the New Frontier of Power*. London: Profile Books.

Notes

1. 'They invent a people, write them into being as a curious body of correlated attributes, grouped into clusters derived from data that are themselves fabulatory devices.' (Amoore 2020: 158)

2. Its ground is constantly shifting like rapid sands. For more on the topic of 'surplus data' see Weatherby et al. (2022): 'Fake news, conspiracy thinking and practice, police brutality, and speculative market bubbles are all the logical products of surplus data.'

3. Big data companies peddle the misconception that 'truth' will spontaneously arise from the correct algorithms.

4. 'The force of [algorithmic objectification] inheres not in [its] correspondence with some external reality, but in [its] ability to directly produce a new, distinct social reality. For example, what matters most about credit reports is not their ability to accurately describe an individual's creditworthiness, but their ability to produce a world that corresponds to their priorities by limiting access to capital.' (Joque 2022): 81.

5. 'It is not just about the mind (*Geist*), which produces technology (*Technik*), but also about technology (*Technik*), which produces mind (*Geist*).' (Blumenberg 2009, 78-79).

6. In his article 'Dogmatische und rationale Analyse von Motivationen des technischen Fortschritts' Blumenberg very much defends technical and scientific progress and the incremental futurity of the scientific method as being part and parcel of human self-assertion in the modern age.

7. It is worthwhile mentioning that in his article Blumenberg sought in part to respond to Husserl's *Crisis of European Sciences*. In it Husserl described how a spiritual crisis had arisen in the wake of the technisation of the world. This technisation, according to him, which could be traced back to Galileo's 'mathematization of nature', had devolved into a scientism that obscured the human 'life-world' of subjective and more intuitive life, oblivious to human questions and concerns. For Husserl, a renewed transcendentalism would help heal this rift. As we will see, Blumenberg opted for a different approach.

8. Drawing on Husserl, Blumenberg describes the concept of life-world as the 'universe of self-evidence' or 'the inexhaustible supply of unreflective and immediate existing, intimate, and unknown precisely in this intimacy' (Blumenberg 2015: 178). See also

Fleming (2020: 1): The obviousness which governs 'our everyday pretheoretical world of common affairs and pre-understood interactions'.

9. Commenting on the growing mis-fit between technical sphere and human life-world, Blumenberg writes: 'Today we live in a scientific-technological world with a largely pre-scientific and pre-technological consciousness' (Blumenberg 2009: 28).

10. 'The legitimacy of the modern age is, therefore, the awareness that only the hiatus between existence and theory, revealed by Platonism, can produce the antidote of spiritual work capable of gradually filling it.' (Carchia 1996: 14)

11. 'The whole horizon becomes equivalent as the totality of the directions from which 'it can come at one." (Blumenberg 1985: 4)

12. Monod (2009: 222) speaks of an 'interdit anthropologique'.

13. 'Man in the modern age is the inundated creature; his concept of reality aims at avoiding the unexpected, at containment, at producing consistency against the case of inconsistency.' (Blumenberg 2020: 124)

14. Blumenberg elaborates on the persistent need for myth: 'That there is, after the work on myth, never the end of myth, does not have to be accounted for or proven by the continued production of mythical models' (Nicholls 2016: 183). In fact, for Blumenberg, the predominance of discursive reason could be grasped as a myth itself.

15. Helbig (2019) traces how Blumenberg conjoins the history of ideas with the logic of technics.

16. 'What is readable, the document, is the absolutely improbable in its surroundings; the probable is chaos, noise, de-differentiation, decay.' (Blumenberg 2023, 338)

17. Blumenberg speaks of a 'contempt for realism' (Blumenberg 2014: 44, trans. by Nicholls 2016: 235).

18. Rüdiger Campe comments: 'Metaphors and rhetorical twists render the processing of meaning even more complex and therefore slower. Technization accelerates the process of history by erasing meaning, rhetoric slows historical processes down by complicating meaning.' (Campe 2000: 110)

19. 'Pensiveness means: everything is not as obvious as it was. That is all.' (Blumemberg 2020d: 516)

20. 'My conclusion – since I must present one because of my profession – is that philosophy has something to preserve, if not revive, from its life-world origin in pensiveness. Philosophy must not be bound, therefore, to particular expectations about the nature of its product.' (Blumenberg 2020d: 515-16)

21. 'Then the world's meaning corresponds to taking the paths of the superfluous.'

22. 'We think about where we stand because we were disturbed in not thinking about it.' (Blumenberg 2020d: 516)

23. Blumenberg's understanding of the world is one of perpetual indeterminacy and postponement which refrains from issuing definitive answers or closures.

24. Blumenberg in fact welcomes science's ability to free us from totalising worldviews but cautions against extending scientific insights into worldpictures.

25. 'Precisely through that which the fable forgoes, it provides us with the space for the play [*Spielraum*] of pensiveness' (Blumenberg 2020d: 515). 'The finitude and historicity of human consciousness mean that the terminus ad quem, the "correct" and final position according to which earlier theories are assessed and toward which they are seen to progress, will never be reached.' (Nicholls 2016: 117)

26. See on this point Galloway 2021. Galloway explores the rapport between computable and uncomputable – including lived experience, intuition, flesh, and affect – seeing them as co-produced modalities.

27. Blumenberg's emphasis on disruption echoes Gilbert Simondon here. 'Technical ensembles are characterised by the fact that in them a relation between technical objects takes shape at the level of the margin of indeterminacy of each technical object's way of functioning. This relation between technical objects is of a problematic type, insofar as it puts indeterminacies into correlation, and for this reason it cannot be taken on by the objects themselves; it cannot be calculated, nor be the result of a calculation; it must be thought, posed as a problem by a living being and for a living being.' (Simondon 1983: 152)

28. 'The brain is an automatic machine, and it is a machine capable of disautomatising its own functioning.' (Stiegler 2016: 134)